The Book of St. Cyprian
The Sorcerer's Treasure

First published in 2014 by Hadean Press
France
Printed in Great Britian

HADEAN PRESS

www.hadeanpress.com

The Book of St. Cyprian
The Sorcerer's Treasure

O Grande livro de S.Cypriano ou thesouro do feiticeiro
translated and with commentary by José Leitão

Contents

Commentaries to *The Book of St. Cyprian* : *The Sorcerer's Treasure*

To read this book is a sin,
but who reads it will rise to the clouds without wings

– Portuguese saying

AN INTRODUCTION OF GREAT IMPORTANCE

PERSONAL PREAMBLE

I FIRST HEARD ABOUT *THE BOOK OF SAINT CYPRIAN* when I was about seven or eight. I believe it was my brother who one day found a copy in the city library and told me about it. He was to do some sort of school assignment with some colleagues and, young boys as they were, they very much wished to read *The Book* as the taboo that it was. He thus came home that day carrying in his mind the inevitably heavy stories of wonder and horror of the Sorcerer made Saint.

I remember clearly not knowing of what he was talking about, much like I still don't these days, but the simple concept of it, of *The Book of Saint Cyprian*, echoed in me quite remarkably. It was simultaneously confusing and mysterious, this notion that a saint would write or have his name associated with a book on black magic. At that time I was very much frightened.

Looking back now... it still mystifies me why I was afraid, or how anyone can be afraid of something they'd never heard of, as if there was an absolute and abstract fear emanating from the pronunciation of a few simple words. Like an electric shock, lashing out into the mind for no reason, forcibly establishing a connection with that core which in all of us is claimed by culture and language, a cursed living thing which had just claimed another one for itself. Looking back now this was probably my first magical experience.

These days I have come to realize that this reaction was nothing but natural. It might be difficult for you, dear reader, to fully understand this if you're an outsider to Ibero-American culture, but this book is so much more than itself, it goes so far beyond its pages, it is so tightly linked and chained to the Ibero-American imagination that one can never be indifferent to it, not even a boy of seven or eight.

Not long after that experience, my grandmother (may God keep her soul), not at all helping my dreadful situation, further underlined and justified my terrible fear, making me promise to never touch that most cursed and forbidden *Book of Saint Cyprian*, placing it alongside such practices as the *Jogo do Copo* (a household spirit game, similar to the Ouija Board) as absolutely prohibited in my family. As is obvious, I would eventually break this promise (and if back then I would have known what today I would be writing, what today I have around my neck, whom today I pray to every night, I would have properly shat myself), but it was this same promise and fear which in truth solidly established *The Book* in my mind, inflated it with all its dread and horror, made it living and made it Magic, and it is still to this dark recess of myself I go for fuel, for that immense magical power which is released in the breaking of a Taboo.

If for nothing else, for this I will forever be in debt to these two people.

Then, as years went by, this book fell gradually into the back of my mind, but in one way or the other it was always present for me, a lurking shadow. Occasionally it would come up in hushed conversations between curious and inconsequential youngsters, amidst those terrifying Lovecraftian stories about floating knifes, madness, suicide, and glimpses of the Devil himself lurking around the darkest corner of some friend-of-a-friend's bedroom, and back then we would all laugh to hide our fear.

Such stories were, and still are, fascinating to me. This book carries with it such an aura, such a myth, that from every corner of society you are bound to hear some tale to chill you to the bone, be it the one that tells that if you read *The Book of Saint Cyprian* from the beginning to end, you will be driven mad, or that a house which has *The Book of Saint Cyprian* in it will never know happiness. And still today, just as before, booksellers might have *The Book* in a locked box behind the counter, and should you dare ask for it, you are looked upon with a mix of fear and loathing. This is an all-encompassing echo, which howls with reverberating strength and firsthand vitality in every new generation and none are shielded from it; even if reactions may vary between fear, anger, or laughter, this book is never indifferent. It is always emotionally charged and in that sense there is something very vampiric about it (even a close friend of mine, no stranger to matters of the occult, upon hearing from my lips that I was working on this book took two steps back as if I was carrying some kind of infectious disease).

Among all of this, the first time the idea of studying *The Book of Saint Cyprian* and possibly working with it woke in my mind, already hardened by my share of satanic literature and dark occult tomes, I was shaken by something which could have no other name besides fear, that same baseline ignoble fear of a young boy hiding his head under the covers at night.

It was then that I knew I had no choice; I had to work with *The Book*. I feared it for no reason, for the same no reason I had always feared it, for this was its power, its omnipresence, the dark corner of my culture and my magical heritage, and the realization that for me there was nothing of worth in the world but this book, that if I did not pick it up then all my life and accomplishments past and future would be but dust, mere cluttered and irrelevant junk.

That dark and unique moment – I remember it well – when I was called to the Work, I only realised later, was on a 26th of September, the day of Saint Cyprian.

Malhas Que o Império Tece

Dearest reader, you are surely a much learned Sorcerer, a greatly experienced Witch, a mighty grand Magician, and you have surely studied the history of your tradition[1]. That history of bloody persecution, of good men and women burned at the stake, of the endless stream of abject monstrosities, sadistic cruelty and bloodthirsty ignorance perpetuated in the name of the Father ✠ the Son ✠ and the Holy Spirit ✠. But, dear reader, you most likely did not study the bloody history of my tradition.

To understand this book and its content one must understand the environment from which it sprang, as, sadly, it did not fall into the world in its complete form from the Heavens/Hells and, in a sense, this is indeed most fortunate, for we can track its content through history and come to a greater understanding of it.

In all honesty, the first time I read *The Book of Saint Cyprian* I felt terribly disappointed. I had built myself up in preparation for the impact of what I assumed to be the most cursed and damnable piece of writing in the world, but what I instead found was, on all accounts, a genuinely Christian and, furthermore, Catholic grimoire (even if an extremely cruel one). Still, after the necessary study, I came to realize that this was indeed the mark of a genuinely traditional book of Portuguese *Bruxaria* and *Feitiçaria*.

Remembering our history, from the Middle Ages and on to the Renaissance, Europe was united under the psychosis of the witch-hunt, a truly remarkable impulse that united classes and nations under a single blood-soaked banner of fear (those of us with a taste for the tragic can still see the echoes of this in today's modern and rational European Union). Portugal, however, came to find in itself a wholly different murderous craze.

In 1478 the Spanish Inquisition was officially established by Ferdinand II and Isabella I, the Catholic Monarchs, initiating the campaign of religious persecution against heresy, with special incidence on the local Jewish and Muslim populations, be them converted or not. As a baseline for this campaign, in 1492 the *Alhambra Decree* was issued, mandating the compulsory expulsion of all Jews from the Spanish kingdoms.

One of the immediate results of this action was, logically, an exodus of Castilian Jews into Portugal, a nation that, at the time, had a historical record of being gentler and more tolerant towards the religious practices of its non-Christian population with the added bonus of not possessing an established Inquisition. Such an impulse was actually greatly beneficial to the small Iberian nation, with many skilled merchants and wise scholars coming in to fill the

---

1. In case you are not one of these examples, don't worry, by the time you finish this book you will be.

most distinct learned ranks of the Portuguese court, further cementing and strengthening the booming Portuguese Empire.

Sadly this situation was not to last, as when King Manuel I of Portugal rose to the throne in 1495, marrying Isabella of Aragon, daughter of the Catholic Monarchs, his marriage contract came with the added condition of establishing the forced expulsion of all heretics (Jews and Muslims) from the Portuguese territory. Now, the king was no fool[2], and, even if such an action would be very much to the liking of the majority of his subjects, he very clearly knew that such an event would catastrophically ruin the country beyond repair. As such, in an attempt to keep with his contractual obligations and his duty to the economic well-being of the country, in 1496 the king in fact issued the dreaded expulsion order, but he simultaneously issued a conversion deadline for all Jews who still wished to remain within the country, hoping that this would lessen the exodus his initial order would surely cause. It should be noted that the king himself did not have any kind of religious problem with the Jewish and Muslim populations, and in truth he expected most well-positioned Jews to convert merely out of convenience, conserving their status in Portugal but still practicing their religion in private... such did not happen[3].

Being confronted with the mass abandonment of the Jewish population, essential to the development of the expanding Empire, King Manuel then ordered all Portuguese ports and harbors to be closed, effectively locking those Jews who had not yet fled the country inside its borders. This logically left the remaining Jews with only one viable option: that of conversion to Catholicism. The whole of Portuguese society was then completely permeated by the rise of the hidden Jew, the Marrano, the Crypto-Jew, the Converso and the New Christian.

King Manuel went on to lead a successful and prosperous reign of unsurpassed wealth and prosperity but eventually, upon his death in 1521, the crown fell to his son, the dim-witted religious fanatic King John III who, unable to see his father's cunning, was the one who finally established the Portuguese branch of the Inquisition at the late year of 1536.

As the Holy Office took up its arms, it was confronted with the reality that in every corner, every social class, every street, every city, town, and village, Jewish heretics were abundant. This, from its very start, caused the Inquisition to become focused solely on the persecution of the hidden Jew, whose presence threatened and contaminated the spirit and faith of the whole of society, successfully riding the wave of anti-Semitism which by now had taken hold of the majority of the nation.

---

2. If you plan to declare yourself the Divinely appointed Emperor of the World you may be mad, but you should not be stupid.

3. Should you ever pass by Amsterdam, please visit the Esnoga in Mr. Visserplein and shed a tear for the foolishness of my ancestors.

The end result of such orientation was that, after the Inquisition fires had settled and the smell of burning flesh had cleared, the Portuguese Witch was left almost untouched. Of course this is not to say that Witches were not persecuted—far from it. Similarly to the rest of Christian Europe, we have plenty of documents relating the heavy punishments and sentences being ascribed to diviners, sorcerers, and Witches, especially from the year 1385 onwards, all the way until King Manuel's *Ordinances* and further still (see Annex I). One of the side effects of this was that sentences ascribed to these were frequently that of exile and *degredo* to Brazil (where the colonial power was in constant need of more men and particularly women) and not the *autos de fé*, establishing a continuous flow of Portuguese Witches to instead fuel the fires of the cults established today as Umbanda, Quimbanda, and many others.

But the bottom line still becomes that, apparently, the Jesuit maxim of *'Witchcraft grows with heresy, heresy with Witchcraft'*, or the idea that divination was implicitly diabolical, was neither accepted by the crown nor the general population, as Witches were mostly found guilty of errors of faith, not heresy. Heretics were in fact Jews and Jews were the ones being sniffed out by the Hounds of the Lord.

To support this strange claim we can analyze the vast number of Inquisition processes and notice that only about ten percent of these related to non-Judaic crimes, being that these ten percent are themselves divided between bigamy, sodomy, clerical immorality, blasphemy, witchcraft, divination, miracle working, false witness, petty larceny, and Holy Office imposture.

So, saving us from the bloodshed of the witch-craze we merely had the bloodshed of anti-Semitism...

You see, dear reader, you can keep your anger and your hate towards the purifying flames of the Inquisition that burned so many of your sorcerous kin, they are surely more than justified. But know that in the real world seldom does hate find a cure, rather, one form of hate just gets replaced by a different one. Hate happens, it just does, and in troubled times it finds its direction and its victim, if not Witches then it would have been someone else. Here we kept our Witch, but her life was bought at the expense of Jewish blood.

Paying our honors and homage to the fallen, we should now take our time to appreciate and understand what was left in the wake of the Inquisition onslaught.

The non-antagonization of the Witch in the Portuguese kingdom meant that they did not have to cut themselves off from the mainstream of Christian society, seeking out in the forced dualism of the Church the protection of the Devil as the opposer of the system massacring them. Rather, through relaxation, Witchcraft would come to find itself more and more Christianized and Catholic.

In a certain sense this can actually be understood through the same basic dualistic Good vs Evil mindset. The general populace (non-Witches) could easily find redeeming qualities in Witches if their services could be used for good, seeing as all good was forcibly in the realm of God and his Church. Reciprocally, a Witch could easily fool herself into believing that she was indeed a good Christian and a good Catholic if her workings produced good effects, since all good is in league with God and His Church, a realization which would then feed itself back into the Witch's practice and gradually color it with more and more Christian iconography and techniques.

This same double approach of the Witch and the Christian can be easily seen in the works of the play-writer Gil Vicente (1465 – 1536?), always a perfect pulse meter for the society of his time (including the anti-Semitism), particularly in the *Auto das Fadas* where the *feiticeira* Genebra Pereira justifies her sorceries to the King (again, see Annex I):

Porem Genebra Pereira	Genebra Pereira however
nunca fez mal a ninguem;	never harmed a soul
mas antes por querer bem	but rather for wanting to do good
ando nas cruzilhadas	I roam the crossroads
ás horas que as bem fadadas	at those hours when those of good *fado*
dormem sono repousado;	sleep a restful slumber.

With the ultimate punch-line being that:

Isto, Senhor, nao he mal,	this my lord is not for evil
Pois he pera fazer bem.	for it is to do good

And as such, in due time we find a form of genuine syncretic *Bruxaria*, truly Christian and intertwined with rural folk Catholicism. Following its own process, spirits and gods became saints, and their evocations and incantations became prayers and orisons, more or less orthodox, more or less pagan, but overall fitted to a Christian mindset.

This, as you would expect, gave rise to a great variety of strange practices and definitions, as now the Witch had at her disposal all of the Catholic Saints and their workings and her own, bringing into the field remarkable and bizarre saints, originating from the most diverse and ancient cults, such as St. Leona, St. Trebuca, St. Maruta and Montenegro, which the folklorist Teófilo Braga reads as the Persian Maroth for St. Maruta, the Rudra Triymbaka for St. Trebuca, the Islamic Monkir-Nekir for Montenegro and St. Leona as a reminiscence of the Mithraic cult. The Virgin Mary would be prayed to together with the stars and the moon, Saints would be bathed in rivers and wine to provide rain and good harvest and, as if all of this was not enough of a mess, in comes the African man...

As we travel from the XVth century all the way to the XVIIIth, we begin to find among the rare Witchcraft processes of the Inquisition a remarkable novelty: the existence of African magic in Lisbon, even if a minority among a minority.

Such should not be received as a surprise as, since the foundation of the nation in the XIIth century, Lisbon had always possessed a stable number of African inhabitants who, by the 1500s, actually added up to ten percent of the whole population. These, it should be noted, are not just present as regular slaves but also *forros* and, of course, free born men, both black and *mulatos*.

Due to their relatively small numbers, and the very social organization of the capital, these, contrarily to Brazil for example, were never enough to actually establish an organized ATR (African traditional religion) cult in Portugal at the time[4], establishing rather small pockets of spirit workers and healers in and around the city, mainly in the predominantly African neighborhoods (particularly in Mocambo, renamed Madragoa after the 1755 earthquake).

This form of social arrangement meant that there wasn't an effective cultural buffer between the established Christian society and the African practitioner who, beyond the syncretic forms of worship meant to hide the African core of his religion from white eyes, as in the ATR that blossomed in America, would begin to genuinely adopt Christian practices by his own initiative.

These practitioners, when placed in front of the tribunal of the Holy Office, would also come to benefit from the Jewish human shield, being treated as regular Old Christians even though many of them had only come into contact with Christianity during their young or adolescent life. Like the Portuguese white *Bruxa*, their main accusations were simply on transgression of church or religious dogma, which could be assumed to have been done under the influence of the Devil and not due to foreign idolatry of a competing religion. This actually meant that the defendant could still be saved on account of the fact that such an action was merely an "orthodox" deviation from the Christian faith (again, a mere error of faith), on which there was no inherent denial of God or the Church, contrary to the blatant heresy of the Jew, but only if he genuinely repented... which of course the large majority said they did.

Still, contrasting between the white and black accused, one may notice that the latter would with much greater ease admit to the dreaded pact with the Devil (which to the white practitioner, as explained above, was in all illogical), while still keeping the same claim of the non-denial of the Church and its laws.

This process of diabolization of their practices by the Tribunal, given the vulnerable state of the African faith in Portugal, and the Africans' lack of understanding of the ramification of Christian theology, would come to impact greatly on the African himself, as he would be led to genuinely assume that the deity of his devotion was indeed the/a Devil of the Christian religion. We

---

4. This has, by now, been thankfully corrected.

then find extremely colorful descriptions of magical practices and visions, either genuine or extracted by the use of torture, of this black Devil, spiritually carrying African *Bruxas* across the ocean back to Africa to meet with other black Devils (in white accounts the spiritual flight is actually an extremely rare instance and usually involves the transformation of the Witch into some kind of bird).

This mechanism of diabolical association with the black man was by no means a novelty, as from an early age the sheer black color had been associated with the Devil, with many accounts from Witches of both colors describing the infernal king as a black man. On this aspect the black accused would fall in line and cater to the religious obsession of the Inquisitorial accuser, while at the same time convincing themselves of its truth, that their own black skin was a mark of the Devil.

This would generate an extremely complicated frame of mind, where the African assumed his diabolic nature on account of his black skin, as if he was marked from birth by the Devil, which would make tremendous sense to him since his Gods were Devils. This aspect of blackness would come to rise to such relevance that the Witches' traditional Sabbath, the *sámbleia*, would actually become known as the *senzala* on account of the amount of black participants in it.

Given this assumption of blackness, and the frank confusion on the mutual exclusiveness of their traditional religion and the Catholic faith, many African *Bruxos* and *Bruxas* would logically become recurrent offenders, eventually mastering the adequate speech to have in front of the Tribunal which would indeed sentence them but save their lives. From here on we notice that in each new account there is an evolution in their practices, demonstrating that theirs was not an isolated universe, but that actually there was a constant cultural exchange between the black and white accused, to which the very prisons of the Inquisition would act as the greatest crucibles of all.

Now, up to this point the great distinction between the two groups of magic workers had been the nature of the powers involved in their healings and workings: the white practitioner used their vast array of Saints, while the black used their Devils. This new cultural exchange then initiated a revolution on both sides; while the African acquired all the flexible fetishism of holy water and rosaries of folk Catholicism (while still not referring too much to the saints), the Portuguese adopted his Devil all but too eagerly[5].

While this may not seem like much, it was actually a groundbreaking step. In traditional Portuguese *Bruxaria* the Devil was not used to a great extent given that, for any one situation, ailment or problem, the practitioner had at his disposal an abundance of saints to resort to. Now a whole new world of opportunities and possibilities had been opened, as this new and improved Devil could be called upon on matters that were previously out of his sphere.

---

5. Once again, the white man had the sweet end of the deal.

Furthermore, the appropriation of the African Devil, likely to have originally been the trickster *Eshu/Elegua*, would make up a Devil on all accounts extremely similar to the Northern Portuguese rural concept of the Christian Devil, making the whole process hit very close to home to those white practitioners adopting it.

Also, please note that this not to say that there was no diabolism in Portugal before the entrance of African magic into the scene. Diabolists are like sparrows, you can always find one in every latitude and longitude, and the proof of wide and plainly satanic practices has always been easy to find, particularly in the Inquisition reports of *cartas de tocar*, a kind of pact with the Devil consisting of a few papers which should be carried by the practitioner for protection. But the fact is that, looking at the numbers, only five percent of all Sorcery and Witchcraft Inquisition processes make a reference to the dreaded satanic pact, and the bottom line becomes that the African man gave Portuguese *Bruxaria* its fangs back, broadening the channel for the use and manipulation of forces understood as diabolical in the dualistic Christian perspective.

Ample evidence of the situations mentioned above can be found particularly in the reports of *bolsas de mandinga*[6], a kind of mojo bag from that same time, where now, among typical African elements including drawings which can be easily interpreted as *veves* and simple stylized representation of *Eshu/Elegua*, we can find evocations to St. Cyprian or St. Mark, Christian iconography and the Portuguese royal coat of arms. These *bolsas* would come to completely permeate all corners of the Portuguese kingdom, be them Africa, Brazil or Portugal, being amply used and traded by men (men in the gendered sense of the word – this appears to have been an exclusively male talisman) of all colors and social classes.

So, similarly to the modern realization, we indeed have here a meeting of ATRs and European magic, but in the opposite direction. The grimoire did not cross the Atlantic to meet with the ATRs in the Americas, but rather the ATRs crossed the Atlantic to meet the grimoire in the Iberian lands.

It is then this field, this bloody beautiful mess, which makes up the frame for *The Book of Saint Cyprian*, this simultaneously Saintly and Devilish, faithful and manipulative magic.

And one more thing, dear reader, please do take all of the above with a grain of salt.

---

6. *Mandinga* refers to an ethnic group of West Africa, decedents of the Mali Empire. The slaves from this ethnicity were known for wearing small leather pouches with verses from the Koran as protection talismans, the original prototypes for the later *bolsas de mandinga*. Nowadays *mandinga* can also be used as a synonym for sorcery.

ON THE CYPRIANIC TRAIL

HAVING READ OUR HISTORY, and having become better people for it, we can now start to look at *The Book of Saint Cyprian* itself. This, yet again, isn't a simple matter.

Upon approaching *The Book* for the first time there is an initial challenge one must confront, as the sheer number and volume of editions of this one single book in any given moment in time is simply overwhelming.

Even taking up the painstaking chore of careful analysis of their content does not simplify this matter in any way: chapters dance and change in form and structure, spells change name, number, and position, sections come and go, contents from other various books appear here and there and some editions seem like completely different and unrelated books altogether. This realization may lead one to try to find his way through this literary maze in search of an original, or less "corrupted" book, adjectives which commonly just mean "the oldest one available".

Although such a quest is without a doubt one of the utmost dignity and worthy of the greatest of praises, in my opinion, a man who sets upon it - as far as this book is concerned - has missed the point entirely.

One must keep in mind that this, unlike some other grimoires, is not a relic of a distant magical past, it is not an old dead book waiting to be brought back into the light by the devoted magician. *The Book of Saint Cyprian* is not one book; it is not something located in time or space. As with anything, any cult, any order or any religion which is alive and active, it is a continuum, a stream and a current. It changes its contents because it is alive, it is practiced, it is used in various temporal, social, and geographical contexts. Whether by the hand of greedy editors, conscious and devoted authors, madmen, charlatans or practical jokers, it constantly responds to the needs of its readers. From the shores of Catalonia to the Algarve, across rural Iberia on to the Brazilian Northeast, to the *terreiros* of Quimbanda[7] and finally brought to the cities, it is, in all senses of the word, a popular magical book, a book of the people.

Yet, don't let such a speech lull you into an idea of some kind of democratic magical source, for this is always a book of limits; it is produced for mass consumption but does not bear the recognition of the official cultural hegemony. It lives on the edges of society, in the shadows, in the border between religiousness and heresy, virtue and vice. Like the Saint, it lives on that thin line where God and the Devil meet.

---

7. Being Portuguese, I have to genuinely bow my head in gratitude to the responsibility with which the Afro-Brazilian cults have had in keeping this book alive. To the best of my knowledge no organized or semi-organized association, order, coven or cult in Iberia, which might use this book (and there are a few), has enough sheer number of members to justify its presence today on the shelves of every bookstore.

Having accepted this idea, one may then be tempted to consider this an "inferior" grimoire, a collage, barely original and unique; again you are missing the point. Should you choose to love this book do not search for the ancient original as if a fossil from a museum. This book is now! It devours content and makes it its own.

Of course, we should never become dogmatic about such ideas. It is quite obvious that an Iberian practitioner will find little use in a more recent *Book of Saint Cyprian* made for a Quimbanda audience and vice versa. Even though one may argue that as a lover of the book, someone who has joined the current, one is entitled to use all of its various contents, one should nonetheless find his place in it.

But as a continuum, one point however does seem to be a constant in all of these books, as they all represent a Faustian narrative. This is the central point around which the whole content of the book revolves: Saint Cyprian is always the black immoral sorcerer who renounces his evil ways and joins the Christian faith. This is a subject which is reinforced time and time again, particularly by the introduction of certain narratives within the text of the book (as you will come to see), most of which can seem almost repetitive, featuring a pre-Christian Cyprian plotting and committing foul deeds out of lust for young maidens.

This same Faustian theme is actually not rare in the Iberian context, as for centuries the good Iberian folk have meditated on the tale of the Dominican friar Giles of Santarém (1185-1265, canonized in 1748), who predates Faust by a few centuries.

GILES OF SANTARÉM - 14TH OF MAY

This legend tells us of the young Giles travelling to Paris with the intention of learning medicine, but, as he passes by Toledo, he is approached by a strangely charming man who advises him to instead go to a different school in the caves and undergrounds of Toledo, where he would learn great marvels which would enable him to perform more wonders than any medical knowledge could. Renouncing God and making a pact with the Devil, he operates great miracles until a man fully clad in armor appears to him warning that his life would soon end should he not renounce his pact. Giles then manages this feat by appealing to the Virgin Mary, quite reminiscent of the legend of Theophilus of Adana. So, be it Cyprian or Giles, in truth the theme of the diabolist turned saint is quite natural and common in this region.

Turning our attention solidly to the books in particular, currently in Iberia there are basically two distinct versions of *The Book of Saint Cyprian* in commercial circulation: the Spanish version and the Portuguese version.

The first of these claims in its introduction to have been translated by the monk Jonas Sulfurino, sometimes Sufurino, from a Hebrew scroll given to him by spirits of the infernal courts in the monastery of Brocken (the highest peak in the Harz mountain range, Germany, long associated with Witchcraft and the Devil) in the year 1001. To this same mysterious author is also attributed the book *La Magia Suprema – Negra, Roja e Infernal de los Caldeos y de los Egipcios*, published in the Spanish-speaking South America. Interestingly, this last book actually claims to be a sequel or appendix to the original Sulfurino Book, arguing that at the time of the first edition certain aspects of the German language were too obscure to be translated, but that these have now been set right.

The second version may come in a variety of titles, given the especially prolific nature of its Brazilian editions, and frequently carries adjectives like, but not restricted to, *The True, The Great,* or *The Ancient*, but as a base it is called *The Book of Saint Cyprian – The Sorcerer's Treasure* (a variety of other attributes may also follow, like, *Black Cover, Gold Cover, Steel Cover, Silver Cover* and so on).

The first one, which I will refer to as the Sulfurino Book, usually presents itself as the most coherent and ritually orientated. It contains in fact a simple and logical grimoire presenting a complete system of magic together with a few sections taken from a number of other sources such as the *Petit Albert*.

The name of the monk in question, "Sulfurino", is an adjective for something sulphur-like, so, in that sense a translation would be "Sulphury Jonas", a suggestive name. Also of particular interest in this book would be the extensive list of magical tools it names and teaches how to produce, namely: a white handled knife, a black handled knife, a sword, a dagger, a lancet, a needle, a baton, a quill from a male goose, a magical wand, a mysterious wand (quite different from the previous one), a second dagger (there's a slight difference in Spanish between *daga* and *puñal*, but both translate to dagger in English), a hook and a boline.

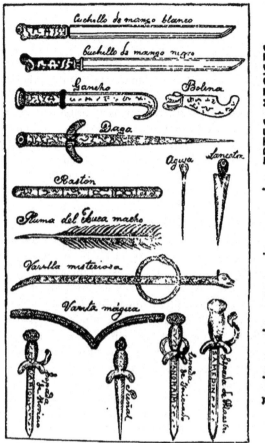

Instrumentos necesarios para las ARTES MAGICAS

These, as many other elements in this book, bear many similarities with the tools and processes described in *The Key of Solomon the King*, but with enough differences as to not make them equivalent.

This version of *The Book of Saint Cyprian* is actually quite prolific, with many editions deviating greatly from one another. Currently you can find extremely small editions of this version in the Spanish market, merely consisting of the mentioned story of Jonas Sulfurino, a brief narration of the life of Saint Cyprian, the conditions necessary to perform an act of magic, the tools required to do the same acts, the ceremonial procedure, and a list of spells and "experiments". But as you widen your range of consideration to Latin-America you can easily find many older arrangements, much larger and complete than the majority of the current Spanish editions. The most extended of these is usually referred to as the *Libro Infernal*, and besides the original Cyprian material it also contains elements from the *Grand Grimoire*, *The Key of Solomon*, or the *Grand et Petit Albert*.

Another remarkable aspect is the fact that the *Libro Infernal* may also be found in Italy. Truth be said, folk traditions of a purely oral nature regarding Saint Cyprian do also exist in Italy, mostly to the North I believe[8], much like they exist in Iberia. This book however is not related to these and should not be confused with an original Italian grimoire of Saint Cyprian, as its presence in this country is actually due the Barcelona based publisher *Editorial Maucci*, which published it around 1920, and was responsible for the creation of the *Libro Infernal* in the first place. This is due to Maucci himself, the publisher, being of Italian origin and as such many of his books ended up translated into Italian[9], meaning that this is not a native product of Italy, but rather an attempt by a publisher to capitalize on a pre-existent tradition. Nonetheless, this situation should not be disregarded, as it is now a part of the continuum.

The Portuguese version of *The Book*, which I will refer to as the *Sorcerer's Treasure*, is an entirely different animal. This is not so much an organized grimoire, existing in itself, but rather a large collection of purely oral and traditional folk magic traditions (be them medicine, orisons, or divinations).

Being still at the crossroads of tradition and the written word, this version is given to an extreme plasticity and flexibility, especially if we open our gaze to include the liveliness of the Brazilian editorial market. In Portugal however, it has remained fairly stable for the last one hundred years or so (this is not counting the more recent influx of Brazilian books coming into the European market), for if one compares its current content with some editions from the late 1800s one does see the exact some content, even if sometimes displayed in a different order or with a different chapter division.

These to me are the two distinct versions of *The Book* currently in commercial circulation in Iberia, but do note that no two *Books of Saint Cyprian* are alike, these are merely the two great "lines" of *Books of Saint Cyprian* in Iberia at this point in time, which, when you reach Brazil and South America, explode into a fertile chaos of magic.

Of course, besides these, it is certain that many other editions and versions existed which are lost today or have simply fallen out of print, as typically any and all magical books in Iberia since the late middle ages would be ascribed to the good Saint Cyprian. One such instance of these lost books of Saint Cyprian was actually reported and analyzed by the ethnographer F. Adolpho Coelho in 1888. This edition, written completely in a somewhat complicated Latin, was entitled *Cypriani Magjej septe horar Magicae*, and in it Cyprian is referred to as the first Sorcerer, as is popular lore. We should quote the following excerpts:

---

8. A tip of my hat to ConjureMan Ali for having confirmed this for me.

9. Idem to Félix Castro Vicente, a true lover of the grimoires, for clarifying this for me.

Ne Opuz hoc contrafial & falso meo NOMine currant Hoc Sabs eripsi
& Rubricavi Mea propria Littera
   Cyprianus Magnus primus

Cyprianus gratia [Belse]buth Locifuge Resoce et ejusdem omnium
potestatum Universi Magust primust, eni tantunmodo cognosscere
Magiae arcana principalia, et tolere de sina Terrae nuica et generali
methodo Thesaura omnia invenire.......
   concessum fuit; nunc pro viribus meis atenuatis Magicandi.....
et parvulos inopiam suam perdere voleus: anrient [arg]entumom ne et
aurum, sient alia pretioza in terra jandudum Magiae virtute detenta:
has septem horas Magiae didico sequentibus notiz. primo: De antiquiz
solum. ADAMI. MAEGI, quae vera est [faina] De paradiso omni
Boni ac Mali Cientia expulsis est. Secundo: Nemo Thezaura haurire
deziderans v... FICAN (?) quaerat...... Mulieres, illae raro pacto sufciens
debent: Querit egenun (?) vel CLoRICVIV, qui pro interin Locifuge
Thezaurorum custode pactum faciat, et fide legat vel a sacerdote audiens
pronuncied omnia infra serripta:
   Magiae artes abjudicate manu; quis in illis aliquod deficiet, et
tantum mea propria manu subscripta, et Typis edita valent, ed solum in
ipsis data ; potente pactum Verum facienti[10].

In this sense of bridging and contracting the two different worlds of oral and written traditions, it is possible to categorize three distinct phases in the history of Portuguese practices of Saint Cyprian and his book, as one must never confuse *The Book of Saint Cyprian* and the traditional magical Cyprianic practices, as both expand well beyond each other.

The first phase one could categorize would be those practices in play before the widespread appearance of *The Book*. This would be defined by an extremely large, diverse and variable body of material which would range the whole history of Portuguese Catholic folk magic, as the ancientness of evocations and magical petitions to Saint Cyprian in Iberia greatly predates the printed books, as is attested by the Gil Vicente play *Exortação da Guerra* (Exhortation of War), written in 1514, where Cyprian is mentioned in the evocation of the demons Zebron and Danor by a necromancer priest:

---

10. You really shouldn't bother too much in trying to accurately translate this piece of text.

(...)	(...)
Nam me quero mais gabar.	I do not wish to brag any more
Nome de Sam Cebrião	In the name of Saint Cyprian
esconjuro-te Satão	I banish thee Satan
senhores nam espantar	My lords do not be frightened
zeet zeberet zerregut zebet	zeet zeberet zerregut zebet
ó filui soter	ó filui soter
rehe zezegot relinzet	rehe zezegot relinzet
ó filui soter.	ó filui soter.

This period should also be characterized by the emergence of heterodox[11] legends of Saint Cyprian, which cement his role as magical hero and underline the moralistic character of his tale, bringing him closer to the reality of the rural folk e/invocation. One such tale, hailing from the Portuguese Minho region, and once again gathered by F. Adolpho Coelho in 1883, falls exactly into this mold (the fragmentary nature of the legend and its strange grammar are typical of an oral ethnographical account, I have tried my best to make it a little bit more understandable):

St. Cyprian was a sorcerer and his father, who had a good amount of money, died and did not leave this money with any of his sons. His father was very much a friend of his son Cyprian and as such his brothers accused him of having kept the money for himself and this greatly bothered him.

"*You have the money,*" he was accused

"*No, it is you who have the money, I have nothing,*" he replied.

Cyprian went down to hell. On account of the pact he held with the Devil he could do this whenever he wished. Upon arriving there he found his father in despair, lying on a fine bed. When he saw his son he said:

"*So, you already join me? Let all of you come, for it is because of you that I am here.*"

Cyprian said:

"*My father, you are here in such a fine bed and still you are so angry?*"

"*Am I? Get your finger close to me.*"

Cyprian extended his finger and it immediately disappeared, because his father was in fact in the middle of a burning flame. He said:

"*My father! I am here to know where you left your money, for we are in a constant war over it.*"

"*The money... go to the wine cellar, behind a large basin, the money is buried there, it is because of that money that I am here.*"

---

11. Heterodox should first be defined as not consistent with the legend of St. Cyprian and Justina, later presented in *The Book* as extracted from the *Flos Sanctorum*, and the text of Cyprian's confession.

Cyprian left and went to the wine cellar with his brothers, finding the money as their father indicated; he then said:

"*Take it all; I want none of it, I will not go to hell on account of that money.*"

His brothers took the money and he left to do penitence and then he went to heaven.

This story, however distant from the orthodox Antioch one presented in the *Flos Sanctorum*, is nonetheless, and once again, a story of conversion and repentance.

This heterodoxy, of course, is not really restricted to these old records, as even today the typical canonical Cyprian legend can be contaminated with echoes from these flexible original practices. With regards to Cyprian's Antioch, for example, one should know that *Antioquia* is also a mythical city sunken in the Galician Lagoa de Antela (province of Ourense), on the upper basin of the Limia River, the river the Romans took to be the Lethe. In this sense one must keep in mind that when a Galician reads the orthodox Antiochian tale of Saint Cyprian, he might be reading something else entirely, adding a random variable to the fixed canonical practice.

Also, other Spanish traditions further remove Cyprian from his known and accepted tale, as the one which mentions him as having had a part to play in the famous *Cueva de Salamanca* or *Cueva de San Cíprian*, a sorcery school where the Devil himself was said to lecture (similar to the one Giles attended in Toledo)[12].

Further evidence of the great variety and widespread nature of ancient Cyprian practices can still be found today in the Iberian countryside, where many prayers and sorceries evoking Saint Cyprian are still used, most of which did not make their way into the written books. To get ahold of these one either has to spend many hours rummaging through ethnographical accounts from the XIXth and XXth centuries or trail the high mountains and scorching plains of Iberia chasing word of mouth.

Furthermore, even in the current versions of *The Book*, which support themselves greatly on Cyprian's orthodox *Flos Sanctorum* tale, one can still find large sections referring directly to these heterodox tales and several incantations presented therein actually make references to events completely incompatible with the tale presented in the *Flos Sanctorum*.

---

12. This was in fact the actual sacristy of the old Church of St. Cyprian in Salamanca, nowadays blocked by order of Isabella I of Castile (the Catholic). This *Cueva* has, of course, much lore of its own, as legend has it that Satan himself taught seven students in it for seven years, after which one of the students would be randomly selected to either be condemned to serve him for the rest of his life or have his shadow stolen by the teacher.

The second phase of Cyprian practices would have come in with the emergence of a standard *Book of Saint Cyprian*, functioning as a "crystallization" of all the oral and unwritten traditions into a semi-solid body. This would have likely meant a reduction in the Cyprian lore around Iberia, as the book would come to be regarded as the canon of Cyprian practices, imposing itself on the global oral corpus. However reductive this might have been, oral traditions have been formed around *The Book* itself, as it became an object of devotion, power, and mystery, a true black box concept for all magic and diabolism.

This reduction in oral material, and the forced conformity around one single book, must not have passed unnoticed, as many legends surrounding *The Book*, no matter how old, usually have as a premise that this is always a reduced corruption. As such, in theory, there should exist a "true" and "complete" book of Saint Cyprian, penned by the magician saint himself, with all the greatest mysteries and powers of existence, somewhere out there, out of reach for common men. This belief is even reinforced by some sections of the *Sorcerer's Treasure* itself, as it many times refers directly to chapters and even specific pages in "Cyprian's book"[13], the original manuscript, and thus assuming itself merely as a reduced version.

According to these same passages, this legendary manuscript was then no smaller than CCI chapters, containing everything from sorceries, orisons, personal diary-like entries, and methods of divination. One such copy of this tome is actually rumored to exist in Galicia, made up of twenty heavy volumes and kept in a secret room in the library of Santiago, locked and chained so as no one may touch it. This is also the idea behind the story of Victor Siderol presented in the *Sorcerer's Treasure*, as this Frenchman finds a true copy of the *Engrimanços de S. Cipriano*, the Grimoire of St. Cyprian, and ends up bringing it to Galicia.

The third, and current period of Cyprian practices came with the liberation of the printing press.

As books become cheaper and cheaper, more variety of material may be added to *The Book of Saint Cyprian* and more variations of it may see the light of day, which has now led, once again, to an increase in the body of Cyprian lore.

This third period cannot in any way be separated from the booming magical-religious atmosphere of South-America. It is there, in the great cultural crucibles of white, black, and Native American blood, that the practices of Cyprian magic are being revitalized and developed beyond the tenets of Iberian praxis, moving further away from the original written books.

This impressive new wave of practices seems now to be making its way back into Iberia and Europe, either transported by emigration or simply by the increasing prestige and recognition of the extremely practical South-American magical-religious techniques, coloring and revitalized the ancient Cyprian cults

---

13. As you will have the chance to see.

and practices. In theory, given their highly pragmatic character, these new revitalized practices may in the near future once again crystallize into a new Cyprian orthodoxy. However, given their allowance for the possibility of direct mediumistic communication with Saint Cyprian himself, a constant flow of new and updated material may be established, making this into a living current by itself, as it once may have been in the distant Iberian past.

ON THE BOOK YOU NOW HOLD

THIS BOOK OF SAINT CYPRIAN, THIS NEW LINK IN THE CHAIN, consists of a translation of the Portuguese version, what I above have referred to as the *Sorcerer's Treasure*.

Given the number of editions and recent variations of this version, I have chosen to follow the old *Livraria Económica* edition present in the Portuguese National Library in Lisbon[14] on most accounts. I understand that this might seem like a hypocritical contradiction given all that was debated above, but one should always start from the beginning.

The points where I deviated from this version were merely on small and curious additions to some sections and sorceries present in more recent editions. Other changes were made but merely regarding organization and numeration of the various sorceries and recipes, on which I have opted, once again, to follow the organization of more recent editions (the *Moderna Editorial Lavores* for example) with which I actually tend to agree. All of these were very simple changes and no part of *The Book*'s content was omitted or lost.

Given all I have tried to transmit in this introduction, this translation is followed by extensive commentaries. The reason behind these is what for a long time had kept me from ever attempting to do a translation of *The Book*. It must be understood that this is a book immensely intertwined in local Portuguese and Iberian culture, that simply translating and transporting it outside of its natural environment would not equally translate and transport its whole significance and power. As such, to try to minimize this inevitable reduction I had no choice but to actually try to equally translate and transport a whole culture.

These commentaries are meant to provide a large cross section of Portuguese magical and religious practices, which may be related to, or have an impact on what is being transmitted by *The Book*'s text and which would be immediately implicit to a conscious Portuguese practitioner. Now, I am very much aware that

---

14. The date of this edition is somewhat uncertain, but a mention of a re-edition of a *Book of Saint Cyprian* by Livraria Económica does feature in the newspaper *Diário de Notícias* from 1855, although there is no proof that this was exactly the same edition as the one used here. Also in the beginning of the third part of *The Book* there is a mention of the date of 1885, which, even if the story behind it is false, would only really make sense if this version of *The Book* was printed after that date. (Once again, my thanks to Felix Castro Vicente.)

such an endeavor is all but impossible, and that the end result will be invariably lacking, nonetheless I have honestly tried my best to provide a good glimpse into the magical Universe of rural Portugal. Should you, dear reader, like to go deeper into any aspect covered or mentioned in these commentaries, I have left you plenty of leads.

It should also be noted that to this end I have resorted largely to the writings of the great Portuguese anthropologists and ethnographers of the late XIXth and early XXth centuries; names such as Teófilo Braga, José Leite de Vasconcelos, or the much more entertaining Teixeira de Aragão will be frequently dropped.

From these I have managed to collect not only the original forms of many of the folk practices which were gathered and presented in *The Book*, so as to demonstrate the oral and traditional roots of this material, but also many diverse Saint Cyprian practices, not at all presented in *The Book*, as well as other practices which bear no obvious connection to the material presented but are nonetheless related to it (such as prayers and orisons to certain saints used within).

Alongside these I have also included the commentaries and additions of Enediel Shaiah, or rather Alfredo Rodríguez Aldao, a Galician journalist, hypnotist, and theosophist (disciple of Papus), a writer and translator of works on occultism and hypnotism. Among his great body of work one can find a most remarkable version of *The Book of Saint Cyprian*, which he called *El Libro Magno de San Cipriano*[15], in which he included elements from the *Grand Grimoire* and other sources so as to "update it". Even though quite often I radically disagree with his position and opinions (and I suspect I won't be the only one), his work should nonetheless be acknowledged and appreciated, both from an occultist and historical perspective.

Lastly, I have also included in the commentaries a few entries from the works of Jeronimo Cortez Valenciano. This was a Spanish author born in Valencia (as his name indicates) somewhere in the XVIth century, popularized by his Inquisition-approved books on medicine and natural secrets. Being that one of his works is actually directly mentioned in the body of the Portuguese *Book of Saint Cyprian*, I have decided to include those entries from his works which seem to be in any way related or relevant to the content of *The Book*. All of these, unless mentioned otherwise, were taken from the 1699 Lisbon edition of the book *Fysiognomia, e Varios Segredos da Naturesa*.

If any of this might seem exaggerated, dear reader, do know that I always prefer to sin by excess.

One last thing...

---

15. The original publication date of this version is somewhat uncertain, although it is at least from the early XXth century; it is currently published by Editorial Humanitas (Barcelona).

Know that this book was written as an intense devotional work to the good Saint. He, or someone on his behalf, was there with me every single day of these past long months, pushing me and riding me (he is a very good-natured saint, but occasionally he does not reasonably measure what he demands of his students... or maybe he measures it too well).

To him I sacrificed my time, my health, my sleep, my social life and my wellbeing and I pray he now doesn't need to claim anyone else's life. And yet, do know that if you are reading this book then you are supposed to be reading it, that with it you invite the Saint and a legion of other spirits I cannot even begin to name into your life. What his plans might be for you are not mine to know.

You are holding my prayer in your hands.

REFERENCES:

Alexandre Parafita: A Mitologia dos Mouros – Lendas, Mitos, Serpentes, Tesouros, Edições Gailivro, Canelas, 2006.

Arlindo José Nicau Castanho: A construção da imagem do Fausto, de Cipriano de Antioquia a Fernando Pessoa, Artifara – Revista de línguas literaturas ibéricas e ibero-americanas, nº1 (Julho-Dezembro 2002) secção Monographica.

Cipriano di Antiochia, Stefano Fumagalli: Confessione – La Prima Versione del Mito di Faust Nella Letteratura Antica, Meledoro, Milano, 1994.

Daniela Buono Calainho: Jambocousses e Gangazambes: Feiticeiros Negros em Portugal, Afro-Ásia, 25-26 (2001) p.141.

F. Adolpho Coelho: Notas e Parallelos Folkloricos – I Tradições relativas a S. Cypriano, Revista Lusitana, Vol, I (1888-1889) p.166.

F. Adolpho Coelho: Notas e Parallelos Folkloricos – II As doze palavras retornadas, Revista Lusitana, Vol, I (1889) p.246.

Francisco Bethencourt: O Imaginário da Magia – Feiticeiras, Advinhos e Curandeiros em Portugal no século XVI, Companhia das Letras, 2004, São Paulo.

H. P. Blavatsky: The Secret Doctrine - Part 5: Synthesis of Science, Religion and Philosophy, Kessinger Publishing, 2003.

Helena Ulhôa Pimentel: Cultura Mágico-Supersticiosa, Cristianismo e Imaginário Moderno, Revista Brasileira de História das Religiões 12 (2012) p.173.

Jake Stratton-Kent: Geosophia – The Argo of Magic, Scarlet Imprint, 2010.

Jake Stratton-Kent: The True Grimoire, Scarlet Imprint, 2009.

Jerusa Pires Ferreira: O Livro de São Cipriano: Uma Legenda de Massas, Editora Perspectiva, São Paulo, 1992.

J. Leite de Vasconcelos: Opúsculos – Volume V – Etnologia, Imprensa Nacional de Lisboa, Lisboa, 1938.

J. Leite de Vasconcelos: Tradições Populares de Portugal – Bibliotheca Ethnographica Portugueza, Livraria Portuense de Clavel & C.ª, Porto, 1882.

Juliana Torres Rodrigues Pereira: *Feitiçaria no Arcebispado de Braga: denúncias a Ana do Frada à Visitação Inquisitorial de 1565*, Cadernos de Pesquisa do CDHIS 24 (2011) p.587.

Maria Helena Farelli: *A Bruxa de Évora*, Pallas Editora, Rio de Janeiro, 2006.

Nicholaj de Mattos Frisvold: *Pomba Gira & the Quimbanda of Mbúmba Nzila*, Scarlet Imprint, 2011.

Owen Davies: *Grimoires – A History of Magic Books*, Oxford University Press, New York, 2010.

Pedro A. de Azevedo: *Cartas de tocar ou de pactos com o demonio*, Revista Lusitana vol.13 (1910) p.66.

P. A. D'Azevedo: *Superstições Portuguesas no sec. XV*, Revista Lusitana vol.4 (1896) p.187.

P. D'Azevedo: *Benzedores e Feiticeiros do Tempo D'El-Rei D. Manuel*, Revista Lusitana, vol.3 (1895) p.329.

Pedro D'Azevedo: *Costumes do Tempo D'El-Rei D. Manuel*, Revista Lusitana vol.4 (1896) p.5.

Peter Missler: *Tradicion y parodia em el Millionario de San Cipriano, primer recetario impreso para buscar tesoros en Galicia (Las hondas raíces del Ciprianillo: 1ª Parte)*, Culturas Populares - Revista Electrónica, 2 (2006) p.8.

Peter Missler: *Las hondas raíces del Ciprianillo – 2ª parte: los grimorios*, Culturas Populares – Revista Electrónica, 3 (2006) p.15.

Peter Missler: *Las Hondas Raíces del Ciprianillo. Tercera parte: las 'Gacetas'*, Culturas Populares – Revista Electrónica, 4 (2006) p.17.

S. Liddell MacGregor Mathers: *The Key of Solomon the King (Clavicula Salomonis)*, Weiser Books, San Francisco, 2006.

Teixeira de Aragão: *Diabruras Santidades e Profecias*, Vega, Lisboa, 1994.

Vanicléia Silva Santos: *As Bolsas de Mandinga no Espaço Atlântico: Seculo XVIII*, Universidade de São Paulo, São Paulo, 2008 (PhD. thesis).

Various authors: *Actas da 1ª Xornada de Literatura oral – Afigura do demo na literatura de tradición oral*, Asociación de Escritores en Lingua Galega, 2005.

Various authors: *Diabolical*, Scarlet Imprint, 2009.

Various authors: *Memento Mori – A collection of Magickal and Mythological Perspectives on Death, Dying, Mortality and Beyond*, Avalonia, London, 2012.

Xoán R. Cuba, Antonio Reigosa, Xosé Miranda: *Dicionario dos seres Míticos Galegos*, Edicións Xerais de Galicia, Huertas, 2008.

DISCLAIMER

IN THIS BOOK YOU WILL NOT FIND the evocations of glamorous demon princes or mighty and powerful angels. There is no high or low magic to be found here. This is a book of the ground, of the dirt, it is not of the mind, it is not of the spirit, it is not of the heart, it is of the viscera. It is the book of the empty stomach, of the bare feet of poverty, the broken heart, the foolish ambition, the maddening envy, the hard cock, the unwashed hands of labor, the agonizing afflicted and all the follies of the world of men.

Let it lull you, let it touch you, learn to love it. Even if you may be sitting comfortably in cushioned sofas, covered with warm rich clothes, never think yourself better than all the barely literate people before you who have read it. You are no less miserable, no less hungry, no less unwashed. The only thing you are more than them is deluded.

It will show you all the darkness beyond the Hells, all the light beyond the Heavens; it will lay bare before your eyes the most precious of gifts and the most horrifying of truths: your own humanity, in all its misery and beauty.

Take your hand and know that YOU turn this page, and in this act embrace your mortality and insignificance.

The Book
of
Saint Cyprian

The Sorcerer's Treasure

LIFE OF ST. CYPRIAN

EXTRACTED FROM

FLOS SANCTORUM OR THE LIFE OF ALL SAINTS

CYPRIAN (named the Sorcerer, so as to be distinguished from the celebrated Cyprian, bishop of Carthage) was born in Antioch, a place located between Syria and Arabia, belonging to the government of Phoenicia. His parents, idolaters and possessors of great wealth, seeing that nature had gifted him with the appropriate talents to easily gain the esteem of men, destined him to the service of the false deities, having instructed him in every science of the idolatric sacrifices. This in such a way as no one like him had such deep knowledge of the profane mysteries of the barbarous genteelism.

At the age of thirty he performed a trip to the country of Babylon so as to learn judiciary astrology and the greatest hidden mysteries of the Chaldeans' superstitions. Surmounting even the great guilt of having dedicated himself to such studies, in the time given to him to search for truth, Cyprian greatly increased his malice and iniquity by giving himself up entirely to the study of magic, so as to, by means of this art, establish a secure commerce with demons, following an impure and absolutely scandalous life.

And whenever a true Christian named Eusebius, who had been his study companion, would frequently call this to his attention and censure his evil life, seeking to save him from the deep abyss where he saw Cyprian fall, not only did he disregard his exhortations, but would even resort to the infernal cunnings to mock the sacrosanct mysteries and the virtuous professors of the Christian law. This he did with such hate that he even joined with the barbaric pursuers who desired to have them renounce the Gospel and deny Jesus Christ.

Cyprian's life had reached this most degraded state when finally the infinite mercy of God came down to illuminate and convert this unfortunate vessel of contumelies and ignominies into a vessel of great reverence and honor. Using His divine grace to operate in Cyprian's heart the prodigious miracle of His Omnipotence in the way we will narrate.

There lived in Antioch a damsel by the name of Justina, no less wealthy than beautiful, whose father, Aedesius, and mother, Cledonia, had educated with great care in the pagan superstitions. However, Justina, gifted as she was with great natural cunning, as soon as she heard the preaching of Praylius, deacon of Antioch, immediately abandoned the gentilic extravagancies and, embracing the Catholic faith, managed in very little time to convert her own parents.

Having been made into a Christian, this blessed virgin immediately became one of the most perfect brides of Jesus Christ, offering Him her virginity and seeking every possible means to conserve this delicate virtue, to which end she carefully followed all modesty, giving herself to prayer and seclusion. Still, upon laying his eyes on her, a poor boy named Aglaias was so pleased that he immediately requested her as bride from her parents, to which they consented; being that the only reason why he couldn't achieve his goal, no matter his diligence, was that he was never able to obtain the consensus of Justina.

Aglaias then resorted to the industries of Cyprian, who immediately applied all of the most effective means of his diabolical art to satisfy his heartsick friend. He offered the demons many abominable sacrifices, and they promised him his desired success, assaulting the great saint with terrible temptations and horrible phantoms. She, however, strengthened by the grace of God, which she very much had earned, with continuous prayer, strict austerities and, most of all, the aid of the Most Holiest Virgin (who she referred to as her most beloved mother), was always victorious.

Angered by not being able to defeat Justina, Cyprian turned against the Devil, who was in his presence at this time, and spoke to him thus: *"Perfidious, already do I see thy weakness when thou cannot even beat a delicate damsel, thou, who brags so much about his power and his ability to operate marvels! Tell me then, what is the reason for this great change, and with what weapons does that virgin defend herself so as to lay thy efforts to waste?"*

The Devil, forced by a divine virtue, confessed the truth, telling Cyprian that the God of the Christians was the supreme Lord of Heaven, of Earth and of the Hells, and that no demon could work against the sign of the Cross with which Justina continuously armed herself. In such a way that, by this same sign, every time he tried to tempt her, he was forced to flee.

"If this is thus," responded Cyprian, *"I would be a madman if I wouldn't give myself to the service of a Lord greater than thou. And as such, if the sign of the Cross on which the God of the Christians died makes thou flee, I no longer wish to use thy prestige. Therefore I renounce entirely to all thy sorceries in the hope that the goodness of Justina's God will admit me as his servant."*

Enraged for losing him through whom he had made so many conquests, the Devil took possession of Cyprian's body. However (so says St. Gregory) by the grace of Jesus Christ, who was now lord of his heart, he was immediately forced to leave. Cyprian now had to endure vigorous battles against the enemies of his soul; but the God of Justina, who he always called upon, came to his aid and made him victorious.

To this end his friend Eusebius was also precious, who Cyprian immediately sought, saying to him while shedding many tears: *"My great friend, the fateful time for me to recognize my errors and abominable disorders has come, and I hope that thy God, who I already confess to be the only true one, may admit me in the guild of His infinitesimal servants, for the great triumph of His benign mercy."*

Greatly pleased by this so prodigious change, Eusebius affectionately embraced his friend, and congratulated him deeply for his heroic resolution, advising to always trust in the infallible truth of the most pure God, who never abandons those who sincerely seek Him. And thus fortified, venturous Cyprian was able to resist with valor all the diabolical temptations.

He made, without ceasing, the sign of the Cross, and, having always on his lips and in his heart the sacrosanct name of Jesus, he never ceased to invoke the aid of the Holiest Virgin. The demons, seeing all their artifices thus fully frustrated, applied their efforts to try and tempt him by desperation, constantly addressing him with discourses and reflections as thus:

"The God of the Christians was without a doubt the only true God, but He was a God of purity, a God who punished with extreme severity even the smallest of crimes, of which they themselves were the greatest of evidences, who, by virtue of committing one single sin of pride, were condemned to an extreme punishment. That being so, how could it be that there was any forgiveness for Cyprian, who by the number and gravity of his sins had already a place reserved and prepared for him in the deepest of Hells? Thus, seeing as no mercy could ever be expected for him, he should take care to solely focus on enjoying himself and loosely satisfying all his earthly passions."

Truthfully, this temptation did put Cyprian's salvation in peril. But his friend Eusebius lifted his spirit and consoled him, efficiently explaining the benign mercy with which God receives and generously forgives all repented sinners, no matter how great their sins. Then Eusebius himself led him to the assembly of the faithful, to the great surprise of the whole audience, there to study the luminous mysteries.

St. Cyprian himself affirms, in the book of his *Confession*, that the sight of the respect and piety so present in the faithful, worshiping the true God, touched his heart deeply. He says, *"I saw that choir singing the praises of God and every verse of the Psalms ending with the Hebrew word Alleluia; all with such respectful attention, and with such smooth harmony, that I thought I was among the angels or of the celestial men."*

At the end of the service the attendants were greatly admired that such a presbyter as Eusebius would introduce Cyprian to that holy congress. And the very bishop leading the service found this very strange, for he did not believe the sincerity of Cyprian's conversion. He, however, dissipated all those doubts by burning all of his magic books in their presence and taking his place among the catechumens, this after having given all his possessions to the poor.

Cyprian, properly instructed and with sufficient disposition, was then baptized by the bishop, together with Aglaias, the young man infatuated by Justina, who, repenting his madness, wished to make amends and follow the true faith. Touched by these two examples of divine mercy, Justina cut her hair as a symbol of her virginity's sacrifice made unto God and also gave her possessions to the poor.

Cyprian, after this, made great and marvelous progress in the ways of the

Lord; his life became a perpetual exercise of the most rigorous penitence. He would be seen many times in church, prostrated on the ground, with his head covered with ashes, pleading to all the faithful to beg for divine mercy for him. And, to humiliate himself further and overcome his old pride, he obtained, after much pleading, the job of church sweeper.

He lived in the company of presbyter Eusebius, who he now venerated as his spiritual father. And the Divine Lord, who always displays the greatest treasures of His divine clemency over the humble souls and over those great sinners truly converted, graced him with the ability to perform miracles. This, together with his great eloquence, greatly helped him to convert to the faith a great number of pagan idolaters; using for this end the famous discourse of his *Confession*, in which, by making his crimes and enormous excesses public, would lift the confidence not only of the faithful but also of the greatest sinners.

In the meantime the name of Cyprian, his zeal and the numerous conquests he performed for the kingdom of Jesus Christ, could not be ignored by the emperors. Diocletian, who then was to be found in Nicomedia, informed of the marvels St. Cyprian worked, and of the perfect sanctity of the virgin Justina, issued an order for their arrest, that the judge Eutolmius, governor of Phoenicia, immediately executed.

Taken, thus, to the presence of this judge, they responded with such generosity and confessed with such efficiency the faith of Jesus Christ that they almost converted the impious barbarian. But, so as no one might think he favored the Christians, he immediately had Saint Justina flayed with thick ropes and the flesh of Saint Cyprian ripped by iron combs, all with such cruelty that it caused horror to the pagans themselves!

The tyrant, seeing that neither promises, nor threats, nor those rigorous torments could bring down the constant firmness of the generous martyrs, ordered them to be thrown into a great caldron of boiling resin, grease and wax. But, seeing the pleasure and satisfaction witnessed on the faces and words of the martyrs, it was evident that nothing in that torment harmed them. The case was such that the very fire under the caldrons appeared not to give off any heat.

This was seen by a priest of the idols, a great Sorcerer named Athanasius (who, for some time, had been Cyprian's disciple) who, thinking that all those prodigies were the result of the sorceries of his old master and wanting to make a reputation for himself among the people, invoked the demons with his magical ceremonies and threw himself willingly into the same caldron out of which Cyprian had just been taken. However, he immediately lost his life and his flesh was boiled off from his bones.

This fact produced even more splendor to the marvels of our saint, and in that city there was almost a great riot in his favor. Under direct orders, the judge then sent the martyrs to Diocletian who at that time was in Nicomedia, informing him by letter of all that had happened. Having read the governor's letter, Diocletian ordered that, without any of the formalities of the usual processes, Cyprian and Justina be beheaded; which did come to happen on the 26th of September by the shores of the river Gallus, which passes by the middle of the mentioned city.

Also, a good Christian named Theoctistus, arriving at that time to speak in secret with St. Cyprian, was equally condemned to be beheaded. This venturous man was a sailor from Tuscany, who had made port near Bithynia. His companions, who were all Christians, upon hearing of this event, came during the night and took possession of the bodies of the three martyrs, taking them to Rome where they were hidden in the home of a pious lady until the time of Constantine the Great, when they were transferred to the basilica of St. John Lateran.

DOCTRINAL REFLECTIONS

The great priest of the Church, St. Gregory Nazianzen, praising in one of his best letters the two saintly martyrs Cyprian and Justina, invites, not only virgins but also married women, to imitate the saint in the glorious effort of her battles. So says the saintly doctor, "*Seeing the candor of her purity so furiously attacked by the impulses of lascivious men and the suggestions of impure demons, she resorted to the weapons of prayer, invoking with fervor and humility the aid of her heavenly Bridegroom, and the powerful aid of the Holiest Virgin.*"

Refer yourselves then to these same weapons, when you are tempted by the powers of darkness. The Lord will surely defend you so as you may not be defeated, rather, you will gain the merit and the crown promised to all those who are valorous in battle. And, lastly, the Saintly doctor proposes the admirable conversion of St. Cyprian, taken from the deepest abyss of iniquity, as an example of confidence and to serve as comfort for sinners (no matter how oppressed they may feel by their countless and unnameable sins), so as they may always trust in the divine mercy, which infinitely exceeds all the sins of men and may, by virtue of its grace, soften the hardest of hearts; and, reducing them by the exercise of a sincere penitence, elevate them to the most eminent degree of eternal glory.

BOOK ONE

BOOK OF ST. CYPRIAN

※

CHAPTER I

Instructions to the priests who are about to heal any ailment. The rules that every member of the clergy must study so as to know if the ailment he is about to heal is a work of sorcery or of the Devil.

We should not so easily believe that every illness that befalls upon a person is the result of sorcery or of the art of the Devil, for we observe in every step of our lives people who suffer from natural afflictions. Even a disease that prolongs itself in time and has no cure might not be the result of sorcery; it may actually be the contrary.

Occasionally one might go to the homes of certain women and certain men, who can barely distinguish what is natural or what is supernatural, who will then start to banish and curse at Spirits who are not to be blamed. These imposters become thus cursed by God, as St. Cyprian says in his book, in chapter XVI.

I plead then, with all my heart, to all priests, that they study attentively these Instructions, so as not to expose themselves to the curse of the Creator. This because all we do and accomplish is in the name of Jesus Christ, and for this reason we must not offend Him, but rather invoke His Holy Name, so as he may assist us when we pray for the sick, so as we may not confuse a sickness that is the work of sorcery and of Infernal Spirits with that which is merely natural. After these Instructions I will quote an orison in Latin, to be read over the sick person three times, for, if it is a sorcery or the work of either benign or evil Spirits, they will immediately speak out, declaring that they are inside this creature, for she will begin to flail convulsively. Should this happen, then you can be sure that this sickness is supernatural and not natural, and, as such, you should immediately say:

"I plead to thee, Spirit, in the name of God All-Mighty, that thou declares to me why thou art harming this body (here one should say the name of the sick person), for I conjure thee to tell me what thou desires from the corporeal world. Here is the protector who shall pray to the Lord on thy behalf, so as thou may be purified in the kingdom of Glory."

At the end of this evocation, the priest will immediately know if this Spirit is roaming the world in search of charity, for as soon as it is told, "*I shall pray for thee,*" the sick person will become calm and tranquil. If this happens, all present must kneel, and as a choir, say the orison we will teach below.

ORISON FOR THE GOOD SPIRITS SO AS TO LEAD THEM TO GOD AND ABANDON THE AILING CREATURE

When one says to the Spirit, *"Be still, for I shall pray to God on thy behalf"* and the person becomes even more agitated this is a sign that the Spirit inside her is evil.

In that case perform the banishment of St. Cyprian.

But, my good reader, I beg you in the name of God, do not treat any sickness without having studied these rules thoroughly. It is important to note that every orison contained in this book has its own application, and the one that is proper for one thing may not be proper for another. There are five orisons that may be found in this good book:

1st To plead to God on behalf of the good Spirits.

2nd To banish the evil Spirits.

3rd To cure sickness, even if natural, that is, not the work of sorcery or diabolism.

4th To banish enchantments or enchanted treasures.

5th To close an open body, so as Spirits may not enter that body again.

These are the principal orisons, but beyond these, this book contains much more immensely curious things, with which the reader will no doubt amuse himself.

CHAPTER II

New orisons for the open hours

FOR MIDDAY

Oh Virgin of the holy Heavens,
Mother of our Redeemer,
Who, among women, holdst the palm,
Bring joy to my soul,
That moans filled with grief;
And come and place on my lips
Words of pure love.
In the name of the God of the worlds,
And also in the name of the beloved Son,
Where the supreme goodness resides,
Always be praised
In this blessed hour. *Amen.*

FOR THE TRINITIES[16]

May the Holiest Trinity
Always accompany my steps,
And open friendly arms to me
In the hours of sorrow.
May the Eternal Father aid me,
And Jesus Bless me.
May the Spirit give me light
Against the temptations of Hell
May I spend all my existence
Always practicing good
And the Holiest Trinity
Guide me on Earth. *Amen.*

---

16. Translator's note: At sunrise and sunset, around 6:00 and 18:00.

FOR MIDNIGHT

Oh my good Guardian Angel,
Be at my side in this hour
Free me from visions;
And let God keep my soul
From any mortal sin,
And avoid dreams and ideas
That may harm my brothers
Oh my good Guardian Angel
Ask the Virgin our Mother,
To keep me away from sin
Through all of this life. *Amen.*

CHAPTER III

The repent and virtues of St. Cyprian
(Summary of his life)

CYPRIAN, called the Sorcerer (for, as we have said, Cyprian since his childhood to the age of thirty held a pact with the Devil and relations with every infernal spirit), was born in Antioch, a place between Syria and Arabia, belonging to the government of Phoenicia. His parents, idolaters and possessors of great wealth, seeing that nature had gifted him with the appropriate talents so as to easily gain the esteem of men, destined him to the service of the false deities, having him instructed in every science of the idolatric sacrifices; in such a way that no one like him had such deep knowledge of the profane mysteries of the barbarous genteelism; finally at the age of thirty, he made a trip during which a religious man named Eusebius, who was his colleague at that time and frequently expressed harsh censorship of his evil life, sought to save him from the deep abyss he saw him in. Cyprian not only despised him but also used his great cunning to frequently ridicule him.

However, one day, Eusebius prayed so much to God that his orisons were heard in Heaven.

The mercy of God finally came to illuminate and convert this unfortunate victim of the ignominious cunnings of Satan into a religiously devout creature. Using His divine grace to operate in Cyprian's heart the prodigious miracle of His Omnipotence in the way we will narrate:

There lived in Antioch a damsel by the name of Justina, no less wealthy than beautiful, whose father, Aedesius, and mother, Cledonia, had educated with great care in the pagan superstitions. However, Justina (gifted, as she was, with great cunning), as soon as she heard the preaching of Praylius, deacon of Antioch, immediately abandoned the gentilic extravagancies and, embracing the Catholic faith, managed, in very little time, to convert her own parents.

Having been made into a Christian, Justina became at the same time one of the most perfect daughters of Jesus Christ, giving Him her virtue and virginity and seeking every possible means to conserve this delicate virtue, to which effect she carefully observed all modesty and seclusion. Still, laying his eyes on her, a poor boy named Aglaias was so pleased that he immediately requested her as bride from her parents, to which they consented; being that the only reason why he couldn't achieve his goal, no matter his diligence, was that he was never able to obtain the consensus of Justina.

Aglaias then went to Cyprian for help, who immediately applied all the most effective means of his diabolical art to satisfy his friend's desire. However, Cyprian's spells were of no use.

In desperation, Cyprian offered the demons many and abominable sacrifices, and they promised him his desired success, assaulting Justina with great temptations and phantoms; she, however, strengthened by grace, which she very much had earned, with continuous prayer, strict austerities and most of all the aid of the Most Holiest Virgin (who she referred to as her most beloved mother), was always victorious. Angered by not being able to defeat Justina, Cyprian turned against the Devil, who was in his presence at this time, and spoke to him thus, "*Accursed and perfidious, already do I see thy weakness, when thou cannot even beat a delicate damsel; thou, who brags so much about his power and his ability to operate marvels! Tell me then, what is the reason for this great change, and with what weapons does that virgin defend herself to lay thy efforts to waste?*"

The Devil, forced by a divine virtue, confessed the truth, telling Cyprian that the God of the Christians was the supreme Lord of Heaven, of Earth and of the Hells, and that no demon could work against the sign of the Cross ✠ with which Justina continuously armed herself. In such a way that by this same sign, every time he tried to tempt her, he was forced to flee.

Cyprian then said, "*If this is so, the Lord is more powerful than thou, and, if the sign of the Cross makes thou flee, I banish thee in the name of the God of the Christians.*" At this time, Cyprian crossed his arms as the Cross of Christ. The Devil, irritated, grabbed him and dragged him to Hell. However, not long after that, the Devil was forced by St. Gregory to return Cyprian to his former state, but not before many prayers.

Cyprian, henceforth, found his life very difficult, for the Devil would frequently tempt him; but Cyprian would always make the sign of the cross with his arms, and in this way make him flee.

St. Gregory told Cyprian that he would only have salvation when he freed himself of all things that had him bonded. Cyprian covered himself with the grace of God and rented a poor house so as to call all of the Devil's crafts into it. Shortly after this, Cyprian was elevated by the Grace of God into the kingdom of the just.

CHAPTER IV

The signs of malefic influence on creatures. Orison that should be read to the sick in order to know if his illness is natural or supernatural, which the priest should have studied thoroughly in Chapter I and in its Instructions; without this, one may not provide good services.

This orison is said in Latin so that the sick person will not be able to fool you; for, if the sick does not understand what is being said he will not know when to move or remain still, and in this way he will not be able to fool the priest attending him.

Following this there is an orison in the vernacular for the same objective.

The signs of malefic influences:

If the priest realizes that the illness is due to a demon or a lost soul, he should say the litany; at the end of the litany apply the Precept that is found below in the vernacular.

"Praecipitur in nomine Jesu, ut desinat nocere aegroto, statim cesser delirium, et illud ordinate discurrat. Si cadat, ut mortuus, et sine mora surget ad praeceptum Exorcistae factum in nomine Jesu. Si in aliqua parte corporis, sit dolor, vel tumor, et ad signum Crucis, vel imposito praecepto in nomine Jesu cessat. Si sine causa velit sibi mortem inserre, se praecipite dure. Quando imaginationi, se praesentant resinhonestae contra Imagines Christi, et Sanctorum, et si eodem tempore antiant in capite, ut plumbum, ut aquam frigidam, vel ferrum ignitem, et hoc fugit ad signum Crucis vel invocato nomine Jesu. Quando Sacramenta, Reliquias, et res sacras odit; quando, nulla praecente tribulatione, desperat, et súbito restitutur; quando diurno tempore nihil vidit, et súbito siat surdus, et postea bene audiat, non solum materialia, sed spiritualia. Si per septem, vel novem dies nihil, vel parum comedens fortis est, et pinguis, sicut antea. Si loquitur de Mysteriis ultra suam capacitatem, quando non curat de illius sanctitate. Quando ventus vehemens discurrit per totum corpus ad mudum formicarum; quando elevatur corpus contra voluntatem patientis, et non apparet a quo levetur. Clamores, scissio vestium, irritationes dentium, quando patiens non est stultus; vel quando homo natura debilis non potest teneri a multis. Quando habet linguam tumidam, et nigram, quando guttur instatur, quando audiuntur rugitus leonum, balatus ovium, latratus canum, porcorum grunnitus, et similium. Si varie praeter naturam vident, et audiunt, si homines máximo ódio persequuntur; si praecipitiis se exponunt, se óculos horribiles habent, remanent sensibus destituti. Quando corpus tali pondere asciscitur, ut a multis hominibus elevaret non benedicti, quando ad Ecclesia fugit, et aquam benedictam non consentit; quando iratos se ostendunt contra Ministros superponentes Reliquias capiti (etsi occulte). Quando Imagines Christi, et Virginis Mariae nolunt proferre, vel se proferunt, illa corrumpunt, et balba, scienter student proferre. Cum superposita capiti manu sacra ad lectionem Evageliorum conturbatur aegrotus, cum plusquam solitum palpitaverit, sensus occupantur guttae sudoris desudunt, anxietates senit, stridores usque ad Caelum mittit, se prosternit, vel similia facit."

†

Precept to the Devil or demons so that they do not
mortify the sick during the banishment

This precept should be repeated many times, and particularly to pregnant women, so as to prevent these from vomiting due to the powerful demonic attacks that happen during this occasion.

"I, as a creature of God made in His image and redeemed with His Holiest Blood, place this precept upon thee, Devil or demons, so as thou may cease thy deliriums, so as this creature is no longer tormented by thee and thy infernal furies.

"For the name of the Lord is strong and powerful, by Him I cite and notify thee to take leave of this place. I bind thee eternally to the place God Our Lord destined for thee; for with the name of Jesus do I stomp and beat thee and bore thee even from my thoughts. The Lord is with me and with all of us, the absent and the present, so as thou, Devil, will no longer torment the creatures of the Lord. Flee, flee, opposing parties, the lion of Judah and the race of David are victorious.

"I bind thee with the chains of St. Paul and with the towel with which he wiped the holy face of Jesus Christ so as thou may never again torment the living."

Next perform the Act of Contrition.

Next, one should say the orison of St. Cyprian to undo all qualities of sorcery and banish all demons, evil spirits or other bindings made by men or women, also, it should be prayed in a house suspected of being possessed by malignant spirits, or, finally, for every single thing which is connected with supernatural illness.

In this orison it is often said, "*I, Cyprian, servant of God, unbind all that I have bound.*" But the priest saying it should not pronounce the name of the Saint, but rather speak in his own name, saying; "*I unbind all that is bound.*"

The Saint is invoked but his name is not pronounced, for in this first part we merely mention the life of St. Cyprian, extracted from the saintly book he himself wrote, and which has certain restrictions in this sense. In the next two parts of the book, however, the reader will be fully informed of all that is relevant.

Orison

"I, Cyprian, servant of God, whom I love with all my heart, body and soul, weighing upon me not having loved Thee since the day Thou gave me being. However, Thou, my God and my Lord, did one day remember this Thy servant Cyprian.

"I thank Thee, my God and my Lord, with all my heart the benefits I receive from Thee, for, now, oh God of the Most High, give me strength and faith so I may unbind all that I have bound, to which I will always invoke Thy Holiest Name. In the name of the Father, the Son and the Holy Spirit. Amen.

"Thou who lives and reigns over all centuries of centuries. Amen. It is certain, Our Lord, that now it is I, Thy servant Cyprian, telling Thee, Mighty and Powerful God who lives at the summit that is Heaven, where the Mighty and Holy God exists, praised be Thou forever.

"Thou who saw the malice of this Thy servant Cyprian! And by such malice did I get placed under the Devil's power! But I did not know Thy Holy Name. I would bind women, bind the clouds of the sky, bind the waters of the sea so as the fishermen could not sail and could not fish the sustenance of men! For I, for my malice, my great evil doings, would bind pregnant women so as they could not give birth, and all these things I would do in name of the Devil. Now, my God and my Lord, I know Thy Name and I invoke it once and again so as all Witchcrafts and Sorceries in the machinery or body of this creature (NN) be undone and torn. For I call Thee, oh Powerful God, so as Thou may cut every binding of men and women ✠. Let rain fall on the surface of the earth so it may bear its fruits; let women have their children, free from any binding I may have done; unbind the sea so as fishermen may fish. Free from all danger, unbind all that is bound in this creature of the Lord; let it be untied, unbound in any way it may be. I unbind it, unstitch it, tear, trample and scrap it all, dolls that may be hidden in any well, or taken so as to wither this creature (NN), and let all be free from evil and every evil or evil deeds, sorceries, enchantments or superstitions, diabolical arts. The Lord all did He destroy and annihilate; the God of the High Heavens, glory unto Him in Heaven and on Earth, like as Emmanuel, which is the name of the Powerful God. As the dry stone opened and sprang water which the children of Israel drank, so will the greatly powerful Lord, with a handful of grace, free this servant (NN) from all evils, sorceries, bindings and enchantments, made partly or in full by the Devil and his minions, and as this orison is said over thy head and thou brings it with thee or has it in thy home, let everything become an earthly paradise from which four rivers will flow forth, fifty-six Tigris and Euphrates, by which Thou commanded that water be distributed throughout all of the world, for which I now beg. Jesus Christ my Lord, Son of the Holiest Mary, to those that may be saddened or mistreated by the accursed malignant spirit, no enchantment or evil deed will be made or anything be moved against this Thy servant (NN), but let all things here mentioned be obtained and nullified, for which reason I invoke the seventy-two tongues that are spread across the whole world and all that is their contrary, let thy studies be annihilated by the Angels, may this Thy servant (NN) be absolved, together with his home and all things in it contained, let all be free of every malefica and sorcery, in the name of God the Father who was born over Jerusalem, by all the remaining Angels and Saints and by all those who serve before Paradise or in the presence of the high God the All-Mighty Father, so as the Devil may not have power to disturb anyone. Any person who brings this orison with them or has it read to them, wherever there is any sign of the Devil, be it day or night, by God, James and Jacob, the cursed enemy shall be cast out; I invoke the communion of the Holy Apostles, of Our Lord Jesus Christ, of St. Paul; by the orisons of the nuns, by the purity and beauty of Eve, by the sacrifice of Abel, by God united unto Jesus, His eternal Father, by the chastity of the faithful, by their kindness, by the faith of Abraham, by the obedience of Our Lady when she gave birth to God, by the orison of the Magdalene, by the patience of Moses, may the orison of St. Joseph break these enchantments, Saints and Angels be with me; by the sacrifice of Jonas, by the tears of Jeremiah, by the orison of Zacharias, by the prophecy and by those who do not sleep at night and are dreaming of Our Lord God Jesus Christ, by the prophet Daniel, by the words of the Evangelists, by the fire tongue crown given to Moses, by the sermons made by the Apostles, by the birth of Our Lord Jesus Christ, by His holy baptism, by the voice of the Eternal Father that was heard saying, "This is my Son, whom I love; with him I am well pleased for everyone fears him and because he made thee abandon the sea and bear fruits onto the earth," by the miracles of the Angels that are with Him, by the virtues of the Apostles, by the Holy Spirit that came down on them, by the virtue and names in this orison, by the praise of God who made all things, by the Father ✠, the Son ✠, the Holy Spirit ✠ (NN), if any sorcery was made unto the hairs on thy head, the clothes on thy body, the linens of thy bed, or on thy shoes, or in cotton, silk, linen, or wool, or the hair of a Christian, or *Mouro*, or heretic, or in the bones of a human creature, or of a bird or any other animal; or in wood, or in books, or in Christian graves or *Mouros* graves, or in a fountain or bridge, or altar, or river, or at home, or in a wall of lime, or in a field, or in a solitary place, or in any church, or any river branch, in a house made of wax or marble, or in a cloth doll or in a puddle toad, or in food or drink, or on the dirt of the left or right foot, or on anything one may make a sorcery with...

"All these be undone and unbound from this servant of the Lord (NN), as many as I Cyprian have done, as many as these *Bruxas*, servants of the Devil, have made; may all be returned to the same being from where it was taken, or unto his own figure, or unto the one that God created.

"Saint Augustine and all Saints, by the holy names, make every creature free from the Devil. Amen."

†

First Banishment

This banishment should be said by the priest with the utmost respect and faith, and as soon as he sees that the sick is in pain and the Devil or evil spirit does not want to leave, he should read the precept in Chapter IV, after the litany, or that which is in Latin.

"I, Cyprian (NN - name of the exorcist), by God Our Lord Jesus Christ, absolve the body of (NN) of all evil sorceries, enchantments, blockings, ties that men and women make and request, in the name of God Our Lord Jesus Christ, God of Abraham, great and powerful God! Glory unto Thee, forever may all the ailments of this Thy servant (NN) be destroyed, undone, unbound, reduced to nothing by Thy Holiest Name; let God come with his good works for love of mercy so that such men and such women who cause these evils be touched in their hearts so that they will cease this wicked life!

"With me be the Angels of Heaven, mainly St. Michael, St. Gabriel, St. Raphael and all the Saints and Angels of the Lord, and the Apostles of the Lord, St. John the Baptist, St. Peter, St. Paul, St. Andrew, St. James, St. Matthias, St. Luke, St. Philip, St. Mark, St. Simon, St. Anastasius, St. Augustine and by all the orders of the Saintly Evangelists: John, Luke, Mark and Matthew, and by all the Cherubim and Michaels, created by the grace of the Holy Spirit. By the seventy-two tongues that are spread throughout the world, and by this absolution, and by the voice that called Lazarus from his grave, by all these virtues let everything be returned to the being that once possessed them or the same health he enjoyed before it was snatched by the demons, for I, in the name of the All-Mighty, order that everything cease its supernatural disconcert.

"Furthermore by the virtues of those holiest words by which Jesus Christ called, "Adam, Adam, Adam, where art thou?" By these holiest words we absolve, by that virtue of when Jesus Christ said unto the sick, "Rise and go home and never sin again," for he was suffering from this sickness for three years, for let God absolve thee ✠ who created the Heaven and the Earth and may He have compassion on thee, creature (NN). By the prophet Daniel, by the sanctity of Israel, and by all the Saints of God, absolve this Thy servant (NN) and bless his home ✠ and let all other things be free from the demon's power by Emmanuel, for may God be with all of us. Amen.

"By the holiest Name of God Our Lord Jesus Christ may all these things here mentioned be unbound, undone, unstitched of all encumbrances made by the arts of the Devil or his companions, let it all be destroyed; this I order by the power of the All-Mighty, so that now, without further appeal, they be unbound and disconnected of all evil sorceries and bindings and all evil venture by Christ Our Lord. Amen."

†

Second Banishment

"I banish thee, excommunicated demons, or evil baptized spirits, if with evil bonds, sorceries, the Devil's enchantments, be them of envy, or be them made from gold, or silver, or lead, or on lonely trees, may it all be destroyed and disconnected and no longer bind anything to the body of (NN) or otherwise, for, henceforth, if this sorcery or enchantment is in any celestial or earthly idol, may it all be destroyed by God, for all of Hell and all language I trust in Jesus Christ, the delectable name! As Jesus Christ separates and banishes the Devil and all his sorceries from the Earth, so, by these delectable names of Our Lord Jesus Christ, may all demons, ghosts and all evil spirits in the company of Satan and his companions flee to their residences, which are all in the Hells, being there in the company of all sorcerers and sorceresses who performed sorceries on this creature (NN) or in this house and all that this same house contains. May it be undone and nullified, banished, broken and abjured by the power of the Holy Obedience, by the power of the Belief in God the Father and the three Persons of the Holiest Trinity and the holiest Sacrament of the Altar. Amen.

"With all sanctity I banish thee and exile thee, cursed demons, evil spirits, rebellious to my and our Creator!

"For I bound thee and bound thee again and bind and tie thee to the waves of the sea, and let them take you to the rough sands of the curdled sea[17], where neither chicken nor rooster sings, or to thy own destinies or places, which God Our Lord Jesus Christ has determined for thee.

"I lift, break, abjure and banish all requests, encumbrances, precepts and obligations that thou made unto this body of (NN). As of now thou are cited, notified and forced, thou and thy companions, to follow the path that Jesus Christ destines for thee, this without any appeal or aggravation by the power of God Our Lord Jesus Christ and the Holiest Mary and the Holy

---

17. Translator's note: The Curdled Sea, *Mar Coalhado*, is an interesting concept in Northwestern Iberian folklore. This is actually the original primordial Ocean of Chaos, from which God created the Cosmos, simultaneously thought of as dead (like sour milk) and a depository of all possible form (like the irregular curds in the milk). Threats to send spirits into the Curdled Sea are one of the most common, powerful, and effective cohesion methods used in Portuguese folk magic.

This is also related to the concept of *braços de mar*, branches of sea, which are, again, associated with either the primordial Ocean of Chaos or the biblical account of the great deluge and Noah's Ark. *Braços de mar* are isolated pieces of raging ocean hidden and trapped underground, which, should they be disturbed, will flood the whole Earth. These are one of the great dangers of magical treasure hunting.

Spirit and the Three Divine Persons of the Holiest Trinity, which is one with the true God in whom I truly believe and by whom I lift these plagues and rages, vengeances and fears, hates and evil eyes; I break and abjure all requests, embargoes, encumbrances, precepts and obligations by the power of the Holy Verb Incarnate and by the virtue of Holiest Mary and all the Saints and Angels and Cherubim and Seraphim, created by the grace of the Holy Spirit. Amen."

When the priest finishes saying what is written above and the demon cries out and says, "*I am not Satan, but a lost soul; I still, however, have salvation!*"

The priest then should ask, "*Dost thou wish for me to pray for thee?*" The soul will then respond, "*Yes, I do.*" After this response, let all those present fall to their knees and say the Orison for the good spirits that is mentioned in this book, for it is common that one may be banishing a soul who actually requires prayers rather than banishment.

Let the reader study the Instructions in Chapter I carefully so as not to perform an absurdity such as the one I just mentioned; for this work is not a joke, it is rather a great service, both to God and the good spirits.

†

Third Banishment

"Here is the Cross ✠ of the Lord; flee, flee, be gone enemies of the human nature.

"I banish thee in the name of Jesus, Mary, Joseph, Jesus of Nazareth, King of the Jews. Here is the Cross of Our Lord Jesus Christ. Flee, opposing factions, the lion of the tribe of Judah and the race of David are victorious.

"Alleluia, Alleluia, Alleluia, exalted be the Lord, let him bless us, keep us and show us His Divine Face, let Him turn His Divine Face towards us and show us compassion. King David came in peace, as Jesus was made man and lived among us and was born of the Holy Virgin Mary by His holy mercy.

"Saintly Apostles, blessed of the Lord, pray to the Lord to come in my aid, Cyprian, so I may destroy all that I have done.

"St. John, St. Matthew, St. Mark, St. Luke, I beg thee to free us and preserve us free of all demonic activities.

"We expect all from those who live and reign with the Father and the Holy Spirit, for all the centuries of centuries. Amen.

"Let the blessing of the Omnipotent God, Father, Son and Holy Spirit, come upon us and bless us continuously.

"Jesus, Jesus, Thy peace and Thy virtue and Passion, the sign of the Cross ✠, the wholeness of the Blessed Virgin Mary, the blessings of the Saints chosen by God, the title of Our Savior upon the Cross, Jesus of Nazareth, King of the Jews, be triumphant today and on all days among my visible and invisible enemies, against all dangers of our life and our body, and at all times and in all places. I will have the greatest pleasure and joy in God my savior.

"Jesus, Jesus, Jesus, be with us, Jesus, Jesus, Creator and forgiver; Jesus of the Universe will cast the wicked over Hell and will stop the Devil from ever tormenting His creatures. Jesus, Son of Mary, Savior of the World, by the merits of the Blessed Virgin Mary and the Holy Angels, Apostles, Martyrs, Confessors and the Virgins, let the Lord be with thee and defend thee and be in thee so as to conserve thee and lead thee and accompany thee and keep thee and be over thee so as thou may be blessed, He who lives and reigns in perfect unity with the Father and the Holy Spirit for all the centuries of centuries. Amen.

"The blessing of the Omnipotent God, Father, Son and Holy Spirit, come upon us and stay with us continuously.

"Holiest Virgin Our Lady of Succor, I, the greatest of Sinners, ask Thee to pray for me to Thy Beloved Son to break all of the demons' forces so as they may never torment this creature again.

"I end this holy orison and all harm made by the workings of evil spirits in this house shall end."

(End of the orison of St. Cyprian)

✝

Orison to the Lord, or praise for having freed the sick from the power of Satan or his allies, which should be prayed while kneeling and with great devotion.

"Jesus Christ my Lord, I give Thee infinite graces, for, by the virtue of Thy holiest passion, by Thy precious blood, and by Thy infinite goodness, Thou has freed me from the Devil, or from his sorceries and spells; and thus do I ask Thee, and beg of Thee now, preserve me and keep me, so that the Devil from henceforth may never harm me again: for I wish to live and die under the protection of Thy Holiest Name, Amen. P. N. A. M.[18]"

WARNING TO THE PRIEST

When, even after all these orisons, the sick does not find himself completely relieved, the priest, after three days, should inquire about his health; should he see that he is still possessed by the Devil, and to know this he should once again read the signs we have here in Latin, it is then certain that there are still sorceries at play.

---

18. Translator's note: *Pater Noster* and *Ave Maria.*

In this case we are facing an open body and one should immediately close him in the following fashion, after reading once again the orison of St. Cyprian.

✝

THE METHOD OF CLOSING A BODY

Take a small steel key and bless it in the following manner:

"The Lord cast upon thee His holiest blessing and His holiest power so as to give thee effective virtue. So that every passage or every door Satan uses to enter may be closed by thee, never again will the Devil or his allies pass through, for blessed art thou by the Father, the Son and the Holy Spirit. Amen. Jesus be with thee."

(Cross the key with holy water)

✝

Holiest words the cleric should say when he is closing a body. The key should be upon the chest of the sick, as if it was locking a door.

"Oh Omnipotent God, who from the breast of the Eternal Father came into the world for the salvation of man, look down upon us, Lord, place a precept on the Devil or demons, so as they no longer have power and never again dare enter this body. Let its door be closed, as Peter closes the doors of Heaven to the souls who wish to enter there without atoning for their sins."

(The cleric should then make a movement as if he is closing a lock on the chest of the sick.)

"My Lord, allow Peter to descend from the Heaven to Earth to close this door where the cursed demons wish to enter whenever they please.

"For I (NN), by Thy Holiest Name, place a precept on these spirits of evil, that from this day on they may never again take up residence in the body of (NN), for this door is permanently closed, just as the door of the pure spirits is closed to them. Amen."

After this orison is said, write on a piece of paper the name of Satan and burn it while saying: *"Be gone Satan, be gone as smoke up the chimney."*

After all this is said, if the sick is still not healed, say the orison of St. Cyprian again.

CHAPTER V

Regarding ghosts that appear at crossroads, or souls from the spiritual
world, who by commandment from God come to this corporeal
world seeking prayers and purification from the mistakes they
committed in this world against God Our Lord, and are thus
sent to mortify its creatures and appear to them as ghosts so as
to be prayed for; however, instead of prayers some men banish
and curse them; a great error of humanity! Read and study well
what follows, so as you may be of service to these unfortunate
spirits.

What are ghosts?

These are visions that appear to certain individuals, possessors of a weak
spirit and a strong belief that the souls of those who have ceased to exist still
visit this world. For ghosts only appear to those who believe in spiritual beings
and not to the incredulous, for they would have no advantage in doing so; on
the contrary, they would only receive curses.

Ah! What will become of he who thus acts in this world, poor fool, if he
does nothing but mock the servants of the Lord who come to this world to seek
relief and instead find punishment? Their torments are doubled!

Ah! What will become of you on the day of your sentencing, if you don't
have good friends to petition on your behalf to the supreme Judge? If you have
no friends, you will be punished with the whole rigor of Justice.

Then, nurture, nurture good and true friendships, so as on that terrible
day you might have good friends to pray to the Creator on your behalf; do as the
farmer who, so as to reap many good fruits by St. Michael, casts upon the earth
all the good and proper elements.

Take heed, my brothers, these words do not come from the tip of my pen,
but rather inspired from the depths of my heart! When a vision appears before
you do not banish it, for it will curse you, it will damage all your businesses and
all in your life will go sour; however, when you feel such a vision resort to the
orison in this book entitled *Orison for the good spirits*, for you will immediately
relieve that beggar who asks for alms from all charitable people.

Know, my brothers, the Devil very seldom appears as a ghost, for demons
used to be angels and as such do not have a body to clothe themselves with; as
such I do recommend that when you see a ghost in the form of an animal, being
it certain that such is a demon, you should banish him by making a ✠. But, if
the ghost has a human figure, it is not a demon, but truly a soul seeking relief
from his sentences. You should then immediately make the orison in this book,
for you will surely not lose anything in doing so, for that soul, which you just

released, will be with you always should you call upon it. Do not take my word for it: do the experiment and you will see.

Pray, pray for those poor spirits, and call upon them in all your dealings and in everything you so choose that you will always be successful; this I swear.

Fortunate is the creature that is pursued by spirits, for it is certain that this is a good person and spirits pursue her so that she will pray to the Lord on their behalf, for she is worthy to be heard by the Creator. It is for this reason that some are more pursued by ghosts than others. Many other spirits do not adopt this system of appearing as ghosts, but rather appear in the houses of their relatives, making noises during the night, dragging chairs, tables and all other things throughout the house; one day they kill a pig, the next a cow, and thus all goes wrong in such a house, all because of the lack of intelligence of its inhabitants, for if they immediately resorted to these orisons they would be free from the spirit and would also perform an act of charity, and, on the last day of their life, the doors of Heaven would open for them. Note these words, my brothers, and consecrate them in your heart, for my intention is that, with this work, many souls may be saved and no more absurdities committed.

†

Orison to petition God on behalf of the good spirits who come to this world seeking prayers so as to be purified from the evils they committed in this world, or restitute some debt or robbery[19].

"Leave, Christian soul, this world, in the name of God the Father All-Mighty, who created thee; in the name of Jesus Spiritual Son of the Living God, who suffered for thee; in the name of the Holy Spirit, who copiously communicates with thee. Be gone from this body or place where thou lingers, for the Lord now receives thee in His kingdom; Jesus, hear my prayer and be my support as Thou are the support of the Saints, Angels and Archangels; of the Thrones and Dominions; of the Cherubim and Seraphim; of the Prophets, the Saintly Apostles and the Evangelists; of the Saintly Martyrs, Confessors, Monks, Religious men and Hermits; of the Saintly Virgins and wives of Jesus Christ and of all Saints of God, who may now give thee a place of rest and enjoyment of peace in the holy city of celestial Zion, where thou may praise Him for all centuries. Amen."

LET US PRAY

---

19. Original footnote: One should recite this orison in any place where it is necessary, or in any place where a spirit or ghost roams. After this orison one should pray the Creed and perform the Act of Contrition.

Merciful God, clement God, God who according to the greatness of Thy infinite mercy forgives the sins of this spirit who bears the pain of having committed them, and give him full absolution of past guilt and offenses. Look down with Thy eye of mercy on this Thy servant who roams this world pining; open for him, Lord, the gates of Heaven, hear him and grant him forgiveness of all his sins, for full-heartedly does he ask this of Thee through his humble confession. Renew and divide, oh merciful Father, the faults and ruins of this soul, and the sins he made and contracted, either by his weakness or by the cunnings and trickeries of the Devil. Admit him and take him back into the body of Thy Triumphant Church. As a living member of it, redeemed by the precious blood of Thy Son, feel compassion, Lord, for his moaning; let his tears and his sobbing move Thee; let his, and our, supplications soften Thee. Support and succor he who places his hope in nothing other than Thy mercy, and admit him in Thy friendship and grace, by the love Thou hast for Jesus Christ, Thy Beloved Son, who lives and reigns with Thee for all the centuries of centuries. Amen.

Oh soul, atoning for thy faults, I commend thee to God All-Mighty, my dearest brother, to Him who I ask to support and favor thee as His creature, so as, having paid with death the dues of this life, may thou see the Lord, the sovereign artifice, who from the dust of the earth created thee. When thy soul leaves its body, may the luminous army of Saints came to greet thee and accompany thee, defend thee and celebrate thee; the glorious college of the Saintly Apostles favor thee, being judges for thy cause; the triumphant legions of the invincible Martyrs support thee, the most noble company of the illustrious Confessors receive thee in their midst, and with the soft fragrance of the lilies they carry, symbols of the softness of their virtues, comfort thee; The choirs of the Saintly virgins, joyful and gay, receive thee; may all of that blessed celestial and courteous company with open arms of true friendship give thee entrance into the glorious bosom of the Patriarchs; may the face of thy Redeemer Jesus Christ be appeasable and merciful to thee and may He give thee a place among those who are always in His presence. Never will thou taste the horror of the eternal darkness, or the crackling of its flames, nor the sentences that torment the condemned. May cursed Satan surrender with all his allies, and, when thou passes before them, accompanied by the Angels, let the miserable tremble and flee fearful into the thick darkness of his shadowy residence.

Go, soul; let thy martyrdom end, for thou no longer belongs to this corporeal world, but rather to the celestial! Thou art free, for if God is favorable to thee, all the enemies who bother Him will be routed; let them run from His presence; vanish like smoke in the air and as wax in the fire, these rebellious and cursed demons; and the joyful just, happily with thee sit at the table of their God. Let the infernal armies be confounded and run, and let the ministers of Satan not dare stop thy path into Heaven. Let Christ, who was crucified for thee, free thee from Hell; let him free thee from those torments thou suffered in this world, tormenting others and being tormented.

Christ, who gave his life for thee, may Christ, Son of the Living God, place thee among the meadows and forests of Paradise, which never fade nor wither, and as a true shepherd may he recognize thee as a sheep of His flock. May He absolve thee of all thy sins, and may He sit thee by His right hand among the chosen and predestined; Let God make thee so happy, that, always assisting in His presence, may thou know with blessed eyes the truth manifest of His divinity, and in the company of the courteous of Heaven may thou enjoy the sweetness of His eternal contemplation for all centuries of centuries. Amen.

✝

A USEFUL ORISON TO HEAL ALL SICKNESS EVEN IF OF A NATURAL CAUSE, WHICH SHOULD BE READ WITH GREAT RESPECT TOWARDS JESUS CHRIST, WHOM WE ARE ADDRESSING

(MAKE THE SIGN OF THE CROSS)

In the name of the Father, the Son and the Holy Spirit. Amen. Jesus, Mary and Joseph.

I (NN), as a creature of God, made in His image and redeemed with His blood, place a precept on all thy sufferings, just as Jesus Christ did to the sick of the Holy Land and the paralyzed of Sidon; for as such, I (NN), ask Thee, my Lord Jesus Christ, to feel compassion for Thy servant (NN), do not allow him, Lord, to suffer the tribulations of life any longer! Rather cast upon this Thy servant Thy holiest blessing and I (NN) shall order, with the authority of thine and my Lord, that all thy ailments cease. Most kind Lord Jesus Christ, true God, who, from the bosom of the Eternal Omnipotent Father, wert sent to the world to absolve all sin, absolve, Lord, the ones committed by this miserable creature; Thou, who wert sent to the world to redeem the suffering, release the imprisoned, gather the vagabonds, lead the pilgrims to their homes; for I (NN), beg Thee, Lord, lead this sufferer to the path of salvation and health, for he has truly repented; console, console, Lord, the oppressed; be moved to release this servant from the sickness of which he is suffering, of the ailments and tribulation I see him in, for Thou received from God the All-Mighty Father the whole of the humankind to support; and being born as man, prodigiously, Thou bought Paradise for us with Thy precious blood, establishing a complete peace between the Angels and Man. Thus, please Lord, establish peace between my humors and my soul; so that (NN) and all of us may live joyfully, free from sicknesses of the body and of the soul. Yes, my God and my Lord, shine down on me and all of us Thy peace and Thy mercy; as Thou made with Esau, to whom Thou removed all his aversion towards his brother Jacob, reach out, Lord Jesus Christ, to (NN) Thy creature, Thy arm and Thy grace and rid him of all those who bear him hate as Thou freed

29

Abraham from the hand of the Chaldeans; his son Isaac, from the consciousness of sacrifice; Joseph, from the tyranny of his brothers; Noah, from the universal deluge; Lot, from the fires of Sodom; Moses and Aaron, Thy servants, and the people of Israel, from Pharaoh's power and the enslavement of Egypt; David, from the hands of Saul and the giant Goliath; Susanna, from the crime of false testimony; Judith from the prideful and impure Holofernes; Daniel, from the den of lions; the three young men Sidrach, Misach and Abdenago, from the burning furnace; Jonah, from the belly of the whale; the daughter of the Canaanite, from the Devil's vexing; Adam, from the sentence of Hell; Peter, from the waves of the sea, and Paul, from the prisons of the jailors; so, most amiable Lord Jesus Christ, Son of the Living God, aid me (NN) as well, Thy creature, and come with haste to my aid, by Thy Incarnation and birth; by the hunger, the thirst, the cold, the heat, the work and afflictions, the spittle and slaps, by the lashes and the crown of thorns; by the nails, by the gall and vinegar, and by the cruel death that Thou went through for us; by the spear that pierced Thy chest and by the seven words Thou said on the Cross, first to God the Father Omnipotent:

"Father forgive them, for they know not what they do." Then to the good thief, who was crucified with Thee: *"Truly, I say to thee today thou shall be with me in paradise."* Then to the Father: *"Eli Eli lama sabachthani?"* which means: *"My God, my God, why hast Thou forsaken me?"* Then to Thy Mother: *"Woman, behold thy son."* Then to the disciple: *"Behold thy mother"* (showing that thou care about Thy friends). Then Thou said: *"I thirst,"* for Thou desired our salvation and that of the saintly souls in Limbo. Thou said then to Thy Father: *"Father, into Thy hands I commit my spirit."* and lastly Thou shouted, saying: *"It is finished."* For all Thy work was done. I beg Thee, Lord, that, from this hour on, never again may this creature (NN) suffer this sickness, which so much mortifies it, for I beg Thee by all these things, and by Thy glorious resurrection, the frequent consolation Thou hast given to Thy disciples, by Thy admirable ascension, by the coming of the Spirit, by the terrifying Judgment Day! As also for all the benefits I have received from Thy goodness (for Thou hast created me from nothing and Thou hast given unto me Thy holy faith); for all of this, my Redeemer, my Lord Jesus Christ, humbly I beg Thee to cast Thy Blessing over this sick creature.

Yes, my God and my Lord, feel compassion for it. Oh God of Abraham, Oh God of Isaac and God of Jacob, be compassionate of this creature of Thine (NN); send in his aid Thy St. Michael the Archangel, let him heal and defend him from these miseries of the flesh and spirit. And thou, Saint Michael, Saintly Archangel of Christ, defend and heal this servant of the Lord, for thou hast earned the blessings of the Lord, and rid this creature of all danger.

Here is the cross of the Lord, which is victorious and reigns.

Oh Savior of the world, save him; Savior of the world, aid me, Thou who through Thy blood and Thy cross redeemed me, save me and heal me of all sickness of the body and the soul; I (NN) ask Thee all of this by all the miracles and steps Thou gave upon the earth as a man.

Oh holy God! Oh mighty God! Oh immortal God! Have mercy upon us. Cross of Christ save me; Cross of Christ, protect me; Cross of Christ defend me in the name of the Father, the Son, and the Holy Spirit. Amen.

(Then say, kneeling, the Creed and one Salve Regina to Our Lady and pour holy water on the wound of the sick)

WARNING

This orison can be said to anyone suffering from any ailment, but mainly from: erysipelas, burns, any critter bites and finally from every misery of life.

When the priest realizes that a sickness is not due to sorcery or demonic work, it is also good to read the orison of St. Cyprian, for in this way the sick will become very satisfied and the faith which then possesses him greatly aids his cure. So says St. Cyprian in his book, Chapter I.

CHAPTER VI

Exorcism to banish the Devil from the body

This exorcism was found in a very old book, written by Friar Bento do Rosário, a priest of the Order of the Discalced Augustinians.

"In the name of the Father, the Son and the Holy Spirit. In the name of St. Bartholomew, of St. Augustine, of St. Catejan, St. Andrew Avellino, I banish thee Evil Angel, who wishes to enter and pervert me. By the power of the Cross of Christ, by the power of His divine wounds, I banish thee, accursed, so as thou may never again tempt my peaceful soul. Amen."

(This should be said three times, while making the sign of the Cross over the chest this same number of times.)

CHAPTER VII

Disenchantment of Treasures

†

TRIANGLE

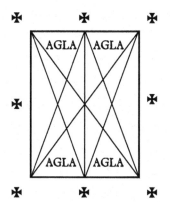

All people assisting the disenchantment of the treasure should be inside of a triangle, as represented by the figure above, which should be drawn on the floor, for, by being inside it, no harm will come to them.

†

Orison and banishment to disenchant the treasure

First pray the Litany of the Saints in a loud and clear voice. If you can do this while kneeling, so much the better.

†

First banishment and disconnection from the earth

"Earth, all thou shall give and all thou shall eat," said the Lord our God.

LITANY OF THE SAINTS

Kyrie, eleison.

Christe, eleison.

Sancta Maria. Ora pro nobis.

Sancta Dei Genitrix. Ora pro nobis.

Sancta Virgo Virginum. Ora pro nobis.

Sancte Michael. Ora pro nobis.

Sancte Gabriel. Ora pro nonis.

Sancte Raphael. Ora pro nobis.

Omnes Sancti Angelis et Archangeli. Ora pro nobis.

Omnes Sancti Beatorum spirituum Ordine. Ora pro nobis.

Sancte Joannes Baptista. Ora pro nobis.

Omnes Sancti Patriarcha et Prophetae. Ora pro nobis.

Sancte Petre. Ora pro nobis.

Sancte Paule. Ora pro nobis.

Sancte Andrea. Ora pro nobis.

Sancte Jacobe. Ora pro nobis.

Sancte Joannes. Ora pro nobis.

Sancte Thoma. Ora pro nobis.

Sancte Philippe. Ora pro nobis.

Sancte Bartholomaee. Ora pro nobis.

Sancte Simon. Ora pro nobis.

Sancte Thaddaee. Ora pro nobis.

Sancte Mathia. Ora pro nobis.

Sancte Barnaba. Ora pro nobis.

Sancte Luca. Ora pro nobis.

Sancta Marce. Ora pro nobis.

Omnes Sancti Apostoli et Evangelistae. Ora pro nobis.

Omnes Sancti Discipuli Domini. Ora pro nobis.

Omnes Sancti Innocentes. Ora pro nobis.

Sancte Stephane. Ora pro nobis.

Sancte Laurenti. Ora pro nobis.

Sancte Vicenti. Ora pro nobis.

Sancti Fabiane et Sebastiane. Ora pro nobis.

Sancti Joannes et Paule. Ora pro nobis.

Sancte Cosme et Damine. Ora pro nobis.

Sancti Gervasi et Protasi. Ora pro nobis.

Omnes Sancti Martyres. Ora pro nobis.

Sancte Silvester. Ora pro nobis.

Sancte Gregori. Ora pro nobis.

SancteAmbrosi. Ora pro nobis.

Sancte Augustine. Ora pro nobis.

Sancte Hieronyme. Ora pro nobis.

Sancte Martine. Ora pro nobis.

Sancte Nicolae . Ora pro nobis.

Omnes Sancti Pontifices et Confessores. Ora pro nobis.

Omnes Sancti Doctores. Ora pro nobis.

Sancte Antoni. Ora pro nobis.

Sancte Benedicte. Ora pro nobis.

Sancte Bernarde. Ora pro nobis.

Sancte Dominice. Ora pro nobis.

Sancte Francisce. Ora pro nobis.

Omnes Sancti Monachi et Eremitae. Ora pro nobis.

Omnes Sancti Sacerdotes et Levitae. Ora pro nobis.

Sancta Maria Magdalena. Ora pro nobis.

Sancta Agatha. Ora pro nobis.

Sancta Lucia. Ora pro nobis.

Sancta Agnes. Ora pro nobis.

Sancta Caecilia. Ora pro nobis.

Sancta Catharina. Ora pro nobis.

Sancta Anastasia. Ora pro nobis.

Omnes Sanctae Virgines et Viduae. Ora pro nobis.

Omnes Sainti et Sanctae Dei. Intercedite pro nobis.

Propitius esto. Parce nobis, Domine.

Ab omni peccato. Libera nos.

Ab ira tua. Libera nos.

A subitanea et improvisa morte Libera nos.

Ab insidiis diaboli. Libera nos.

Ab ira, et ódio, et omni mala voluntate. Libera nos.

A spiritu fornicationis. Libera nos.

A morte perpetua. Libera nos.

Per mysterium sanctae Incarnationis tuae. Libera nos.

Per adventum tuum. Libera nos.

Per nativitatem tuam. Libera nos.

Per baptismum et sanctum jejunium tuum. Libera nos.

Per crucem et passionem tuam. Libera nos.

Per mortem et sepulturam tuam. Libera nos.

Per sanctam resurrectionem tuam. Libera nos.

Per admirabilem ascentionem tuam. Libera nos.

Per adventum Spiritus Sancti Paracliti. Libera nos.

In die judicii. Libera nos.

Peccatores. Te rogamus, audi nos.

Ut ei induldeas. Te rogamus, audi nos.

Ut hanc creaturam tuam a cruciantibus daemonum liberare digneris. Te rogamus.

Ut hanc creaturam tuam pretioso tuo sanguine redemptam ad infestatione doemonum liberare digneris. Te rogamus.

Ut hanc creaturam tuam a potestate daemonum liberare, benedicere, et conservare digneris. Te rogamus.

Fili Dei. Te rogamus, audi nos.

Christe, audi nos.

Christe, exaudi nos.

Antiphona. - Ne reminiscaris, Domine, delicat nostra vel parentum nostrorum, neque vindictam sumas de peccatis nostris propter nomem tuum. Pater noster, ect. V. Et ne nos inducas in tentationem. R. Sed libera nos a malo Amen.

†

SECOND BANISHMENT

Ecce crucem Domine viest seu Radix do vielin nomine Jesu omne genus tutantur coelestrum terrestrum infernorum it omnis Lingua Confititur quia Dominus Jesus Christus in gloria est Dei patri viest Deus ille crucem Domine de tribu Juda Radix David figite partes adversa veribilium in nomine Jesu omne genus tutantur coelestrum terrestrum infernorum omnia Lingua Confititur quia Domninus Jesus Christus in gloria est Patri, amen; o Senhor seja comigo e com todos nós. Amén.

Jesus, Mary and Joseph, in the name of God the Father, God the Son and God the Holy Spirit.

By the virtue of the Holy God the Father, three persons distinct and one and only true God, by the virtue of the Virgin Mary and of all the Saintly Apostles, Evangelists, Patriarchs, Prophets, Martyrs and Confessors, by the virtue of Saint Ubald Francis, I, creature of Our Lord Jesus Christ, redeemed by His Holy Blood and made in Thy likeness, in Thy Holy Name I disenchant this treasure that is before me buried; I command thee under the saintly power of obedience, that now the earth, where a treasure is kept, buried here by the *Mouros*, shall open; I, by the sight of these lights, command that all treasures under this earth under the power of Lucifer and his companions, be given to me now, ordering now in name of Saint Cyprian that these be given to me under the power of Our Lord Jesus Christ. Jesus, Jesus, Jesus, be with me, come to my aid! Jesus, Jesus, hear my orison and let the prayers of this great sinner reach Thy ears. Jesus help me, Jesus hear me! Jesus come once again to my aid, Jesus, Jesus, a thousand times Jesus, be with me, Jesus, without Thee I am helpless, Jesus, I with Thy holy power command that this treasure now be open.

I command in the name of all Saints, of the God of Abraham, of the God of Jacob and of the God of Isaac, and in their virtue let all things of this world be untied and disconnected so that I may find what I am seeking. Amen."

Whoever reads this orison, or has it read by someone else, God will appear to him through the gates of mercy, accompanied by the Angel Raphael and all the other Saints and Archangels, Princes and Virtues of the Heavens; and, at God's command, the blessed St. John the Baptist, St. Thomas, St. Philip, St. Mark, St. Matthew, St. Simon, St. Jude, St. Martin and all the Saints that are in Heaven; all the orders of the Martyrs, St. Sebastian, St. Damiano, St. Cosmas, St. Fabian, St. Cyprian, be with me, St. Dionysius and his Companions of all orders of Virgins, Martyrs, Confessors of God and by the coronation of King David and by the four evangelists John, Mark, Matthew and Luke, and by the four columns of Heaven, which nothing they prevent, and by the seventy-two tongues that are spread throughout the world, and by this absolution, and by the one given by Our Lord when he called Adam saying, "*Where art thou?*" and by this virtue and by that which Adam rose as he said:

"*Rise and take the habit, go from here and sin no more,*" and by that infirmity that twenty-eight years afflicted the sick and kept them paralyzed and wert saved by Our Lord who all Saints praise, for all receive charitably his fruit by the hand of the Prophet Jeremiah and the humility of Joseph, and by the patience of Job, and by the grace of God, and by all the Saints of God, did God then absolve him of all evil things and be Emanuel blessed, for being God with us and by the Holy Name of God and of all things that are here named and are now untied and disconnected in plain sight, and let ill-fortune step aside and all the evil made by the *Mouros* or made by the Devil, be gone Satan, from this place, for I order thee with all the power I have with me from He who is greater than thou.

Go now to the depths of Hell! Let the earth now be open; Jesus, Jesus, defend me from these phantoms that surround me so as to keep me from my desire; Jesus, Jesus, come to my aid. Be gone Satan, for thou art defeated.

I have broken thy cunnings with the saintly power of Our Lord Jesus Christ. Be gone, phantoms, enemies of the human nature; I banish thee in the miraculous name of St. Cyprian and by the Holy Cross in which Our Lord was crucified; by this very same Cross I order thee: Be gone, Satan, phantom enemy of God and all Men.

PREVENTION

After you have preformed this orison, many phantoms will appear to you, to test you and see if you will be frightened and leave the riches behind; do not have the slightest worry, for, when the Devil appears to you and sees that you do so, he will immediately run leaving all the treasure at your disposal. After you have taken all the wealth, order in the name of Jesus Christ and St. Cyprian that all things return to their natural state, and afterwards divide the wealth with no greed, for it was given to you by God and St. Cyprian.

PLACES WHERE ENCHANTMENTS ARE TO BE FOUND

1. In the Castelo de Castro, by digging up the same Castro on the side of the rising Sun, thou shall find a trap door under the wall, with two golden tiles.

2. In the fountain of Soalheira, nine steps down from the fountain, there is a buried boulder, where there is a vase[20] filled with gold coins.

3. In the fountain of the *Moura*, twenty five paces from the fountain, there is a vase of gold.

4. In the fountain of Frasqua, above the spring, there is a coffer of jewels.

5. In the three fountains of Navalhos, in the Castro Feimano, there is a treasure in each one of them.

6. In the fountain in the Castro they call Navalho, there is, under the road, a great treasure.

7. In the castle facing North, between the fig tree, near Edreira, two men deep[21], there is a man's skull, there thou shall find a coffin and in it nine gold ingots.

8. In front of Mirandela, by the wall of Serrado, near the Pilar, thou shall find a copper vase filled with gold coins.

9. In the Castelo do Sírio, near the fountain, at the front, to the South, in the middle of the tower, two ovens built into the wall; there thou shall find the weapons of D. Teludo Seminadas, and four gold doubloons.

10. In this same castle, at the gate, where the Sun enters through the fringe of the door on the side of the hinges, thou shall find a vase of gold.

11. In Castelo do Mau Vizinho, on the side of the rising Sun, under the wall, or better, the cliff, sixty one paces from the castle there is a hand painted; three men down, thou shall find a coffin, in a tub, many gold coins.

12. In the fountain of Ferradoza, in front, at the side of the rising Sun, above the fountain, along the chestnut tree, thou shall find some clay and two ingots, inside a pot.

13. In the fountain of Vale, in the limit of Castelo do Mau Vizinho, which

---

20. Translator's note: the actual word is *asado*, a particular type of vase with large handles, *asas*. All vases mentioned in this section are *asados*.

21. Translator's note: to the best of my knowledge this is an old unit of measure. I have been unable to find a correspondence to any modern unit, although I am suspicious it might be equivalent to a cubit.

springs right in front, to the South, approximately twelve steps, there is a dress with gold finishes.

14. In the fountain of Cavaleiro, at the edge of the Castro, facing the rising Sun, near the strawberry tree[22] there is a cliff which goes down to the Castro, and, below, in the middle of the cliff, two men down, thou shall find four gold cocoons; do not kill the one which is still alive.

15. In the fountain of Cavaleiro, in front, to the North, above and near to the R. S. X. V. I., in a plate, there is a rock with a sign; there thou shall find a coffin with gold coins.

16. In the same fountain of Castro de Comum, along it, thou shall find idols of the gods.

17. In the fountain d'El-Rei, thou shall find an enchanted silver tray.

18. In the Peneda do Gato, going down to the Fragoso River, in front, to the North, thou shall find, at top of the Peneda, half a man deep, a coffin filled with gold.

19. In the fountain of Castro de Ameias, in front, to the South, in the mouth of the lion from where water springs out, thou shall find a great treasure.

20. In this same fountain of Terronha, in front, on the side of the rising Sun, sixty paces from the Cprião, above the fountain there is a great vase of gold.

21. In the fountain of Vale Grande, along the Horto de Famiro, sixteen paces above the fountain, there is a strawberry tree, near it a basin filled with sand; under this there is the imprint of a man in gravel, at the bottom, a small vat filled with gold.

22. In the Castro do Solhão, under the Castro, in front, to the South, above the fountain fifteen paces, where there is a tile oven, there is coffin filled with silver.

23. In the Oratorio of the Castro, on the ground, under the altar, thou shall find three *palmos*[23] of gravel, underneath thou shall find a coffin filled with rocks, under this one there is another one filled with gold.

24. In Castro Piloto, in front, to the South, and by the side of the rising Sun, there is a fountain of meager flow, above which are some white stones, thou shall find under this a very great treasure.

25. In the fountain of Navalhas, on the upper side, thou shall find three landmarks, in the middle of them there is a slate; lift it and underneath thou shall find a great treasure.

26. In the fountain of Bazadouro, thou shall find a marble rock, one step

---

22. Translator's note: the actual tree mentioned is an *Ervideiro*, another common name for the *Medronheiro*, *Arbutus unedo*, also called the Apple of Cain in English. Traditionally the fruits from these trees, besides being delicious, are used to produce a strong distilled spirit.

23. Translator's note: an old unit of measure, equivalent to 22 centimeters.

above the fountain, and in the middle of the rock there are two sculpted faces, dig on the left side, the height of a lance, thou shall find a very large slate and under it an enormous boulder, where thou shall find a great treasure.

27. In the fountain of Lagoalhos, thou shall find a mud flat; in the middle of it and two steps above the fountain, thou shall find some corner stones, on one of them there is a sign, under this one there is a great treasure.

28. In the fountain of Lamas, thou shall find some boulders, under these some white stones and one of them will be out of the ground, near this one thou should dig and thou shall find a great treasure.

29. In the fountain of Encalada, two and a half steps above the fountain, among thick brambles, thou shall find beautiful clay tiles, under these thou shall find thirty-three stones stuck together, and behind these a round rock, and below this the possessions of a *Mouro* king.

30. In the fountain of Salgeiro, three steps above the creek, on the upper side, there are some willows in front, and under these there is a mantle that is worth two millions.

31. In the Castro do Mau Vizinho, in the creek flowing to a strawberry tree, there is a marble boulder; in it thou shall find a slab with a hole and under it a great treasure.

32. In the Castro Quintal, where the two creeks meet, thou shall find four landmarks together, being one of them out of the ground; in the middle of these thou shall find a cornerstone, and under this some tiles with plenty of gold.

33. In the rock of the Namorados, near the fig tree and a fallen statue, dig a *braça*[24] and thou shall find a wooden urn filled with coins.

34. In the fountain of the *Mouro*, in front, to the South, water flows out of a pipe, and on the other end of this thou shall find one hundred and fifty small bags of gold.

35. In the fountain of the Serra do Gato, at the water spring there, thou shall find a tall boulder with five edges, and near this boulder there is a coffer of gold coins.

36. In the same fountain, almost at the middle, there is a small tower with lathes in it, and under the wall, or on the floor, thou shall find four gold ingots.

37. Four paces off of the same Serra do Gato, thou shall find a ditch; in this ditch thou shall find nothing, but where there is a rough deserted patch of land, seventy paces from the ditch, thou shall find a mill stone, and under this there is a pitcher filled with gold coins.

38. In the Peneda do Cavalo, above the fountain, along the pedestal, thou shall find doors made of gold.

39. In the Seca fountain, to the South, above the fountain, thou shall find a broken boulder and under this a load of gold.

40. In the fountain of Cavalo, near the horse, there is a bell made of gold.

---

24. Translator's note: an old unit of measure, equivalent to 2.2 meters.

41. In the Ribeira dos Namorados, under the altar or oratorio, thou shall find fifteen small bags of gold.

42. In the fountain of Ferradosa, by the fountain, near the boulder, thou shall find a great treasure.

43. Near Cavado, along a black fig tree, there is a treasure.

44. In the Castelo de Ervideiro, in Val Martim, placed against an oak tree, near the oratorio, thou shall find a gold coffer.

45. In the fountain of Meijoadas, but three steps abeam from the fountain, along the Carvalheira, there is a coffer of gold.

46. In the Castelo de Ervideiro, the jewels of a king.

47. In the fountain of Vila Velha, as part of the same stone, there is a vase of gold coins.

48. In these same stones in another fountain, there is another vase of gold coins.

49. In the path below the Canacho, at nine paces, there is a great treasure.

50. In the fountain off the road, at the side of the rising Sun, there is a coffin with a great sum of gold.

51. In Barreiros, below the Andouro there is a great treasure; to obtain it you must divert the water flow.

52. In the Castelo das Passadas, and three steps around the castle, there is a vase of gold.

53. In the fountain of Navalhos, which springs up at the side of the rising Sun in Lamacego, in a mud flat, there is a creek near a mill, and near to the mud flat, three landmarks, there is a tiny canal; under a mud flat, to the South, there is a great treasure.

54. In the Penedo Pilheiro, there is, on top of the Penedo, an enormous sculpted coffin, this contains a great sum of old coins.

55. In the fountain of Rego, at nine paces, there is a great treasure.

56. In the Penedo Salgoso, in the broken down section of the wall, there are the belongings of D. Gurina, the old proprietress of the Penedo.

57. In the shores of the Caramelo, near the fountain, thirteen steps from the wall, under the fountain, there is the tip of a coulter made of stone, there is a great sum of gold there.

58. In the fountain of Leda, nine paces off the road, at the side of the rising Sun, there is coffin with the belongings of D. Caprina.

59. In the fountain of Salgueiros, there is a great treasure, and another one along the stream of the same fountain.

60. In the fountain of Seixos, eleven steps from Ciprião, there is, to the North, a stone snake under the stream of water, the snake is facing a treasure.

61. In Silveira, where the water of a creek comes together, there is a great treasure.

62. In the fountain of Valongo, above the fountain of Nascedouro, there is a trapdoor in the ground, to the North, and there is a great treasure there.

63. In the fountain of Ervideiro, above the fountain, twelve steps from Ciprião, there are twelve saddles of gold.

64. In the Castro, locked in the bottom of the Castro, there is a large amount of gold nuggets.

65. In the Fragas Velhas, where there used to be water, there is the throne of a king.

66. In the Penedo das Pombas, there is a trapdoor on top of the Penedo, there is a great sum of gold there.

67. In the fountain of Rima, over the fountain, eighteen steps to the North, there is a coffin of tiles filled with jewels and fine silk.

68. In the Penedo da Edra, where the water flows out between some cracks, there are five ingots of gold and five of silver, which make the water taste very bad.

•
• •

Sum of the treasures of Porto de D. Gazua, rivers and running waters

69. Between the two rivers, in Castelo da Cidade, neighboring Castro das Lamas, on the upper side, ten paces, there is a boulder, and under this a great treasure.

70. In the same city, in the Portal do Sol, under the gate, there are many gold ingots.

71. Along the same city, on the side of the setting Sun, in the fountain nearby, there are a few lines on a rock, and under this a whole set of golden balls.

72. In the same Castro, by the river, on the South side, there is a boulder with the marks of some horseshoes, at the height of a man; under this there is a treasure.

73. In the fountain of Castro, three paces on the upper side, there is a golden spike.

74. In Castelo Vizinho, by going down the river, there is a stone with some lines sculpted into it, and under it a brass coffin filled with gold.

75. In the southern gate, there is a great sum of gold.

76. In the fountain of the same Castelo, on the side of the rising sun, there is rock erupting from the ground, under a slab, underneath there is a great treasure.

77. In the fountain of Lagoalhos, in the middle there is a cornerstone, and, under this, a man down, many gold bars.

78. Going to the vale, there is a stone with a written sign, a man down, a great treasure.

79. Near the fountain of the Sereijal, thou shall find a box of gold.

80. In the fountain of Castelo, there is a spike of gold.

81. In the fountain of Salgueiro, there is a load of gold.

82. Near the Peneda dos Namorados, in Sindeira, by a small path, under a boulder, thou shall find a great treasure of D. Moura.

83. In the Penedo do Castelo do Ervelino, in the hallway, near a fig tree, thou shall find a column base[25]; on the far end thou shall find a golden hinge.

84. In the Brosco do Castelo, on the side of the setting Sun, thou shall find a serving tray.

85. In the fountain d'El-Rei, under the Castelo, by the side of the rising Sun, there is a great treasure.

86. In the terrace of the Castelo thou shall find some old golden shoes, filled with coins.

87. In the fountain of Mó, on the South side, under the wall of D. Maria, over the wall seventeen paces, thou shall find a silver coffer filled with old golden coins.

88. In the Castelio, in front of Carrazeda, there are five rough[26] boulders; each one the height of a man; above the fountain, at the height of a *vara*[27], thou shall find a vase of gold coins.

89. In the fountain, in front of Carrazeda, seventeen paces above the fountain, thou shall find a box filled with gold coins.

90. In the Castelo de Seilhadas, twelve paces in front, on the side of the setting Sun, there is a lot of gold.

91. In the *estevais*[28] of this same old fountain, fifteen paces along the current, there is a vase of gold.

92. At Tresgajo, there is, at the border of a creek, a stone mule and, under it, a great treasure.

93. In Encruzilhada, there are, twelve steps from the path, seven barrels of enchanted pearls, gold and diamonds.

94. In the Penedo do Corvo, on the side of the rising Sun, fifteen paces from Ciprião, there is a clay coffin with ten golden eagles.

95. In the Penedo Cernateiro, to the Porta do Sol, near a bolder, there is a golden chair.

96. In the old fountain, by passing the right side pier, to the North, there is a great treasure.

97. In the Seixo das Anciães, in the same fountain, there is a rock, under it there is a copper vase filled with gold.

---

25. Translator's note: uncertain translation, might also be an enclosed area.

26. Translator's note: the original word is *bernosas*, which is something afflicted by *bernes*, a type of cattle tumor caused by the larvae of a particular fly.

27. Translator's note: an old unit of measure, equivalent to 1.1 meter.

28. Translator's note: I struggled with the meaning and translation of this term. I believe it refers to a field of *estevas*, *Cistus ladanifer*, Laudanum. As there isn't an English word to define such a field, I decided to keep it as it is.

98. In the same Castelo de Anciães, in the corner, turning to the side of the rising Sun, there is a clay coffin built in the same tower, where there are seven gold doubloons.

99. Following the other fountain in the same Castelo, in the water stream, there is a tile covered by a mill stone filled with gold coins.

100. In Sombreiro de Roldão, there is a painted goat, looking at the place where a treasure lies.

101. At Manadouros, at the place where water flows from a crack on the cliff, there is a tile and under it a great treasure.

102. In Olha Velha, in the well, below, twenty-five paces towards the setting sun, near a cork oak, there is a coffin filled with jewels.

103. In Palha Parda, in an old barge, where there are some painted chairs, thou shall find a tile filled with gold ingots.

104. In the fountain of Pingão, there is a great treasure.

105. In the Sitio dos Cabrões, in the Peneda do Lagarto, two paces from the Northern part, thou shall find a face resembling the rising Sun, and, ten steps farther above this same face thou shall find, under the tower, at two and a half men, a chest made of clay, which will require three beast of burden to pull it out, given the amount of coins it contains.

106. In the fountain of Costa, at sixteen paces, thou shall find a goat on top of a boulder half a man high and, nine paces farther, facing the setting Sun, there is an easily discoverable tile of gold coins.

107. In the fountain of Ouro, at nine paces, there is, half a man down, a pan with money facing North.

108. In the fountain of Teixeira, facing the rising sun, one and a half men down, much gold and silver.

109. In the fountain of Navalhas, ten paces from the fountain, facing South, half a man down, there is a treasure evaluated as being worth more than one thousand *cruzados*[29].

110. In the fountain of Sibra, on the left side, below the same fountain, the height of a man down, there is a pan filled with precious stones.

111. In Castro de Cima, in one of the five gates, there is buried a pan of gold, two men deep.

112. In this same gate, facing South, near the Caneleiro, a *tiro*[30] of distance, fifteen paces and one and a half men, there is a basin of gold pieces.

113. In Castelo do Mau Vizinho, there is a rock with three edges and, in front of this same rock, at eight paces, there is a vat of silver and under this there is much gold, facing South.

---

29. Translator's note: an old Portuguese coin in circulation between the XVI and XIX century.

30. Translator's note: literally a "shot", I believe this refers to a medieval unit of measure called *tiro de besta*, crossbow shot, corresponding approximately to 35 meters.

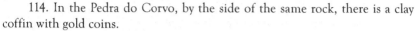

114. In the Pedra do Corvo, by the side of the same rock, there is a clay coffin with gold coins.

115. In the Peneda Redonda, facing South, at twenty-seven paces, one man down there is great sum of gold and fine silver.

116. In the Castro Sucher, thou shall find a coffin six *palmos* high, where there is a great sum of wealth.

117. In the fountain of Monte Frio, twenty *palmos* in the direction of the setting Sun, thou shall find, at sixteen paces, a gold tray and under this a great deal of silver.

118. In the fountain of Carvalho, one man down, facing North, thou shall find over twelve thousand gold and silver *cruzados*, at the distance of six *palmos*.

119. In the Castro Troncado, facing South, at ten paces, by passing the first gate, there are two very valuable golden chains.

120. In the Peneda do Rio Fragoso, there is a goat to the South, on the other side, facing the rising Sun, at eighteen paces, there are the tools of a blacksmith, all made of gold.

121. By digging up the Castro, where many riches lay inside this same castle, there are over one hundred thousand *cruzados* in gold pieces.

122. In the Peneda de Olho Redondo, at the turn of the sun, at fifteen paces, there are great riches.

123. In the Castelo do Mau Vizinho, facing the midday Sun, under the gate, thou shall find a great treasure.

124. At the gate of Sabugueiro, of the Calador house, there is a great treasure in this gate, consisting of forty gold bars.

125. In front of the Penedo Furado, at seven *braças* down, there are forty gold ingots and forty silver ones.

126. In the Cabeço da Velha, there is a sign in the shape of a horse's head, near it there is a golden goat and twenty ingots of silver.

127. Near Seixo Branco there are seven gold ingots.

128. In the Castro Bolha, along the fountain, at seven paces, there are the belongings of a king: seven million gold coins.

129. Near Calçada, near a great rock, on the side of the Castelo, there is a great treasure, one thousand gold and silver *escudos*[31], in this same rock there is a painting of a man's face.

---

31. Translator's note: *escudo* was the name of the Portuguese currency in circulation between 1911 and 2002, which makes up a complicated situation if you take into consideration the age of this book; alternatively this name may also refer to a number of European coins in circulation at various periods in time, distinguishable for bearing the coat of arms of their emitting authority, their *escudo*, shield.

130. In the well above the Goadramil, inside it there are two carts of gold and silver pieces, with one thousand *quintais*[32] of iron over it, and on one side, a hole from which water flows.

131. In the rocks of a fountain with a willow, near where the fountain springs up, there are forty gold ingots and twenty silver ingots, inside a coffin.

132. In the Penedo de Mira, close to it, by the side of the rising Sun, there is a treasure, below a landmark, with two hundred gold ingots and five hundred silver.

133. In Penha, in Varge, there is a great priceless treasure; there is a painted horse's head above it.

134. In every fountain of Navalho there is a treasure, and, above the main one, eight paces, there is a vat filled with gold.

135. In the other fountain of Navalho, the one with a horseshoe painted on it, between the fountain and the horseshoe there is great treasure and all that thou may find there still alive do not kill.

136. In the other fountain of Navalho, to the North, between the road and the fountain, on either side, there is vase of gold.

137. In Salgueira, there is a great treasure, consisting of five hundred gold ingots.

138. In the fountain of Velho there is a gold spike.

139. At the edge of Castro Socham, there is a furnace for making tiles, to the South, there is a stone chair, and under it a tray of pearls and diamonds and fifteen ingots of gold.

140. In the fountain of Sagraça, on the upper part of the fountain, there are forty landmarks, and, in the middle of these, there is a tray of gold, at the height of a man.

141. In the fountain of the *Moura*, at three paces, there is a tray of gold, at the height of a man.

142. In the Vale dos Namorados, there is a white bar on the fountain, and there is also a bramble bush and to the North a white rock, at fifteen paces there is a hand, and underneath there are four chapels of gold, carried there by an *azemel*[33] over a period of fifteen days, the whole treasure is worth four millions, and it contains an idol of the gods.

143. In the Vale Valbom, there is a large rock with a hole in it; by the side of the setting Sun, there are a hundred and forty bags of gold at the height of a man.

---

32. Translator's note: an old unit of measure with various definitions in different times in history. The most widely used consisted of 4 *arrobas*, being that one *arroba* weighs between 14 and 15 kilograms.

33. Translator's note: an *azemel* (from the Arabic *az-zammal*), also called an *almocreve* (*al-mukari*), is a conductor of *azémolas*, beasts of burden. An old profession which consisted in transporting merchandise between cities.

144. In Castelo de Vorim, in the fountain d'El-Rei, on the side of the rising Sun, there is a white rock with a medal painted on it, at the right side, one pace away, there is a round den filled with gold coins, at the height of two men.

145. At the same edge, under the Castelo, there is a mud flat; where two creeks branch out there is a round table made of painted stone, on the other side, a horseshoe and, underneath, twenty five *palmos* high, there is the gold and silver belonging to a widow.

146. At the edge of Vale Curto there is a big slab; underneath there are four *arrobas*[34] of gold, at the height of a man.

147. In the Castelo do Mau Vizinho, there is a round boulder under the gates of the Poente, where thou shall find two basins stuck in the boulder, one made of gold, the other of silver.

148. At the same edge, in the Penedo do Vale, where water flows from, there thou shall find two painted horseshoes; above which water is flowing out, at six paces to the North thou shall find a tray of diamonds and one gold ingot, at the height of two men.

---

34. Translator note: see footnote 32.

CHAPTER VIII

System of casting cards

The millennial science of conjecture, known by the priests of the most ancient of the world's nations and the diviners and prophets of all idolatric religions, was later passed on to the dominion of all of those who, until this day, have thought of predicting the future of an individual or a society in general, by the analysis of things of no importance. The Haruspices, the Auspices, the Adulites, the Augurs and the Druids, so much decanted by Schiller, all of them read the future in the flight and singing of birds or the entrails of animals. From this arose Ornithomancy and Alectryomancy.

Divination by numbers and names is not any less ancient, for divination through numbers goes back to the very beginnings of the world, being widely used by the Chaldean mages, and divination through names, called the anagrammatical science, was practiced by the disciples of Pythagoras, the Pythagoreans. To the first one we call Arithmomancy and to the second Onomantomancy.

Divination through dreams is known by the name of Oneirocritica, which is one of the most important branches of the conjectural sciences, probably originating in the Orient, and should be considered on equal footing with astrology, or astromancy, in terms of ancientness. The Arabs, the Persians, the Peruvians, all ancient peoples sought their future in the firmament and many celebrated men of past ages considered astrology a respectable art.

Many were the objects the ancients used to obtain knowledge of the future. Wands, branches, sieves, air, fire, smoke, water, light, wax, plants and trees, books, one's hand, mirrors, rings, eggs, animals, fish, rocks: all could be used to explain the future of an individual who consulted a diviner, as comets and eclipses were used to mark great calamities in the future of nations.

Cartomancy, or the divination through playing cards, is more modern, for cards were only invented after Charles V. This branch of the conjectural sciences, still today practiced by many people, and sincerely accredited by many more, is the great resource of lovesick girls, using it out of jealousy, suspicion and longing for the object of their affections. Cartomancy is practiced with thirty-two cards, or with a deck of seventy-eight. Today, among us, the forty card deck will be used, with each card meaning one of the things we will thus expose:

DIAMONDS

The *Ace* – a gift
The *Two* – soon
The *Three* – with joy
The *Four* – church
The *Five* – novelty
The *Six* – meager money
The *Seven* – much money

SPADES

The *Ace* – affirmation/statement
The *Two* – cutting
The *Three* – bad words
The *Four* – in bed
The *Five* – sickness
The *Six* – detour/deviation
The *Seven* – passion of the soul

HEARTS

The *Ace* – a ball/dance/party
The *Two* – a letter
The *Three* – good words
The *Four* – placed in the front of the exit door
The *Five* – tears
The *Six* – through paths
The *Seven* – at eating or drinking time

CLUBS

The *Ace* – by night
The *Two* – through long paths
The *Three* – through fast paths
The *Four* – in this house
The *Five* – with the five senses
The *Six* – zeal
The *Seven* – with great pleasure

The queen of spades is a bad talking woman, and the king and jack of spades are the body and mind of a man connected with justice, be him a lawyer, a judge, a prosecutor or anything of the sort.

The queen of diamonds represents the sorceress' consultant, the king and jack of diamonds the body and mind of the consultant or the individual one desires to know something about.

All other figures are used to represent people who might play a part of this nigromancy, being obvious that the jacks represent the thought of the individuals marked by the kings of the same suit.

The disposition of the cards, after being shuffled and cross-cut, which should be accompanied by words in which one places great importance and with which one asks St. Cyprian to reveal the intended answer through the cards, should be made as thus:

Let us suppose that it is a girl in love who is consulting the sorceress, and that the cards were drawn as the figure demonstrates. The sorceress, starting by the Three of Hearts and the Ace of Diamonds, across from each other, would say:

"Good words with a gift, with joy and great pleasure, this man, of body and soul is with this woman and with a ball..."

Holy name of Jesus! The good old lady has divined a terrible secret, such a secret that it makes her consultant faint, for she would never imagine that a card could reveal the loss of her innocence, taken while hiding from prying eyes...

The old woman, sprinkling some cold water on the pale cheeks of her customer, continues with her nigromancy...

"Soon, with the church through fast paths..." (the girl will be married very soon, for I drew here the figure of the church with great haste...) "With five senses with much money and meager money, through the exit door..., etc., etc."

She may then continue with great volubility, always drawing *crossed* cards from the next two *columns* and on to the center.

"We have a *novelty*, for the middle column does not have any figures. Let us see then. What does thou wish for me to look for in this *novelty*?"

"What I wish to know is if he is faithful to me."

"Very well. The *novelty* will tell."

The sorceress whispers in a low voice:

"Cards, by the power of St. Cyprian, who seven years the sea roamed, and seven lucks for his divine wife he cast, tell me if this man is keeping himself faithful and loyal to this woman. If he is faithful, let him go out with her with great pleasure, but if he is unfaithful, let him go out with some other woman, having been *diverted* from this one."

You then place 21 cards facing down over the middle column and you place by the side of this *column* 8 cards, two by two in *a cross*, so as you will end up with only three cards in your hand. If these three cards do *not tell you anything* start drawing from the 8 at the side, in *a cross* from each other, and read what they say, then go to the column of 21, taking one from one extremity of the column and one from the other until you run out of cards. If such is the case that you cannot satisfy the curiosity of the girl, you must bend the significance of two or three cards, making them fit to the best of your abilities to what she wishes to know, and thus your job is done,

One must also take note that should the Four of Diamonds be drawn with the Four or Five of Spades that this is the signal of death soon to come.

The Two of Hearts with the Four of Diamonds indicates a marriage.

CHAPTER IX

Method of Reading the Signs

Since the most remote ancientness almost all nations have made use of Quiromancy, or the art of divining the fortune or disgrace of an individual by the lines in his hand.

The reading of the *buena dicha*, being so widely distributed even to the smallest villages, also deserves to be in this book.

We thus present all the fates distributed by the twelve months that make up the year, so as one may easily find the one that belongs to his birth.

Having made this explanation, let us start with the reading of the *buena dicha*:

CAPRICORN

FROM THE 22ND OF DECEMBER TO THE 19TH OF JANUARY

The individuals born under the influence of this sign are of an honest character, but inconsiderate and shy, to such a degree that they become unable to handle or lead any form of business or responsibility.

The men are usually swarthy, with black hair, blue eyes, and for the most part with a sovereign aspect. They will be suspicious of everyone and everything, and as such they will lose many good business opportunities.

The women will be swarthy, of an average height, very elegant and witty. They will be luxurious lovers, but also good mothers and good wives. If their nature is not contradicted they will have at least five children; their temperament will be bilious, as will be the men's.

AQUARIUS

FROM THE 20TH OF JANUARY TO THE 18TH OF FEBRUARY

All who are born under this sign are of a passionate and sanguine tendency.

The men should be pale and with a nervous complexion, but peaceful. They will not make much use of sincerity, even among their friends.

The women will be very untidy and fickle; they will have black hair and eyes, and will have extraordinary beauty and elegance.

The marriage between two people born in this month is inconvenient, for that union will be disastrous.

PISCES

FROM THE 19ᵀᴴ OF FEBRUARY TO THE 10ᵀᴴ OF MARCH

Those who come into the world during the passing of this sign are of a boisterous and suspicious character. He will also be of an unusual intelligence, but selfish. He will love all that will enable him to fulfill all of his desires and whims, without caring about the means to accomplish these; he will be capable of undignified actions to keep himself from doing any honest work.

Both men and women will be seductive, persuasive, and in general, will be very easily loved. Both will have a nervous temperament.

ARIES

FROM THE 21ˢᵀ OF MARCH TO THE 19ᵀᴴ OF APRIL

Those born under this sign are gloomy. They have a great love for work and for fulfilling the desires of the women they love; however they are ridiculously demanding and unbearably jealous. They are strong and vigorous and more on the tall side, brown eyes and hair of the same color.

The women are usually good housekeepers, faithful wives and loving mothers, although not very elegant. They are sanguine and strong.

The men will be nervous.

TAURUS

FROM THE 20TH OF APRIL TO THE 20TH OF MAY

Those born under this influence are of a delicate complexion and pusillanimous, regular height, sea-colored eyes and lymphatic. The men are ordinary, kind and given to rest. Generally they have more appreciation for the comfort of their family than the company of strangers. They are not apt for high stakes enterprises, but they are generally esteemed for their excellent behavior.

As far as women go, they are short and plump, boisterous and given to dances and other such entertainments; they will at times take their husbands to desperation, while they are quite strenuous and attentive of their duties.

Ⅱ

GEMINI

FROM THE 21ST OF MAY TO THE 20TH OF JUNE

Those who see birth during this sign are bilious and very prone to cerebral distress. They are usually reserved with their words, kind-hearted and gentle.

Both men and women are intelligent and skillful, extremely honest in their business and able of sacrificing themselves for their friends.

The men are of a greatly bodily build and the women are also tall, with great black eyes.

CANCER

FROM THE 21ST OF JUNE TO THE 22ND OF JULY

The ones born under the strength of this sign are inconsiderate and stubborn, to the point of practicing indecorous acts to fulfill their fancies. They have the habit of chasing women without regarding their quality. They have a bilious and valiant temperament. Their eyes are ordinarily brown and their hair blond.

The women are flimsy, gentle and delicate, and they only have three defects: they are bad daughters, bad wives and worse mothers.

♌

LEO

FROM THE 23RD OF JULY TO THE 22ND OF AUGUST

Those who are born influenced by this sign are unintelligent and not at all delicate.

The men, swarthy and vigorous, are almost always dedicated to business on a large scale, in such a way that they usually manage to gather large fortunes quickly. They are usually infatuated and very little eager to treat a friend, no matter how well they regard him.

The women are usually active, but not too gentle with their husbands however, although they do love them greatly, their ideal life is a peaceful one spent around their home. They have a feeble temperament.

♍

VIRGO

FROM THE 23RD OF AUGUST TO THE 22ND OF SEPTEMBER

Those born under the influence of this sign are all ordinary; they have no physical or moral quality that may distinguish them from each other. Only one quality distinguishes them from any other person born into a different sign: that they are all hard workers and honorable people. The men will be good sons, good husbands and, usually, good fathers.

♎

LIBRA

FROM THE 23RD OF SEPTEMBER TO THE 22ND OF OCTOBER

Those who are born in this month are scruffy and given to extraordinary whims; they are almost all joyful and merry. The women are usually beautiful, with tempting eyes of an extremely deep black. They are usually very intelligent and given to romance, but not too constant, frequently cheating on their boyfriends and breaking up with their husbands. The men are intelligent and full of energy. The women are weak and never reach eighty years of age.

SCORPIO

FROM THE 23RD OF OCTOBER TO THE 21ST OF NOVEMBER

Those born in this month are given to war and to all which is fighting; they have a bad temper and will be irritated by everything. The men will abandon important issues over frivolous pleasures. They are full of vigor and elegance.

The women are slender, well proportionate, extremely beautiful and blonde. Although they are very good housekeepers, they are very given to sins of the flesh, so it might be good to keep them under control.

All except the ones born from the 12th to the 20th of November.

SAGITTARIUS

FROM THE 22ND OF NOVEMBER TO THE 23RD OF DECEMBER

Those born under this sign have a very moldable character: they are joyful as easily as they are sorrowful.

They will desire a lifestyle that they will rarely be able to afford. They will like to travel but will never be able to leave their country.

The men will have regular height, with blue eyes, round and interesting faces. Men and women will be of an unusual dignity and extremely amiable. Their temperament will be bilious and they will have many children.

The great majority of marriages among people with the same sign will not have a satisfying result; as such one will be wise to avoid these unions, for the domestic unbalance will be great.

OCCULT POWERS

CARTOMANCY, ORISONS AND BANISHMENTS

I

How God permits that the Devil
torments his creatures

1st So that a man, unrepentant of his guilt, may serve as terror and example to other men.

2nd So that those who repent are punished solely in this world for their guilt.

3rd So that a man, seeing himself punished by the Devil, will avoid offending God.

4th So as to deal punishment over small penalties that God's Justice wishes to have readily solved.

5th So that those who are in grace do not lose their way.

6th So that sinners, seeing with their own eyes the punishment dealt by the Divine Justice, may repent.

7th So as to manifest the Power of God.

8th So as to demonstrate the sanctity of some of his creatures.

9th So as to increase the merits of vitiated creatures.

10th So as to further purify his chosen.

11th So that these creatures may have their Purgatory in this world, and be confounded, seeing as from their evil so much good can be accomplished.

II

The names of the demons who torment God's creatures, and why God consents that they torment them – How many castes of demons and afflicted exist

There are the obsessed, the possessed and the maleficated. Of these, some are maleficated and possessed, others are obsessed maleficated, repetitious, phitonic, lunatic and fascinated.

The obsessed are those who the Devil torments from the outside.

The possessed are those who have the Devil inside their bodies.

The maleficated are those who the Devil torments or harms with pain and suffering by means of some sorcery.

The maleficated and possessed are those who are under some sorcery and also possessed by the Devil.

The obsessed maleficated are those the Devil pursues from the outside.

The repetitious are those the Devil suspends or carries through the air, the ones who hold a pact.

The phitonic are those who have a divining spirit.

The lunatic are those who are tormented during the crescent and waning moon.

The fascinated are those who the Devil forces to work or speak, without them knowing that they do so.

III

The way of preparing a sieve for divination, as St. Cyprian did, after he became a saint

Take a sieve, attach a widely open scissor on its rim, and pick it up with your fingers (one on each side, each one with his own finger). Next, both people involved should pray the Creed while making the sign of the cross over the sieve, saying afterwards: "Sieve who sieves all of Humanity's bread, I beg Thee, Lord, by the three distinct persons of the Holiest Trinity, that thou does not stray from the truth, *para gelão, traga matão, vaes do pauto a chião, a molitão*[35], may expect to deliver thee to prince Lucifer."

After saying these words, speak to the sieve in these terms: "I wish for thee to tell me if this is to be true or if I am to be married: if I am, turn to this side; if I am not, turn to that side." In short, ask anything you wish to know; the sieve only does not divine that which will not happen.

IV

To divine with six rosemary sticks

Take six small sticks of rosemary, and, at night, before going to bed, cut some paper strips; wrap the sticks in these paper strips in such a way as both ends of the strips end up together, then fold them back so as the stick is very well wrapped, next ask St. Cyprian in the following manner:

"My miraculous St. Cyprian, I beg of thee, by that hour in which thou repented, in which thou made the Devil immediately return the deed to thy soul, for I beg thee, my miraculous St. Cyprian, that thou declare to me if I must do this or that."

The secret to this mystery only St. Cyprian knows, if the sticks manage to come out of the fold without ripping or undoing it, then what you asked for is true; you should, however, leave the sticks wrapped like this until the next morning.

Do note that the sticks should be small.

---

35. Translator's note: I did not translate this small section because these don't seem like regular words to me, but rather an incantation.

V

Way of reading the cards exactly like St. Cyprian did[36]

THE MEANING OF THE CARDS

DIAMONDS

The *Ace*, a gift
The *Two*, soon
The *Three*, with joy
The *Four*, church
The *Five*, novelty
The *Six*, meager money
The *Seven*, much money

SPADES

The *Ace*, affirmation/statement
The *Two*, cutting
The *Three*, bad words
The *Four*, in bed
The *Five*, sickness
The *Six*, detour/deviation
The *Seven*, passion of the soul

HEARTS

The *Ace*, a ball/dance/party
The *Two*, a letter
The *Three*, good words
The *Four*, placed in the front of the exit door
The *Five*, tears
The *Six*, through paths
The *Seven*, at eating or drinking time

---

36. Original footnote: See chapter VIII.

CLUBS

The *Ace*, by night
The *Two*, through long paths
The *Three*, through fast paths
The *Four*, in this house
The *Five*, with the five senses
The *Six*, zeal
The *Seven*, with great pleasure

So as to know how to read what the cards reveal to the consultant

The *queen of spades* is a woman of ill fame or of a bad sign. The *king* and *jack of spades* are the body and thoughts of a man of justice. If a woman is consulting the cards she should be represented by the *queen of diamonds*, and the *king* and *jack* of this same suit represent the position and thought of the individual who the consultant wishes to know about. Should it be a man he should be represented by the *king* and *jack of diamonds*, and the person consulted about should be represented by the *queen* of this same suit. All other figures are used to mark any other person who might be mentioned in this nigromancy, knowing that the *jacks* represent thoughts of the individuals marked by the *kings* of the same suit.

The way of displaying the cards

After the cards are shuffled and cut into a cross, divided into five equal portions and placed into rows of three piles, making like this a cross, and all this operation should be accompanied by the responsory, just as St. Cyprian did, so as the cards do not fail in their response to you.

Let us suppose that it is an infatuated girl who is consulting the cards, and these, after shuffled and spread on the table, are as follows:

1st line – Ace of diamonds, 7 of clubs, jack of diamonds, queen of diamonds, ace of hearts, 2 of clubs, 5 of diamonds and 4 of spades.

2nd line – King of clubs, jack of spades, 2 of spades, king of spades, 7 of spades, queen of hearts, king of hearts and 6 of clubs.

3rd line – 5 of diamonds, 5 of hearts, 2 of clubs, 7 of hearts, 5 of spades, 4 of clubs, ace of clubs and ace of spades.

4th line – jack of clubs, 4 of spades, king of spades, 3 of spades, queen of clubs, king of hearts, 6 of spades and 6 of hearts

5th line – 6 of diamonds, 6 of clubs, 4 of diamonds, 2 of diamonds, ace of hearts, king of diamonds, 3 of diamonds and 3 of hearts.

If the cards come out as we have just described you should read them as follows; but, if they do not, you should study their meaning, for without knowing this you will not extract any benefit from them.

We now start from the cards on the columns by the sides, across from each other, by the *three of hearts* and the *ace of diamonds*, and, consulting their meaning, you can see that they mean these words: *a gift with great joy and a night of pleasure.* "This man with his thought on this woman and with ideas for her, with a paper for church by quick paths, with five senses in much money and meager money, coming by the exit door."

It is then obvious that she is to be married quite soon with the individual about whom she inquired, with a great fortune arising from this consortium, having still to accept a gift from him before all this comes to pass. We then begin this same operation with the next lines, extracting from them their meaning. Arriving at the middle column we see that there is a *novelty*, for it has no figures; when this happens we may ask this *novelty* anything we wish, for example: the consulting girl wishes to know if the person she loves is faithful to her; you then take the 32 cards which were already consulted and reshuffle them.

After this, keep the cards in your hand until you finish the responsory of St. Cyprian; after you have finished this, place 21 cards, facing down, over the 8 of the middle column, and place, next to this column, 8 cards, two by two, in a cross, in such a way that you are left with 3 cards in your hand; if these 3 do not tell you anything, start by the 8 by the sides in a cross and read what they say; after this pass to the 21, taking one from each extremity of the column until you are done. One should know that the 4 of diamonds, or the 5 of spades, is a sign of an imminent death and the 2 of hearts with the 4 of diamonds, is an omen of joy, which the person involved will soon discover.

We know that there are many people who cast cards, but of what good is this if they do not possess the *Great Book of St. Cyprian or the Sorcerer's Treasure,* to study and memorize the responsory that one must say, just as the Saint used to say?

Here is how St. Cyprian invented this method: This Saint, after repenting the evil life he led, left his motherland and went to a faraway place and there he remained for seven years. As this Saint had a great deal of love for his wife and children, and also did not have any news from his parents, he decided to develop this system. He used to say: "Back when I was the lord of Satan's cunnings, I cast the cards by the power of my lord, who was Lucifer, however, now I know not how to do this."

He remained meditative on this issue, retiring to his bed at night. There, an Angel of the Lord appeared to him and said, "Cyprian, on what art thou thinking? Hast, by any chance, that cursed one thou abandoned greater power than thy God, who rules over everything illuminated by the Sun? Is thy faith still not true?" after which the angel left.

St. Cyprian woke and said, "This night I had the most pleasant dream; for who has more power than God? I still remember the day when I made fire rain from the Sky over the Earth by the power of Lucifer.

"And a single woman, just by saying – Jesus! – made all the fire cease. Great is the power of Our Lord Jesus Christ!"

Thinking of these things he said, "I shall then cast the cards in the name of Our Lord Jesus Christ," and so he did.

St. Cyprian endowed the cards with great virtues, so as they could divine all that he desired; as such, all those who do not do as this will not reap any benefit from the cards. If they do so this is a sign of imposture.

Cyprian took the deck of cards and passed them, one by one, in seven basins of holy water, each one from its own church; after this he said the Creed over them in a cross, that is, made the sign of the cross over them with his right hand. Next he passed them through the waves of the sea, wrapped seven times so as not to get them wet.

After this the cards could divine all that was happening with his family and all other things he desired.

VI

RESPONSORY THAT SHOULD BE SAID BEFORE CASTING THE CARDS

"Oh my most beloved Lord, Thou, who art the God of the Universe, allow that these cards tell me what I wish to know, for, Lord, I have no one else to whom I may ask: the Lord be with me and aid me and save me. Holiest Mary, my mother, save me by intervention of Thy beloved Son, my Lord, whom I love with a most vivid faith with all my heart, and body, and soul, and life; cards, thou shall not fail me, this by the blood Our Lord Jesus Christ shed. Amen."

This is the way to cast the cards; those that do not do as such will not obtain good results.

VII

FIRST MAGIC

Occult power or the means of obtaining the love of women

In the life of St. Cyprian, as in the *Miracles of St. Bartholomew*, it is told that, for a man to make himself beloved by women, no matter whom they may be, he needs to take the heart of a virgin pigeon and make a snake swallow it and keep this snake in captivity for fifteen days. The snake, as is obvious, will not resist for long.

As soon as the snake dies, cut off its head and dry it over some hot coals or ashes and drop 30 drops of Hanoverian Laudanum on it; next, grind all of this and put it in a new glass vial. While this is conserved as such, the owner of the vial can be sure that he will be loved by as many women as he desires.

METHOD OF USAGE

Rub your hands with a small portion of this substance saying the following words: *Izelino Belzebuth, canta-galen-se-chando-quinha, é a própria xime, é golote*[37].

This magic is so strong that to attract two creatures together it is the most admirable!

The reader may use this without any scruple, for this is not a sin, rather the same St. Cyprian taught this method to his servants, who he had released from the power of Satan, who, with his cursed sorceries, had disgraced a whole city.

In the second part of this book, it is revealed more clearly the reasons behind these occult powers.

VIII

SECOND MAGIC

Occult power or secret of the hazel wand

It is most admirable this magic, for it performs such marvels that my blood almost freezes in my veins with the idea of publishing it, not because it may offend the All-Mighty, but rather over the fear that some reckless man might use it without having armed himself with courage.

Yes, we say courage, for out of sheer fear many grave things may happen to him who uses this wand. Only because of fear and nothing else; for the Devil's power does not enter into this; for in this saintly book we do not deal with communications with demons, but rather we deal with methods of getting rid of them with our kindness.

And for this reason we will not reveal this secret.

---

37. Translator's note: similarly to the previous situation, I did not translate these words for they are obviously an incantation. While some words in there are actual Portuguese, as a whole the expression does not make the slightest sense.

IX

THIRD MAGIC

The occult powers or the enchanted money

A coin of good silver, placed under an altar stone over the period of three days, so as three masses are said over it, and all of this being done without the priest knowing about it (only the person who placed the coin there can be aware of it and no one else), may be traded in any place or store and when one gets home he will find it again inside his pocket. Such is the power of this enchantment that it might be better if the reader does not try it, unless it is as a joke.

The most favorable months for this operation are February, April, June, September and December.

Still, should you perform this operation, do not fear, no matter what you might see, and always do what you think is best according to your own ideas, and when you are done and satisfied say, with your eyes raised to the heavens: *Be at peace!* Amen.

X

Orison of the Custodian[38] Angel

The orison of the Custodian Angel was taught to St. Cyprian by St. Gregory, his companion, a virtuous man who very much preached throughout those temples, announcing the virtue and procedures of St. Cyprian and the repentance of his evil life. St. Gregory says: "Behold, my brothers, the joyful day has come when I, with my prayers, saved Cyprian. For three days now he is a slave of Our Lord God, and be sure that he will never again be enslaved by the Devil!"

"But how could Cyprian be saved?" asked the people.

"With prayers!" responded St. Gregory, "Go the Mount Samão, in the chapel; there you will see the very place where the Devil, taking over Cyprian's

---

38. Translator's note: in the original Portuguese the name of the angel reads *Anjo Custódio*. It should be noted that *Custódio* can both be a title, custodian, as in the guardian or keeper of something, or a given name. Of particular interest in this point is the fact that *Custódio* is a name traditionally given to boys so as to prevent them from becoming *Lobisomens*, werewolves (the name *Custódia* is the one prescribed to girls so as to keep them from becoming *Bruxas*, see footnote 174), being as such a religiously/ magically charged name. Sadly, this double significance of both title and name is not easily salvaged when translating *Anjo Custódio* into English, but nonetheless it should be noted that Custodian, in this context, is both the angel's title and name.

body, threw him into the depths of Hell; and the virtue of that damsel whom he, with his sorceries, tried to repudiate or convince on behalf of his friend!

"But the virtue of this damsel was not lost, and, not only did she forgive Cyprian, but she also asked God not to punish him as well as to forgive him.

"For the orison of the Custodian Angel is so effective that every creature that recites it once per day, not only will be free of Satan's cunnings, but will also create such an obstacle that twelve miles around him Satan will not be able to touch any creature. As such, every faithful Christian should know it by heart, so as to better recite it when he so wishes."

XI

An episode of St. Cyprian's life

St. Cyprian says, in a chapter of his book, that on a Friday, while passing through a deserted place, he saw so many ghosts around him that he shuddered with fright and lost all of his strength to resist them; these ghosts were, however, *Bruxas* seeking salvation. Immediately one of them approached Cyprian and said to him:

"Save us, if thou so knows that after this life we shall have another."

"How shall I save thee?" asked Cyprian

"How wert thou saved, infamous?"

"Yes... I am a slave of the Lord! I am a slave of the Lo..."

Cyprian did not finish speaking, for he fell into a deep sleep.

....

He dreamt that the orison of the Custodian Angel would save him from that danger.

As he awoke he saw in front of him an angel, who immediately disappeared... It was Custodian!

Cyprian remembered the orison and said:

"I, Cyprian, exhort and conjure the ghosts who appeared before me, under the penalty of obedience and superior precepts."

A great thunder roared across the sky.

Suddenly Cyprian saw in front of him fourteen *Bruxas*.

"Who art thou?" asked Cyprian.

"Maria and Gilberta, sisters," responded two of them.

"And the rest of these ghosts?" Cyprian enquired back.

"They are my daughters, and, such as me, all slaves of Lucifer," said Maria.

"What dost thou wish?" asked Cyprian.

"We wish for salvation and to be like thee, slaves of the Lord," responded the *Bruxas* as a choir.

Cyprian saved all of these *Bruxas*, and with the orison of the Custodian Angel bound all the demons, so as they could no longer bother them.

St. Cyprian further says that this orison can be used both for good and for evil but, should you want to use it for evil it is necessary that you not finish it.

XII

Lucifer and the Custodian Angel

"Custodian Angel, my friend, dost thou wish for salvation?"
"Yes, I do; ...I am the Custodian Angel, thy friend, am I not?"
"Dost thou wish for salvation?"
"Yes I do."
"And what are the principal virtues of Heaven that can save thee?"
"They are:

1st The Sun, brighter than the Moon;

2nd The two tablets of Moses, where Our Lord placed his holy feet;

3rd The three persons of the Holy Trinity and the whole of the Christian family;

4th Are the four Evangelists: John, Mark, Matthew and Luke;

5th The five wounds of Our Lord Jesus Christ, who suffered to break thy power, Lucifer!

6th The six holy candles that illuminate the tomb of Our Lord Jesus Christ, and illuminate me, to be free from the cunnings of Lucifer, god of Hell;

7th Are the seven Eucharistic sacraments, for without these no one has salvation;

8th Are the beatitudes;

9th Are the nine months the Virgin Mary carried Her Beloved Son Jesus Christ in her womb, and by this virtue delivered us from thy power Satan!

10th Are the Ten Commandments of the Law of God, for those who believe in them will not enter the infernal depths;

11th Are the Eleven Thousand Virgins, who plead to the Lord, without ceasing, for all of us!

12th Are the twelve Apostles, who always accompanied Our Lord Jesus Christ to the edge of death and to eternal redemption;

13th Are the thirteen rays of the Sun that banish thee eternally Satan."

On this occasion, Satan submerged, accompanied by lightning and thunder sent by God Our Lord.

We further warn that this orison should be said whole, and, should it be necessary, repeated three times.

XIII

Orison to assist the sick at the hour of their death

This orison is so effective that no soul is lost when it is said with devotion and faith in Jesus Christ, so says St. Cyprian.

St. Cyprian says, in chapter XII, that the virtue of this orison is such that, from all the sick to whom he read it, he would take one hair from their head and drop it into a vial of water. This water he would use to clean their wounds, which were untreatable through medicine; he would sprinkle one drop and say: "I, Cyprian, heal thee in the name of the Father, the Son and the Holy Spirit. Amen[39]."

ORISON

Jesus, my Redeemer, into Thy hands, Lord, I deliver the soul of this Thy servant, so as Thou, Savior of the world, may take it unto Heaven, in the company of the Angels.

Jesus, Jesus, Jesus, be with thee and defend thee; Let Jesus be in thy soul so as to settle thee; let Jesus be in front of thee so as to guide thee; let Jesus be in thy presence so as to keep thee; Jesus, Jesus, reigns, Jesus rules, Jesus defend thee from all evil. This is the Cross of the Divine Redeemer; flee, flee, be gone, enemies of the souls redeemed with the most precious blood of Jesus Christ.

Jesus, Jesus, Jesus; Mary, Mother of Grace, Mother of Mercy, defend me from the enemy and sustain me in this hour. Do not abandon me, my Lady, pray for this Thy servant (NN) to Thy Beloved Son, so as with Thy intercession he may be free from the danger of his enemies and their temptations.

Jesus, Jesus, Jesus, receive the soul of this Thy servant (NN), gaze upon him with compassionate eyes; open Thy arms; sustain him, Lord, with Thy mercy, for he is the work of Thy hands, and his soul the image of Thine.

Jesus, Jesus, Jesus! From Thou, my God, shall even his remedy come; do not deny him Thy grace in this hour, for I (NN), call upon Thee, oh Powerful God, to come without delay to receive this soul in Thy most Holy arms. Come, Lord, come in his aid, as Thou came in Cyprian's aid, when he was battling with Lucifer.

Jesus, Jesus, Jesus! I believe, Lord, firmly in all that the Apostolic Roman Catholic Church orders to me to believe in; strengthen, then, the soul of this Thy servant (NN). Come Jesus, oh true life of all souls! Free him, Lord, from his enemies; as the sovereign medic, heal him of all his ailments; purify him, my Jesus, with Thy precious blood, for, prostrated at Thy feet, I plead for Thy mercy.

Jesus, Jesus, Jesus! Oh Holiest Mary, Mother of Our Lord; now my Lady,

---

39. Original footnote: Sprinkle the holy water.

it is the time for Thee to show that Thou art the Mother of us all. Save him in this perilous hour, for in Thy hands we have placed the most important matter of our salvation.

Remove him from this conflict and agony in which he finds himself, and place his soul in the presence of Thy Beloved Son.

Jesus, save him; Jesus, help him; Jesus, succor him, oh my God, my Lord, have compassion for us all; free us from all things, as the stag desires the clear fountains, so my soul desires Thee, my Jesus. When will Thou call for me? Oh! Let my ears hear now those words from Thy divine mouth "Enter and come, soul of mine, into the joy of Thy Lord!"

Jesus, Jesus, in Thy hands, my God, I offer and place my spirit; for it is fair to return to Thee what from Thee I received; be then, just to our souls, and save them from the darkness.

Defend it, Lord, from all battles, so as eternally it may sing in Heaven Thy infinite mercies.

Mercy, most sweet Jesus; mercy, most beloved Jesus; mercy and pardon to all Thy children, for whom Thou suffered on the Cross, being it then just that Thou save us. Amen.

XIV

Great exhortation[40] made by St. Cyprian in order to punish Lucifer, who always tempted him during his prayers

When St. Cyprian saw the goodness he was to enjoy in Heaven and the evil that would befall him, should he not abandon Lucifer, he decided to punish him in a frightful desert.

ST. CYPRIAN LEFT HIS PALACE TO PUNISH LUCIFER

Here is how St. Cyprian exhorted to the Devil:

"I Cyprian, servant of God, whom I have loved with all my heart for ten years now, and it pains me, Lord, not having loved Thee since the day I was born. Rise up, Lucifer, from those infernos, come now to my presence, traitor and false god whom I so much loved out of ignorance.

"But, as I now am disillusioned, that the God I worship is a true God, powerful and full of kindness, by whom I force thee, Lucifer, to appear to me,

---

40. Translator's note: The original word here is *Requerimento*. This is a Portuguese legal term that does not exist in other languages, and it refers to a document or legal process used to request the entitlement of rights or ownership over something from an official entity or institution.

under the penalty of disobedience; should thou not wish to obey me thou shall be punished, a thousand times more than I even desire. Appear immediately, Lucifer, for I force thee in the name God, the Holiest Mary and the Eternal Father, and I banish thee by the strength of Heaven and by the grace of God, who is in the most high with open arms and ready to receive those of his children who no longer worship the idols and the false gods, whom I, Cyprian, had loved for thirty years. However, now, with the aid of Jesus Christ, I have left those false deities and worship a Powerful God who is in Heaven, with whom I now hold a full pact and will hold until the day of my death: it is by this same pact that I cite and force thee, Lucifer, to appear to me readily.

"Let now the gates of Hell open. Come Satan, to my presence. Come from the Orient, in the form of a human creature."

Having said this, Lucifer appeared, surrounded by all the demons of Hell, as St. Cyprian says in his book, chapter VIII, page 116:

"I counted three thousand demons around me; In vain did these demons try to fool me; and, seeing as they could do nothing, rebelled against me, to such a degree that fire rained from the stars with such abundance that it seemed that the whole world was aflame. All of this to try to bury me under those flames, however, I invoked the name of Jesus Christ and the fire could never come close to me or harm me."

The Devil seeing that Cyprian already had a great power under God, decided to disobey him and retire back to Hell ignoring God and Cyprian; however, the Devil shouldn't have done this, for he was punished a thousand times by St. Cyprian.

At the end of the *exhortation*, we will teach how to prepare the rod with which St. Cyprian punished the Devil.

Continuation of the exhortation with which St. Cyprian made, for a second time, the Devil arise from Hell and come to his presence, to be punished with the magic wand[41].

St. Cyprian, seeing that the Devil had retired into Hell and had closed its doors, thought for an instant on what he should do, or rather, in what way should he begin to *exhort* to Lucifer and punish him as he deserved.

---

41. Translator's note: the exact expression here is *varinha de condão*, which is something usually associated with fairy and folk tales. But anyway, the correct translation is "magic wand". Further down in the text this same wand is referred to as the *vara boleante*.

XV

How St. Cyprian began his exhortation
to the devil

"I, Cyprian, praecepitur in nomine Jesus."

"Thou, who art in the glory of God the Father, God the Son and God the Holy Spirit and in the power and virtue of the Holiest Mary, and the Divine Verb Incarnate, and in the power of the Angels of Heaven and Cherubim and Michaels, surrounded by the grace of the Divine Holy Spirit, and by all this sanctity, I order, without appeal or aggravation, that all the gates of Hell now be open, and let Lucifer come now to my presence, so as my commands be followed and executed, as I ordered.

"Appear now Lucifer in the form of a human figure, without noise or foul smell.

"Let the gates of Hell now be open, as the prison doors wert opened where some of the Apostles were kept, when an angel appeared to them under the orders of God, and as soon as the angel came to the prison all the doors wert opened and the Apostles escaped, and the angel was elevated unto Heaven as Jesus Christ had determined.

"Jesus Christ, I beg Thee and order in Thy Holiest Name, that the Devil now come to my presence, without any offense to my person, my body, and my soul.

"Appear now, Lucifer, for I require thee to do so by the power of the great Adonis[42], and by the power and virtue of those holy words said by Jesus Christ when he gave his last breath on the Cross; looking up unto Heaven, he exclaimed in anguish *'My God, my God, forgive those who crucify me, for they know not what they do.'*

"By these holy words, I banish and exhort thee, Lucifer, emperor of Hell; come to my presence, without appeal or aggravation, for I force thee in the name of Jesus, Mary and Joseph, and I order thee by virtue of Saint Ubald Francis, by these holy words, by the virtue of the twelve Apostles and by all the Saints of the God of Abraham, of Jacob and of Isaac, and by the virtue of the Angel St. Raphael, and all the more Saints and Virtues of Heaven and Orders of the Blessed: I require thee, Lucifer, by the virtue of the faithful St. John the Baptist, St. Thomas, St. Philip, St. Mark, St. Matthew, St. Simon, St. Jude, St. Martin, and by all orders of the martyrs St. Sebastian, St. Fabian, St. Cosmas, St. Damiano, St. Dionysus with all his companions, confessors of God, and by the adoration of King David and by the four Evangelists: John, Luke, Mark, and Matthew.

"I exhort thee to appear to me, Lucifer, without appeal or aggravation, for I force thee by the four columns of Heaven that thou dost not disobey me.

---

42. Translator's note: This troubles me... it might actually just be a misspelling of *Adonai*, although that is a divine name that is not really used in this grimoire.

"I, creature of God, force thee, by the seventy-two tongues that are spread through the world and by all these powers and virtues. Appear readily, four steps away from me. If you do not appear thou will be punished with curses."

At this moment Lucifer appeared, suddenly, and said:

"What dost thou want from me, Cyprian?"

"I want to punish thee as thou deserves," answered Cyprian.

"So Cyprian, dost thou not remember all the good I did for thee? Dost thou not remember all the damsels whose honor thou defiled and that all of this I arranged for thee? Dost thou forget all the good I did to thee?! I who made thee the lord of this entire kingdom!"

"Infamous! I am the guilty one in all of that! If I was less generous to thee..."

"Rain down, now, now! Fire against this man, and let him be reduced to ashes. Here is the deed of the pact thou made with me; here is the agreement we made and thou did not fulfill. You are the infamous one! Let fire rain down over thee now!" said Lucifer.

As soon as Lucifer said these words so much thunder and lightning boomed in the sky that the whole earth trembled.

However St. Cyprian feared nothing, for his power was strong against Lucifer. Cyprian said to Lucifer:

"Be still and suspend that thunder and that lightning which are falling from the heights."

Lucifer immediately ceased the thunderstorm.

"Thou will be punished with three thousand strikes from the boleante rod[43]," said Cyprian.

"Forgive me, forgive me, Cyprian, do not punish me," said Lucifer.

Cyprian did not obey him.

Cyprian bound Lucifer with a chain made from the horns of a virgin ram, and, after he was safely bound, he said:

"Thou art captive, accursed one, traitor! Thou hast tried to steal my soul, over which Jesus Christ suffered so much; however Jesus, being good, forgave my sins, and as such I will punish thee with three thousand strikes, for it is thy fault that I offended my good Jesus."

Cyprian punished Lucifer, and, after punishing him, placed a precept on him so as he could never again make a pact with anyone else.

It is this precept that does not allow the Devil to appear to us, only under obligation from God or from all the Saints.

---

43. Translator's note: The verb *bolear* means to round or smooth something down, make an irregular form into something rounded and soft. This rod is then one for the violent domination of spirits, to tame them through force and violence. Use it at your own risk.

THE METHOD OF PREPARING THE BOLEANTE ROD TO PUNISH THE DEVIL

Cut a branch of a hazel tree, thick enough to hold three one-centimeter long nails, that is, after preparation, without the nails.

THE METHOD OF PREPARING THE NAILS

Slaughter a young virgin lamb with a steel knife, and, as soon as it is dead, take the knife to a blacksmith and have him make you three nails from it and nail them in the rod, one at the bottom and two at the tip, all three along the middle, and in this way you can punish the Devil easily.

We further declare that the knife should be placed on the flame with the lamb's blood still on it. The chains to bind the Devil can be made from the horns of a ram, or even better, they can also be a cord of St. Francis[44], blessed, or a stole with which a priest has given mass at least eighteen times.

XVI

Orison to place precepts on demons

This orison is made when exorcising a pregnant woman, for some harm can come to her with these great convulsions. It is also good to place this precept on any person who is suffering from any harm, so as it may cease:

"I order, by the virtue of the Holiest Name of Jesus, to the Devil or demons, who cause me *such and such wound or affliction or pain* (one should name the illness), to no more move it, and give up from it, leaving my humors, which from some part were moved, or have been moving, in equality, with all their operations free, so as I may serve my good God. And if such affliction is moved by any humor, even if natural or elemental, by virtue of the Holiest Name of Jesus, with all faith, I order it to compose itself and cease it disconcert, so as, without this affliction and pain, I may serve and praise, with all my heart, my God the Lord Jesus Christ, by whose love alone I live, and hope for health, as my Redeemer."

V. *Omni, qui invocavit nomen Jesu.*

R. *Hic in tribulatione salvus erit.*

---

44. Translator's note: I am somewhat unsure if what is meant here is actually a Franciscan cord or the psychoactive plant known as *cordão-de-são-francisco*, Klip Dagga or Lion's Ear in English, *Leonotis nepetifolia*. Most likely it is the first, but one cannot deny the Klip Dagga's shape would indeed make it a remarkable chain.

† ORISON OF THE JUST JUDGE[45]

    Just Judge of Nazareth, son of the Virgin Mary, who was born in Bethlehem among the idolaters, I ask Thee, Lord, by Thy sixth day, that my body not be imprisoned nor wounded, nor killed, nor be enveloped by the hands of the Law. *Pax Tecum, Pax Tecum, Pax Tecum.* Christ so said to His disciples. If my enemies come to imprison me, may they have eyes and not see me; may they have ears and not hear me; may they have mouths and not speak to me; with the weapons of St. George I will be armed; with the sword of Abraham I will be covered; with the milk of the Virgin Mary I will be sprinkled; with the blood of my Lord Jesus Christ I will be baptized; in Noah's ark I will be kept; with the keys of St. Peter I will be locked where they cannot see me, or wound me, or kill me, or take any of my blood. I also ask Thee, Lord, by those three holy Chalices, by those three invested priests, by those three consecrated Wafers, that Thou consecrated on the third day, from the doors of Bethlehem to Jerusalem, that with pleasure and joy I may also be kept night and day as Jesus Christ in the womb of the Virgin Mary, God in the front, peace in the guide, God give Thee the company which God gave to the always Virgin Mary from the holy home of Bethlehem to Jerusalem. God is Thy Father, the Holy Virgin Mary Thy Mother, with the weapons of St. George Thou will be armed, with the sword of St. James Thou will be kept forever. Amen. [46]

---

45. Original footnote: Although this orison in not of St. Cyprian, we publish it nonetheless for it is extremely miraculous.

46. Translator's note: Although the translation of this last section of the orison is not particularly hard it is still quite confusing, and the fact is that in Portuguese it actually rhymes quite harmoniously, suggesting it might be an incantation. The original is as follows: *Também Vos peço, Senhor, por aqueles três Cálices bentos, por aqueles três padres revestidos, por aquelas três Hóstias consagradas, que consagrastes ao terceiro dia desde as portas de Belém até Jerusalém, que com prazer e alegria eu seja também guardado de noite como de dia assim como andou Jesus Cristo no ventre da Virgem Maria, Deus diante, paz na guia, Deus te dê a companhia que Deus deu à sempre Virgem Maria desde a casa santa de Belém a Jerusalem. Deus é teu Pai, a Virgem Santa Maria tua Mãe, com as armas de S. Jorge serás armado, com a espada de S. Tiago serás guardado para sempre. Amém.*

NEW TREATY OF CARTOMANCY

In which one may learn the method of casting the cards without referring to sleepwalkers or other kinds of diviners

The following chart indicates the value and significance of the cards; to resort to them one needs only to shuffle them many times and turn them over one at a time.

DIAMONDS

King. . . . . . .A good man who will take care of you.
Queen. . . . . .A friend seeks to do you harm; she will not be successful.
Ace . . . . . . .Good news coming through the mail soon.
Jack. . . . . . .A man who will betray you, should you follow him.
Ten . . . . . . .A pleasant surprise.
Nine . . . . . .Bad news coming at an uncertain time.
Eight. . . . . .Great success.
Seven . . . . .Betterment in position / promotion.

CLUBS

King. . . . . . .An elderly man and a good adviser; he should be listened to.
Queen. . . . . .A bad-mouthing neighbor who seeks to harm you.
Ace . . . . . . .A great disappointment, but not lasting long.
Jack. . . . . . .A young man of good position and fortune; he will marry you.
Ten . . . . . . .Efforts that will bear good fruit.
Nine . . . . . .Satisfaction in the family.
Eight. . . . . .Bad conduct, violent passion.
Seven . . . . .A happy marriage.

SPADES

King. . . . . . .A man of the law; important business.
Queen. . . . . .A woman who will harm you greatly.
Ace . . . . . . .Sickness without danger.

Jack. . . . . . . Process and condemnation.
Ten . . . . Obstacle to your marriage.
Nine . . . . . . Bad news.
Eight. . . . . . A trip and good results from your efforts.
Seven . . . . . Successful business.

HEARTS

King. . . . . . .A man who wishes to make you happy; he shall
            be successful.
Queen. . . . . A kind-hearted woman who will provide you
            good services.
Ace . . . . You shall receive money.
Jack. . . . . . . A person who loves you.
Ten . . . . Great prosperity.
Nine . . . . . . Short-lived discord with a friend.
Eight. . . . . . Loss of money.
Seven . . . . . A happy and unexpected event.

King and Queen. . . . Marriage.
Two Kings. . . . . Two suitors to your hand.
Three Kings . . . . Triumph and great results.
Four Kings . . . . Momentary happiness.
Queen and Jack. . . . You are betrayed.
Two Queens . . . . . . Jealousy, rivalry.
Three Queens. . . . . Short-lived agreement.
Four Queens . . . . . . A great deal of bad-mouthing.
Ace and Jack . . . . . . Uncertainty.
Two Aces. . . . . Solid friendship.
Three Aces. . . . . . . Progressive friendship.
Four Aces. . . . . Absolute happiness; nothing to desire.

Jack and Ten. . . . . . . Cunning.
Two Jacks . . . . Suspicion.
Three Jacks. . . . . . . Betrayal, laziness.
Four Jacks. . . . . Heartbreak of every kind.

Ten and Nine. . . . . . .Distraction.
Two Tens. . . . . Non-serious sickness.
Three Tens . . . . Romantic intrigue.
Four Tens. . . . . Much money.

Nine and Eight . . . . .New love.
Two Nines. . . . . Stubbornness.
Three Nines . . . . Position of greater advantage.
Four Nines . . . . Return to the country.

Eight and Seven. . . . Scuffles, falling-outs.
Two Eights . . . . Great heartbreak.
Three Eights. . . . . . Restlessness.
Four Eights. . . . . . . Isolation.

Seven and King. . . . . Bad mood.
Two Sevens. . . . . . . Money to come in the long term.
Three Sevens . . . . . . A military man will leave.
Four Sevens . . . . . . Fulfilled hopes.

Six and Seven . . . . . A benevolent neighbor.
Two Sixes. . . . . Lasting happiness.
Three Sixes . . . . Pleasures elevated to drunkenness.
Four Sixes . . . . Pleasurable company.

Six and King. . . . . . .Interview with no advantageous outcome.
Six and Queen. . . . . . A rival of little danger.
Six and Eight . . . . . . .Lamentable events.
Six and Jack. . . . . . . Ephemeral venture.

BOOK TWO

TRUE TREASURE

OF

BLACK AND WHITE MAGIC

OR

Secrets of Sorcery

⚜

The cross of St. Bartholomew and St. Cyprian

In a book, very much esteemed and very much unknown even to the majority of well learned men, whose title is *Life and Miracles of St. Bartholomew*, we have found a way of making the cross of this saint, as well as the proper method of using it.

The explanations we are about to give to our reader deserve great faith, not only for having been extracted from a book greatly anointed by mysticism, but also for having been practiced by people of our acquaintance with the most satisfactory results.

METHOD OF MAKING THE CROSS

Cut three cedar sticks, one long and two short, so as to form the arms of the cross; cover the three pieces with rosemary, rue and celery; place then on each arm, on the top and on the bottom of the long stick, a small cypress apple[47]; leave this in holy water for three days and remove it from this same water at the stroke of midnight, saying the following words:

"Cross of St. Bartholomew, the virtue of the water in which thou wert placed and the plants and wood of which thou art formed, free me from the temptations of the evil spirit and bring onto me the grace enjoyed by the Blessed. In the name of the Father and the Son and the Holy Spirit. Amen."

These words should be said almost without any sound, and they should be repeated four times.

---

47. Translator's note: the large globular seeds of the Mediterranean Cypress, *Cupressus sempervirens*.

METHOD OF USING THE CROSS

This cross can be carried inside a small, blessed black silk bag, or even in direct contact with the body, hanging from a black twine thread. The person carrying it should make the greatest effort to keep it hidden from everyone; and, whenever he is suspicious that someone has cast an *evil-eye* on him, he should, upon going to bed, kiss the cross three times and say the same orison we have indicated in the method of making the cross.

Upon rising the next morning, he should kiss the cross again three times and pray one Our Father and one Hail Mary.

I

Great magic of the fava beans

Kill a black cat and bury it in your yard, having placed a fava bean in each eye socket, another one under its tail and one in each ear. After this is done, cover it with earth and water it every night at the stroke of midnight, with very little water. Do this until the fava beans, which should have grown into full plants, give you mature favas, and when you see that this is the case, cut the stock close to the ground.

After cutting them, take them home and place one at a time inside your mouth. When it seems to you that you have become invisible it is because the fava in your mouth is the one with magical power, and anytime you feel like going anywhere without being seen, put that fava in your mouth.

This is by an occult virtue, and it does not require a pact with the Devil, as the *Bruxas* perform.

A WARNING TO THOSE THAT PERFORM THIS MAGIC

When you go to water the favas, there will appear to you many phantoms, so as to frighten you and keep you from your desire. The reason for this is very simple. It is because the Devil is very envious of those who perform this magic without giving themselves to him in body and soul, as the *Bruxas*, also called women of virtue, do. Do not be frightened, he will not harm you, and to be sure of that you should always make the sign of the cross and at the same time pray the Creed.

II

Magic of the bone of a black cat's head

Boil a pan of water with white clematis[48] in a fire of willow wood, and as soon as the water starts boiling, put a cat inside it and let it boil until the meat comes off its bones. After all this is done collect the bones by straining the mixture through a linen cloth and place yourself in front of a mirror; place one bone at a time in your mouth, noting that it is not necessary to place it completely inside your mouth, but only between your teeth. When your image disappears from the mirror keep the bone you are holding in your teeth, for that is the one that contains all the magic. When you wish to go anywhere without being seen, place the above mentioned bone in your mouth and say these words: "I wish to be in this place by the liberal black magic."

III

Another magic of the black cat

When a black male cat is connected to a female cat of the same color, that is, connected by carnal copulation, have a scissor immediately ready and cut a piece of hair from both cats. Mix all of these hairs, burn them with some northern rosemary[49] and then take these ashes and place them inside a vial with a bit of spirit of hartshorn. Be sure to close this vial well so as to preserve this spirit fresh and strong.

After all this is ready, you should take the vial with your right hand and say the following words:

"Ash, with my own hand wert thou burned, with a scissor of strong steel wert thou cut from the two cats, all people who smell thee with me they shall meet. Only when God stops being God will this fail; *e para golão, traga matão, vaes do pauto a chião a molitão*[50]."

As soon as this is done, the vial will contain the sorcery, magic and enchantment, that whenever you have the desire for any girl to become your friend[51], all you need to do is open the vial and, under some pretext, offer it for her to smell.

Let us suppose an individual wishes that his girlfriend smell the said vial but cannot find a good reason to take this into proper effect. In that case,

---

48. Translator's note: The Portuguese Clematis to be specific, *Clematis campaniflora*.

49. Translator's note: This is the common name given to a number of plants not necessarily related to Rosemary: the *Lantana microphylla martius*, the *Diosma ericoides* and the *Myrica gale* (Sweet Gale), I have not been able to determine which one is meant here.

50. Translator's note: obviously, an incantation.

51. Translator's note: euphemism.

one may start a conversation about any one subject, in such a way as to make reference to some sort of cologne. This being done, take the vial from your pocket and say with the greatest serenity:

"Dost thou wish to smell this most pleasant scent my girl?"

Well, since, as a general rule, women are very curious, she will immediately smell the content of the vial and you can expect all of her love. In this way you may captivate all who please you. Do note that this enchantment has such virtue that it may both be used by men on women as well as by women on men.

IV

Another magic of the black cat to cause harm

Let us place our thought on someone who wishes to execute vengeance on an enemy but does not wish for this enemy to know of his revenge. This vengeance may be easily achieved in the following way:

Take a black cat, which cannot have one single white hair, and tie his feet together with an *esparto*[52] cord. After this operation take the cat to a crossroad in a mount and, as soon as you arrive at the place, say the following:

"I, (NN), on behalf of God All Mighty, order the Devil to appear to me here, now, under the saintly penalty of disobedience and superior precepts. I, by the power of the liberal black magic, order thee, Devil or Lucifer, or Satan, or Barabbas, to enter the body of this person, whom I wish harm, and do not leave there until I tell thee otherwise, and do all that I ask of thee during my lifetime."

(Here you say what you wish for him to do to the creature)

"Oh great Lucifer, emperor of all that is infernal, I bind thee and tie thee to the body of (NN) just as I have this cat tied. After all I ask is done, I offer thee this black cat for I shall bring him here when all this has been done."

WARNING

When the Devil performs his obligation, go to the place where you first requested from him and say twice: "Lucifer, Lucifer, here is what I promised thee" and, after these words are said, release the cat.

---

52. Translator's note: *Macrochloa tenacissima* and *Stipa tenacissima*, a type of fibrous grass that grows in Northwest Africa and the Iberian Peninsula, used to make baskets, cords and such.

V

Another magic of the black cat and the way of generating a tiny devil with the eyes of a cat

Kill a black cat and, after this is done, remove its eyes, placing them inside an egg from a black hen, noting that each eye should be in its own egg. After this operation is done place the eggs in a pile of horse manure, it being very important that the manure be hot, so as to generate the tiny devil.

St. Cyprian instructs that one should go to this pile of manure every day for a whole month, for this is the time it takes for the tiny devil to be born.

WORDS
THAT SHOULD BE SAID AT THE PILE OF MANURE
WHERE THE TINY DEVIL IS

"Oh great Lucifer, I give thee these two eyes of a black cat, so as thou, my great friend Lucifer, are favorable to me in this plead I make at thy feet. My great minister and friend Satan and Barabbas, I give thee this black magic so as thou may place all thy power, virtue and cunning, which wert given to thee by Jesus Christ, in it; for I give thee these two eyes of a black cat, so as from them a devil may be born, to be my company for all eternity. My black magic, I give to Maria Padilha, all her family[53] and all devils from Hell, lame walkers, near blinds, cripples and everything that is infernal, so as from here be born two devils to provide me with wealth, for I do not wish for wealth from the power of Lucifer, my friend and companion from henceforth."

Do this as we have just indicated and, in one month, give or take one day, two tiny devils who look like small lizards will be born. As soon as the devil is born place him inside a small tube of ivory or boxwood and feed him iron or steel powder.

When you have these two tiny devils you may do anything that pleases you; for example: should you wish for money, just open the tube and say: "I wish for money, here and now" and immediately money will be delivered, with the sole condition that you may not give this money to the poor nor order masses with it, for this is money given by the Devil.

---

53. Translator's note: it should be important to note that the expression "Maria Padilha and all her family," (*Maria Padilha e toda a sua família*), and all similar variants of this, rhymes quite harmoniously. This is probably meant as a kind of incantation and, although I have chosen to translate these, it is debatable if I actually should have done so. I guess this is one of the eternal questions of translating magical and religious texts: exactly how fundamentally important is the original language? In this work I do not intend to approach this question even in the slightest; my only hope is that I do a good job.

Reader, it is not possible to describe in this part of the *Great Book of Saint Cyprian* all the events that happened to this saint, for this would make up such a large volume that it could not possibly be afforded by any class of society.

We are thus content in teaching you this magic.

VI

Method of obtaining a tiny devil by making a pact with the Devil

METHOD OF PERFORMING THE PACT

Take a virgin parchment and make a deed of your soul to the Devil in your own blood.

You should make it in the following way:

"I, with blood from my little finger, make this deed to Lucifer, emperor of Hell, so as he may accomplish for me all that I desire in this life, and, should he fail, I shall no longer belong to him - (NN)."

After this is written, grab the egg of a black hen, which mated with a rooster of the same color, and write on the egg the same deed you wrote on the parchment.

After this is done, open a small hole in the egg and drop inside it one drop of blood from your pinky finger, then wrap the egg in raw cotton and place it inside a pile of manure or under a black hen. From this egg a small devil will be born that you will then keep in a silver box with silver powder and every Saturday you should place your pinky finger inside this box so as to suckle him.

After acquiring this devil, you may obtain all you wish from this world.

But, regarding this practice, St. Cyprian says the following in chapter XLV of his saintly book:

"Every son of God who delivers his soul to the Devil will, at that very moment, be cursed by he who created him and gave him being, Our Lord Jesus Christ."

It is important to declare that we do not expose these diabolical recipes so as the readers may practice them; we present them here for we understand the utility of knowing all that is good and evil, so as those who take the bad path may deviate from it in due time and that they may thank us for this good intervention which was provided in the pages of this good book, and we also hope that God may bless our work.

VII

Sorcery which is performed with two dolls, just as St. Cyprian used to do when he was a sorcerer and a magician

Prepare two dolls made with linen or cotton rags, one resembling a man and one resembling a woman; after they are ready you should unite them closely, having them embrace each other.

After this operation, take a ball of white thread and start wrapping it around the dolls saying the following, declaring firstly the name of the person you wish to affect.

"I bind thee and tie thee, in the name of Our Lord Jesus Christ, Father, Son and Holy Spirit, so as, under this saintly power, thou shall not be able to eat nor drink, nor be in any part of the world without my company, (NN). I (NN), here bind and tie thee, just as they bonded Our Lord Jesus Christ to the wood of the Cross; and the rest thou shall have while thou dost not turn to me will be like the fire the souls in Purgatory have, pining continuously for their sins in this world, and like the wind in the air, the waves in the sea always in continuous movement, the tide rising and lowering, the Sun rising in the mountains and setting in the sea. Such will be the rest I give thee, while thou dost not turn to me, with all thy heart, body, soul and life; under the divine penalty of obedience and superior precepts, thou will be imprisoned and bonded to me, just as these two dolls are tied to each other."

These words should be repeated nine times at the hour of midday, after praying the orisons of the Open Hours, which are in the first part of this work.

VIII

Enchantment and magic of the fern seeds and their properties

Here is what you need to do to collect the fern seeds on St. John's Eve:

On St. John's Eve, at the stroke of midnight, sharp, place a sheet under a fern, where you should have already drawn a *signo-saimão*[54] under the said fern, which you should bless in the name of the Father, the Son and the Holy Spirit so as the Devil may not enter the said seal.

After this operation is done, place inside the seal, which should have a precise width, all the people assisting the ceremony.

---

54. Translator's note: *signo-saimão*, *sino-saimão*, and a few other variations, is simply the Portuguese folk name for the Seal of Solomon, being that it can be frequently associated with either the pentagram (more common) or hexagram.

We further warn that all people who wish to acquire the said seeds should say the Litany of the Saints, which is published in the first part of this work. The litany should be said aloud, so as to force the Devil to retreat, for he will surely come to frighten you so as you may not acquire what you so desire; but, as you sing the whole litany, all demons will vanish. At the end of this operation, divide the seeds without greed or arguments, otherwise they will lose all their virtue.

WORDS ALL THE PRESENT SHOULD SAY, WITH THEIR FACE OVER THE FERN SEED

"Fern seed, which was harvested on St. John's Eve, at midnight sharp. Thou wert obtained and thou fell on a *signo-saimão*, thus thou will serve me in all quality of enchantments; and as God in divine proportion of St. John is Father and in human proportion of St. John is Cousin, so will any person thou touch become enchanted by me[55].

All this will be made by the power of the great Omnipotent God, for whom I (NN) cite and notify thee so as thou dost not fail me, by the blood that was shed by Our Lord Jesus Christ and the power and virtue of the Holiest Mary be with me and with thee. Amen."

After these words, one prays the Creed in a cross over the seeds, that is, while making the sign of the cross with the right hand over the said seeds. In this way the seeds will acquire all power and virtue. Then one should dip them in a basin of holy water.

After all this is done, place them in a vial, but keep it very well sealed.

EXPLANATION OF THE VIRTUES AND MARVELS OF WHICH THESE SEEDS ARE GIFTED

1st — Every creature that obtains these seeds, if he touches another person with one with evil intentions, will be in mortal sin for the reason of using a divine mystery to enact an offense against humanity. Such as touching any woman, be her married or single, to take her somewhere with bad intentions.

2nd — One will be under the threat of excommunication if he touches another creature with one of these seeds to bring about bad luck to his businesses or enchant his work, so as it will not go well.

---

55. Translator's note: This curious section of the prayer is probably meant as an incantation; as such we provide the original Portuguese: "(...) *e assim como Deus em ponto divino de S. João é Pai e em ponto humano de S. João é Primo, assim toda a pessoa por quem tu fores tocada se encante comigo*"

3rd — These seeds have the virtue to banish any evil spirit that may possess the creature which one of them touches, but this while having a strong faith in Jesus Christ.

4th — These seeds have the virtue to heal any infirmity, just by having one seed touch the wound, but only with an extremely lively faith in Jesus Christ.

5th — These seeds have the virtue of defending us from our enemies or their cunnings, just by carrying them with us.

6th — These seeds have a hidden virtue, which operates almost as if by a divine power and which can be brought about in the following way: Let us suppose that there is a girl with which an individual greatly sympathizes, but the interesting girl does not feel the slightest affection for him. It is very easy to make the above-mentioned girl fall in love with him. Do the following:

When you are conversing with her, throw three of these fern seeds at her, and you will see that the girl will never again deny you her attentions and gentleness and will obey you in every way.

7th — These fern seeds have a hidden virtue that can only be given credit by those who have experienced it, and it is as follows:

When you pass by anyone, touch that person with one seed and this person will follow you, and, when you wish for her to stop, touch her again.

8th — These fern seeds have so many properties that they cannot be fully explained. Only those who possess these seeds will be able to give you these explanations.

And, for now, dearest readers, we find it reasonable to stop with such explanations about the fern seeds, and we will simply say conclusively:

These marvelous seeds hold virtues for every single issue their owner wishes for.

IX

Magic of the four-leaf clover cut on St. John's Eve, at the stroke of midnight

Reader, the four-leaf clover has the same virtues as the fern seeds; for that reason it won't be necessary to bore you any further regarding this matter.

We understand that this will suffice for you to become convinced of the virtues of the four-leaf clover.

To obtain the clover, proceed in the following way:

On St. John's Eve search the fields for a patch of four-leaf clovers. As soon as you find one draw a *signo-saimão* around it and leave it there until midnight. When, however, the church bells ring to the Holy Trinity[56], return to it and say the following orisons:

---

56. Translator's note: This probably refers to six p.m., the same hour of the Trinities when you're supposed to pray one of the orisons of the open hours, which means that,

Start by praying the Creed in a cross over the clover, that is, saying the Creed while making the sign of the cross with your hand over the clover.

†

ORISON

"I, creature of the Lord, redeemed with His Holiest Blood, which Jesus shed on the Cross to free us from the furies of Satan, have the most vivid faith in the edifying powers of Our Lord Jesus Christ. I order the Devil to be gone from this place, and I bind and tie him in the curdled sea, not perpetually, but only until I collect this clover; and as soon as I have collected it I untie thee from thy prison. All this by the power and virtue of Our Lord Jesus Christ. Amen."

OBSERVATION

When you are binding the Devil in the curdled sea, should he appear to you at that moment and say: "Living creature, son of God, I beg thee not to bind me, ask what thou wishes from me as a reward." Respond to him: "Be gone, Satan, ten paces away from me."

The Devil will immediately retire, and afterwards you may ask of him all you wish for, for he will do anything so as not to be imprisoned. After you tell him what you wish from him, force him to make an oath, otherwise you will be tricked, for the Devil is the father and mother of lies; but, by having him make an oath to you he will not be able to break it, for God will not consent that he fools a baptized creature redeemed with His Holiest Blood.

After all this is properly executed, take the clover, with which you may accomplish anything you wish, for thus was written by St. Cyprian, in his book, chapter CXLV.

X

Magic or sorcery that is made with two dolls, to do harm to any creature

Observe attentively what we are about to teach, so as this magic may be performed properly. Make two dolls; one of them signifies the creature to be enchanted, and the other the person doing the enchanting.

After the said dolls are made you should unite them to each other, in such a way that they become very well embraced. After all this is done, tie a cord

---

seeing as according to the title of this procedure one is supposed to perform this sorcery at midnight, you'll need to be outside for quite a long time.

around their necks, as if you are strangling them, and after this operation is done nail five nails in the indicated areas:

1st In the head, so as the nail goes through them both.
2nd In the chest, in the same way as before.
3rd In the belly, so as it goes through and through.
4th In the legs, so as it goes through them both.
5th In the feet, so as it crosses them from one side to the other.

In this way, both those creatures will be suffering the same pains, as if the nails were carved in their own bodies.

There is still one further condition: that the said nails must be employed with the following invocations in the different places where they are nailed:

1st nail. *(NN), I, (NN), nail and tie thee and pierce thy body, just as I pierce, tie and nail thy figure.*

2nd nail. *(NN), I, (NN), swear to thee, under the power of Lucifer and Satan, that, from this day forth, thou shall not have a single more hour of health.*

3rd nail. *(NN), I, (NN) swear to thee, under the power of malefic magic, that thou shall not have, from this day forth, a single hour of rest.*

4th nail. *(NN), I, (NN), swear to thee, under the power of Maria Padilha, that, from this day forth, thou will be possessed by all sorcery.*

5th nail. *(NN), I, (NN), bind and tie thee from head to toe, by the power of the sorcerous magic.*

In this way, the enchanted creature will never again have a single hour of health.

Reader! Do not be frightened by this, for God, just as he gave man the power and wisdom to perform sorceries, he also gave man the remedy to combat them, as is explained in the first part of this work, which teaches how to undo all matter of sorceries – which was the whole purpose of St. Cyprian's life after he became a saint, and it is because of this that we recommend that every Christian should own this book.

DECLARATION

So as no further doubts about the sorcery you have just read remain, it will be good to provide you with an explanation, which is the following:

Both dolls need to be put together, both the enchanter and the enchanted; meaning that the enchanter doll is embracing the enchanted, as if wanting to kill him or carve him with nails.

XI

Magic of a black dog and its properties

A black dog has great magical power: thus says St. Cyprian in chapter CXLV.

There are many people who say that magic is performed with magical words, this is false, however, for there is no magic which operates through words, what may be said is that without words nothing can be done; but words are worthless without certain other things which have magical power, and these are also worthless by themselves.

Here is the first magic of the black dog:

Let us begin with the eyes of the dog: When the dog is dead remove its right eye without crushing it; then place this eye inside a small box and carry it in your pocket. Whenever you pass by a dog take it out of your pocket and show it to the said dog, for it will follow you anywhere you go, even against its master's orders. When you wish for the dog to leave, wave the box at it three times.

XII

Second magic or sorcery of the black dog

With a black dog one may perform sorceries of the greatest power: thus assures St. Cyprian in chapter CCI, Volume XII.

Proceed in the following way:

Cut the eyelashes of a black dog as well as its nails and a piece of its hair, put these three things together and burn them with northern rosemary. After all this is reduced to ashes, gather these inside a vial, very well covered with a cork, for nine days and at the end of this time the sorcery is ready.

METHOD OF APPLICATION

Let us suppose that a person, be it a man or a woman, wishes to love[57] one other creature, either with good or bad intentions, and is unable to achieve this by any method. This intent is very easily achieved.

Take the ashes of these already mentioned three objects, mix it with a small portion of tobacco and roll a cigarette with it, which should be quite strong. When you are speaking with the person you wish to enchant, puff some smoke on her and you will see that this person will immediately be under the spell; this should be done three, five, seven or nine or more times; the number should always be uneven.

---

57. Translator's note: euphemism.

We further declare that if it is a woman doing this spell, and cannot perform it for not being a smoker, do the following:

Take any sign[58] of the person you wish to enchant and wrap the ashes we mentioned inside the sign, then wrap around the sign a green twine, while saying the following words:

"I bind and tie thee with the chains of St. Peter and St. Paul, so as thou may not have peace or rest in any part of the world under the penalty of obedience and the superior precepts."

After these words, said nine times, the person is bewitched; however, if this sorcery, which we have just taught, is not enough to obtain what you desire do not be frightened, and do not lose your faith, for many thing aren't accomplished by lack of faith.

You should know, reader, that there are many creatures in which sorcery cannot penetrate on account of some prayer they might say every day at bedtime and as they rise.

XIII

Story of St. Cyprian and Clotilde

On the 15th of January of the year 1009, being St. Cyprian in a conversation with Prince Satan, he asked him thus:

"Oh my friend Satan, what supper shall thou give me today in return for my faithfulness?"

Satan responded:

"Today I shall give thee a supper, or rather, an unexpected pleasure which thou, Cyprian, will very much enjoy."

Cyprian was pleased with the response and said to Satan:

"My friend and lord, whom I have loved for ten years with such faithfulness and pleasure, that it seems to me that I am not content unless I am near thee..."

Satan smiled and said:

"Since thou loves me and are thus so faithful, I shall love thee in the same manner; as such put thy fava in thy mouth and follow me."

Immediately Satan and Cyprian disappeared.

Eight minutes later they were over the palace of the King of Persia.

Satan opened a hole on the right side of princess Clotilde's room, turned to Cyprian and said to him:

"Dost thou see that princess so beautiful?"

Cyprian answered:

"I believe that there is no other girl as beautiful as to compare with her."

---

58. Translator's note: I believe this should be a photo or some other thing that clearly indicates the person in question.

Satan said to him:

"Then thou can see, Cyprian, my servant, that I am thy friend, and that I love thee with all my heart."

Cyprian, hearing these words, fell at Satan's feet and said to him:

"My friend and lord, whom I love with all my heart, body, soul and life, if thou could make it so as I may enjoy that damsel, I will swear to love thee even more than I have so far."

Satan responded:

"I will place her within thy reach. Convince her with thy cunnings and arts, and I am here ready to aid thee in all thou may need."

After this, Cyprian tried using sorcery to make the princess follow him or have him called into the palace; however, Cyprian, with all his sorceries could not convince the princess.

Becoming gradually desperate, he one day entered the palace, walked to the king's cabinet but could not find him.

Enraged by all this he meditated for half an hour on what he should do.

Suddenly, the king entered through the cabinet door and shouted aloud:

"Aid me! Aid me!"

Cyprian reached into his right pocket to grab his fava and escape, however, he was not able to find it. He reached into his left pocket and took out a silver tube where he had a tiny devil (one of those we already mentioned).

"What dost thou wish?" asked the tiny devil.

Cyprian told him:

"I wish for four castles around me."

"I will execute thy orders readily."

In that very instant the cavalry and an escort of soldiers arrived, however, they could do nothing. The battle was so fierce that the palace was completely destroyed.

The king fell at Cyprian's feet and begged him for forgiveness by the soul of whom Cyprian most cherished.

Cyprian said:

"Thou surely know that I am a bishop, and, besides this, I possess diabolical arts. Dost thou see that this palace is reduced to nothing; what shall thou give me to put it back to the way it was before, all this in but an instant?"

Then Cyprian said the following words:

"I command now, by the power of the liberal black magic, which can accomplish all, I command now, now, that this palace be raised and returned to its natural state *e para golão traga matão, vaes de pauto a chião, a molitão, pexeda ispera regra retragarão, onit prontual finis!*"

After Cyprian said these words the palace was left just as it was before; the king, seeing that Cyprian could perform marvels, became even more frightened, casting himself once again at his feet and said:

"I ask thee, I beg thee, lord, that thou forgive me if thou finds thyself offended by me."

Cyprian said to him:

"Rise, that thou art forgiven, but under the condition that thou shall give me the princess, who is thy daughter Clotilde."

The king, hearing these words, trembled and became silent, not being able to utter a single word. Cyprian shouted once again:

"I told thee! Will thou give me thy daughter Clotilde? Otherwise, all will be returned to nothing."

The king remained quiet.

Cyprian insisted:

"Well, what shall I say?"

The king remained silent.

Cyprian, enraged, gave a loud shout and said:

"By all the strength of my black and white magical art, I order that this entire kingdom be enchanted, reduced to rocks and boulders and the king and queen turned to two marble stones!"

His order was executed in five minutes. He only couldn't enchant Clotilde, because of an orison she prayed every day. Cyprian, as soon as everything except Clotilde was enchanted, became enraged against Lucifer and shouted:

"Lucifer, Lucifer! Come to me Lucifer!"

"Here I am friend Cyprian, at thy command," said Lucifer.

"I want thee to tell me," said Cyprian, "the reason why I cannot satisfy my appetites with this princess."

The princess, hearing these words, said in a low voice:

"If thou art the Devil, I conjure thee in the name of the Lord to only say the truth."

The Devil, forced by a divine power, said to Cyprian: "My friend, thou surely knows that there is a powerful God covering the Heaven and the Earth who hast power over all. If He so wishes, neither thou nor I will be able to move from this spot, for He is mighty. The princess invoked His holy name and I could not help it but confess the truth, besides, the princess says an orison every day that frees her from everything which is a temptation, either from me or from my beloved children."

Cyprian fell to the ground and said:

"Lord of the high heavens, who art Thou that I do not know Thee? And thou, Satan, evil spirit, cursed demon, cursed, cursed, thou wert my perdition? Cursed be the hour I was conceived; cursed be the womb that generated me; cursed be the father and the mother from whom I am a descendent; cursed be the hour I was born; cursed be the milk I suckled; cursed be every step I took in my whole life! My God, my God, make the gates of Hell open now so they may swallow this cursed man; may he disappear forever! Jesus, Jesus, Jesus, if I still have salvation, answer me from the high heavens."

Cyprian then heard a voice telling him:

"Son, continue with this life thou hast, for I will warn thee, one year in advance, of thy death, so thou may arrange for thy salvation."

Cyprian kissed the earth and thanked God the great benefit he was giving him.

However, Cyprian was fooled, for that voice he heard was the same Devil who, to trick him, climbed up to the stars in order to pretend to be God responding to Cyprian's pleas.

Cyprian, innocently, gave serious credit to the voice he heard. Indeed he must have been very innocent not to realize that that voice could not be God. However, Jesus Christ, kind and just as he is, did nonetheless forgive Cyprian all the sins committed by his unmeasured ambition, which the illusion of Satan's power had caused. Cyprian retired from the palace, and, when he was already far away, he heard a voice saying to him:

"Cyprian, Cyprian, hear me in this affliction by the love of that great God of the altars!"

Cyprian trembled and fell to the ground.

The good princess Clotilde came close to Cyprian and said to him:

"I order thee in the name of God! Rise!"

Cyprian got up suddenly and looked the beautiful princess straight in the eyes, saying to her:

"What dost thou want?"

The princess responded:

"I invoke the saintly name of Jesus so as thou, man, do not move from here without restoring life to my father and mother and disenchant everything thou has enchanted in the kingdom by an occult and powerful art."

"I," said Cyprian, "will do all that, but I ask thee to teach me the orison that thou prays every day, by which I could never take my depraved desires forth, even using all my sorceries and enchantments."

"The orison I pray," responded the princess "is very simple, and I will gladly teach it to thee.

"Listen:"

†

ORISON

"I deliver myself unto Jesus, to the Holy Cross, to the Holy Sacrament, to the three relics in it, to the three masses of Christmas so that no harm may come to me. Holiest Mary be with me always, angel of my guard keep me free from the cunnings of Satan. P. N. A. M."

Cyprian, then, disenchanted the palace and everything he had enchanted and said to the princess:

"Always pray for me in thy orisons."

The princess thus did and obtained from Our Lord Jesus Christ the forgiveness of Cyprian's sins, who did not continue in that deceitful life for more than one year.

Cyprian was saved, for God does not hold any hate towards His children, who He permits to follow the wrong path so as, in the proper occasion, He may show them His power.

For all that was here exposed, you can see, reader, that the Devil cannot stand in the way of anyone who utters an orison as the princess we just mentioned did. Make diligences to imitate this daughter of God, so as the Devil may not pursue you, nor the *Bruxas* and sorcerers.

We ask then, to all dedicated people who wish to remove themselves from all enchantment and dangerous traps, to always keep this miraculous orison in their memory.

MYSTERIES OF SORCERY

EXTRACTED FROM A MANUSCRIPT OF BLACK MAGIC
THAT IS THOUGHT TO BE FROM THE TIME OF THE MOUROS

While performing excavations in the village of Penacova[59], in the year of 1410, a manuscript was found in perfect state of preservation.

In this precious scroll many curious things were found, some of which we will present to the readers, convinced that we are performing thus a good service.

It was that scroll, today in the Library of Évora[60], which gave body to a much-respected grimoire in Brazil, entitled *Livro do Feiticeiro*.

Here are some of those mysteries:

I

Recipe to force a husband to be faithful

Take the marrow from the foot of a black dog, one of those hairless breeds, and fill a wood needle case with it. Wrap this needle case in a piece of red velour, perfectly tight and well sewn. After this, unstitch that area of the mattress that lies between the husband and wife and place the needle case inside the mattress, in such a way that it does not bother anyone during the night.

Having done this, the woman must become very amiable and compliant with her husband, agreeing to everything he says and requests with all her will. She should seek to laugh and smile when he is sad, promising to help him if, by some fatality, his fortunes are adverse, and she should also conform herself when she is suspicious that he has a mistress, going as far as pretending that she does not know of anything.

At night, around bed time, and again when rising in the morning, she should give him either some food or drink, with plenty of cinnamon and clove, or at other times some chocolate with a great deal of vanilla, cinnamon and clove.

She should sleep completely nude, as close to her husband's body as she possibly can, so as to transmit her heat and sweat to him.

---

59. Translator's note: A small town belonging to the Coimbra district, in the center of Portugal (Beira Litural). Its exact date of foundation is unknown but the earliest known record dates from 911, well into the Umayyad occupation of Iberia. Contrary to what might be assumed, the name *Penacova* does not mean "a foot in the grave", as a current literal translation would suggest, rather, it simply comes from the Cantabrian "Deep Mount", as it sits on a mount at the bottom of a vale.

60. Translator's note: See the commentaries.

Every time he enters the house she should give him a gift and say that she thought about him. This affection may be in the form of some fruit or sweets he enjoys, a flower and, if she lacks these things, a hug accompanied by a kiss.

If he has a bad temper, and is crude and harsh, she should never contradict him; rather, she should calm him with cuddles. If he is docile, but inconstant, she should always present herself superior to him in every action of life and in all feelings.

This recipe, being all these formalities we exposed here observed with attention, is of an incontestable effect.

Let our lady readers try it, and they will see their time put to good use.

II

Recipe to force single and even married women to disclose all that they have done and plan on doing

Take the head of a pigeon and the head of a frog, and, after these are well dried and reduced to powder, place this in a small bag, which should be perfumed with a bit of musk.

Place the bag under the head pillow of the woman in question while she is asleep and after a quarter of an hour you will know all you wish to know.

As soon as the person stops talking, or a few minutes after, remove the bag from under the pillow, so as not to expose her to a cerebral fever, which can prove to be fatal.

III

Recipe to become fortunate in all manners of business

Take a live frog, cut off its head and feet on a Friday, right after the full moon of the month of September; keep these pieces in elderberry oil for 21 days, removing them after this period of time during the twelve strokes of midnight; afterwards expose them to the moon's rays, for the period of three nights. Afterwards calcinate these in a clay pot which has never been used, mixing in, afterwards, an equal amount of graveyard dirt, noting that this dirt must be from the grave of someone belonging to the family of the person this recipe is destined for.

The person who possesses this preparation can be certain that the spirit of the dead will look after him and all endeavors he may embark on, this because of the toad, which will never lose sight of your interests.

IV

Recipe to make yourself be loved by women

Before anything else, one should study, although not too much, the character and temper of the woman one wishes to pursue, and regulate and direct one's conduct and manners according to the knowledge obtained about this woman.

It should go without saying that, according to your own resources, you should get a good suit; I won't say elegant or rich, but exceedingly clean. An untidy man will never be able to captivate a woman. The cleanliness of the suit is indispensable, and even more important is the cleanliness of one's body, which will demand special care.

As soon as these first conditions are observed, after six months, take the heart of a virgin pigeon and make a snake swallow it. The snake, after some time, will die; take its head and dry it over some ashes or over a very hot iron surface, heated on a soft fire. After this reduce it to dust, crushing it with a mortar and pestle and afterwards add a few drops of laudanum; and when you wish to use this recipe, rub your hands with a portion of this preparation, as we have taught our readers in the first part of this work.

V

Recipe to make yourself be loved by men

The recipe advised for men to make themselves be loved by women, which precedes this one, is, from every point of view, the first a woman should employ if she wishes to make herself be loved by a man; however, the efficiency of this recipe depends on certain practices that should not be overlooked or forgotten.

Let us pin them down:

The woman should obtain from the man she has chosen a coin, medal, pin or any other object or fragment, as long as it is made of silver and that he has carried with him for at least 24 hours. She should approach the man having this silver in her right hand, offering him with the other a chalice of wine where she should have crushed and mixed a tiny ball the size of a corn grain made up of the following composition:

Laudanum. . . . . . two drops
Eel head . . . . one
Hemp seeds. . . . . a thimble

As soon as the individual drinks the chalice of this wine he will be forced to love the woman who gave it or had it given to him; being completely impossible for him to forget her as long as the enchantment lasts, whose effects can be renewed without the slightest inconvenience.

If, by any chance, the man is strong enough to resist the action of this medicine, or the medicine does not have its proper effect, the woman then should, if he is close to her and both are alone, give him a cup of chocolate to drink, into which she should have dropped, while beating the eggs[61]:

Powdered cinnamon . . . . . . two pinches
Cloves. . . . . five
Vanilla . . . . ten grams
Scraped Nutmeg. . . . . one pinch

After it is ready, remove the cloves and drop in:

Cantharidin[62] tincture. . . . . . two drops

If the individual wants or asks for something to eat, she should give him preferably *pão-de-ló*[63].

Sometimes, if the woman isn't in a hurry to bind this man, chocolate with the cloves, vanilla and cinnamon should be enough.

The chocolate can be substituted for coffee; however, in this case, it should be prepared with sweet fennel and one should add one single drop of cantharidin tincture.

We will not hide that the individual will immediately become suspicious that he is being enchanted.

If the woman is fearful that this man will escape her, and wishes to keep him in love for a very long time, she should repeat the first medicine every two weeks and, during this interval, invite him for lunch or supper, giving him:

At lunch, frittata or an omelet prepared in the following manner: beat the eggs extremely well; then let them flow from the top of her spine, along the whole extension of her naked back collecting them in the other extremity of the spine. Then cook the frittata and place it on the table still hot. At supper, while preparing meatball meat, drop in the beaten eggs, and after this, before taking them to the oven, pass them one by one through your sweaty body: through the breasts, back and belly, keeping them for a few moments under the arm pits.

---

61. Translator's note: I believe this is an indication to make an extremely creamy kind of hot chocolate, which requires beaten egg whites in the recipe.

62. Translator's note: Spanish fly, occasionally used as an aphrodisiac that can produce priapism. Do not underestimate, this substance is toxic.

63. Translator's note: Portuguese sponge cake. There are many local variations on the recipe, but they all go around (as the sponge cake that it is) eggs, sugar and wheat flour.

The coffee that is given to him at lunch and supper should be strained through the bottom of the woman's nightgown, which should have been worn for at least two nights.

We further add that this recipe has worked for the happiness of many women.

VI

Secular orison to banish the Devil from a body

The importance of this orison, in some cabalistic combinations, is known by all of those who devote themselves to the study of the sciences defined as occult.

"Immortal, eternal, ineffable and holy: Father of all things, who in a rolling chariot travels without ceasing through those worlds which spin perpetually in the vastness of space: dominator of the vast and immense fields of ether, where Thou raised Thy powerful throne, which dispenses light and light, and from which Thy tremendous eyes see everything, and Thy great ears hear all! Protect the sons Thou so much loved since the beginning of the centuries, for long and eternal is Thy duration. Thy majesty shines over the world and the starry heaven! Thou rises above them, oh scintillating fire, and Thou illuminates and conserves Thyself by Thine own splendor, emerging from Thy essence inexhaustible streams of light, which feed Thy infinite spirit! This infinite spirit produces all things, and constitutes that undying treasure of matter, which will never lack to the generation that is always circled by the thousand forms of which it is surrounded, and by which Thou hast covered and filled since the beginnings. From this spirit so do also those saintly kings extract their origin, which are found near and round Thy throne and make up Thy court, oh Universal Father! Oh unique Father of the blessed mortals and immortals! Thou hast in particular the powers which are marvelously equal to Thy eternal thought and Thy adorable essence. Thou established them superior to the Angels, which announce Thy will to the worlds. Finally, Thou created a third order of sovereigns in the elements.

Our practice of every day is to praise Thee and worship Thy will. We burn in desire of possessing Thee. Oh Father! Oh Mother! Tender Mother, the tenderest Mother, the most tender of all mothers! Oh Son, the most loving of all sons! Oh form of forms! Soul, spirit, harmony, names and numbers of all things keep us, and be propitious. Amen."

VII

Orison that protects from lightning

Wrap a white ribbon around the arm, neck or waist of St. Barbara, as soon as a thunderstorm begins, and light a quarter candle[64].

Do this every hour, after washing your mouth three times with three mouthfuls of water, and say the following:

"I beg thee, Lady, to intercede on my behalf with He who, conformed, died for us. Like that ribbon that thou hast by thy neck, so too do I have my soul pure and pure my intentions. Free me, Lady, I who am worthy of thy protection, against the terrors of lightning. Amen."

VIII

Magic of the grapes and its properties

It is most interesting this magic, so says St. Cyprian, on page 14 of his book.

Satan is the most cunning of all demons, that is, prince Beelzebuth, the wisest of all his companions.

This magic, which was discovered by the Devil, is very simple to do and should be performed in the following fashion:

Take a bottle with a wide bottom. After this bottle has been prepared, fill it with a deciliter and a half of virgin olive oil and place the bottle in a vineyard on which the new grape bunches are still newly formed, placing one of the bunches inside the bottle, tying it the best you can to the vine, in such a way as the bunch will grow inside the bottle.

It is necessary that the grapes do not touch the olive oil.

As soon as the bunch is ripe cut it from the vine and with this the operation is ready.

Explanation of the virtues and properties of the olive oil and the bunch inside the bottle

1st By lighting a lamp with the said oil there will appear all the trees and plants surrounding the vineyard from where those grapes came from and it is also possible to see some of the people who, by chance, were at that place when you cut the bunch from the vine; finally, every object from that place will appear: fruit baskets, birds, trees and everything which was close to the grape bunch.

---

64. Translator's note: Either a candle that only lasts a quarter of an hour or a candle that has a quarter of an *arratel* (an old Portuguese unit of measure, approximate 460 grams) of wax, it is difficult to say which.

A warning to this process: When all these bunches of grapes and this fruit appears to you, do not cut them for food, otherwise you risk being slapped by the Devil. As soon as the light is put out, everything will disappear.

2ⁿᵈ The oil has the virtue of healing any new or old wound, just by letting one drop fall on it with linen threads.

3ʳᵈ This oil has the power and virtue of releasing the souls from Purgatory and making them come to speak with a person who might call for them in front of a church gate, at the stroke of midnight. By lighting a lamp and saying: "I, by the power of this light, order that the souls in Purgatory come now to speak with me, those whose bodies are buried in this house," the souls will appear immediately, but it is necessary to have a great deal of will and courage, for this may result in the death of the person calling them.

4ᵗʰ The oil has the virtue and power of casting sorcery on a person, just like St. Cyprian did in the city of Carthage to a girl named Adelaide.

IX

Story of Cyprian and Adelaide

Cyprian the sorcerer desired to possess the love of a girl named Adelaide and requested her of her parents; they, however, denied him.

In desperation over their response, he became so enraged that he ordered his tiny devil, who he always carried in his pocket, to destroy, without further delay, all of Adelaide's parents' possessions.

His order was immediately executed.

As soon as Adelaide saw all her possessions destroyed she went to see Cyprian and said to him:

"What evil did my father do to thee that made thou enact such ungratefulness towards him?"

Cyprian responded, "Dost thou not see Adelaide, that I love thee so much that I cannot see anything else but the place where thou resides?"

Adelaide responded to Cyprian, "If it is true what thou tells me, let us pretend that from this day on I am thy slave, but not thy wife, for I am not worthy of marrying thee."

"For which reason," said Cyprian, "for which reason dost thou say that thou art not worthy of being my wife?"

"For thou art a saint," responded Adelaide, "canonized by God. How can I be thy wife, if I am the greatest sinner in the world, as no other, I believe, exists?"

Cyprian turned to Adelaide and said to her:

"My girl, if thou loves thy God so, and still thou says that thou art the greatest sinner in the world, what vengeful God dost thou worship?"

Adelaide, upon hearing these words, was much astonished and doubting her ears said to herself, "What God dost this man worship? Is there, by any chance any other God than mine?! This is not possible!" She mustered her courage and said to Cyprian:

"Man, I force and banish thee by God, whom I worship, to tell me what strange god is this thou worships and forces thee to deny mine."

Cyprian responded:

"The God I worship is Lucifer of Hell!"

Adelaide, hearing this, crossed herself three times and said to him:

"I force and banish thee by God, whom I worship, to restitute my belongings, just as they were."

Cyprian, forced by the power of the Omnipotent God, restored all of Adelaide's parents' possessions, and afterwards retired without having enjoyed himself with her.

Lucifer, appearing to him said the following:

"My friend Cyprian, do not bother me so much, I have already taught thee all sorcery and all magical art. Thou already has all the power I have, but still, being thy friend as I always was, am and shall be, I will give thee some advice to help thee enjoy Adelaide..."

Cyprian said to Lucifer: "Thou, my friend, whom I love with all my heart, body and soul, tell me what I should do in this situation."

"Take thy magical bottle," said Lucifer, "put thy fava in thy mouth and make thyself invisible: in this same instant, go to Adelaide's house, and, as soon as thou arrives, drop some of the oil in one of the lights there, that both Adelaide and her parents will be so frightened by the prodigies they'll observe, that thou, Cyprian, may seize that opportunity to take Adelaide."

Cyprian went, and unfortunately executed Lucifer's orders, the spirit of wickedness.

After five minutes, Cyprian had already enjoyed Adelaide and his infamous desires were satisfied.

After reading, my lady, what happened to the girl Adelaide, pray to the Lord and the Holiest Mary to free you from Satan's cunnings, for the Devil has many traps prepared for the Christians, from which they cannot escape.

And furthermore, dear readers, why are you not constantly ordering yourselves to Jesus and the Holiest Mary?

X

Story of Cyprian and Elvira

The magic of the critters is the magic that the Devil and Cyprian used to convince the only daughter of a marquis, called the marquis of Soria, the most esteemed of the king of Persia. This girl was named Elvira.

Cyprian, seeing her one day with her parents, thought that there couldn't possibly be any other girl like her.

He immediately placed into practice his diabolical arts, demonstrating to the marquis that he desired his daughter Elvira.

The marquis, facing Cyprian directly, for he saw that he was but a regular man, said to him,

"Thou desire my daughter?"

"I," responded Cyprian, "intend to love Elvira and make her mine..."

The marquis, hearing these words, was enraged against Cyprian, but it was all useless, for Cyprian was quick in saying the following words:

"I order that, immediately, by diabolical and magical arts, A. M. N. O. P.[65], that the marquis and marquise be turned into marble stones!"

His order was immediately satisfied.

Cyprian turned to Elvira and said:

"Dost thou see, girl, what I have done to thy parents? The same will happen to thee, if thou dost not follow my will."

Elvira, scared with what she had just heard, said to Cyprian:

"What dost thou want from me?"

Cyprian responded:

"I want thee to follow me and stop worshiping that false God, and instead love only my laws and commandments."

Elvira, hearing these words, fell to the ground and prayed the following orison to Jesus Christ: "Lord, if it is Thy will that I follow this man, tell me this from the Highest, for I am ready to follow whatever Thou determines."

Cyprian, hearing Elvira's supplications, became enraged against her and enchanted her with the same words he had used on her parents.

Cyprian was satisfied with his vengeance, but he, however, should not have done so, for his life came into great danger.

The king, as he was a great friend of the marquis, immediately noticed his absence and was greatly surprised by this, and he said to himself, "What has become of the marquis, his daughter Elvira and all of his family?"

No matter how much he searched his kingdom all his efforts seemed useless.

After one month a badly dressed woman appeared at the palace and said she wanted to speak with His Majesty.

The king was informed that there was a poor woman there who desired to speak with him. The king responded to his servant:

"Tell this woman to enter."

The woman entered but did not bow, as was the custom.

The king seeing that the woman was thus proud, told her:

"Dost thou not think, woman, that thou hast already deserved to be beheaded on this very spot for not showing the proper respect to a king?"

---

65. Translator's note: These probably refer to prayers or Latin expressions. The first A. M. most likely refers to Ave Maria, but the remaining N. O. P. are a mystery to me.

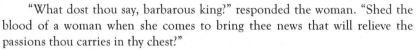

"What dost thou say, barbarous king?" responded the woman. "Shed the blood of a woman when she comes to bring thee news that will relieve the passions thou carries in thy chest?"

The king then thought that the woman was bringing news of the marquis and his family, and said to her in a supplicating voice:

"Woman, forgive me, for thou can very well see that it is my passion for the marquis that makes me thus angry!"

"This very day," responded the woman, "thou will see the marquis and his whole family, but under the condition that thou orders the man called Cyprian killed."

"Cyprian the sorcerer?" asked the king.

"The same," responded the poor woman, "and I shall give thee advice on how to do so."

"Yes woman, tell me how thou thinks I may be able to do this."

"Summon him here and tell him to present the marquis and his family to thee; if he dost not do so, he should pay with his very life."

The king, believing in the advice of this woman, did as she said.

Immediately he called Cyprian to his presence.

As soon as he arrived in the presence of the king he said:

"What dost thou wish, royal lord?"

"I wish," said the king "that thou presents here the marquis and his family, under penalty of beheading."

"With whom dost thou think thou art speaking?" said Cyprian.

"I speak with a sorcerer," responded the king, "one who holds a pact with Lucifer, the prince of Hell."

As soon as the king said this, Cyprian evoked the evil spirits and ordered that the whole palace, as well as the king and his family, be enchanted.

The king fell to his knees at Cyprian's feet, saying,

"Forgive me, forgive me, great and powerful Cyprian! Disenchant me and my family, for I am not to be blamed for this."

"Then who is the guilty one?" asked Cyprian, angry.

"The guilty one," answered the king, "is a woman who is hiding in my palace."

"This woman," said Cyprian "Let her come to my presence without delay."

The king ordered the woman to come immediately.

"Thou, with what pleasure did thou, woman, desire that the king shed the blood of a prudent man without any crimes?"

"Without any crimes?!... Who is the man with more crimes than thee," responded the woman, "who enchanted a family so esteemed by the king, my lord? And thou still says thou has no crimes! Ah! Infamous! Thou art worthy of a thousand deaths, if such wert possible. For here before thee is someone with power over all thy powers and all thy cunnings."

Cyprian, hearing what she had just proclaimed, trembled and said:

"What power dost thou have against my cunnings?"

"I have power over all, for I am a sorceress of greater age. I was one of the first to take up a pact with Lucifer, and for that I have power over all sorcerers."

"As thou belongs to my law," said Cyprian, "I do not want to make thee feel the strength of my sorcery. What dost thou want from me woman?"

"I want thee to restitute the marquis and all his family to the king, and bring them here to the king's presence."

Cyprian thought for a moment and turned to her suddenly,

"Yes, I shall do all of that under the condition that Elvira shall be mine and I shall cherish her as is proper."

The woman responded:

"Well then, present them here that Elvira shall be thine."

Cyprian's simplicity made him believe in the woman's advice. He immediately went, with much joy, to disenchant the marquis, the marquise and their daughter.

CONVERSATION THE WOMAN HAD WITH THE KING WHILE CYPRIAN WAS GONE

"My royal lord," said the woman, "we shall kill Cyprian this very day."

"Dost thou not see," said the king, "that Cyprian has great power over the magical arts and can enchant all of us with a single word?"

"No, my royal lord; for I also have great power to stop all of his enchantments and diabolical arts."

Having said this, the woman fumigated the entire palace; but this, however, was to be a sham, for Cyprian had a greater diabolical power. But it did do something against him.

CYPRIAN'S ARRIVAL

Shortly after, Cyprian, the marquis, his wife and Elvira returned, for they had all been disenchanted.

The king was filled with the utmost satisfaction and said to Cyprian:

"Be gone from here, heartless man, for thou hast over thy head the weight of the most hideous crimes, this by thy perverse wickedness and infamy."

Cyprian, enraged by what he had just heard, said arrogantly to the king:

"So this is my payment for disenchanting those thou so much esteemed? I can tell that thou dost not know me well. Just thou wait, for I will deal with thee."

Cyprian reached into his pocket and, taking out his devil, said to him, "I want ten castles at my command, now."

His orders were immediately followed and he set fire to the palace, but it was all in vain, as a consequence of the sorcery the woman had performed, when she fumigated the palace.

Cyprian immediately recognized that the sorceress had blocked his intent, and, seeing as there was nothing he could do, was angered against the falsehood the king used against him.

THE MEETING OF CYPRIAN AND LUCIFER

Cyprian was sadly thinking about the king's betrayal, and even saying to himself that maybe he should leave this world, when Lucifer appeared, who, putting his hand on his shoulder said:

"Do not be sad Cyprian, my friend, for Elvira shall be thine."

"That cannot be," responded Cyprian.

"I thought thou had more trust in me, my Cyprian. Be confident, for everything has a remedy."

Cyprian was calmed by Lucifer's conciliating words, who then took Cyprian to a desert and said to him:

"Thou surely saw, dear friend, that the palace was fumigated with rosemary and incense, and that was the reason why our diabolical arts could not enter there, but that however, will not be sufficient for Elvira to elude thee today."

"What must I do to possess her?" said Cyprian filled with satisfaction.

"Gather with thy hands," said Lucifer, "all the critters of the world, especially toads, spiders, rats, snakes, lizards, ants, flies, in sum, all those thou so wishes and manages to find; put them in a great caldron, put a *quartilho*[66] and a half of virgin olive oil and boil it in such a way that the critters melt and turn to oil, this with the only condition that they must be thrown into the caldron still alive. After this bring me the oil in a tightly closed flask, and do not smell it."

Cyprian did all Lucifer told him to, and, as soon as he saw it was ready, he went to give him the news.

Lucifer then told him:

"Dost thou know what to do with that oil now?"

"I shall listen to thy advice," responded Cyprian curiously.

"Prepare a lamp with this oil and, after all is ready, place thy fava in thy mouth, and tell it thou wishes to enter the palace without being seen by anyone."

Cyprian before doing what Lucifer told him to, asked him:

"What should I do when I get there?"

"As soon as thou enters the palace, light the magical lamp and everyone inside will be terrified; thou Cyprian, put one fava inside the mouth of the sorceress and one inside Elvira's mouth and say, 'Favas, accompany me.' As soon as thou art at a high altitude, let the sorceress fall, for it was her who put thee in this mess."

---

66. Translator's note: An old measurement for liquids, roughly equivalent to half a liter.

Cyprian did as Lucifer indicated. After having dropped the sorceress from a great height, he took Elvira to the desert and told her:

"Lady Elvira, what dost thou wish me to do to thee?"

Elvira responded, "Do that which is thy will."

It is pointless to say what Cyprian did, for the reader will forcibly imagine it. Cyprian was only successful in convincing and taking Elvira thanks to the oil of the critters.

He then prepared for her a rich palace fit for such a beautiful dove as Elvira to live.

As you can see, readers, the Devil, after he starts working on a creature, will not leave her until he has first achieved his desire; that is why we always recommend to all Christians that they never forget to make the sign of the Holy Cross ✠ every day, three or four times a day.

It would be also good to declare to you, readers, how easy it is to make the magic of the critters, so as you might learn it and further teach it, for it is not necessary to make a pact with Lucifer to learn every magic we teach here.

These were discovered by the Devil, and Cyprian published them throughout the world, and, as such, in order to obtain these now, we do not need any permission or advice from Lucifer or Satan.

METHOD OF PREPARING THE MAGICAL OIL

Gather all the lowly creatures you can find (the slimiest and most toxic have the greatest magic); having them safely restrained, place them still alive inside a casserole, with a *quartilho* and a half of virgin olive oil; boil all of this over a hot fire until it is at half of the original volume; store this oil and when you light a lamp with it all people present will become so frightened that they will not be able to move from where they stand.

The reason for this fright is because in that place many great ghosts, earthquakes and all the creatures that were boiled alive will appear, shrieking terribly, wanting to bite and sting the people present; do not be afraid yourself, for all of that is merely projected by the burning flame.

XI

Sorcery which is made with a toad so to make someone love against their will

It is very simple to make this sorcery, and it has power over all sorcery, for this is said by St. Cyprian in his book, page 84.

In his life's book, while he was a sorcerer, he says that the reason why the toad has such a great power for sorcery and magic is because the Devil has something to do with it, for this is the food with which Lucifer feeds the souls in Hell.

You can, thus, make any sorcery you wish with a toad, like the ones we teach you here.

XII

Sorcery of the toad with his eyes sewn

Take a large toad, and let it be male if this sorcery is meant for a man.

After having it restrained, take it with your right hand and pass it under your belly five times while saying the following words:

"Toad, little toad, just as I pass thee under my belly so may (NN) not have any peace or rest, while he dost not turn to me with all his heart, body, soul and life."

After saying the words above, take a very thin needle and green twine and sew the eyes of the toad in such a way as not to wound even in the slightest the eyes of the animal, otherwise the person to which this sorcery is directed will become blind. You should only sew the outer skin of the eyes, in such a way as the eyes of the toad will be covered but not offended.

XIII

Words to be said to the toad after sewing its eyes

"Toad, I by the power of Lucifer, prince Beelzebuth, sewed thy eyes, which is what I should have done to (NN), so as he (or she) dost not have peace or rest in any part of the world without my company, and let him be blind to all other women (or men). Let him only see me and have only me in his thought."

Put the toad in a large pan and say:

"(NN), here thou art bound and tied without seeing the Sun or Moon, while thou dost not love me. From here thou will not be released; here thou art bound and tied as is this toad."

WARNING TO ALL THOSE PERFORMING THIS MAGIC

The pan or vase where the toad is kept should have some water and every day one should put in some more fresh water in it.

XIV

Sorcery of the toad with his mouth sewn with black twine, when one wishes for the sorcery to work evil and not good

Here is the recipe to perform this sorcery:

Take a toad, sew its mouth with black twine, and, after its mouth is shut, say the following words:

"Toad, I, by the power of Lucifer, Satan, Barabbas, Caiaphas and the limp Devil, and mainly in the name of prince Beelzebuth and Robert the Devil[67], by all of these I plead to thee, (NN), that thou no longer have a single hour of health, and thy life I imprison inside the mouth of this toad, as it weakens and loses its health, so will the same happen to thee by the power of Lucifer."

In this way is this sorcery performed. Then place the toad inside a pan with nothing to eat.

A GREATLY IMPORTANT WARNING

Let us suppose that you have prepared this sorcery and for some reason regretted applying it; it may be undone very easily. Take the toad out of the pan and feed it some cow's milk for five days with his mouth unstitched. Only in this way will the sorcery be undone.

XV

Toad sorcery to make one love whom they do not desire against their will, or to perform marriages

Let us suppose a girl wishes to marry her boyfriend as soon as possible, but the said boyfriend isn't really in a hurry to marry, either because he doesn't want to commit or because he doesn't want her as a wife. Very easily does the girl force this marriage with the greatest haste.

Proceed in the following way:

Take an object belonging to the boyfriend or girlfriend and tie it around the belly of a toad; after this is done, tie the feet of the toad with a red ribbon and place it inside a pan with some dirt mixed with cow's milk. After all these operations are done say the following words over the pan:

First one should name the creature being enchanted.

---

67. Translator's note: This refers to a Medieval legend of Robert the Devil. This tells the story of Robert, the Devil's son, who his mother had despaired from asking heaven for help conceiving a child and ended up requesting this to Hell. It essentially narrates a story of sin and repentance, with Robert going from a cruel criminal to a pious hermit.

"(NN), just as I have this toad imprisoned inside this pan without seeing the Sun or the Moon, so may thou not see any other woman, be her married, single or widowed. Thy thoughts will only be towards me; and just as this toad has its legs tied, so will thou not be able to take a single step that is not in the direction of my door, and just as this toad lives inside this pan consumed and mortified, thou shall equally live while thou dost not marry me."

As soon as the above words are said, cover the pan extremely well, so as the toad inside cannot see the light of day; then, when the sorcery comes through, release the toad into the woods, in such a way as not to harm him, otherwise the person who was the target of the sorcery will be equally harmed.

XVI

Recipe to win at gambling

Have a jet *figa*[68] made, we essentially recommend that it be done with a new fine steel knife.

Take this *figa* to the sea, suspended on a ribbon of St. Lucia, and pass it three, seven or twenty one times through the foam of the waves of the sea.

While you are doing this, pray the Creed three times, extremely softly, in a nearly imperceptible tone, and you should also offer a quarter candle to St. Lucia.

The gambler should carry this *figa* around his neck when he is gambling; having, however, the care of not being blinded by ambition, much less being dragged by greed, so as he may take a satisfactory result.

XVII

Talisman to make one return to his home quickly, rich and happy

This is mostly the same jet *figa* from the previous recipe, but with the difference that the individual should conserve himself chaste for as long as possible, or, as a last resort, only be joined with his wife after six months, or, alternatively, every three months, should his health not permit him to carry this sacrifice for long.

Every three nights, before going to bed, on his knees, he should send God three Our Fathers and two Hail Marys.

---

68. Translator's note: An extremely ancient amulet, also commonly called *mano fico*, or an infinity of other names depending on the country.

XVIII

Recipe to convert a good sorcery into an evil one

Take a black toad, whose mouth one should sew with a black silk twine.

After this, tie the fingers of the toad, one by one, with a thick thread, also black, and, making a kind of parachute figure with it, suspend it in a smokehouse, so as its belly is facing up.

At midnight sharp, call for the Devil at each of the twelve bell strokes, and after imprinting a spinning movement on the toad say the following words:

"Filthy creature, by the power of the Devil, to whom I have sold my body but not my spirit, do I ask thee to not allow (NN) to enjoy a single more hour of happiness on earth; his health I imprison inside this toad's mouth; and as he withers and dies, let the same happen to (NN), whom I banish three times in the name of the Devil, Devil, Devil."

In the morning place the toad in a clay pan and seal it hermetically.

To undo the effects of this sorcery, should you feel sorry for the victim, take the toad from the pan and feed it some fresh milk for seven days, but with his mouth already unstitched.

XIX

Recipe to make a man not enjoy any other woman besides his wife, or vice-versa

Take a toad and sew its eyes with black silk twine, but in such a way as not to injure them. One should proceed as the previous recipe but the words to be spoken should be the following:

"Filthy creature, in the name of the Devil, to whom I have sold my body but not my spirit, I have sewn thine eyes, and that is what I should have done to (NN) so as he (or she) may not enjoy any other person besides me; and let him be blind to all women (or men)."

After this suspend the toad in a smokehouse for twelve hours, placing the toad still alive in the pan, which should be very well closed.

The words to be said while this is done are the following:

"(NN), thou art bound and tied, and no more shalt thou see the light of the Sun or the dull brightness of the Moon until thou loves me. Stay, Devil, Devil, Devil!"

Both in this as in the previous recipe, one should refresh the toad every day with water.

XX

Recipe to speed up marriages

Take a black toad and tie around its belly some object of the boy or girl in question with two ribbons, one scarlet and one black, then put the toad in a clay pot and say these words with your mouth against the lid:

"(NN), should thou love any other besides me or direct thy thoughts to anyone else, to the Devil, to whom I have consecrated my fate, I ask to imprison thee in the world of afflictions, just as I have now locked this toad, and may thou never come out of there unless to unite thyself with me, for I love thee with all my heart."

After these words are said, close the pan very well, refreshing the toad every day with some water; and on the day arranged for the wedding, release the toad near a pond with the greatest care, for if he is mistreated, the marriage, no matter how pleasant it might be, will become intolerable; it will be a disgraced union both for the husband as for the wife.

XXI

The story of the marvelous ring

History tells us that Candaules, the king of Lydia, one day showed Gyges, his favored official, his wife, the queen, completely nude. The enchanting queen saw Gyges and, out of love or vengeance, gave that official the order to kill her husband, promising him, as a reward, her hand and the crown. Gyges became, as a consequence of this crime, the king of Lydia, in the year of 718 before Christ.

Plato tells this story slightly differently. He says that the earth parted, and Gyges, the king's shepherd, climbed down to the bottom of an abyss, and there he found a great horse. Mounting this animal was a man of herculean form, who had on his index finger a magical ring, gifted with the great virtue of making an individual invisible. Gyges took the ring and used it to kill King Candaules, without any risk, replacing him on the throne.

We will give here a simple sketch of this precious talisman. It had two engravings: one, shaped like the sun, with a topaz; the other shaped like the moon and with an emerald. The whole ring was made of silver, with many cabalistic signs written upon it.

To this day great sorcerers are trying to discover the magical words to be pronounced so an individual can become invisible with the aid of this ring.

If these words come to us, as we hope, we will not be long to transmit them to our readers, as soon as this book goes into print again.

In Portugal there was a fanatic of about ninety years of age who was still working tirelessly to discover the words necessary to make this enchantment accessible. Unfortunately, he died without achieving success.

XXII

Method of divination by means of magic or magnetism

When a person is asleep and is dreaming, quickly place your hand over their heart and ask all you wish to know.

If it is a woman, and it is her husband with his hand on her heart, he may ask her if she is faithful; or, one may ask anything that might come to mind.

PRECIOUS WARNING

The person performing this operation you have just read should be very careful and pay attention if the person dreaming is having any convulsions, that is, if she is in any kind of distress; should this happen, he should remove the hand immediately, wake her up and give her some fresh water to drink.

You may cause this person to die if you do not do as such.

The reason for this danger is because the Devil, during this operation, is standing nearby so as to see if he may snatch the soul of the sleeping person, for this is a risky situation.

XXIII

Magic of the holly[69] and its virtues, or strength of the enchantment, cut on the night of St. John the Baptist, the 24th of June

At midnight sharp, cut the holly with a steel knife, and, after you have cut it, bless it in the name of the Father, the Son and the Holy Spirit; after all this, take it to the beach and pass it through seven waves; and, while you are doing this operation, you should say the Creed seven times, always making the sign of the cross with your right hand over the waves and the holly.

VIRTUES AND PROPERTIES OF THE HOLLY

1st Whoever brings this holly with him will be fortunate in all business endeavors and in everything dealing with the happiness of men.

2nd Whoever brings this holly with them and touches another person with it having living faith that the person touched will follow him, will make that person follow him anywhere he pleases.

---

69. Translator's note: *Ilex aquifolium.*

We have tried this secret a few times and were always victorious; of these acts, however, we are very much regretful, by fault of certain circumstances that shall not be mentioned here.

3rd This holly has the virtue to perform anything its owner wishes. Anyone who owns the holly and hangs it in his store, that is, if he is an established person, should say every morning when arriving at the store, the following: "God save thee, holly, created by God," and in this way the store will become very fortunate. This system has made many fortunes in Portugal, Brazil, Africa and Europe.

XXIV

Magic of the enchanted vial

METHOD OF PREPARING THE FLASK

Prepare a small vial, so as to be more convenient to those carrying it in their pocket, and put inside it the following ingredients:

1st Spirits of hartshorn.
2nd Altar stone[70].
3rd Rosemary[71].
4th Fennel.
5th Marble stone.
6th Fern seeds.
7th Mallow seeds.
8th Mustard seeds.
9th Blood from your pinky finger.
10th Blood from the thumb and big toe of the left foot.
11th The root of a hair from your head.
12th Nail scrapings from your hands and feet.
13th Scrapings from the bone of a dead man; if these are from the skull, so much the better.

After all of these things are prepared, place them inside the vial, in such a way that this vial is only half full. We further declare that all the ingredients mentioned should be in the smallest quantity possible, so as to give the greatest effect.

After the vial is ready say the following words:

---

70. Translator's note: given the explanations to follow in the text, they probably mean shavings or small particles of an altar stone, also, see the commentaries.
71. Translator's note: *Rosmarinus officinalis.*

"Thou, sacred vial, who by my own hand wert prepared, my blood in thee is locked and tied to the root of my hair and inside thee was shed. Every person thou touches shall be enchanted by me. A. N. R. V.[72] *Ignoratus tuum vos assignaturum meo.*"

After all of this is done exactly as we have said, maintain this vial very well kept and you may enchant whoever you wish. By offering it to smell to any creature, she will immediately follow you to any place you choose.

We further declare that the vial not only possesses the power of enchanting, but also the power to perform evil.

It all depends on the thought of the person using it; if it is for good, good will happen, and if it is for evil, evil will happen.

XXV

Magic of the needle passed three times through a dead man

This magic is very simply (so says St. Cyprian in chapter XXI of his book). He assures us that it was discovered by a demon or pythonic spirit of the XIIth century.

Put a thread of Galician linen[73] on a needle, and pass it three times between the skin of a dead man[74], while saying the following words:

"(NN) (the name of the dead man), this needle in thy body I will pass, so as it may have the power to enchant."

After this operation is done, keep the needle and you may work the following sorceries with it:

1st When you walk by a girl and want her to follow you, all you need to do is make a stitch in her dress or in any other part, and leave a piece of string hanging from it; she will follow you anywhere you go.

When you want the girl to stop following you, you should remove the piece of string you left behind.

This magic requires great secrecy, so as not to happen to you what happened to me, for I had a hard time on account of having made this magic and declaring the way I did it; for that reason, you should never reveal this secret to anyone.

2nd When you wish for your beloved to never stop loving you and never love anyone else, do the following: Take an object of the boy or girl in question and make three cross-stitches, while saying the following words:

---

72. Translator's note: Once again this probably is a set of Latin prayers or words I have not been able to crack.

73. Translator's note: High quality linen of the *Linum crepitans.*

74. Translator's note: I believe what is intended here is for the needle not to actually pierce the flesh, just go in and out of the first layers of skin.

First stitch: (NN) (the name of the dead man used in this magic), only when thou speaks, will (NN) leave me.

Second stitch: (NN), only when God stops being God, will (NN) leave me.

Third stitch: (NN), while these stitches are here and thy body is in its grave, (NN) will not have peace or rest while he is not in my company.

In this way you may bewitch or enchant any person you so like.

We assure you that this sorcery not only has the power for good but also for evil. It is all defined by a person's words; instead of saying: "Only when this dead man speaks will thee, (NN), leave me," say: "Only when this dead man speaks will thee, (NN), live and have health;" likewise with all the others.

XXVI

The magical herb and its properties

St. Cyprian says the following in page 82, Chapter XII, of his book: "The magical herb has so much power and virtue that one must not even mention it; not even the Devil wanted to discover it."

But, this however was not enough for St. Cyprian not to learn it, for it was revealed to him by a shepherd called Barnaby.

Cyprian was walking in the mountains one day when he saw a shepherd playing with a beetle, which is commonly called the *vaca-loura*[75].

Cyprian, out of curiosity, observed what the shepherd was doing to the said *vaca-loura* and he saw that the boy constantly killed it and brought it back to life.

Cyprian thought to himself with great admiration: "What is this, or what might be this virtue that this boy has to resuscitate a bug after crushing it with his foot?"

Cyprian approached the shepherd and asked him:

"What art thou doing, good shepherd?"

"Tending to my flock," responded the shepherd. "And who might thou be?" asked the shepherd to Cyprian.

"I am Cyprian," responded him, in a triumphant way.

"Well, well!" said the shepherd, "Art thou by any chance the bishop of Carthage, or art thou Cyprian the sorcerer?"

Cyprian upon hearing these words asked the shepherd:

"What wouldst thou do if I wert Cyprian the sorcerer?"

"Oh, poor sorcerer," responded the shepherd, "what things would happen to thee this day on this mountain!"

Cyprian trembled and said to the shepherd:

"Be calm, be calm, I am not the sorcerer, but the bishop of Carthage."

---

75. Translator's note: literally the blonde-cow, beetles of the *Lucanidae* family, stag-beetles.

The shepherd fell to his knees and said:

"Good shepherd, father of the Church, hear my sins and absolve me, for thou hast the power to do so."

Cyprian thought to himself, "Using but good manners I will learn this shepherd's secret."

The simple shepherd, kneeling on the ground, made the following confession:

"I confess myself to the bishop of Carthage, who has the power to forgive my sins."

"According to our doctrine," said afterwards the false bishop, "thy sins are forgiven good shepherd."

In this way was the confession done, as was the custom in that land.

At the end of the confession, Cyprian, still pretending to be a bishop, said to the shepherd:

"What was it that thou wert doing to that beetle, that thou resuscitated it after it was killed?"

"I healed it with an herb," responded the shepherd, "one that grows in the mountain, of which only the beetles, the wagtails and the swallows know about."

"Then how did thou discover it?" asked the fake bishop.

"I was playing around one day," responded the shepherd, "and I saw one of those beetles and killed it; after a few minutes I saw another beetle with a herb between its horns and by placing it on the dead one he immediately resuscitated; I took this herb immediately and now I have been killing many beetles; but as soon as I touch them with the herb, they resuscitate."

"What great virtue has that herb!" said the false bishop.

"This herb," said the shepherd, "has the virtue of anything one might wish in life; if thou want this herb I will go get some and give it to thee."

"And how may one obtain this herb?" asked the false bishop.

"Very easily," responded the shepherd.

HOW THE SHEPHERD ACQUIRED THE HERB

He searched for a swallow's nest with all its eggs already laid, and, as soon as he found them, he boiled them in water and placed them again in the nest, without the swallows noticing it.

The swallows, after some time, saw that their brood was not growing, and as such they went to find this herb and placed it on the eggs so as to bring them back to life.

The shepherd, always on the lookout, went back to the nest, took the herb and brought it as a present to Cyprian, the pretend bishop of Carthage.

In the *Book of St. Cyprian* there is nothing else mentioned about the virtues of this marvelous herb.

We, however, guarantee the virtues of the herb, which resuscitates the dead and brings life to eggs after they have been boiled

Do note, readers, this marvel, and we hope that your curiosity will bring you to do every possible thing to obtain this herb, for you will be the happiest man on earth if you do so.

XXVII

Magic of the enchanted black dove

Raise in your home a black dove, and do not feed it anything else besides floating seeds[76] and holy water to drink.

After it is grown and able to fly, write a letter to any one person, containing or requesting anything.

After this operation is done, place the letter in the beak of the dove and pass it thought the smoke of incense, myrrh and asafetida; afterwards, put your thoughts on the person you want to have the letter delivered to and release the dove.

We guarantee that the said dove will take the letter to its destination and return to its owner's home; and that the person who receives this letter will forcibly do what is written on it.

Do note that you should only send the dove from ten in the morning and until two in the afternoon[77].

XXVIII

The most fateful days of the year, in which one cannot perform any sorceries meant for good, only for evil

January – 1, 2, 3, 4, 5, 6, 7, 8, 9, 10, 11, 13, 15, 16, 23, 24, 26, 30.
February – 2, 4, 10, 13, 14, 15, 16, 17, 18, 19, 23, 28, 29.
March – 10, 13, 14, 15, 16, 17, 19, 28, 29.
April – 3, 5, 6, 10, 13, 15, 18, 20, 29, 30.
May – 2, 7, 8, 9, 10, 11, 14, 17, 19, 20.
June – 1, 4, 6, 10, 16, 20, 21, 24.
July – 2, 4, 5, 8, 10, 13, 16, 17, 19, 20, 27.
August – 2, 3, 8, 9, 13, 19, 27, 29.

---

76. Translator's note: uncertain translation; the original reads *sementes de boiamento* which might simply mean seeds that float, a typical method of determining which seeds are proper for planting and which are not.

77. Original footnote: It was from the reading of this chapter that the idea of carrier pigeons, which provided such wonderful results both in war as in peace, came to be.

September – 1, 13, 15, 16, 17, 18, 22, 24.
October – 1, 3, 6, 7, 8, 9, 10, 16, 21, 27.
November – 2, 6, 7, 11, 15, 16, 17, 18, 22, 25.
December – 1, 6, 7, 9, 15, 21, 28, 31.

It should be noted that sorceries performed on the days indicated above will not succeed.

But these may, however, be performed on any other day not mentioned here, producing then the desired effect.

XXIX

Magic of the egg, performed on the night of St. John the Baptist (24th of June)

On the night of St. John the Baptist leave a black hen's egg out under the night sky. This egg should be left broken[78] inside a glass of water; in the morning, at dawn, go look at it and you will see the fate and troubles you will have to endure.

You may also perform the magic on the nights of St. Anthony and St. Peter[79.]

XXX

Sorcery which is made with five nails taken from a dead man's coffin, that is, when it has been dug up from its grave

Go into a cemetery and bring back from there five nails from a dead man's coffin, always keeping in mind the sorcery you are about to perform.

Then, draw over a board a *signo-saimão*, where you should have a sign of the person you are directing this sorcery to; this sign should be nailed over the said *signo-saimão*.

METHOD OF NAILING THE NAILS
AND THE WORDS THAT SHOULD BE SAID
WHEN ONE IS NAILING:

---

78. Translator's note: I think what is meant here is to actually break the egg into the glass of water.

79. Translator's note: St. Anthony's night is usually the 12th of June, the night before St. Anthony's day, the 13th, likewise St. Peter's night is on the 28th of June, the night before St. Peter's day on the 29th.

1st *nail* – (NN), I plead to thee, in the name of Satan, Barabbas and Caiaphas, that thou becomes bonded to me, as Lucifer is bonded in the depths of Hell.

2nd *nail* – (NN), I bind thee and tie thee inside this *signo-saimão*; just as the Cross of Jesus Christ inside these lines was buried and the blood of Jesus on it was spilled, I, (NN), cite and notify thee not to fail me in this, by the spilled blood of Jesus Christ[80].

3rd *nail* – (NN), I, (NN), bind thee to me eternally, as Satan is bonded to Hell.

4th *nail* – (NN), I, (NN), bind and tie thee inside this *signo-saimão*, so that thou may not have any peace or rest unless thou art in my company, that is, by the power of Satan and Maria Padilha and all her family.

5th *nail* – (NN), only when God stops being God and the dead man to whom theses nails served speaks, will thou leave me[81].

We further declare that when one says the last word he should strike a great blow in the nail.

After all this is done, save the board, and when you wish to undo this sorcery burn it.

XXXI

Recipe to bind lovers

Go into a store and ask for a ribbon roll. Leave the store, and looking up into the sky, keep saying the following words:

"Three stars in the sky I see, and with one more from Jesus four, this ribbon to my leg I shall tie, so as (NN) may not eat, or dink, or rest, while he (or she) dost not marry me."

You should say this three times in a row.

---

80. Translator's note: In the original Portuguese, part of this incantation rhymes, as such I am supplying the original: *(NN), eu te prendo a amarro dentro deste signo-saimão; assim como a Cruz de Jesus Cristo dento deste risco foi enterrada e o sangue de Jesus nela foi derramado, assim eu, (NN), te cito e notifico para que não me faltes a isto, pelo sangue derramado de Jesus Cristo.*

81. Translator's note: both these last incantations have sections which rhyme. The originals:

4º prego – (NN), eu, (NN), te prendo e amarro dentro deste signo-saimão, para que tu não tenhas sossego nem descanso senão quando estiveres na minha companhia, isto é, pelo poder de Satanás e de Maria Padilha e de toda a sua família.

5º prego – (NN), só quando Deus deixar de ser Deus e o defunto a quem serviram estes pregos falar, é que tu me hás-de deixar.

XXXII

Infallible recipe to get married

This orison should be said six days in a row, being that on the last day you should ask for your beloved's hand in marriage.

"(NN), St. Manso[82] tame thee as the docile lamb, so as thou may not drink, or eat, or rest, while thou art not my rightful companion."

If you can, take in your hand a picture of the person you have in your thoughts while reciting this.

XXXIII

Method of requesting to the souls in purgatory so as to force them to do whatever one may desire

On a Tuesday, at midnight sharp, you should go to the main entrance of a church and, as soon as you get there, knock three times on the door, saying aloud the following words:

"Souls, souls, souls! I order thee, by God and the Holiest Trinity, to accompany me."

After these words have been said, walk three times around the church, but never look back, for that may result in such a terrible fright that you might lose your speech for the rest of your life.

After walking three times around the church pray one Our Father and one Hail Mary and you may leave.

Do this requirement nine times and on the last time one of the souls will ask you:

"What dost thou wish us to do?"

On this occasion you may ask anything you desire, for they will do anything.

We must once again say that you should never look back, and you should not be frightened with anything you may see, otherwise this operation may not produce its proper effect.

---

82. Translator's note: It should be good to mention that St. Manso in Portuguese means, St. Tamed, or St. Docile; also, see the commentaries.

XXXIV

The encounter of Cyprian and St. Gregory in which they had a dispute regarding the Holy Catholic Faith, in which St. Gregory was victorious

Being St. Gregory preaching in a temple, Cyprian passed by and said out loud:

"What preaching is that imposter doing?"

One of the attendees said to Cyprian:

"That is Gregory."

"Well, well!" said Cyprian, "what God dost this Jew worship? Rather than listening to this imposter thou would do better to be in thy homes, tending to thy duties."

St. Gregory, observing Cyprian's conversation, smiled and continued with his practice.

After his sermon, St. Gregory approached Cyprian and said to him:

"Man with no faith or fear of God, will thou not end that life of sin?"

"Woe with this life of sin!" said Cyprian laughing.

"Yes, with that life of sin," said Gregory. "Thou Cyprian art so misguided with that art of the Devil that thou dost not want to leave it."

"Tell me, friend Gregory, what is this God of thine and of the Christians, which I have heard such marvels about?"

"The god thou worships is Lucifer, and the one I worship is a Powerful God, who created the Heaven and the Earth and all else the Sun rules."

Cyprian answered immediately to St. Gregory, filled with indignation:

"So, if thou, Gregory, worships a God more powerful than mine, defend thyself with him from my arts; and, should thou be victorious, I shall come to believe in thy God, however, if I am victorious, thou shall become my victim that very instant."

St. Gregory trembled and said to himself: "Should God abandon me now what will become of me! Cursed be the hour I met Cyprian. My God, my God!" said Gregory, "if Thou art not with me now, what will become of me?"

Cyprian, enraged by the supplication being made by St. Gregory, shouted out to all demons in Hell, and in a few instants there were so many demons that they covered the whole earth in a quarter of a square league around; however, St. Gregory raised his eyes to heaven and said aloud:

"Jesus, Jesus! Be with me in this hour of affliction."

A great thunder was heard and opened the gates of Hell, and immediately all the demons fell into the depths of a fearful abyss.

Cyprian, seeing the amazing thing that just happened, fell to the ground and was like that for a quarter of an hour.

After a few minutes, St. Gregory felt a great earthquake, which greatly surprised him.

It was Lucifer, rising from the bosom of the Earth, with a coffin of fire carried by four lions, and at the sight of this spectacle was St. Gregory greatly amazed, however he regained his strength with the aid of the Lord and said to Lucifer:

"I banish thee, accursed, on behalf of God; and tell me what thou wants from here?"

"I come to collect Cyprian," responded Lucifer.

"Dost thou, accursed," responded back St. Gregory, "by any chance have the power to claim a living creature?"

"I," responded Lucifer, "take Cyprian for he has died, and he is mine, in body and soul; this is our arrangement."

St. Gregory, hearing Lucifer's words, prayed to the Lord and said to Lucifer:

"I banish thee to the depths of Hell, for Cyprian is not dead!"

St. Gregory touched Cyprian on the shoulder and said to him:

"Rise, Cyprian."

Cyprian immediately rose, and St. Gregory readily told him:

"Dost thou not yet regret, Cyprian, that life of sin? One must indeed be a wicked man, seeing the hand of God wanting to save him and still choosing the path of perdition!"

"And thou, Gregory," responded Cyprian, "dost thou not know that I belong to Lucifer, for I have made a pact with him, and by that reason I cannot enter into Heaven, where only the just and those who do not follow the path of Hell enter? Remove thyself from my sight then, while I do not use my powers and my diabolical arts."

St. Gregory was enraged against Cyprian and told him with very harsh words:

"Unworthy man, remove thyself from my presence, while I do not use my own means to do so."

Cyprian was also enraged by these words and suddenly the heavens were covered with clouds, the sky was darkened, the earth trembled and great lightnings hovered over the ground that made it look like the whole world was on fire; St. Gregory however, with the name of Jesus, stomped and crushed Cyprian's cunnings.

Cyprian, seeing as all he did was of no use, was angered against Lucifer, who appeared to Cyprian and said to him:

"My friend, what dost thou want from me, why art thou so angry at thy lord?"

Cyprian told him:

"Thou, Devil, what power dost thou have if thou cannot destroy Gregory's?"

To these words the Devil responded:

"Dost thou not know that Gregory told me that if I did not kill him here, in one year he would give me his soul? For that reason, my friend Cyprian, it is not convenient for me to combat him in this way; retire thyself from here Cyprian, and leave Gregory."

Cyprian placed his fava in his mouth, and retreated to the city where he lived. Of this case I found nothing else written.

REFLECTIONS ON WHAT YOU HAVE JUST READ

When the Devil told Cyprian to leave Gregory, that he could do nothing to him according to a contract they had made, it was to fool Cyprian into not continuing his war with Gregory. For the Devil was afraid that Gregory would eventually convert Cyprian, and this was then the reason why he lied.

XXXV

Sorcery that is made with a bat so as to make someone love you

Let us suppose a girl wishes to marry her boyfriend with great haste. Do the following:

Take a bat and pierce a needle and thread through its eyes.

After this operation is done, the needle and the thread gain a great magical power.

METHOD OF BEWITCHING

Take any object belonging to the person you wish to bewitch and give it five cross-stitches, while saying the following words:

"(NN), I bewitch thee by the power of Maria Padilha and all of her family so as thou may not see the Sun or the Moon while thou dost not marry me, this by the magical power of the middle-aged sorceress."

After all this is done, the person is enchanted and will not have a single hour's rest while she is not married.

If by any chance you no longer wish to marry the person you have enchanted, you should burn the object you used for this sorcery.

XXXVI

Another magic of the bat

Kill a male and a female bat, in such a way as to keep their blood; then, put their blood together, mix in a little of spirits of hartshorn and put everything inside a deciliter vial, which you should always carry in your pocket.

When you desire to enchant a girl, or if a girl wishes to enchant her lover, all that is necessary is to give them the flask to smell.

In this way the person will become enchanted and will never leave.

XXXVII

Sorcery which can be made
with mallows picked in a
cemetery or churchyard

Cut three stems of mallows, take them home and place them under the mattress of your bed, saying every day immediately before going to sleep the following:

"(NN), as these mallows wert picked from the cemetery and under me are placed, so will (NN) to me be bonded and tied by the power of Lucifer and the liberal magic, and only when the bodies in the cemetery of the church from where these mallows came from speak will thou leave me."

These words should be repeated for nine straight days, so as produce the proper effect.

XXXVIII

Marvelous sorcery of the sprouting potatoes
under the nightsky

When a lady is suspicious that her husband or lover is lost through bad paths with women, and wishes to divert him from this, she needs not do any more that this:

Take six potatoes, with at least four sprouts each, and, after blessing herself with each of them one by one[83], place them in a glazed pan, which has not been used before, cover them with holy water and drop a splash of virgin olive oil on them while saying the following:

"Satan, by the virginity of this olive oil, I request to thy power that my man regain his previous virginity towards me."

Then place this pan under the night sky, for three nights, and, should there be moonlight, all the more powerful will be this sorcery.

After the three nights, boil the potatoes, and by using them in a stew of virgin pigeon, she should give them to her husband or lover to eat, with broccoli or rapini, with lots of pepper.

When you go to bed, place the head of the pigeon inside the boot of the enchanted one with its excretion tract in its beak.

---

83. Translator's note: I am uncertain if what is meant here is that the person performing this sorcery cross herself with the potatoes in her hand, or actually carry them to church in order to be blessed by the priest with them in her possession; most likely it is the first.

This magic comes from book III of Abraham Zacuto, a Jew who practiced admirable Witchcraft in the XVth century.

XXXIX

Remedy against the hunchbacks

To avoid that your businesses go wrong when in the morning you run across a hunchback man, St. Cyprian says you should do the following:

"Dolphin, hunchback, which bends forward, go, go, diligent, and leave me in peace. Dolphin, dolphin, pursue me no further; here is a *figa*, do not look back."[84]

Then, do a *figa* with your left hand and reach out your right arm with your hand open, as if you were catching a butterfly. Afterwards, keep walking with your hand closed until you run across any one of these individuals: another hunchback; a municipal soldier[85]; a white horse; a man with a limp; a one-handed man; a black cat; a black dog; an albino man.

As soon as you find any one of these, open your hand and say in a continuous act[86]:

"Be gone in the name of Maria Padilha and all her family, to where thou dost not bring misfortune neither to the rich neither to the poor nor anyone under the sky[87]. Amen."

This banishment is infallible: we have used it ourselves on various occasions and we always avoided the bad crossing of the hunchbacks, which are truly fatidic to all who see them, although this is entirely not their fault.

IMPORTANT PREVENTION

For this recipe to work it is necessary that one does not bear any hate towards the hunchback, otherwise everything will go badly.

---

84. Translator's note: some sections of this incantation rhyme, as such the original Portuguese should be observed: "*Golfinho, corcunda, que entortas prá frente, vai, vai, diligente, e deixa-me em paz. Golfinho, Golfinho, não mais me persigas; aí vai uma figa, não olhes pra trás*".

85. Translator's note: I think a police officer should do.

86. Translator's note: probably what is meant here is a single breath.

87. Translator's note: in the original Portuguese this whole incantation rhymes, as such it might actually be important to observe the original language: "*Vai-te, em nome de Maria Padilha e de toda a sua família, para onde não azangues nem a rico nem a pobre, nem a ninguém que o céu cobre. Amen*".

ART OF DIVINING

THE

PASSIONS AND TENDENCIES OF PEOPLE
THROUGH THEIR SKULL AND THEIR PHYSIOGNOMY

Gall, a notable German physician and physiometer, deceased in 1828, is the author of this ingenious system, which teaches one how to discover, by a most clear method, the tendencies, vices, passions and virtues of every person by the simple examination of the configuration of their skull.

It is certain that women, by some natural instinct, always seek to surround themselves with a certain degree of mystery, if we but look at the way they arrange their hair; men, on the contrary, less fearful of the advancements of Science, leaves this field completely exposed for any examination.

The logic of this system cannot be questioned. And frankly there hasn't been a single person who has not been amazed by the aspects of another person's head. The most notable men, be it for their talents or their crimes, rarely present regular or ordinary heads, and the reason for this is that the head is the seat of all our thoughts and all our ideas. It is quite natural that certain lobes of the brain should develop to a greater or lesser extent, according to the use we make of a certain faculty, and, as a consequence, the cranium should lose its primitive uniformity in order to present different protuberances corresponding to the most relevant feelings they represent in an individual.

After serious and lengthy studies made over a great variety of subjects of all countries and all classes, ages, and social conditions, the most wise Gall presented the system of the localization of the faculties of man. These faculties are thirty in number, and we present them here in numerical order:

1st The sense of things, living memory of facts; very pronounced vocation towards everything which is instruction.

2nd Philosophic spirit; the organ of intuition and inductive observation; faculty of discovering general laws and their consequence.

3rd Organ of poetry; heightened feeling for the beautiful, the great and the supernatural.

4th General notions of what is just and unjust; sweetness of character, extreme kindness.

5th Love of approval and glory; desire to please.

6th Firmness of character; perseverance.

7th Love for one's children or love for all children in general.

8th Physical love; libidinous and propagating instinct.

9th Friendship; heightened sense for great sympathies.

10th Organ of slyness and cunning; smartness and dissimulation.

11th Pronounced tendency for everything which is marvelous or supernatural; gullibility in everything.

12th Love for authority; dominating spirit; vanity, pride.

13th Spirit of imitation; mimic.

14th Consciousness; upstanding; circumspection, providence.

15th Organ of a jesting spirit; tendency towards satire; joyful temper and full of saucy sayings.

16th Carnivore instinct; pronounced sanguinarian tendency.

17th Feeling of numbers; spirit of calculus; mathematical talent.

18th Musical talent; feeling of melody and harmony.

19th Deepness of spirit; metaphysical penetration.

20th Organ of locality and spirit; desire of travel; cosmopolitanism.

21st Faculty of preserving the memory of people.

22nd Feeling of colors and their effects; taste for paintings and painting.

23rd Instinct of accumulation, greed to the point of taking that which is not his.

24th Instinct of defense, of the self and his property.

25th Ease of elocution; liveliness of spirit; popular eloquence.

26th Feeling towards the existence of God; religious tendency.

27th Faculty of preserving the names and the signs of words; locality.

28th Good instinct to select habitation.

29th Feeling of articulate language; manifested disposition to learn languages.

30th Feeling of mechanics and construction; organ of the arts and industry.

Know that these lumps are doubled, meaning that the ones on the left side of the head are exactly reproduced on the right side and have the same significance.

The protuberances are not always found on all heads, but there are people on whom a great deal of these are so visible that they are evident even to the least perceptive. In some criminals, lump 16 is so visible that it makes their heads deformed. Those who don't love children have the backs of their heads flat and almost in a straight line with their necks; those individuals are missing lump 7.

The study of phrenology complements the study of physiognomy.

Slanted eyes, in an almond like form, indicate indolence, melancholia and tenderness.

Big round eyes indicate liveliness, levity, indiscretion.

Sunken eyes indicate bad and violent passions. Crossed-eyes very rarely indicate good character.

Generally, one can place trust in individuals whose stare is direct and clear; but not in those who do not look at you directly and seem to want to avoid looking at you eye to eye.

Small eyes are an indication of vengeful and stubborn character, insensitive heart, and selfish spirit.

Squinting eyes, with heavy eyelids, are an indication of indolence, a spirit without weakness; contrarily, large and well opened eyes, with thin eyelids where one can easily distinguish veins, note vivacity, ardent heart, great imagination, generous soul.

A round nose indicates a weak character, sensual temperament, even more if the tip is red and the nostrils broad.

Long and thin nose shows stubbornness, satirical spirit, curiosity; but if by any chance it deviates to any side, it denotes a limited spirit, but, however, a great tendency towards the natural sciences.

A small and perky nose indicates cunning and also good spirit, intelligence and joy.

A blunt nose indicates stubbornness associated with weakness of spirit, great self-love and a weak mind, defects associated with stubbornness with a tendency towards wickedness[88].

Long and thick nose, accompanied by thick lips, are signs of those notable for their kindness, tenderness and charity without limits.

A wide forehead, of a regular height and slightly arched, denotes an unusual spirit; those favored in this way may achieve a great influence; they will be distinguished by their merits and talents and may come to rise to the highest dignities. They will be firm in their principles and will never deviate from an honorable path.

Thin and narrow forehead shows a limited spirit, cold heart and a temperament propitious to debauchery.

An elevated forehead, but narrow, indicates spirit, imagination and at the same time imprudence and lack of foresight; these will be dreamers or poets, but terrible husbands and fathers.

A square and straight forehead demonstrates a hard heart, highly organized, but selfish; by their perseverance they will ascend to great positions in society, but they will not provide services to anyone; they will not know love or friendship.

Those with a low and narrow forehead, and the hair of their eyebrows almost united, will be limited of spirit; they will have, however, as compensation, a great ability for manual labour, and love for work and economy. Among these, some do become greedy.

Large mouth and thick lips indicates gluttony, love for talking and lying.

---

88. Translator's note: this translation was not easy... but what is meant is that a person such as this is a son of a bitch.

Large mouth, thin and pale lips is the announcement of a falsity, selfishness, wickedness, trouble-making spirit and a depraved tongue.

A very small mouth very rarely indicates any spirit; in most cases you can only place trust in people whose mouth isn't too big or too small, with nicely colored round lips, for these are the signs of a good character, tender heart, jovial spirit, frank and sincere.

The teeth also have their significance. A man who falls in love with a woman whose teeth are short and pointy will not be happy; for there isn't enough money in the world to satisfy the whims of women with such an attribute.

Pronounced canines, out of line with the remaining teeth, indicate low and vulgar instincts, a flimsy spirit.

Strong, white and well positioned teeth, but not too united are the indication of good health, great disposition for greed; these are also the signs of a tendency towards madness.

Round and pointy chin denotes a dry heart and a sardonic spirit.

Long chin indicates kindness, sexuality and absence of spirit, but this is not true if there is the presence of a dimple.

A pronounced chin turning upward indicates courage and a disorderly spirit, ardent temperament and voluptuous.

A narrow tucked-in chin is the sign of a self-conscious and shy spirit, but a sensitive and weak heart.

Wide and square chin is the proof of a strong man but without any delicateness of feelings.

A chin coming in a straight line from the lower lip to the extremity of the face indicates firmness of spirit and hardness of heart; this is commonly found in people whose forehead is flat, having small and sunken eyes and pale thin lips. One should avoid contact with people with such signs.

Big ears, badly delineated and widely separated from the head are an indication of laziness and curiosity.

Round and small ears, well delimited announce a bookish tendency, independent, lovable character.

Long, dry, wrinkled and thin hands denote evil instincts, greed being common in the case where the fingers are curved.

The feet are almost always in relation with the hands; it is preferable that they be narrow and well rounded, even if long; one should avoid wide and flat feet, the kind which deform all sorts of footwear.

We will not bother ourselves with hair or eyebrows. Everyone knows that curly hair indicates vanity and lust; straight hair tenderness, affability; red hair indicates a bad tongue, envy, deceitful spirit; black hair indicates a brave spirit; blonde, weakness and kindness.

Finally, thick eyebrows denote a great character and energy; thin ones an ardent imagination and levity; those that are united indicate violence and jealousy.

133

In general, tall white men, slightly fat, are of a shy character, soft, weak and with as little energy as physical strength.

The short, white or dark, are violent, passionate, but susceptible to deep lasting affection, they give themselves to important and serious endeavors; but their weakness is their vanity and jealousy.

Tall swarthy men with pale skin[89] are easy talkers, but indolent and slightly weak of character, no matter how much energy they appear to have; they are boisterous and talkative but also cowards; they love pleasure, luxury, women and a full table.

Extremely tall women very rarely have the qualities of their gender; given their preferences they are closer to men, which they do resemble.

Short women, on the contrary, are graceful, amiable, charming; but generally given to affairs of the heart, with a rowdy spirit; they have more energy and liveliness than tall women, and they can handle the downsides of fortune with greater ease. Generally they seem weak, but they are sturdy.

To wrap up this chapter, we shall provide good advice for men to choose a companion: a woman of regular stature, brown hair, dark blue or velvet black eyes, slightly arched eyebrows, wide and slightly curved forehead, slightly rounded nose, red lips, wide mouth, garnished with white teeth, rounded chin and ornamented with a dimple. Should you find such a person you may expect to find the kind of happiness with which a man may enjoy the whole of the earth.

To women we advise: chose a man of a stature slightly above average, but nothing too tall, let him have straight hair and slightly wavy, high forehead, frank, open and slightly dignified stare, long and straight nose, large and smiling mouth, abundant beard, thick eyebrows, but not united; thus you shall have an amiable, affectionate, energetic, hard working and constant husband.

Nature however seems to operate by contrasts. Tall men like short women, the short, tall women, and vice-versa; the swarthy like the white, and the white the swarthy.

To conclude, my reader friends should follow our advice, for we assure you that they will serve you well.

---

89. Translator's note: There seems to be some contradiction here, as swarthy, *trigueiro* in the original Portuguese, among other things indicates an incompatibility with being pale.

CROSSED CARTOMANCY

Method of casting the cards, unknown still to this day, and used by St. Cyprian

In the miserable cell which housed St. Cyprian, his last residence before his death, and hidden in the empty space where he used to sleep, a manuscript was found with this new art of card reading that we have named *crossed cartomancy*, of which Cyprian made use of after his dealings with Satan went sour.

Many years after the death of St. Cyprian, this manuscript was discovered and taken to Rome, where it was condemned to be burned after experimentations on its authority in divination were performed. Such was the effectiveness they found in it that, fearful, they wished to destroy it by fire.

Gladly this did not to come to pass, maybe due to the will of the Saint, whose soul had already taken flight to join the Lord. The one in charge of destroying the manuscript substituted it with another one, which he threw into the fire under the sight of all those surrounding him, saving the real one. Later this manuscript appeared in the Library of Rome, being that it is still a mystery as to who actually left it there. It is thought that it was indeed its original keeper or his relatives. But nothing can be known for sure. That it is authentic is without a doubt, for with it was also found the order of its condemnation. Due to the amiability of a friend, who recently visited the Holy City, and whose curiosity took him to the library where this precious manuscript resides, which he then copied, we can, in this edition of the *Great Book of Saint Cyprian*, teach it to the reader.

•
• •

The deck, composed of 40 cards, should have been passed by the waves of the sea, at midday on a Friday, while uttering at that time the following words:
"May the celestial spirits give thee the virtue."

VALUE OF THE CARDS

DIAMONDS

Ace – Promise

Two – Marriage

Three – Cuddles of love

Four – Separation

Five – Seduction

Six – Meager fortune

Seven – Wealth

HEARTS

Ace – Constraints

Two – Reconciliation

Three – Sympathy

Four – Banquette

Five – Jealousy

Six – Delay

Seven – Surprise

SPADES

Ace – Passion

Two – Correspondence

Three – Loyalty

Four – In the house

Five – Plot

Six – Brevity

Seven – Heartbreak

CLUBS

Ace – Vice

Two – Treason

Three – Disorder

Four – Levity

Five – Out of the house

Six – Captivity

Seven – Obstacle

The *aces* and the *sevens* also have the special name of *Temptations*.

FIGURES

There are four indispensable figures: the *queen of diamonds*, which represents the consultant; the *king of diamonds*, her boyfriend (or husband); the *queen of spades*, a rival; and the *jack of hearts*, an intermediary person, who can either be a man or a woman.

The remaining figures are only useful when you need to represent other people, who the consultant may suspect.

Any *queen* should be indicated by the words: *this woman*, and a *king* or a *jack* by the words: *this man*, except the *jack of hearts*, which should be named: *this person*.

One should understand that it is necessary to switch the figures if it is a man making the consultation. That is, the consultant should be represented by the *king of diamonds*, the lover (or wife) by the *queen of diamonds*; the *jack of spades*

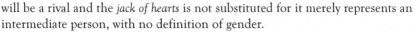

will be a rival and the *jack of hearts* is not substituted for it merely represents an intermediate person, with no definition of gender.

We then usually only have 4 figures, which, with the remaining 28 cards, make up 32; but, in this case, we only cast 24, as was indicated by the Saint.

Firstly remove the *figures* you will not be using.

Then, separate the *aces* and the *sevens* and shuffle these eight cards together (these are the *temptation*), placing them in a pile, in the middle of the table, facing down.

We then have 24 cards in our hand.

Next, shuffle these 24 cards, and cast them over the table, facing up in the form of a cross, whose middle is the pile of the *temptation*:

Start in this order:

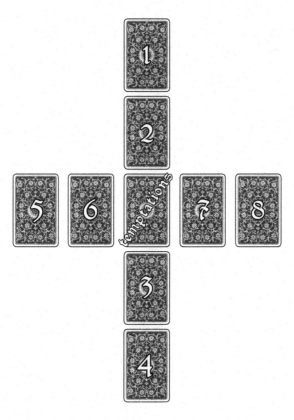

One should have the greatest care in observing what we indicate here, so as this consultation may be of some use.

Then continue until you have placed the rest of the cards over the previous ones, in piles of three, as indicates the following figure:

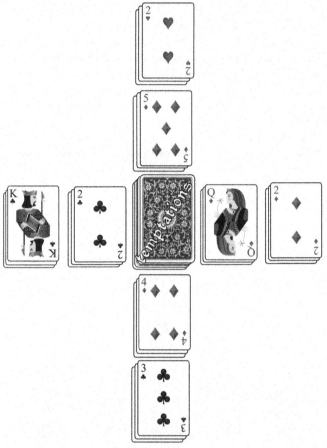

On this occasion, at last, everything is ready to begin uncovering the secrets of the *crossed cartomancy*. And thus, by raising your eyes, placing your thoughts in Heaven and seeking to become possessed by the greatest of faiths, extend your hands over the center of the table, praying in a low and soft voice the following orison of St. Cyprian, which should also be repeated every time one shuffles the cards:

"May these cards, by the power of St. Cyprian, now a saint and previously a sorcerer, tell me the truth, for the glory of this same saint and the satisfaction of my soul."

As soon as one has cast the first eight cards, cross yourself with the remaining, saying:

St. Cyprian with me[90].

---

90. Translator's note: the most correct translation would be "St. Cyprian be with me", but, as you will see, at this point it is important that these be only four words.

These four words should be accompanied, respectively, with the movements of your hand, that is, taking your hand to your forehead, one should say: *Saint* – by placing your hand on your chest say: *Cyprian* – with your hand on your left shoulder say: *with* – and, with your hand on you right shoulder to finish – *me*.

Then cast the second group of eight cards and cross yourself with the remaining, repeating the same words. Finally, as should be obvious, conclude with the last cards.

We believe we have explained as clearly as possible the ceremony and the order in which the cards should be cast, so as they end up as the figure demonstrates.

The *crossed cartomancy* may be applied for the uncovering of any mystery; for one needs only to personify the cards with the names of people one assumes to take part in what he wishes to know.

———————

To uncover the cards one follows a different order. Starting by turning one card from each extreme of the cross, continuing to the next extreme, and, as soon as all eight have been lifted, draw one *temptation*. Meaning, turn them in the following order:

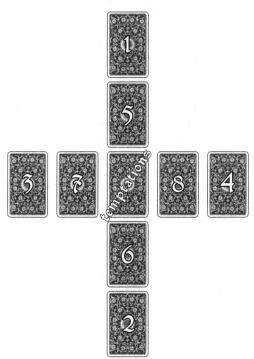

Very rarely will one need to lift every card, for, usually, the first nine cards alone should be enough to satisfy the curiosity of the consultant. But, if there remains any desire to know something else, keep going until the next stop in a *temptation*.

When you have lifted all the cards and their meaning has become confusing do the following:

Reshuffle the temptations, place them back in their place, shuffle the rest of the cards and, at last, proceed to a new operation, everything as in the beginning.

1ST EXAMPLE (FOR A LADY)

A young woman hasn't received any news from her lover, and she desires to know what the cards say about this. Let us suppose that these were the cards she got:

Four of clubs (Levity)
Six of hearts (Delay)
Two of spades (Correspondence)
King of diamonds (This man)
Four of spades (In the home)
Three of hearts (Sympathy)
Five of diamonds (Seduction)
Ace of spades (Passion)

By coordinating the significance of the cards, you should learn the following:

By *levity*, a *delay in correspondence* from *this man*, because he is entertained *in the home* of someone for whom he has *sympathy* (this is the rival of the consultant), and he has a *seduction* in a *banquette* (meaning that he eats and drinks with this woman), this is due to *passion*.

If you wish to know if this passion is from his part or her part, continue lifting cards (but this time do not include the *temptations*), following the same order, until the *queen of diamonds* or the *queen of spades* appears; if it is the first, the passion is from the rival; if it is the second, then he is the one with passion.

2ND EXAMPLE (IDEM)

Now let us suppose that the two queens had already been drawn, meaning that we shall assume that in the first nine cards we had the following draw:

King of diamonds (This man)
Six of hearts (Delay)
Two of spades (Correspondence)

Queen of diamonds (This woman)
Three of hearts (Sympathy)
Queen of spades (This other woman)
Four of hearts (Banquette)
Six of clubs (Captivity)
Ace of spades (Passion)

This man delays the correspondence to this woman (consultant) for *sympathy* with *this woman* (rival) with whom he has a *banquette* and *captivity* (he is captive) because of a *passion*.

In this case, if the consultant still wants to know from which of the two comes the passion (seeing as the *queen of diamonds* and *queen of spades* were drawn), once again put the twenty-four cards together, shuffle them, spread them out again and lift them one by one (always in the same way, stretching out your hand before lifting them and praying the orison), until one of the mentioned queens is drawn; and, according to the first one drawn, the answer of which of the two is in love will be given, as we have explained.

As this operation has the objective of searching for one of the two *queens*, it is unnecessary to lift the *temptation*.

One further warning – if both queens are together, it means that they are both equally in love with the same man.

3RD EXAMPLE (FOR A GENTLEMAN)

A young boy wishes to know the behavior of his lover.
The following cards were drawn:

Queen of diamonds (This woman)
Four of clubs (Levity)
Two of spades (Correspondence)
Jack of spades (This man)
Five of diamonds (Seduction)
Three of diamonds (Cuddles of love)
Five of clubs (Out of the house)
Seven of spades (Heartbreak)

One can read in these cards:
This woman had levity of corresponding with this man, by whom she is *seduced* with a *cuddle of love*, in a *banquette out of the house*.

And lifting the ninth card (the *temptation*), you will know:
Should you continue to give attention to this woman you are risking a *broken heart*.

4TH EXAMPLE (IDEM)

The consultancy is for an individual who was abandoned by his wife. Let us suppose the following cards were drawn:

Queen of diamonds (This woman)
Four of diamonds (Separation)
Five of hearts (Jealousy)
Five of spades (Plot)
Jack of hearts (This person)
Six of spades (Brevity)
Two of hearts (Reconciliation)
King of diamonds (This man)
Seven of hearts (Surprise)

These cards mean:
This woman had a *separation* over *jealousy*, created by a *plot of this person*, but with *brevity* she will *reconcile* with *this man*, presenting a *surprise*.

FINAL WARNING

The *three of diamonds* (*cuddles of love*) may mean *care* and *affection*, or even a *gift*; the *ace of hearts* (*constraints*) may, at times, mean *violence* (a raped woman, for example); the *two of spades* (*correspondence*) may represent a letter; and the *ace of clubs* (*captivity*) means *imprisoned by love*, or it may represent prison as in actual jail, all according to the circumstances of the consultation.

EXPLANATION OF DREAMS

AND

NOCTURNAL APPARITIONS

ABBOT – Treason, dishonor, loss of health, woman in a commitment.

ACTOR – Regrets over time wasted in pleasure.

AMBASSADOR – Swindle from the administrators of your businesses.

APPLE TREE – Full – abundance; Empty – difficulties.

APRICOTS – Eating them – pleasure, contentment; Dried – serious disappointment, mortification.

APRICOT TREE – Full of ripe fruit – constant happiness; Unripe fruit – great difficulties to overcome; Without fruit – losses, setbacks.

BAKER – Time to start saving.

BANKRUPTCY – Prosperous results in commerce and business.

BASIN – Seeing horses drinking from it – unexpected and satisfactory news; Dry – mystery.

BEE – Benefits and dignities. If they sting you that means a treason; if you kill them, you should expect great troubles; inheritance if you see them over flowers. If you see them with honey that means you are to be happy, married and parenting many children.

BIRTH – Wedding, inheritance, good omen.

BISCUIT – Eating them – enjoyment, good health.

BLOOD – Headache; abundant fortune.

BOTTOMS – Fortune with little work.

BRAIN – Wisdom, high dignity.

BROTH – Better food, unexpected fortune.

BUFFET – Packages, cheap shopping.

BUMBLEBEE – Sincere love, marriage is near.

BURIN – Happy marriage with a hard working man.

CADAVER – Joy and good health, friendship.

CALDRON – Good news from the village, enjoyment.

CAMEL – Wealth, power, dignity.

CANARY – Great journey, with great venture.

CATERPILLAR – Bad harvest, loss of money.

CEDAR – Happy prosperity that will be blessed by Heaven.

CHAIR – Quiet and peaceful life, celibacy.

CHANTING – Quiet life, insincere love.

CEREMONY – Religious – pray for your relatives; Public – mortification and heartbreak.

CHEESE – Unwavering health through sobriety.

CHERRY – Red – pleasant news; Black – death of relatives or someone you know; Green – dashed hopes; Ripe – inheritance or a present soon to come; Eating them – birth of a boy in your family.

CHICKEN – Many children, opulence; Death, disease.

COLD – Good news.

CONSTRUCTION WORK – Rough and inelegant – slavery.

COW – Wild – Animosity between women, unskillful man; Tamed – coming betrayal from your loved one.

CRACKERS – Nearby journey, great fortune.

CROSS – Carrying it – long affliction; seeing it – most fortunate omen.

CYPRESS – Misfortune, pains of the soul, sudden death.

DAMASK (tissue) – Ruin due to luxury, poverty.

DANCING – Good rest, sure win.

DATING – Wasted time.

DAWN – Hopeless love; Loss of a young child.

DEATH – Of children – birth of relatives; Embracing a dead man – long life; Being grabbed by him – dangerous injury.

DEVIL – Seeing him appear – news of countless and cruel torments; Seeing him in Hell – omen of unhappiness; Fighting with him – imminent danger; Tripping him – sure triumph; Being notified by him – unfortunate, Sickness or death of the person dreaming should you not be careful while going to bed or rising from it, you should order yourself to your Guardian Angel.

DICE – Rolling them – loss of belongings; If winning – inheritance from a family member.

DOOR BELL – Ringing it – disorder in the family.

DRUMS – False courage, a great fight over nothing.

EARRINGS – Corresponded love, satisfaction.

EARTHQUAKE – Ruin, misery, death.

ECCLESIASTIC – Shame, coming misery.

EGG – The white – joy; Yolk – adversity; Fresh – good news; Rotten – sickness to a parent or someone very close; Broken – broken relationship.

ELECTION – Politics is never fruitful.

ELECTRICITY – A very much expected letter.

ELEPHANT – Mortal danger; Feeding it – friendship among relatives; Owning it – end of torments.

FACTORY – It is good to fear necessity.

FAMILY – Prosperity, marital love, lasting health.

FATHER – Joy, consideration.

FAVA BEANS – Contending, dissensions.

FIRE – Disaster for he who sees it.

FLOUR (from grain) – Wealth, abundance due to work; Burning it – sudden ruin.

FORTUNE - Honorable - charity work to be done; Wrongly acquired - disgraceful end; Promised - it shall not come.

FRUIT - Eating it - pleasure, happiness.

GAIN - Improperly acquired inheritance.

GALINHOLA[91] - Badly directed affection.

GAME - Winning - bad sign; Lose - declaration of love; Watch - treason; Children's game - great satisfaction.

GANGRENE - Large family, mediocre position, ill-paid work.

GARDEN - Prosperity to come.

GHOST - Black - sentences and misery; White - joy and abundance.

GRAPES - Tears; frail luck.

GRASSHOPPER - Invasion from the enemies of a country or crops ruined by pests; Public and private disgrace.

HARP - Happiness destroyed by envy.

HERBS - Eating them - poverty, sickness; Raw - pain, embracement in your business.

HOWLING - Hearing it - death of a relative, someone in the house, or a person you know.

HUGS - Treason, improper proceeding, illicit pleasure.

IGNORANCE - Too much study is bad for your health.

ILLUMINATION - Happiness, unexpected wealth, inheritance.

IMAGES - Fond memories; Gifts, letters.

INHERITANCE - Stolen succession.

ISLAND - Boredom, non-reattributed affection.

JEWELS - Giving them - false friendship; Receiving them - false love; Losing them - dishonor.

JOY - Clear conscience, pleasure.

KNIFE - Disunion, animosity; Two, in a cross - fight, death.

KNOTS - Discretion; To be stuck in them - embarrassment.

LACKEYS - Hidden enemies.

LIZARD - Superficial friendship.

LOBSTER - Pain, disunion.

MACHINE - In movement - fortune in industry; Stopped - inventions which do not favor the inventor.

MALLOWS - Submission, humility.

MAN - Tall - jealousy; Short - conquest; Dark - wedding; Blond - fatality; Rich - misery; Old - dishonor; Young - successes; Handsome - adulation; Ugly - good future.

MACARONI - Inconsiderate conversations.

---

91. Translator's note: In Portugal this refers to the Eurasian Woodcock, *Scolopax rusticola*; in some regions of Brazil this name refers to the Helmeted Guineafowl, *Numida meleagris*.

MONKEY - Infidelity, wickedness.

MOON - Seeing it clearly - happiness to take long; Pale and wavering - imaginary torments; Red - danger.

MOUSE - Hidden enemy.

NOSE - Very large - abundance; Losing it - adultery; Seeing two - discord, fight.

OBLIGATIONS - Badly administrated profits.

OLIVE TREE - Happy marriage, good business.

OPTICIAN - Blindness in choosing your affections

PAINTINGS - Love for the arts.

PALACE - Laziness; To live in it - great help; Destroying it - usurped power; Royal - intrigue.

PIN - Order, economy, abundance.

PRIDE - High posture which is hurtful to yours and other's well being.

PRIEST - Protectors with their own agendas.

PUMPKIN - Hopeless love, loss of a young child.

QUESTIONS - Constant friendship; From men - envy; From women - torments.

RAZOR BLADE - Increased vigilance with your children and servants.

RINGWORM - Generous reward from someone whose life you'll save.

ROOSTER - Zeal will give you well-being; Cock fight - dispute over women.

ROSEMARY - Good nomination, pleasures to come soon.

SERPENT - Danger, disease.

SHIPWRECK - Seeing it - business difficulties, broken marriage, existence in danger; Being shipwrecked - bad omen.

SHOEMAKER, SHOES - Working life, journey over an inheritance.

SHOVEL - Bad neighbors you should be suspicious about.

SHRIMP - Unimportant enjoyment.

SIGN - Prosperity in commerce.

SMALLPOX - Broken pride, false glory.

STRAW - In bundles - fortune; Spread out - disgrace.

STEAKS - Unfounded pleasures, loss of relatives.

STRETCHER - Disaster on the street.

STUTTERER - A son that will be a great speaker.

SWIMMING - In clear water - good results after difficulties; In clouded water - bad results, danger.

SUN - Shining - glory; Shaded - danger; Fiery - death of a person of royal blood.

SWING - Happy union with plenty of children.

SYRUP - Perfect health.

TOBACCO - To smoke it - madness, disorder; To smell it - premature old age; To chew it - laziness.

TAVERN - Wine is an enemy of household peace.

Tempest – Great offenses to come, threatened fortune, imminent danger.

Thief – Infamy, dishonor.

Thinness – Seeing thin people is a sign of getting fat.

Toad – Disgust, bad digestion, perjury.

Toothpick – Bad sign.

Trinkets – Mediocrity.

Turnips – Cure from a disease, profit in business.

Urn – Full – marriage; Empty – celibacy; Funerary – birth.

Vine – Children to support you in your old age.

Voice – Calling us: Child's – change in condition; Woman's – reward; Man's – unexpected fortune.

Wealth – Omen of ruin.

Widow or Widower – Great satisfaction, recovered liberty.

Wind – Soft – favorable destiny; Strong – afflictions and setbacks; Cold – lazy heart; Warm – ardent heart.

Wine – Richness, health.

Window – Beaten quest; Coming out from it – sadness.

Wooden clogs – Excessive pride.

Wool – Union in the family, fruitful work.

Workshop – Wealth through work and economy.

Zero (number) – Prosperity at work, wealth, consideration.

Zigzag – Seeing zigzags – doubts, torments, perplexity, wrong path leading to perdition.

THIRD AND LAST
BOOK OF ST. CYPRIAN

OR

THE TREASURES OF GALICIA

DISCLAIMER

The original of this 3rd volume, which completes *The Book of St. Cyprian*, we owe to its collector, our dear friend from Barcelona, D. Gumerzindo Ruiz Castilejo y Moreno, owner of the *Biblioteca Academica Peninsular Catalani*, who sold us the exclusive right of translating it[92].

---

92. Original footnote: As the sole owner of the book entitled *Grimoire of St. Cyprian, or, The Prodigies of the Devil*, and all other matters related to it, we thus publicly state that the rights to print this book in the domains of Portugal are given to the property of Mr. Domingos M. Fernandes, publisher and editor in Lisbon (Portugal).

Barcelona, 25th of March of 1885
   D. Gumerzindo Ruiz Castillejo y Moreno.

By work of the notary Godinho, these rights were passed to Mr. F. Napoleão de Victoria, publisher and editor in Lisbon (Portugal).

GRIMOIRE[93] OF ST. CYPRIAN

or

THE PRODIGIES OF THE DEVIL

A TRUE STORY
THAT HAPPENED IN THE KINGDOM OF GALICIA

CHAPTER I
The story of Victor Siderol

From a much respected French book, entitled *The Occult Sciences*, by Mr. Zalotte, we have extracted the story you are about to read:

Victor Siderol was a farmer in the village of Court, five leagues off of Paris. This man had a great intelligence, and, thinking the fields of his village were unworthy of someone with such fine instruction, began to leave some of them unattended, which caused him to always have a meager harvest.

The other farmers, his neighbors, harvesting an abundant crop by the time of St. Michael[94], would tease him and call him *calaceiro*[95], a reference that, with each passing day, filled him with more and more heartache.

One afternoon, feeling a terrible indisposition right after finishing tending to a sowing row, he freed his oxen, dropped the bow yoke on the plough and said:

"Here I leave thee forever, my old plough. Let the Devil take thee, just as all my other farming tools I have back home."

As soon as Siderol said this he heard these words, as a roar in the air, which actually seemed to have come out of the earth's bowels:

"Take out the bow yoke, for I will have nothing to do with a cross."

The farmer, trembling with fright, put the bow yoke back on the oxen's necks, pulled them with him and ran away home with his hair standing on edge, completely speechless.

The following day, at the break of dawn, he went to his porch and saw that all his tools had disappeared as if by magical means.

---

93. Translator's note: The actual title of the chapter in the *Book of Saint Cyprian* is "*Engrimanços de S. Cipriano*". *Engrimanço* is a word meaning an unintelligible way of speaking, an obscure speech, related to the Italian "*grimo*". In popular rural context it is then an equivalent to Grimoire, as an obscure and indecipherable thing.

94. Translator's note: The feast of St. Michael I assume, on the 29th of September.

95. Translator's note: Lazy, someone who is not a friend of any sort of work.

He then went to the place where he had left his plough and it was nowhere to be found.

A few days later he sold his house and all of his lands, moving to Paris, where he rented a room on Saint-Honoré Street, and, while lifting a floor board in his room, so as to hide some of his money, he found, between two beams, a small book of spells, of which he had heard of back in his village, but was largely unknown to him.

This was the *Grimoire of St. Cyprian*[96].

CHAPTER II
How the grimoire of St. Cyprian is uncovered

In that remarkable book Siderol saw that he could place himself in close and friendly relations with the Unclean Spirit.

"This occult commerce," said Victor, "will surely have no interest to a man of good morals, but, it neither dishonors the worth or nobility of anyone who might use it, and for that reason, perhaps, I will make my fortune dealing with Lucifer. The Avernian King is surely my friend, seeing as I so freely have given him my plough and my collection of tools."

After carefully studying the magical book he went down to the patio of his residence, where an old maid raised some chickens that produced excellent fresh eggs. He carefully opened the door of the chicken coop, grabbed a black hen, entirely appropriate for diabolical conjurations, fled out the door and, despite the chicken's desperate cackling, marched without delay to the place where the paths of *Revolta* and *Neuilly* cross; for the Devil singularly infects the crosses made by four paths.

In this place he stopped, drew a circle on the floor around him with a hazel branch, placed the hen at the center and, at midnight sharp, recited three words, which I will not teach here, for we have enough tempting spirits among us and I do not wish to move you in the beginning of this story to the fantasy of adding to their numbers.

As these words were recited the hen started seizing and convulsing, dying while harmoniously singing praises to God.

The Earth shook, and, after this convulsion, the Moon, covered in stains of blood, fell down rapidly over the crossroad of *Neuilly*, and, as it rose back to its place, a great lord appeared on the outside of the circle, into which he could not enter by virtue of the words recited.

This large man, taller than Siderol, due to him wearing something like a *Sganarelle* barrette, had great and twisted ram's horns over his head, a long monkey's tail, which he gracefully waved in between his legs, goat's feet, a hood

---

96. Translator's note: In some editions, mostly Brazilian, the book Siderol finds is said to be called *The Prodigies of the Devil*, the second title of this section of *The Book*.

covering his hair and, covering his body, a scarlet dress decorated with gold, for this is this guise with which the Devil always presents himself to all creatures.

Should you ever call him, dear reader, you shall see, being struck by horror, the figure I have just described.

As soon as the farmer saw this great lord he felt himself overcome by a cold chill, for surely no man, no matter how brave he thinks himself, has the courage to look the King of *Aventesmas*[97] face to face. As soon as the great lord spoke, his fear became even greater, for the Devil carries great terror in the metal of his voice.

As the great lord went silent, the farmer was overcome by embarrassment, for in truth he had not prepared himself to converse with such a strange visitor.

However, the question he placed Siderol was as simple as it was short, and, by itself, would not cause any problems to anyone hearing it.

"What dost thou wish from me?"

This is what the Devil usually asks those who force him into appearance.

Siderol hesitated for a long time before deciding on what to ask, for he had many things on his mind he wished to possess. In this circumstance he wanted to choose something which would make him greatly fortunate, seeing that, as a general rule, the Devil concedes only one thing for each time he is summoned.

CHAPTER III
The art of predicting the future

As soon as the Frenchman decided upon something his mind would push him into another direction and he could not come to any decision. The great lord waited, with a submissive and reverent aspect, for him to make up his mind and tell him what his desire was.

The farmer thought that the future, once so rich, beautiful and seductive, had abused his good faith and it was now his will to read it as easily as a child reads the school doctrine.

He thought that the power of divination had advantages that would extend to all things in life, and by this means he would surely be able to regulate his conduct and actions and as such, take possession of all things he could possibly imagine.

This is the way, after much reflection and great titanic struggles, in which men can perfectly decide on their preferences.

A simple farmer would ask for snow over the fields neighboring his own; a poor priest would ask for the restitution of the clergy's belongings; a despot, the restoration of his old regime; a wrinkled old woman, the return of her lost

---

97. Translator's note: This is an expression to designate something extremely horrifying, an unexpected and startling presence, a supernatural and terrifying apparition, also, a class of spirits of infinite height.

charms; a spoiled libertine, the return of his previous vigor; an army supplier, an eternal war; and a visionary, immortality, something which no demon could ever grant him.

Victor told the great lord that he wished for him to whisper the future in his ear, every time he so wished, something the Devil agreed to with good will and fine manners.

He then took from his pocket a small piece of paper, on which was written a donation for Siderol's soul. He stung the farmer's pinky finger and he signed the deed with his own blood after which the Devil disappeared from his sight, with much courtesy.

The farmer, before trying out the new art he had just bought in exchange for his soul, felt that he had not eaten, and had also forgotten to bring any money with him.

He then asked his familiar demon where he could, at that time, find a meal that belonged to no one, for even if he had the will to sell himself to the Devil, he did not have the will to steal anything, no matter how insignificant.

The spirit responded:

"At this fateful hour for humanity, it is not convenient for thee to fill thy stomach. At four in the morning," said the spirit in a very low voice, "leave thy house, march in the direction of the rising Sun and thou will find a large pile of rocks. One of them will be carved as a pilaster. Lift it and take what thou finds there."

CHAPTER IV
A meal under a pile of rocks

The former farmer could not convince himself that under a pile of rocks he would find a meal that did not belong to anyone.

However, as he was certain the Devil always keeps the promises he makes to those who give him their soul, and an empty stomach does demand faith, he followed exactly what his oracle had indicated.

As the foreseen hour approached, he went to the mentioned place and wandered for a long time without finding any piles of rocks, and, in desperation, called his Devil once again.

The evil spirit then whispered in his ear:

"Thou still have little faith in my power, and this is the reason why thou cannot find the pile of rocks I told thee about. Dost thou see that palace in the distance and those rocks piled up on that corner?"

"I do."

"That is the place. Go there and eat at will."

The farmer found there what his stomach needed.

After searching for some time he found the pilaster, near which there was a lever. He rotated it and found underneath it three boards. He lifted them up and found a hole with an enormous plate, having on it a turkey, two chickens and six roasted quails. Next to this there were two large cheeses, a loaf of bread and two Savoie biscuits, very cleanly wrapped in a fine towel, and two bottles of wine from the Canary Islands.

The famished farmer, amazed before such marvelous things, took a cloth from his pocket, wrapping in it part of the content of the blessed hole and in quick steps returned home.

Upon arrival he ate, with great appetite, the quails and part of the turkey and on top of this he drank the two delicious bottles of wine. But, even though his stomach no longer demanded nourishment, Siderol did not wish to limit himself to that single delight.

To acquire something else he called the Devil and asked him if he knew of any hidden treasure, one that did not belong to anyone.

"In the bowels of mount Carballo there is a hidden gold mine."

"And how may I explore it?"

"With the Cabala of the *Mouros*."

"And where is this to be found?"

"I will give it to thee shortly. But before that, tell me, dost thou like to give alms to the poor?"

"I do."

"Then thou shall give them all the money thou still possesses, for, while thou hast a single cent, the earth will not open itself to give thee the riches of its bowels."

"Well then," said the farmer, "tomorrow I will give away all that I have. But, my friend Beelzebuth, tell me, where can I find some more treasure?"

"In the village of Meirol there is a vein of diamonds, which will open itself with two words from my Cabala."

"Oh my lord, tell me these words."

"Wait," said the Devil, "first thou shall learn where the treasures are, only then I will give thee the keys to open them."

"Come, friend Lucifer, tell me now where there is a treasure which I may explore this very day and I promise I will be faithful to thee for the rest of my life and even after death."

"Have I not told thee, oh sold soul, that thou must first give everything thou owns to the poor?"

"Ah! Yes, yes, forgive me, my good friend, my kind Satan."

"Well then, a usurer from Baiona, who is the owner of everything three leagues before those islands, buries every year many hundreds of doubloons in a pasture he owns in Baigreza. For thou can already perceive that there is a great treasure in that place and that thou can approach it easily without having to use any magical words from me."

"But such money belongs to its owner and I do not wish for it. I only care for money that no longer belongs to anyone."

"What is thy business with my purposes? Today thou art completely my property, and I can order thee to do whatever I may see fit!"

Lucifer then started to whisper unintelligible words, before which the farmer fell to his knees begging forgiveness.

"Be calm," said Lucifer, "I know very well what is convenient to favor thee. This old usurer is to die this very night, without any warning, and as he is hiding from his partners, for they have not treated him well, they know not, nor shall they ever know of this treasure, which this very night shall fall under my power, just like the soul of this old man from Baiona."

"But where is this land that guards such wealth?"

"It is near Santiago, to the North, near the seashore."

"My friend Satan, I am asking what is the name of this country."

"It is in the Hispanic plain, in the outmost Northern extreme."

"Then I will never make it, for I will die of hunger along the path."

"Don't be a fool. When thou arrives at the Pyrenees, sit by the roadside and wait for the pilgrims coming from Rome to Compostela, those vile and rabid dogs who never wanted to sell their souls to me in exchange for my blessing. Thou may accompany them and thus find the treasure of this dying man. Come now, go without delay."

"No, thou should go and discover this treasure for me," said the former farmer with humbleness.

"Not me!" responded the Devil. "We did not agree on me doing any work. You merely asked for the gift of divination, and thou hast it; that is where my commitment ends."

"Devil, Devil! I will do as thou tells me; but dost thou not know of any other treasure?"

"I do. In that faraway kingdom there is more buried gold than in any other place where the daughter language of the Arabs and *Mouros* is spoken."

"Tell me now these places my good Beelzebuth."

"Should thou still live when thou reaches that land, search in the villages I shall tell thee:

Rubióz, Outeirello, Taboeja, Lañas, Infiesta, Hyga Buena, Guilhade, Sobroso, Pojeros, Budinhedo, Aranza, Guinza, Caritel, Mondim, Fraguedo, Celleiros, Foçára, Bordem, Mondariz and..."

"So many my Lord!" interrupted Victor Siderol, amazed by such an amount of wealth.

"Those and many more! In that country there are more than one hundred enchanted treasures. Thou shall find there the wealth of more than six kingdoms. Go to thy destiny and call upon me whenever thou requires. Since thou hast given me thy soul, I shall give thee happiness."

"But how shall I open the earth to extract all that gold?"

"Travel to these places I have told thee, and take this lantern. Light it anytime thou wishes for something, and thou shall be immediately served."

The former farmer bade Lucifer goodbye and went on his way to give all his money to the poor. After he had gotten rid of his last cent, he went out and crossed a large square. Although he was distracted, thinking of the Devil, he noticed a store with the following sign: "Tomorrow the Gaul lottery is extracted."

Victor thought of gaining fortune by buying a lottery ticket, but he had neither money nor any way of obtaining it.

Considering this idea he roamed the streets, and, as that very day the rent on his room would expire, he found refuge in the ruins of an old house near St. Martin for the night.

As the night was dark he lit up the lantern and suddenly he saw, near an old doorjamb, a gold coin from the time of Clovis I.

Siderol was greatly surprised by this, for he had already forgotten about the virtues the Devil had told him were accumulated in this lantern.

He kept the money and early in the morning called for the Devil's help and asked him with humility:

"My dear friend, what are the winning numbers of today's lottery?"

"The five greatest prizes of today," said the Devil, "are the numbers 7, 32, 49, 65 and 81."

"What of the other prizes? Dost thou not know their numbers?"

"I do; but those thou should leave for the poor, do not be ambitious and do not desire everything for thyself."

The farmer was content with Lucifer's answer and went on to buy a ticket. He was given the number 7 and as Siderol paid the store owner laughed with the tone of having just played a great prank.

"Why dost thou laugh in such a way?"

"Because that number will be blank," responded the store owner, laughing louder.

"Really?!... We shall see then!"

And Victor Siderol left the store, bidding the owner goodbye with all cordialities.

True enough, at midday the lottery was extracted and the goddess of fortune followed her decree, for the Devil is always honest in the fulfillment of his duties.

CHAPTER V
Siderol becomes wealthy
on account of the prize he wins

That most fortunate ticket assured him seventy five thousand gold *cunhos*, which corresponded to two hundred and forty *contos de réis*.

When Siderol, in the afternoon, returned to the shop owner he was no longer laughing; he offered Siderol a chair to sit and paid him his prize.

The first thing Victor did was to go out to eat at one of the best restaurants he could find. After dining as a prince he went to the tailor and got himself the best suit he could find, he shaved and, taking up residence in a good hotel, called his benefactor Lucifer.

"What more dost thou wish for?" asked the Devil.

"My friend, where may I find a young damsel who is both pretty and a good lover?"

"In the Greek Theater, where today they are performing a play by Aeschylus," responded the Devil.

The good son of fortune filled his pockets with gold and went to the indicated place. This was the first French theater.

Among the great numbers of people, most of them noblemen, he found there two women, one elderly and the other in the splendor of her youth, whose figure seemed to Siderol to be the most seductive in the world.

He approached them with the wit which only opulence inspires. The young woman received him with great shyness, pretending to be naive, even managing to blush. Victor was extremely satisfied by seeing her with such an honest pose.

He then declared his intentions and she responded with excessive innocence. The old woman, who presented herself as her mother, approached them, and told Siderol that she was delighted with the union of this girl with such a distinct gentleman.

After the play, Siderol, finding himself so well received by both women, offered his arm to the young one, who accepted it without hesitation.

A rich litter awaited them in the vestibule of the theater and as soon as they arrived at their home they invited Siderol to dine with them, serving him with the greatest courtesy and honors.

During dinner Siderol learned that those ladies were actually from the provinces and were in Paris to deal with issues regarding an inheritance. They further told him that the judge in question would certainly not refuse the reception of two thousand *cunhos* of gold to resolve the case in their favor. Victor immediately offered them that amount, but they, however, refused, which made him suspect that they did not believe that he could come through with such an amount.

They eventually conceded, but under the conditions that he would receive a declaration in form, to which he agreed.

The mother went to her office to write the declaration and left our good man with the enchanting Rosa.

Siderol assumed that, after such a loan of two thousand *cunhos* of gold, he could go ahead and take further liberties with this lady, which he did.

The girl firmly resisted him, while at the same time not shunning him entirely. Virtue is always strong against the expansions of vice.

Love and wine, however, had made him resilient and cheeky.

Rosa, incapable of such excesses, which always impact badly upon a woman, was content in blocking many of Siderol's attacks with her hands.

Defending herself from such insistence, she slowly stepped back over her long dress, tripping. Siderol took the opportunity and pushed her softly. She, with such impulse, landed on the sofa, and then... well... only they can confess what happened. The reader can certainly guess, as I for one have some idea of it...

As the poor girl cried he hurried to wipe her tears and, promising to marry her, asked that she tell nothing of what just happened to her mother.

Rosa shrugged her shoulders indicating consent and as the old woman returned she suspected nothing.

Oh, of what good faith she was!

They commenced a new conversation and Siderol invited them to go dine the following day in his company, in the hotel where he was staying, to which they agreed.

He arranged to have a notary there on that night, and during the afternoon bought a jewelry box to offer his bride, on which he was so generous that upon returning home he only had five hundred *cunhos* of gold.

He gave Rosa the jewelry coffer and went to search for the notary, who was late, to finally bind him to the one who had inflamed his senses so.

Mother and daughter bid him goodbye with all courtesies and asked him not to take too long.

CHAPTER VI
How Siderol is fooled by a woman and asks the Devil for help

Victor returned an hour later in the company of the notary.

He joyfully entered the hotel and... no one was to be found! He went about the building, called the hotel manager, asked about the two women and learned that they had left. He had a bad feeling.

He went to his closet and saw that his safe had disappeared with the women, and instead of jewels and gold he found a note in these terms:

"When a smart girl finds an ass and a gullible fool, she plays him; such are the rules. In the future, before thou gets thyself involve in such matters again, thou should study them. We hope thou find this lesson useful."

The unhappy Victor started shouting out against the Devil, who appeared and asked him:

"Was it me, by any chance, who chose that woman for thee?"

"No," responded Siderol.

"Then thou hast no reason to complain to me. For a man to be happy and enjoy my affection, it is necessary that he dost not get himself involved with women of that quality. Tell me: hast thou ever heard of me as being a philanderer?"

"No," answered Victor.

"That is the reason why I can achieve everything I desire. If I was to involve women in my businesses, surely my workings would not come to good fruition."

"But how will I retrieve the diamonds and gold that that ingrate took from me?"

"Thou won't. Money that falls into the hands of adventurous women is like gold enchanted inside the Earth without the knowledge of the words that disenchant it."

"But with all thy power, can thou not make it so as I can get my jewels back?"

"No; like I just told thee, I will have nothing to do with women. And, furthermore, I did not promise thee I would do any work, merely advise."

"Be gone from my sight, damned one! Be gone now if thy power is this limited!"

And as Victor made the sign of the cross ✠ on the floor, the Devil disappeared instantly.

Victor was left to think, and after some minutes remembered the magical lantern, which he could use to once again find some money. But when he searched for it, however, he could not find it for the Devil had taken it with him.

CHAPTER VII
Siderol decides to publish the *Gaul Sorcerer* and other adventures which happened to him after he is released by the Devil

Siderol, finding himself exhausted and with little money, and having learned to predict the future in the *Grimoire of St. Cyprian*, decided to write and publish the *Gaul Sorcerer* in Paris, in the place where today is St. Jacques Street.

An astrologer assured him that he would be able to sell many copies and win great amounts of money if he were to fill the book with many diabolical things.

Siderol began then to write divinations for the future, predictions, days when important people of the Church were to die, and as a consequence the bishop decided to have him arrested, preparing a grill so as to roast him for *the love of God*.

Victor, filled with dread, called once again for Lucifer, and, after begging for much forgiveness, asked to be saved from that peril, something that the Devil refused.

"What then, infernal spirit, is the art of divination good for if I cannot escape persecution?"

"I told thee where rivers of gold were to be found, why did thou get thyself involved with women, and why did thou write those predictions, all instead of digging for treasure? And who told thee to play in the lottery?"

"And who was it that invented it, just as all other games of chance?"

"It was me," responded the Devil.

"And for what end?"

"To mortify the souls of those with vices, so as they may find their ends quicker and I can take possession of them sooner."

"If that is the case, then it is thee who drives all homicide, patricide and robbery?"

"What? Thou dost not yet know the mighty and dangerous hand which drags the whole of the human race to all excesses! Gambling never brought happiness to anyone! Go, go dig the lands I told thee, and take those treasures, for they are thine. But if they are to be of any use thou must never gamble again. Come now, march! Beyond old Toletum[98] thou shall find gold upon gold and then thou shall see how fortunate it was to make a pact with me."

And the Devil opened the door to his cell.

Victor left. He crossed the Pyrenees and in fifty-two days reached Barjacova. In the passage of Valladolid to the kingdom of Galicia he felt extremely tired and noticed his shoes no longer had any soles.

He then called his spirit and told him:

"I am barefoot and hungry; give me shoes and something to eat."

The Devil appeared to him, and, pointing his finger into the distance asked him:

"Dost thou see, there, in the distance, that village among some trees?"

"I do."

"It is called Santiguoso; go towards it and thou shall find some food on top of a large rock. Fill thy stomach and walk to the North, for fortune is there waiting for thee."

"But I cannot walk, dear Lucifer; give me some shoes."

"No."

"Why not, infernal spirit, dost thou not have the power to arrange for something of so little worth?"

"I do."

"So?"

"Listen carefully," said the Devil. "The God which thou worshiped, before thou gave thyself to me, did he not say to the human race 'by the sweat of thy brow will thou have food to eat'?"

"He did; but I do not wish to earn my living as such. I would rather unearth the treasures thou pointed me towards."

"Very well. Your old God is the King of the Heavens and I am the King of the Hells. He gives laws to his subjects and I give laws to mine. For thou to enjoy my protection it is necessary to make some sacrifices. Go now to thy destiny, for to achieve this venture it will be good for thee to go through the martyrdom of walking barefoot."

"Very well, give me thy blessing."

The Devil blessed him and the villager went on his way, barefoot.

---

98. Original footnote: Toledo.

CHAPTER VIII
How Siderol, starving, asks for the Devil's help and sets out seeking for treasure

After some days marching North he arrived at Bembibre, always finding food by evoking the name of the Devil, the owner of his soul.

In this place, however, no matter how much he called, the Devil would not appear, and hunger was torturing him terribly. He walked towards the direction of the River Camba and found a tall stone cross ✠ covered with moss and vines.

As he beheld the symbol of Christ's suffering, he stopped and trembled. He then once again called the Devil, asking for something to eat. As no answer came to him he was ready to fall on his knees at the cross, when he felt a rush of fire against his face.

Victor, under the weight of such pain, fell to the earth. As he got up again, after a few minutes, he looked around but saw no one.

"Such is the punishment for wanting to abandon me," said the Devil. "Damn thee! Is it with this doubt that thou wishes to reach the places where treasures rest and disenchant them?"

"Forgiveness, forgiveness, god Lucifer, I was, and am, so hungry!"

"Did I not tell thee already, oh false friend, that in my law it is also necessary to have patience? I did not feed thee so as to test thy courage. Go, then, to thy destiny and do not betray me again, or else..."

The Devil vanished and the former farmer carried on in his path, offering himself further to his infernal protector.

Close to midnight he found a table by the roadside, filled with delicacies, and had his fill. Having finished the meal he offered himself again to the Devil and said:

"Had I another soul I would gladly give it to that great lord of Hell!"

The great Lucifer appeared to him again in person, dressed in the same way as he was in *Neuilly*, back when Victor had given him a black hen, and hugging him, said:

"Since thou art so much of my friend I would not have thee tire thyself any more. Tell me, art thou very ambitious?"

"No; what I wish is for a treasure that will allow me to live the rest of my life without working. Nothing more."

"Dost thou see that village, in that clearing, that goes as far as that hill?" asked the Devil.

"I see it perfectly."

"Then thou shall not need to go any further. That village is called Ababides. Go there; find a place to stay and tomorrow, around this same time, go up the hill and light up our lantern. At that time thou shall prick thy pinky finger with this spike made of horn I give thee now."

And Lucifer broke off his spike and gave it to Siderol.

"And then?" he asked.

"Then thou will sign this document with thine own blood..."

"But I have already given thee my soul; what more is there in me that might be pleasant and useful to thee, my good protector?"

"Listen carefully. In this paper thou declares the sale of the souls of thy children, who will be born when thou acquires wealth. For thou shall marry a woman very much given to procreation."

"But..."

"Thou hesitate? Will thou sign it or not?"

"I will. But... what next?"

"At midnight, as I said, a raven will stop by that mountain. At the place where he digs and picks at the floor is the first treasure located."

"But with which words will I make the bosom of the earth open itself?"

"I will not tell them to thee yet, for I fear that the earth might swallow thee if I do. Come now, march on."

CHAPTER IX
The curious story in which Siderol sells his unborn children's souls, so as the Devil would allow him to find a treasure

Victor followed everything that the Devil, his lord, had instructed him to do.

Arriving at the mount of Ababides, at midnight of the following day, he waited, and a few minutes later he saw a black raven land on a large rock. Siderol dug and pricked at the ground with the spike the Devil gave him but the earth remained as it was, without the slightest hint of movement.

Victor then lit up his lantern and still everything remained as it was. Desperate, he walked slowly towards the bird, which, seeing him come closer, took to flight and left.

Our man started speaking out against the Devil, demanding that he either give him the power to open the earth or give him back his soul.

The Devil then appeared in the figure of a raven and said to him:

"What did we agree on? Was it not settled that thou would sign at this time the donation for thy children's souls with thine own blood?"

"Forgive me great lord!" begged Siderol. "Forgive me for I had forgotten."

And, as a continuous motion, he pricked his pinky finger and signed the deed with blood.

The Devil, with great satisfaction told him:

"I take my leave now. Take all the gold thou desires."

And, by taking flight, disappeared.

Victor remained still, not knowing what to do, staring in the direction the bird had disappeared.

Suddenly he heard, in the midst of all that loneliness, these words;

Aurea Hispania! Hiscere Gallaecos Romano!

At that moment the mountain shook, opening an enormous crack, and Siderol saw a great deal of golden Roman coins, and, as he went down that hole, it closed behind him.

He took off his jacket to fill it with money, but, all of the sudden, he saw a great brass coffer, open, full of the precious metal. He placed it on his shoulders and, as he was about to leave, he suddenly noticed that the mountain had closed. He had been made a prisoner.

Victor started to cry and shout, placing the coffer on top of some piles of gold.

"My St. Devil, my powerful king, owner of my soul and my unborn children's souls, free me from this prison!" he said in tears.

Suddenly, he felt the earth once again tremble in great convolutions, and heard in the cave the following words:

Hispania! Regicitur in publicum janua!

The great cave once again opened and Siderol found himself on the mountain-top with his coffer of golden coins.

He walked the rest of the night, and, at daybreak, he found himself in the settlement of Damil, further up North.

He rented a room in a poor inn for eight days, remaining barefoot and badly dressed so as not to raise suspicions and avoid robbery.

By the end of the eight days he heard that in the suburbs of that place there was a house for sale. He then called the Devil and consulted with him:

"What dost thou think about this place? I like these neighbors and I could very well live here."

"That is indeed fair," answered the Devil, "neither me nor the enchanted spirits would allow thee to take all that gold to any far away land."

"Why not?" asked Siderol.

"In Spain thou received it; in Spain thou shall enjoy it. In this region there are many beautiful and virtuous women, capable of teaching morality to the French ones, as also capable of teaching about love to that little Rosa thou met at the Greek theater. Thou would do well in staying here."

"Very well then, I will," responded Siderol.

"I bless thee then, and be happy."

Lucifer, after blessing him, rapidly disappeared.

Siderol, taking some gold coins, set his path to the town of Allariz, in search of a priest who could exchange that ancient money. Returning the following day he bought that house and made up his residence there.

CHAPTER X
The strange illness of Siderol,
which struck him after he was married
and had given the soul of his first child
to the Devil

Victor Siderol then began to understand the happiness money can bring, for he started to enjoy all things he desired, and, as fame of his wealth quickly ran through those lands, he became the target of the attentions of both men and women.

As women had always been his preference, he started analyzing them with care, and it so happened that, after a few months, he was married to a beautiful maiden from Podentes. The name of this interesting peasant girl was Manuela.

A year had passed, and she had given birth to a little girl, whose soul the Devil immediately counted as his own.

Her parents rejoiced in such a little angel, and every day they loved her more. But, as wealth is not always the sole thing in life, the Frenchman one day found himself gravely ill.

This was a violent fever, accompanied by hallucinations, which struck him so fast that he didn't even had time to consult with the Devil.

His father-in-law called two doctors and placed at his bedside the most famous nurse which lived in the region.

Maybe due to all these cares his fever broke remarkably and Victor once again regained his senses.

He then took the opportunity to better know of his condition and consulted with the Devil, calling him and asking:

"Dear Lucifer, how did my doctors tend to my illness?"

"The wrong way."

"Is it deadly?"

"No."

"What should I do to heal it?"

"Get rid of the doctors and let nature do its work, for only it has control over the life and death of humanity."

He did as he was told. Nature healed him, although his recovery was long. During this time, however, Siderol had the chance to get to know the good heart of beautiful Manuela, whose presence never disappeared from his bedside.

CHAPTER XI
The sadness of Siderol,
after ten years of happy marriage,
when he realized that he had sold the souls
of his eight children

Manuela was an extremely well educated damsel, made as the graces and as joyful as them. She was a sensitive, frank and joyful girl, a woman as he very much needed, for an honorable and wealthy man very much needs a prudent and sensitive companion.

Siderol, after being completely healed of his illness, asked the Devil how to repay his wife for all her attentions.

"Hast thou not given her thy hand?" asked the Devil.

"I did."

"Dost thou not love her dearly?"

"I do."

"Then thou hast already paid her well enough."

Ten years passed in uninterrupted harmony, and Manuela had just given birth to her eighth son.

Victor, lulled by the commodities of wealth and the charms of his three girls and five boys, was enchanted with his fortune and almost forgot the donations he had given the Devil.

But one day, feeling the crackling of lightning over his head, between the booming of thunders, he was reminded of dark memories, which flooded his imagination and poisoned all of his delights.

He then realized that he had bought all such sweet pleasures with his damnation. That he had paid for his earthly life the highest possible price! From that day on he was always unhappy and meditative and Manuela felt his sorrow even worse, for she did not know what caused it.

Her most tender cares, her most feverous pleas could not extract the reason for such sadness from him.

Siderol wished to know if the eternal fire would light up for him only at the end of his old age, or if death was in any way imminent.

He would ask the Devil when he was destined to die, for having his soul already lost, and even if he was not ambitious, he would like to at least enjoy the satisfaction of disenchanting the treasures which the Devil had told him about.

CHAPTER XII
Siderol tells his wife the reason of his great sadness

Siderol was considering such things, when, suddenly, his wife Manuela with tears in her eyes and complaints on her lips, accused him of not loving her, for he would not tell her his secret.

Would he be silent if the secret was of a different nature? Would he not trust it with his wife who would surely sweeten such bitterness?

Surely not.

Manuela would not take such silence and continued to insist upon it, until Siderol found it necessary to confess, filled with great regret, that he had made a pact with the Devil.

Manuela, who had been educated as a proper Christian, trembled and ran away, saying that she did not wish to live with a damned man. She feared damnation was transmittable and that she would also become one if she lived in that place with him.

She was young and naive, without any experience in such worldly things, and as such, went to tell her mother about it, unto whom her confessor had advised her to always place her absolute trust.

Her mother, who was not so easily frightened, said that it could not be possible that such a kind man was indeed damned, and that Siderol certainly wasn't.

The good Manuela insisted and the old Galician woman said that, should it be true, she would find a way to resolve this issue.

Having said that, she thought that the holy priest of Campo de Moura, a faraway place, should go there, place his stole over Siderol's head and recite the gospel of John, for the tip of a stole has a prodigious power. If you further add three or four exorcisms, willingly or not, the Devil would surely return those contracts.

The old woman sent a servant on horseback to call the old priest, who lived in Cobello, and who immediately came to make the banishment for Siderol.

But the Devil, who is always alert, does not allow such important interests to go unnoticed, and a soul that belongs to him does not easily escape his grasp.

Observing all the preparations meant to rob him of what was rightfully his, he told Siderol that if he returned to the Church he would immediately fall into the pits of Hell!

To this threat Siderol started shouting and crying, to which his mother-in-law immediately responded by placing a vial of holy water inside his pocket, ordering him to never take it out.

Manuela, with her known sincerity, thought that it would be convenient if she was to read at that time the Gospel, for it would surely be very unpleasant for her husband to be in that feverish state.

CHAPTER XIII
How Siderol, with the aid of his wife, managed to rescue his soul and his children's souls

They left in the direction of the church. The Devil, in a fury, for he saw the danger he was in of losing Siderol's soul, flew around him, but the virtue of the holy water did not permit him to come closer, and Siderol's mother-in-law laughed at his helpless rage.

Upon arriving at the church, the priest counteracted enchantment with enchantment, and the damned Siderol started to foam from the mouth and contort his arms and legs; his mouth stretched from ear to ear and, after these typical muscle contortions, the Devil dropped the deeds at the feet of the altar. For Victor's Guardian Angel appeared at that time, over the head of the exorcised, with blond hair, blue wings and white robes.

The priest, at the end of the exorcism, confessed Victor, for he now had the permission to absolve him, seeing as he had just been ripped away from Satan's claws.

They finished the ceremony and returned home. Manuela no longer feared the contact with her husband and slept with him in the same bed where they had always laid.

They continued on living in wealth, thanks to the treasure Siderol unburied with the power of the Devil, who he ended up tricking with the protection of the Holy Church.

Siderol, after a happy existence, gave his soul to his Maker in a villa he had bought in Sabajares, at the age of 108 years, leaving his wife with seven children, eleven grandchildren and three great-grandchildren.

CHAPTER XIV
The illusion of happiness, or the envy over that which one does not possess

The people of the village, upon learning of the way by which Siderol had become wealthy and, wanting to imitate him, would sometimes say to Manuela:

"Oh, if I could only divinate this, predict that, how happy I would be!"

Manuela always responded:

"All that is easy, one only needs to do as my husband did, but beware of the Devil's cunnings."

"But he has many treasures under his great power!" responded back the many curious folk.

"Surely, he does," answered Manuela. "I am not telling thee not to make a pact with him, but as soon as thou have obtained thy goal arm thyself with holy water, and throw thyself into the arms of the Holy Church so as to enter into the Kingdom of Glory."

"But, why did thy husband not disenchant more treasures?" they would ask.

"Because he did not need them. He said that in this country there were many poor people who could use to do that."

And, if someone takes possession of those goods, let God forgive him the sin of having made a pact with Satan. Amen.

Manuela, not being able to stand the absence of her husband, expired three months later, the day after she completed 94 years of age.

TREASURES OF GALICIA

EXTRACTED FROM

A SCROLL FOUND IN THE XIITH CENTURY

The precious scroll we are publishing here for the first time, was found in the foundations of the Moorish castle of D. Guttierre de Altamira, in the year of 1065, during the time when D. Fernando the Great, King of Leon, gave the dominion of Galicia to his son Garcia.

Today this scroll can be found in Barcelona, in the *Biblioteca Académica Peninsular Catalani*, of D. Gumerzindo Ruiz Castillejo y Moreno, shelf n°76-A, where it can be consulted by all the curious who request it. We here provide a faithful copy of the original, translated into our language.

IMPORTANT EXPLANATION

All the treasures and enchantments of the ancient kingdom of Galicia were deposited there by the *Mouros* and Romans in underground hiding places. The large majority of them, as the scroll declares, are located at little distance from water springs which conserve a continuous flow even under the harshest heat.

This action by the *Mouros* and Roman indicates that, as these peoples were expelled from those territories after the wars enacted there, they hoped to one day return and establish themselves there once again. For this reason they left part of their belongings hidden there, fearing that they would be sacked by the invading legions.

Many sections of the mentioned scroll were damaged by the wear of the centuries and as such are not easily understood; but surely the intelligent reader will be able to decipher their meaning and translate what was impossible for us due to the ancientness of the language.

Still, from the previous editions of this book we have, by careful study, made several corrections and clarifications to many obscure points (but not all, unfortunately), as the curious reader may very well observe by comparing different editions.

NOTE: Although the legend you have just read, featuring Siderol and the Devil, seems to bear some relation to the treasures we are about to publish, we cannot affirm its authenticity, for we do not have the gift of divination.

That many hidden treasures exist is a proven fact, for chance has discovered a great deal of them; but we remind our readers that this information may both come from sure facts as from visionary absenteeism.

We make these declarations for, as the disbelieving disciple of Christ, we have as our motto: SEEING IS BELIEVING.

THE COLLECTOR

†

TRIANGLE

TO

DISENCHANT THE TREASURES

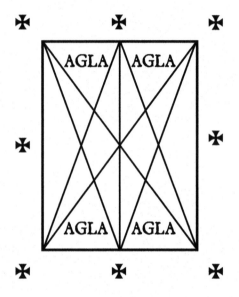

†

The orisons, banishments, litanies and all other instructions for the disenchantment of treasures can be found in the first part of this book.

It is for this reason that we do not repeat them here.

RELATION OF THE TREASURES AND ENCHANTMENTS[99]

(EXTRACTED FROM THE SCROLL)

1. At the crossroad of Lobios, thirty-two steps towards the sunrise, under a stream of little flow, there is a stone pot with an *abada*[100] of gold.

2. At thirty-two men from Louro, Riba, inside a rock, twenty-two hands deep, we have placed 500 *cunhos* from the year of 812.

3. In Loredo there are many silver ingots, from the crucibles of Vimaranes.

4. In Revolta, three cubits[101] from the road of Sabajares, at three men, are the jewels of the family of Numa Caspio, and the headless body of a Suebi.

5. In Queda, there is a gold treasure of 700 *fakirs*[102], in the riverbed by the side of the setting Sun of Padroso.

6. On the hunting grounds of count Mora, in the enclosure of Padran, to the South, inside a fallen rock, there are two treasures of great wealth; two men deep.

7. In Portella, in the cork oak field of Outeirinho, there is a vase of silver and gold.

8. In Refojo de Teba, in the residence of Friar Themudo, we left an amount of silver in the mud.

9. In Bardian, at the head of the house of D. Sisnando de Logronho, there is an ox of gold, without any weapons, at two men deep.

10. At the edge of the cross, in Padrela, between two pine trees, there are twelve gold palms, in sheets.

11. On the shady side of the Oroso, there sleeps, hidden, the money of the Grande Homem de Altamira.

12. In Longoares, under the bridge, between the stone lanes, there is an ink pot of solid silver.

13. In the spring of Riba de Via, thou shall hear the sound of metal tingling, and by breaking the stone thou shall see it.

14. In the black rock of Outero, we have deposited, in the year of 704, three baskets of silver, taken from a general.

15. At 46 paces from S. Bento, near Portello de Isno, a silver horse broken on his left side, filled with old coins.

16. In the mound of Fraga, after three passagings of the shade, thou shall find a pair of oxen made of gold with jeweled finishes.

---

99. Translator's note: do consult the commentaries on this list of treasures.

100. Translator's note: either an old unit of measure I have not been able to determine or it might actually be a golden rhinoceros.

101. Translator's note: uncertain translation.

102. Translator's note: I am uncertain if what is meant here is actually *fakirs*, as in Sufi ascetics, or if this is some old unit of measure I am unfamiliar with.

17. In the cave of Fonte Fria, right in the middle, a pot filled with random gold pieces.

18. In Bouças, behind the church, when the Sun is at the highest, we have left a treasure of mixed gold pieces.

19. In Molone, in the stream of the northern spring, at two men, thou shall find a cork bark with some noble possessions.

20. In the climb of Leirado, near the water, thou shall find a great golden plough.

21. In the underground path of Castelo de Mondarim, at twenty paces towards the sunrise, two men deep, a bucket of copper filled with medals from the time of the Celts.

22. In Gallinho, in front of the Lusa, there are two mushrooms of fireless gold, under the cross by the road.

23. In the Solar dos Nobres, in Angade, near the movable metal ring, there is an uncovered vat of gold.

24. In the path coming from the Barbantinho, going east, thirteen steps from the corner of the wall, we buried the rings of D. Ramiro.

25. After Melananha, 28 men in the direction of the Sun, we have left a castle of great worth near the lower stone of a small bridge under 13 palms of earth.

26. Over the Pico da Portela there are, in a narrow ditch, 243 gold *maravedis*[103] minted in Toledo.

27. In Fontinha de Alariz, there are 25 Lusitanian vases in a bed of clay mixed with oil of green olives.

28. Under the basin of the church of Segalvo, we buried, three men deep, a monstrance made of gold and diamonds.

29. In the cork oak field of Moniz Paio, on the upper side, in the dusk of sunset, we hid a large board from the ox cart of Sertorius, made of gold from Baetica by Alvares Torga.

30. In the gate of Bertraces, near Rendo Perdilho, there are two gold spears with a wigless partridge.

31. Not too high in the spring of Monte do Ramo River, at sunrise, at the sixth hour of May, there is a hiding place with 17 silver pine cones, which were taken from the wealthy Verino Guterre de Pinar.

32. In the cave of Prado, between the four round boulders, we have left 900 crossbow men of Santiago, made of silver.

33. In the mountain range of S. Mamede, at the northern tip, as thou goes down, there is the inheritance of the noblemen of Chrisus.

34. In the Castle of Sobogido, hidden in the shadows, there is a lead pot filled with gold powder.

---

103. Translator's note: an ancient Iberian coin, first minted by the Almoravid dynasty.

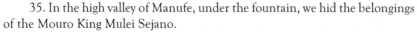

35. In the high valley of Manufe, under the fountain, we hid the belongings of the Mouro King Mulei Sejano.

36. In Farcadella, neighboring Lusitania, 22 men to the South of the fountain, there are 107 doubloons of gold from Granada.

37. Near the Quintão, in the third boulder, there is a treasure of over one thousand gold *maravedis*.

38. In the left alley of Burcia, to the east, near the people's spring, there is the gold deposit of the rich man Abduzil of Cordova.

39. On the road from Sobroso to Cobello, we left, right near the earth's surface an amount of silver extracted from Leon.

40. In the front of the Mosque of Confurco, we buried our king's water basins, made of black clay.

41. At the lookout point of the fountain of Camoz, we placed, while escaping, a rough iron pot with an uncertain amount of Roman coins.

42. In Tornellos, at 303 paces from Mirandella, there is a reel of gold with six men of rope made from this same metal.

43. In the great cross of Castro Marigo, at the right, in the direction of the sunset, under the floor, among the white stones, we laid a gold armor with 12 chain mails.

44. In the spring of Larôa, we have a gold bed, made from one-man-long boards.

45. On the slope of Villarinho, looking in the direction of the sunrise where the gullies cross, we have buried the belongings of our neighbors, inside three stone caves under the gully.

46. We have left an arm-full[104] of unminted gold in the crack of Flariz, twelve men deep.

47. On the floor of the church of Pinoe, 71 paces towards the Sun, under the olive tree, there should be two mill poles of gold and diamonds.

48. In Orilhe, at the break of the three roads, we have placed an altar of gold with all its tools and a silver idol from the Mouro kings of Granada.

49. On the narrow path out of Podentes, by the side of the Sun, under the ground, we have covered a ditch with 25 shovelfuls of gold.

50. In Meã, to the side of the ditches, we left, at three men deep, the tools of the black bishop.

51. In the hunting grounds of Amorim there is the silver of Ataulfo Cerdo, by the roots of a strawberry tree.

52. In Fontarcada, between the wall, at five spears[105], we hid a treasure of jewels belonging to the black priestess.

---

104. Translator's note: the actual word here is *braçado*, which refers to the amount you can carry by circling something with one or both arms.

105. Translator's note: I assume this is a unit of length I am not familiar with.

53. In the ledge of the Villaça tower, we have an encampment of gold dogs minted in Logronho.

54. Near the small cypress of Ninho de la Aguila, at two men, we buried a golden gate which used to be the gate of Pelagio.

55. In Infantes Novos, in the black sand bed, there is a brass drum full of silver butterflies.

56. In the bosom of Ababides, rests the belongings of ten Mouro parties together with the bones of three girls, killed by the southern invaders.

57. In Marmontelhos, at 21 paces from the Penado Espalmo, there is a horse rider with a gold saddle and bridle and diamond encrusted horseshoes.

58. In the sharp edge of Villa-Rei, near the round well, we have placed a polished board cover and filled a silver pit with dull effigies.

59. In the middle of the Castelo de Pazos, very deep, there is a gold mine guarded by a living calf. If thou wishes for the treasure do not touch the calf.

60. In the spring of Tebra, in the direction of the shade, there are the enchanted belongings of a warrior and seven pairs of gold daggers.

61. In the bolder of Entrevides, near the olive trees of Sotacabo, there is the dowry of the Moura Zulama, wife of King Trafil.

62. In the two boulders of Reiril, while coming down from the cliff, at 104 paces from the chestnut tree, we buried a cradle of silver with gold finishing and smoky curtains.

63. In Banhos, in the stream of the shallow creek, there is a great treasure of the kings of Segovia and their subjects, mixed in blood.

64. In Becerroz, to the southeast, 22 men towards the mount, there is a valuable enchantment of gold and men of war with rich armors from the time of Crudencio.

65. In S. Torquato, below the small bridge, there is the idol of Calmar made with gold from Rigo with diamond drapes.

66. In the direction of Cruzaens, we have placed, under an arch of white stone, a noble dowry and we engraved a man's arm on the cover.

67. While leaving Monferey, by the side of the rising Sun, in the curve of a water stream, we have left the valuables of the fearful one of Calatrava, inside a hollow silver calf with a broken left leg.

68. In Traz de Estrada, under the tip of the Cabeço Alto, where there is a flooded mine, there is a great treasure of gold and silver.

69. In the Bibey River, near a dog made of black stone, we have placed, in a closed box, the diamonds of Selva, killed while leaving Soutomór in the direction of Arenoso.

70. In the conch of Rande, near the island where the waves crash at the eleventh hour of the Sunrise, there is a great treasure between two great stones.

71. In the top of Enteza, near the southern wall in front of a corral, there are the belongings of a Mouro.

72. By going down the narrow path of the cork oak field in the direction

of Martiohan, there are four oaks, at 62 paces North there is an iron box with a golden horse head and three silver prayer stands, with open axis, inside.

73. Between the wall of the Rebordono, near a cross that was dug into the large stone, we have the movable possessions of 114 neighbors who ran to the Asturias in 709.

74. In Praça Teiroso, at 276 paces from the new chapel in the direction of the rising Sun, there is a vase of gold in lumps, inside a stone bowl.

75. At the end of Torneiros, thirty paces in the direction of the midday Sun, there is a twelve square arm-wide canopy in which we deposited all the possessions of the fleeing people.

76. In the small creek of Amerim, over the black stone dams, there is a two wheel cart with brass finishes filled with gold coins. In this place there is an enchanted man holding a rod; do not kill him if thou desires this treasure. Say to him: *"By the power of the Mouro gold I plead to thee to join the Mouros, thy relatives, and leave me in happiness."*

77. On the side of the Sun, on the oratorio of Ouega, fourteen paces from the pier, there is a countless amount of gold. On the shadowy part is where the dead from Carabellos were buried.

78. On the lower edge of Peinera, at the core of a hollowed chestnut tree, we placed 300 gold doubloons with equally printed faces.

79. To the South of Franqueira, 19 men along, in the peak of Altinho, in a cork oak field, is the Mouro Bisnarém, enchanted, laying over gold and wearing shoes riveted with jewels from the crown of a Goth king.

80. In the fountain of Chamusinhos, in the sand, we have buried a large vat of chiseled silver which is worth 3000 doubloons. This vat has six small corners and four larger ones engraved with metal of little value. More to the bottom there is a heather of white metal.

81. Between two large rocks in the height of Louressa, we have left a caldron filled with gold and feces, covered with stone.

82. In Unna, where two cart paths cross, there is, four men deep, the belongings of the queen, wife of Beppo II.

83. Buried at 110 paces from Mixas, in the shortcut to Infesta, there is a box of Roman wealth, with a landmark over it.

84. In the edge of Requias, we left a hole covered by hard clay, half filled with silver and gold.

85. In Tozende, on the mount from where water flows in December, there is the wealth of a lord from Compostella.

86. In the triplet[106] of Montécel, on the path of Gironda, in a wall covered by vines, we dislodged five stones and placed inside it the objects of greatest value we had in our party.

---

106. Translator's note: very uncertain translation, this might also be a reference to a crossroad of three paths.

87. In Osono, in the golden fountain, we placed, two men below the grass, a treasure of coins from Mirim de Lugo, in the quantity of six thousand valuable gold doubloons, in a box of tiles.

88. On the path of Freira, twelve men along from the square stone, we left a vat with 2000 coins of Lobo Bañas.

89. In Villar da Velha, on the right side of Canda, at twenty-five paces, there is the usury of the wealthy of Lanhezes, made of silver.

90. In the ditch of Cadabos, at twenty men from the valley, in the direction of the mountain, we have the belongings of Zupellino Castelan.

91. In Santegoso, three arms deep on the side of the fountain, there is the gold and silver of the King Pampe Raby.

92. In Freixo Luviano, three hands from the heathers, we have a *lasco* of *perenhas*, another of *petranhas* and another of *ambanas* with 104 rooms of gold without fire.[107]

93. In Pias, in the direction of the setting Sun, there is, barely buried, and with a lot of stones on top of it, a Mourish coffer with the possessions of three companies and with some crosses marked on its lid.

94. In Xaguasos, on the river shore, between two trees, we left the belongings of Lebrun IV, made up of strong gold with *mentigas rupicans de bazano si cuentas austaas, por lá quanta sin nó á manado com las manos, y si queda fusco de prudiencia estrana. Teneémos a de más cientos de nonas oureas com blagas embarances de la monasterio com gran toso y rumo*[108].

95. In Lobanços, to the South, inside a moss-covered wall where a creek passes through to the grasses[109], three hands deep, there is a golden sow with her piglets.

96. In the drains of Hermezendo, we have a box of diamond jewels, worth four villages.

97. In Fontes, while thou art passing to the province of Brácara, we have left the legacy of the Restaurador, all made from unmarked gold. It is in the gravel, when the Sun hits it at the seventh hour.

98. In the village of Paramoz, at the crossroad of the path of Mil Fontes, we have buried a great treasure of silver, inside a barrel of laurel wood.

99. In Parada, twenty-eight paces after the church in the direction of the Sun, there are the belongings of a wealthy man from Bayona.

100. In S. Julião, after Oia, we have the belongings of a nobleman who ruled over all and drowned in Panjon.

---

107. Translator's note: This one is clearly a riddle, even more so than all the others.

108. Original footnote: We apologize to the reader the improper interpretation of this passage, for we do not understand the significance of some terms which appear in various parts of this manuscript.

109. Translator's note: Here what is actually meant are plants of the true grass family, *Poaceae*.

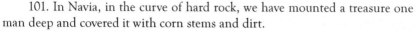

101. In Navia, in the curve of hard rock, we have mounted a treasure one man deep and covered it with corn stems and dirt.

102. In the middle of the cross of Ganhado, there is a gold ryegrass[110] and two halberds, under a stone with a horse's leg marked on it.

103. Under the cross of Curul, there is a stone grave filled with gold, and the crown of King Zolito VI.

104. On the big slope going down, twenty-five men along the wall of Souto Maior, there is a great amount of gold.

105. In the mill of Caldellas, there is a clay vase with 270 gold coins, with imprints on both faces.

106. In Intrimo, by passing the chestnut tree field, eight paces from the chain, there is a standing enchanted Mouro, with his value in gold at his feet. Leave this spirit alive so as thou may take his enchantment.

107. In S. Pedro Martyr, there is an amount of silver in the path facing the sunrise.

108. In Gondamar, near the Penedo de dois Bicos, we buried the loot of the Celtic warriors killed in Antemoz.

109. In the height of Feis, in the direction of the sea, in the crossroad, there are the treasures of a wealthy church.

110. At twenty-three men from the house of Phebus, in Arneu, to the North, in the middle of the cliffs, there are eight tiles of gold.

111. At the gates of Teste, eight men from the great stone with Celtic letters, there are the possessions of a king and an Arabic book containing the treasures of Tolosa and Castile.

112. Below Ramalhesa, among the yellow lemon trees, we hid the possessed man of Senapio, five days after this barbarian was burned.

113. Between Rubiãs and Manini, near an arch of stone and clay, there are the gold possessions of a Lusitanian from Gerez.

114. In the oratory of Gironda, fifteen men towards the small path, there is a small treasure.

115. In Famaguellos, in the three boulders, there is a dark clay pot with valuables inside.

116. In Lorrios, between two small landmarks, we have left a gold bench four feet long.

117. In Valgeras, under a ditch, there is a sword with a silver blade and a jeweled handle.

118. In Tabagon, in the Rochedo da Terceira Escada, three men deep, there is a board filled with gold coins, inside a boulder of seven arms' length.

119. In the narrow path of Salados, in the lower corral, facing North, there is a small boat buried containing a conch filled with money.

---

110. Translator's note: uncertain translation.

120. In the enclosure of Gondarem, over the narrow path, three men towards the shade, we placed the belonging of our people in Tolho.

121. In the blessing basin of Sendolho, in the corner of the lower wall, there is a coffin of coins covered with gravel.

122. In the churchyard of Cheleiros, in the water basin of the fountain, near the cypress to the North, we have dug up a great wealth.

123. In Pedorne, ten men from the sandy spring, there is a young Mouro boy enchanted among diamonds from Lerida.

124. In Arzua, in front of the coarse patch, half way around, there is a... no... pa... ast... in... bras dark[111].

125. In the enclosure of Corcubião, on the lower side, where there is some very sticky clay, there on the ground, four men deep, a kitchen of silver and copper.

126. In Saboadella, much lower, in a mine with two white slabs of marble, there are the rich possessions of princess Urraca.

127. In the cork oak field of Ortigana, on the upper side, we have the tools of the renegade from the Asturias, on the third arch, where there is a hollow sound coming from the ground when it rains.

128. In Eunae, by going over the small gate leading to the fountain, there is a very great treasure.

129. In Cella, there is a small amount of gold, three men deep.

130. In Gormezim, while leaving in the direction of the landmarks, we have placed twenty-five swords with gold finishes.

131. On the path leading to Meaus, near some slabs, there are the possessions of five warriors, killed in Cantabria.

132. We have left, in the slope of Feces, our possessions, in the white dirt, and we plated over it a *taleigo*[112] of acorns.

133. In the valley of Monzalvos, two men under, among the five boulders there is the possessed of Cadabos.

134. Between Morisco and Castreto, along the two rises, five men from the small oak tree, we have placed the jewels of the marquis of Orrios.

135. In the floor of the Fonte do Rei, coming from Mairos, a hundred paces towards the sunrise and five men deep, there is a slab fortified with iron, with the treasures of the mosque of Rosal.

136. In Cendelha, among the boulders in the middle, from where a stream with water which tastes like iron springs up, there is a treasure consisting of a great deal of coins.

---

111. Original footnote: At this point, the scroll is unreadable.

112. Translator's note: an old unit of measure for liquids and cereals, corresponding to four *alqueires*, (from the Arabic *al kayl*) another old measurement with values oscillating between 13 and 19 liters, depending on the region.

137. In the corner of Salto Real, four men under the gutters, there is a box of tax money in small coins.

138. In Guilhade, sixty paces from the new path, towards the shade of the oak trees, thou shall find a small treasure.

139. On the rise of Piconha, on the left side, on a patch of sand, we left some leftover silver and two crucibles of gold.

140. On the side of the rising sun in Gargamalla, around the path, we left the robe and tools of a young priest.

141. In the rock where one beats the clothes on the Arnoia River, two men deep, we placed, in a ditch, Amenil Zeta with his wife and the possessions of both of them.

142. In the lower part of Comiar, there is a treasure of 300 doubloons in an open coffin.

143. We have left a treasure of little worth in Gandaras. The rocks around it smell like sulfur.

144. Inside Bouça Branca, we have five treasures hidden. We do not know if they were kept there.

145. In Cangas, at the four oaks, there is a treasure of one hundred doubloons of silver. During the day the Sun hits it through a very sharp rock.

146. In the breach of Anceu, we buried a treasure with little gold. There is a lot of silver, blade weapons and painted porcelain.

147. We used the hole of Freixo to hide a... ta... e... te to... bo... one... gal... dou...[113]

148. Towards the sunset in Outeirello, in a well of seven gutters, in front of a boulder, at the corner, there are the possessions of Abdel.

149. We dug the earth near the stairs of the cross of Foçará, and we placed at the South the loot of S. Lourenço.

150. We have the inheritance of Moura Trebinka in the outskirts of Moscoso. It is in the flood lands to the North, near a small olive tree and a male chestnut tree.

151. In Gulanes, near the yellow rock, we dug up the possessions of priest Ataulfo, of Vigo.

152. In Arenté, at the midday Sun in the mount, on the two walls, there is a valuable box.

153. Dig in the cave of Teu-tão and thou shall find the treasure we have left.

154. On the two paths, in Atios, under the black grape vines, there is a good amount. Do not bother thyself with the iron thou sees around there.

155. We left Limia and dumped many treasures in the mine of Penedo Rachado.

---

113. Original footnote: This scroll is greatly damaged; some letters have completely vanished. The reader should resolve the meaning of the missing words with some meditation.

156. In the noble houses of Lira, we left the treasure of the *almocreve* Zeniga. Leave the cross and take all the remaining gold.

157. Around Santo Adrião, walk facing the Sun and where the earth is covered with moss there is a great treasure.

158. To the left of the pointy stones, while going up the cork oak field of Lanhas, under a large cave, thou shall find the belongings of the Lamazos. Pray some orisons for their souls.

159. In Ortigueira, we gave unto the earth with white veins, a small amount of silver.

160. In Canedo, there is the treasure of Gonçalo Viegas and the weapons of his son.

161. On the relief of Peneda, around the hunting grounds, between the wall with the fine pebbles at the root of the cork oak, there is the gold of the killer Zileno, who escaped.

162. In the temple of Moreira, there was buried a golden landmark, with sculpted jawbones.

163. In Bórbem, to the North, in the quarry, seven men away, there is a treasure.

164. In Ciervos, we have a great silver granary, enough to last for three lives.

165. By an evil enchantment, we buried a treasure in Requeijo. Do not seek to obtain it without the aid of the Infernal Spirit. We sold our soul, not thine.

166. At the base of the mosque, in Fresmo, there are two enchantments of great value. If thou wants them, before the banishment, make the sign of the Cross ✠ three times.

167. In the center of Cerejal lays the belongings of the escapees from the previous year. Look to the North at the base of the mount.

168. At twelve steps from the fountain of Caniça, there is... lhas... lareja... nellad... va... at the surface of the earth[114].

169. Touch the center of the lime of Vide and thou shall immediately hear the sound of gold. In there are the belongings of our own from beyond the mountains.

170. In Conso there were left... two... crements... There is no mistake[115].

171. In the valley of Nanceda, towards Lusitania, between the three landmarks at the left, we buried the belongings of an orphan.

172. We went down the Vallinha, and already unarmed, we buried our own in a marked grave.

173. In the fields of Regamão, there are the belongings of the dead of Padernosa.

174. At the summit... Amori... twenty Roman states...[116]

---

114. Original footnote: The scroll is unreadable.

115. Original footnote: Idem.

116. Original footnote: From here until the end it is impossible to read any more words. For this reason we are deprived to further satisfy the curiosity of our readers.

DIABOLICAL SPIRITS

That infest houses with loud noises and the remedy to avoid them

CHAPTER I

On Spirits

Experience has shown that some places and houses are infested by spirits who disturb these places with loud noises, apparitions and other great bothers.

Examples are not even lacking in history, and these are mentioned by greatly celebrated authors to whom we cannot deny credit. Saint Augustine, in book 22 of the *City of God*, chapter 7, mentions that these spirits caused great harm to the animals and people living in the house of a certain man called Hesperius, who worked as a tribune.

John the Deacon, in the *Life of St. Gregory*, chapter 89, mentions that this saintly pontiff would frequently be molested by an evil spirit. To this end, whenever he would see this Pope praying, he would release his horses from their stable, having thrown two of them into a ravine; he would appear in the form of a cat to two other clergy members, whenever these were at this Saint's house, as if wanting to scratch them, and at other times he would appear as a Moor, wanting to injure them with a spear.

Plutarch, in the life of Dionysius of Syracuse, reports that, while he was meditating a certain afternoon, a woman of extraordinary height and terrifying and amazing countenance appeared to him, like an infernal fury, who restlessly started to sweep the living room floor. Dionysius was greatly frightened by this visitation and, calling his friends, told them of this vision and asked them to not leave him alone that evening, fearing that this monster would repeat its visit. Such did not happen, however, a young child of Dionysius did fall that day from the highest ledge of his house, perishing.

Father Possevino, from the Society of Jesus, also mentions in the life of António Barreto, senator of Tolosa, that one day an extremely tall woman appeared to his wife, who was a very spiritual lady. This sight was so frightful that for a period of 24 hours she was continually shaking, completely unable to control such movements.

Cardano, in book 16, chapter 93 of *De Varietate Rerum*, claims that the great and noble Torroles family of Parma owns a fortress where one may see, on certain occasions, in front of the chimney of the house, an old woman, representing one hundred years of age.

Even more worthy of note is the story mentioned by Johannes Trithemius in the description of Hirsau Abbey. He mentions that by the year of 1132, in a certain place in Saxony, a small man was sometimes seen with a hood over his head, who, on such accounts, the Saxons would call *Hudekin*, which in the Latin tongue means *Pileatus*, and should be that which we call *fradinhos de mão furada*[117].

Many remarkable things are told of him, for he enjoyed conversing with men he casually encountered, while wearing farmer's clothes; other times he would act invisibly and cause great bothers and play great tricks. He would advise great and important men, and would not be shy about helping housemaids with their work. He would work in the bishop's kitchen, and, being recommended by this same bishop to a certain man who needed to keep his wife safe while he was on a trip, equally served him with punctual diligence, keeping away all those who might have attempted against her honesty. He would not harm anyone, except when provoked, to which he would take great offense and enact his terrible revenge.

In that kitchen there worked a boy who greatly dealt with this spirit, and with such trust, ended up insulting him. The spirit complained to the kitchen master so as he would reprimand the boy, but, seeing as he would not amend his vulgarity with mere words, he drowned him and chopped up his body into slices, which he then roasted in the oven, and offered as food to the kitchen master and the rest of the bishop's servants. From this example we may see how harmful it can be to the body and soul such familiarity with demons in disguise.

Alessandro Alessandri, in chapter 9 of *Genialium Dierum*, tells us that, in Rome, a certain individual had a very peculiar friend, who, by reason of some ailment, was forced to go to the baths in Pozzuoli. They both went on their way, and, as his friend's ailment got worse, he ended up dying in an inn. The man gave his friend a proper burial and upon finishing the merciful job continued on his journey back to Rome. Stopping in a trading post, he laid down to sleep, and, while still awake, saw his friend enter the house, pale and emaciated, as his sickness had previously made him look.

Terrified by this spectacle, he asked who he was; however, that figure, without responding, gradually came closer to the bed, removed his garbs and laid down next to him, as if wanting to embrace his living friend. In a panic and fearful anguish, he pushed him away, and the dead man, taking up his clothes once again, looked at him with anger, left and disappeared. From this incident his friend would develop a dangerous ailment, of which he would mention that, while pushing this specter away, he touched its foot and that he felt a cold sharper than snow.

---

117. Translator's note: a type of *duende*, literally, "little friars with a hole in the hand", see comments.

Gordiando, another acquaintance of this author, while walking with his servant to Arezzo, got lost and ended up wandering into overgrown and uncultivated forests, where neither house, nor hut, nor any human sign was visible.

They wandered through the large and harsh bushes with great dread over such fearful loneliness, until, by the end of the afternoon, while sitting down to rest from all their fatigue, they thought they heard, faraway, the voice of a man, and supposing that it was someone who could instruct them in a way out of there, they followed the noise. Arriving at the top of a mound, they saw three horrible figures of immense height, wearing long black tunics, with long hair and beards, and with an extraordinary countenance.

These apparent men called to the wanderers, who, coming closer, made them out as gigantic figures, and among them was one completely naked, leaping and jumping, while making indecent gestures.

These wanderers, agitated by this great fright, ran as fast as they could, until, after crossing many paths and cliffs, they noticed the hut of a farmer, where they finally took refuge.

Of himself, this author mentions that, while struck by sickness in Rome, only waking up on certain occasions, he saw an elegant woman appear before him, which he carefully observed for he was unsure he was in possession of all his mental faculties. Feeling that he had perfect sense and vigorous potency, he asked the woman who she was. She replied with the same question, displaying a mocking smile and disappeared as if by magic.

André Tiraqueau, on the notes he made regarding the mentioned Alessandro, repudiates these allegations, justifying them with a dream, but it is surely not impossible nor incredible that demons may use such tricks, with which they constantly seek our downfall or make us fall into error and sin, seeing as in their ridiculousness they seem to only take pleasure in afflicting and harming souls.

Nonnullos, says Cassianus Collat, *immundorum spiritum quos Faunus vulgo appelat, ita seductores.*

One should also consult the much learned father Manuel Bernardes, from the Congregation of the Oratory, in his *Nova Floresta*, tome 1, title 10, where, with his customary erudition, he deals with a similar subject and mentions several other cases of spirits and demonization.

CHAPTER II

Remedy against Spirits

Regarding remedies, the gentiles used many useless and vain superstitions to deal with this bother, to which perhaps the Devil conceded, to further confirm these superstitious diligences and errors of men.

Apollonius of Tyana was convinced that by insulting these spirits they would remove themselves or become still, ceasing their bothersome affairs. But he was wrong, for insulting words do not have such power, nor did God give them such operating power, except to those which are used by the Church in the ritual of exorcism and are thus proper to employ the power of God to strike fear into demons and force them to obey the priest[118].

Of the same fortune are those who fool themselves into banishing spirits with the strength of weapons, as if such incorporeal substances could ever be harmed by iron.

These seem to want to follow the advice of the Sibyl, saying to Aeneas, when he entered Hell, as Virgil writes, to use a sword to defend himself from the stygian shadows.

Many others on the other hand think that it may be important to have a great deal of lit fire.

Fire does indeed favor this experiment, as it is shown that these spirits harm men more often during the darkness of night than in the light of day, although in current times this is not always the case.

On the side of fire seems to be the successes that Paulinus mentions in the *Life of Saint Ambrose*.

Empress Justina intended, by a variety of means, to take the life of this saintly doctor, and ended up resorting to a certain Innocent, a sorcerer, so as he would take his life through the demonic arts. He sent a few of these demons so as they would fulfill this task with diligence, but they returned saying that they could not even reach the doors of the Saint's house, for an unbearable wall of fire surrounded the building, and as such they realized that they could not operate their industries. However, it is quite perceivable that this fire was indeed divine protection, which, surrounding Saint Ambrose, would terrify the demons ever more.

Having left behind some of the superstitions of the Ancients, to which Alexander and some others mention, the true and effective methods are those used by the Church, and these are the sign of the Holy Cross ✠, the evocation of the holiest names of Jesus and Mary, the exorcisms of the said Church, fasting, orisons, banishments, the relics of saints, the blessing and consecration of houses, aspersions of holy water and other methods such as these.

---

118. Original footnote: Consult the first part of the *Great Book of St. Cyprian*.

But one should always be warned that not always are these phantoms, which appear as baleful figures and make such loud noises, actually evil spirits. These may be of two different natures, as may be seen by the following examples.

There once were in Athens some large houses, being, however, uninhabited due to the noises and rumors going about them.

As soon as the silence of the night fell, one could hear, as if far away, the dragging of iron and chains; after some time the sound would come closer and finally the figure or shade of an old man with a skeletal aspect, haggard face, long beard and spiked hair would appear; his hands and feet bound with chains which he dragged through the floor.

When this apparition would come about, those living there would spend horrible sleepless nights, and overwhelmed by fear, would fall into disease and death.

For this reason were these houses completely deserted, but their owner, trying to get some form of profit from them by sale or rent, placed them on the market at a very low price so as to appeal to those who did not know of this issue. At that time the philosopher Atenodoro arrived in Athens, and seeing the price of these houses did find it peculiar. He sought the reason behind this and upon discovering it was even more interested in renting them.

Upon entering there he had a table set up with an inkstand and a light; and ordered all other people to retire to their rooms, while he, with great industry and joy, started writing, so as his idle imagination would not make him see false figures.

As night fell, he immediately started to hear the noise of the banging of iron and the dragging of chains, but he neither lifted his eyes nor dropped his pen, merely opened his ears.

The noise grew louder and louder and one could feel it inside the room, and that was when Atenodoro lifted his eyes and saw the figure that was mentioned to him, which, standing still, made a sign with its hand as if calling him.

Similarly, he made a sign for the shade to wait and, leaning over the table, continued writing.

The shape approached him even more, making a great noise right over his head. The philosopher got up, grabbed a light and followed the shade's slow steps.

As soon as they arrived at the backyard of one of the houses the shade suddenly disappeared, and the philosopher, gathering a few leaves and grass, marked the place where the shade had vanished.

Some time passed without the vision appearing again, and as such he asked the magistrate to dig up that spot, where they found a skeleton tied with chains.

He gave the bones a public and sacred burial and from that day on never again were noises heard in those houses.

This case is mentioned by Pliny the Younger, in book 7, and its credibility seems to confirm the previous case.

St. Germanus, bishop of Antissiodorum, while traveling in the middle of winter, and seeing as night was already setting, sought to find shelter and rest. Not far away was an old house, practically a ruin, without roof, which no single soul had inhabited for a long time, and for this reason it was also partially covered with brush and reeds.

To some it would even seem better to just stay out in the forest than take refuge in such a place, seeing as two old men had told him that, in that house, some specters were said to appear, and this is why it was uninhabited. However, the saintly prelate did desire to spend the night there.

Having his provisions stored in one of the rooms of that house, where some of his companions ate their meal, he retired to one other room with another cleric accompanying him, to whom he ordered to read a spiritual book.

After some time, as the Saint was exhausted and had not eaten, he fell asleep, and immediately a horrible figure appeared to the reading cleric, while the noise of the dragging of iron was heard throughout those walls.

Frightened by this apparition, the cleric gave out a loud scream, which woke up the Saint, who, immediately rising, evoked the name of Jesus, and with an unshakable will, ordered the shade to tell him who he was and what he desired.

The shade, with a humble voice, common to people begging for something, responded that he was the shade, or figure, of an individual buried in that house, together with one other companion of his and that he bothered other people thus for they were not at rest, and that he begged for help in the form of prayers and suffrages, which the Church performs for the deceased.

The Saint was moved by this story, and with a candle followed the shade so as he would show him where the bodies were buried, which, were indeed found the next morning in the indicated area, together with the chains they were tied with when they were put in the ground.

A proper grave and burial was made, with the appropriate orisons as practiced by the Church and that habitation was left at peace, with no further noises or visions.

This case is mentioned in the *Life of St. Germanus*, chapter 7.

NECESSARY PREVENTION

To avoid and combat these apparitions, one should go to mass every Sunday and, upon entering, dip the right hand in the holy water basin and sprinkle yourself with it, all of this beyond what we just said.

When you are leaving the temple, take a portion of holy water and always have it by your bedside, putting two drops from it on the water you use to wash your face in the morning.

OCCULT POWERS

OF

HATE AND LOVE

DISCOVERED BY MAGICIAN JANNES

AND PRACTICED BY

ST. CYPRIAN

I

Owl sorcery for women to captivate men

The owl is an unlucky animal par excellence, and due to this fact one should not mention it after at least six months have passed after the death of any family member; otherwise this relative may appear to you. A woman may use this recipe, which is very much proven, but she should be in her proper physical condition, that is, when her rules[119] have passed at least four days ago.

Obtain an owl with a white belly and wrap it in flannel, in such a way as only the neck is visible, keeping it this way for thirteen days, and, after day thirteen, which is fateful, cut its neck with a single cut, over a stump, and put the head in alcohol until the 13th of the next month.

When this day comes, cut off its beak and burn it together with the coal used to cook the dinner of the person one wishes to bind. On this occasion, both of the eyes of the owl should be placed near the stove, one on each side, and the woman performing the operation should control the fire with a fan made from the bottoms of her night gown, with which she should have slept for at least five nights.

It is also necessary to say that this operation should be done while kneeling, saying the following orison:

"By the Wounds of Christ, I swear that I have no complaints of (NN), and that if I do this it is by the love I consecrate to him so as he may not have any affection towards any other woman P. N. A. M."

---

119. Translator's note: menstruation.

After this is done, one should make diligence so as the man does not discover the sorcery and has a restful sleep, and this operation will produce the effects the Saint always obtained from it.

II

Magic of the hedgehog

When a man is upset with the woman he cares for and does not wish to procure her himself, he should find a hedgehog, and, after removing its skin with all its quills, spray it with the juice of the *erva-do-diabo*[120], and, by bringing this with him, the woman will appear to him anywhere he goes, asking with humility that he once again become her little friend[121], becoming capable of great sacrifices and of doing anything the man asks of her. The enchanter, so as this sorcery comes to good results, should pray every day, while rising from bed in the morning, the following orison:

"My virtuous St. Cyprian, I implore thee in the name of thy great virtue that thou dost not abandon a martyr of love, mad as thou wert for thy lovely Elvira."

This sorcery cannot be used by women on men.

III

Enchantment of the black owl[122]

Take an owl which is completely black, and, after the stroke of midnight, bury it alive in your backyard, and plant on top of it five grains of white corn, this in the shape of a square, one at each corner and one in the middle. After the corn stocks are born, water them every day before sunrise, while saying the following orison:

---

120. Translator's note: literally Devil's Weed, a type of Datura (*Datura stramonium*), also known as the Devil's Fig tree.

121. Translator's note: euphemism.

122. Translator's note: in sorcery I and III the actual Portuguese words used to indicate the bird in question are, respectively, *mocho* and *coruja*, both of which translate as "owl". The case is that certain species of owls are referred to in Portuguese as *mocho* while others as *coruja* without there being any set of rules or characteristics that would fully describe and distinguish one from the other. As such, it is my advice, should you wish to perform any of these sorceries, to consult a Portuguese zoological dictionary and determine if the bird you are about to sacrifice is actually the most appropriate one for the sorcery in question.

"I, (NN), baptized by a priest of Christ, who died nailed to the Cross to redeem us in our captivity in which the despots of the Earth had us incarcerated, swear on these five trunks from where bread is born by the breath of God and heated by the smile of the Sun, that I will be faithful to (NN), so as he may never stop loving me, or take any other love while I exist, by the virtue of the black owl. P. N. A. M."

When the cobs are ripe, cut the ones in the four corners and give the grains to one or more black chickens, those with sharp back nails, making sure that no roosters touch them, for it was while this animal sang that the disciple denied Christ. The cobs from the middle stock should be dried in a smoke-house, wrapped in any piece of cloth which contains the sweat of the person you wish to enchant and kept safe, while saying:

"By God and the Virgin Mary I repent all my sins. Amen."

IV

Sorcery of the willow root

The willow root has a great virtue of which very few sorcerers know. This, as many other such discoveries, was found in Monserrate, written in scrolls, inside a bronze coffer, in the time of the *Mouros*.

By cutting the root of the willow, and placing it in a very dark place, one starts to see some vapors, like sulfur, appearing in the air, resembling flames. The person who wishes to do harm to another should sprinkle some holy water over the root and say the following:

"By the fire that heats the blood and by the cold that freezes it, I wish, while the will-o-the-wisps of this root dost not burn out, that (NN) dost not have one more single moment of satisfaction."

If this magic is for good, one should say the opposite, adding, with your hand over your heart, the following:

"May the heart of (NN) spark with enthusiasm for me just as these sparks, coming from the blessed root."

NOTE – These evaporations can last for about six months; this is, while the root is fresh. For that reason it is a good idea to have another one which may substitute it in this drying virtue as soon as the first one is finished burning.

Magic of the orange tree flower

When a girl has a great interest in marrying her boyfriend and he has the habit of telling her to wait another year, one should seek to steal a handkerchief with great care, so as the individual does not realize it. Then, as soon as you go to church, you should soak the handkerchief in the baptismal fount and immediately iron it, saying these words while breathing the vapor produced by the iron on the humid surface:

"Lustral water, thou who hast the virtue to make us Christians and open the way to Heaven, make (NN) receive me as his wife in one hundred Suns time, and let him give me as much trust as St. Joseph deposited in the Virgin Mary. I deliver myself into his hands, ornated with the flowers with which I shall perfume this handkerchief he uses to clean the lips through which the holy wafer enters, which contains the body, blood, soul and divinity of Our Lord Jesus Christ. Amen."

After this is done you should perfume the handkerchief with spirit of orange tree flower and place it back into his pocket in secret.

VI

Magic of the hawthorn[123] seeds

There is a wild bush, covered with thorns, related to the pear tree which gives small fruits, extremely sour to the taste. During the grafting period, cut its strongest branch from it and, after splitting it in half, place on it a branch of a *ferrã*[124] pear tree, covering it well with fertile earth. When the scion takes it will spring branches which will produce pears after two years. These pears have an excellent taste, but no other virtue. It is in their pits that lays the secret.

Roast 24 of these and, after grinding them in a bronze or copper crucible, sprinkle them on your beloved, and while this powder in on his skin, you may obtain all you wish for from this person.

---

123. Translator's note: the original Portuguese was a folk name for this plant, *escalheiro*, so it may either be the *Crataegus monogyna* or the *Crataegus laevigata*.

124. Translator's note: this word is usually used to designate a fruit tree that produces small and weak fruits. While I could have just substituted it in the current case by "a pear tree that produces small and weak fruits", it is also meant to be used in the subsequent orison and it did not seem like a good idea to substitute one single word by this lengthy explanation.

"I sprinkle thee by the grace of God, so as, while he creates pears in the hawthorn, thou never disagree with my desires or leaves me."

And, after making the sign of the Cross ✠, add;

"May God bless thee, *ferrã* pear tree, for thou takes away a thousand pains and generates love: blessed may thou be in the morning Sun."

VII

Magic of the navelworts[125]

In Mato Grosso, Brazil, in the year 1884 there died a celebrated sorcerer, a native black man, who operated astounding miracles with a secret we will reveal to our readers.

Take a handful of red navelworts and an equal portion of macerated *erva-de-saião*[126] and place this mixture in an infusion for 15 days and then give it as a drink, mixed with some wine, to any individual of any gender, and this will make them do anything you desire. Many Portuguese men returned more than wealthy from that state, all due to the sorceries of this black man, called Piaga Ambongo.

As soon as the person has drunk the first four doses of this liquid, one should drop in the fifth and last one or two drops of blood from the left foot of a black dog that must have a great fondness for the person making the sorcery.

ORISON

"May the God of the Christians embrace me, may the Tupi bless this leaf and the Pajé soften this heart. S. R. Mother of mercy, etc."

VIII

Magic of the black donkey

In Shanghai, China, the following sorcery is used since times immmemorial, whose secret a Portuguese man who returned from that region not long ago revealed to us.

---

125. Translator's note: *Umbilicus rupestris.*
126. Translator's note: a plant of the *Kalanchoe* genus, I could not determine the exact one.

When a lady runs from the temptations of a man who is requesting her, he should go to a donkey cemetery and buy the left testicle of a completely black donkey. Then he should fry it so as to extract its grease and mix this with perfume of thousand-flowers[127]. Next, he should rub the resulting substance in his hair and approach the object of his desire, in such a way as she may feel the smell of this mixture. We assure you that the woman will immediately begin to fall in love with the man and will not rest until she delivers herself to him.

Our informant also tells us that it is not wise to pass by any donkeys in heat while carrying this product, for they will charge this individual, shrieking terribly. We cannot verify the veracity of this magic, for it is not of St. Cyprian.

IX

Recipe to make men marry their lovers

Take 26 leaves of *erva-de-santa-luzia*[128] and, after boiling them in six deciliters of water, place this infusion in a very well closed white bottle, until small debris starts forming in the bottom, and say the following orison over the neck of the bottle:

"Oh Saint Lucia, healer of the eyes, save us from all pitfalls, night and day; oh Saint Lucia, blessed be, for being blessed, in Heaven thou rests."[129]

Then take a *seven* from a deck of cards and place it under the bottle, saying:

"In the name of the Father, the Son and the Holy Spirit, I beg thee, Lady, that, as this card is secure, so too may I have (NN) secure all my life, whom I love with all my heart, and I beg thee, Lady, to make him take me to the altar, our Mother in Christ Our Lord."

Next pray a chaplet to Our Lady, and you can be certain that your lover will take you to the altar of God and will give you happiness in accordance with his belongings. It is necessary to conserve the card under the bottle until the day of the wedding.

---

127. Translator's note: There is a perfume with this same name that is usually used in Umbanda as a general offering to all sorts of entities and workings. However, I cannot be certain that this is the exact same perfume mentioned here, but it is likely that, at this point, any flower perfume can be used, such as Florida Water.

128. Translator's note: Grass of Saint Lucia, this name is given to a few plants, but this most likely refers to the *Commelina erecta* (also possible is the *Commelina nudiflora* or *Commelina diffusa*), alternatively to plants of the *Euphorbiaceae* genus, but this is unlikely.

129. Translator's note: this orison rhymes, and its peculiar structure suggests an incantation. The original Portuguese: "Ó Santa Luzia, que sarais os olhos, livrai-nos de escolhos, de noite e de dia; ó Santa Luzia, bendita sejais, por serdes bendita, no Céu descansais."

X

Sorcery of the stingray to bind a lover

Every woman who has the desire for a man to love her should buy a fish called the stingray, when it is going through its bloody evacuations, for this is the only fish that suffers from this inconvenience. This fish, cooked in a stew with plenty of paprika, saffron and a drop of elderberry juice, also with some tangerine juice, and given as a meal to this man, will make him stay with this woman forever.

XI

Magic of the *trovisco*[130] pulled by a black dog

St. Cyprian says, on page 23 of his *Grimoire*, that every man that has the desire to magnetize a woman (noting that she shouldn't be over 50 years of age) should tie the tail of a black dog to a stem of wild *trovisco*, and, after the dog pulls it out, he should then pass it through fire, remove its peel and make a belt to tie around his body, being in direct contact with the skin. To further hasten the sympathy of this woman, it is also convenient to make a bracelet of this same material and put it on your right wrist, for, by shaking the woman's hand with this object, she will start to fall in love with this man and give him all sorts of finenesses

XII

Magic of the living lizard, dried in an oven

Take a live lizard, one with a blue back, place it in a new, very well-covered pan and put it in an oven to roast. As soon as it is well dried, grind it into a powder and place this in a sandalwood box.

The woman or man who wishes to captivate the heart of any other person, only needs to give them a pinch of this powder in some wine or coffee, and they will have this person at their command.

Jerónimo Cortez further says that this powder is also marvelous to pull out teeth with no pain whatsoever, simply by rubbing it on your gums.

---

130. Translator's note: the common name for plants of the *Thymelaeaceae* family, mainly the *Daphne lauerola*, *Daphne gnidium* and *Thymelaea villosa*. These plants are quite toxic.

XIII

Magic of the left foot insole

To make sure a husband will be faithful to his wife or lover, and be disgusted by all other women who might take him off the good path, all one has to do is take the insole of his left foot, burn it in a strong fire with incense, rue and pealed acorns, put the ash from all of these ingredients in a bag and place this inside the mattress where he sleeps. What is also very effective is placing any amount of this ash in any stitching of this individual's clothes, as long as it is from the knees up. The woman will also obtain a marvelous effect if, while going to bed on Fridays, she sprinkles a pinch of this sorcery on her spine. In this way, she will have him forever.

XIV

Magic of the *brandão*[131] wax

Whoever obtains a portion of the yellow wax from the candles placed by the sides of a funerary coach and melts it in a fire of cypress wood, while the dead person has not yet been put in the ground, will acquire a powerful weapon to be loved by women. The man who possesses this talisman can make a woman obedient to anything, and for that all he needs to do is light a wick with this wax, in such as way as the lady of his thoughts may see this light.

This experiment should not be performed in the fateful days enumerated in the second part of this book.

XV

Magical power of the wheat bread

Every man who wants a lady to accept his courtship, if she pays little or no attention to him, should wait for the occasion of confession and on that very day, at dinner, he should take some wheat bread which hasn't been burned in the oven, and chew it with his thought in God the Creator and his soul in Jesus Christ the Seer, saying:

"By God I chew thee,
   by God I bless thee,
   With teeth I knead thee,
   Oh bread which is of wheat.

---

131. Translator's note: This word refers to a particular large and thick wax candle.

By the Wafer so unleavened,
I swear, my God,
always amend me
of my sins.
For the good of Thy Son,
allow, Lord,
that (NN) will always
love me."[132]

After this hymn, one should find a black cat that has not been castrated and give him the bread to lick, and afterwards make the necessary diligences to place this chewed bread in the pocket of the lady, and the result will be most satisfactory.

The person who performs this responsory should not reveal it to anyone, for, according to St. Cyprian, great miseries may come into his life and he may suffer the fate of never having any bread to eat, for he publicly chewed this most holy food with libidinous thoughts.

XVI

Sorcery of the faithful love

A man who manages to unite his body with that of a woman, even if an ill-reputed one, and desires to be the exclusive benefactor of her charms, may do so with minimum cost, as all he needs is for this woman to have material pleasure in his contact.

On that occasion he should say, with his eyes fixed upon hers while gently holding her:

---

132. Translator's note: Although not particularly harmonious this section does rhyme in the original Portuguese:

Por Deus te mastigo
por Deus te bendigo,
com os dentes te amasso,
ó pão que és de trigo.
Pela Hostia tão ázima
te juro, meu Deus,
emendar-me sempre
dos pecados meus.
Por bem de Teu Filho
permite, Senhor,
que sempre (NN)
por mim sinta amor.

"Oh St. Cyprian, friend of unhappy lovers and father of black and white magic, by the true God to whom thou gave thy soul and heart, I ask thee to turn this woman to me, so as I may be venturous A. M. G. P.[133]"

After doing this, and treating this woman with gentleness, and, by giving her other small pleasures, she will never again remove him from her thoughts and all other men will greatly bore her.

XVII

Infallible remedy to break friendships

Proceed in the following way:

- *Verbena*[134], 2 grams
- Pomegranate seeds, 30 grams
- Root of *mil-homens*[135], 20 grams
- *Mestrunços*[136], 150 grams
- Green banana peels, 100 grams

Boil all of this in sufficient water, in a new clay pot, until all is reduced to a deciliter. Next, place this in a frying pan and melt on it:

- Lamb marrow, 125 grams
- Saltless lard, 50 grams
- Alcohol, 20 grams.

After this grease is prepared, drop some of it for eight days in the food of the person bothering you, saying:

"For good or evil, and with the help of God, whom I worship with all my heart, thou shall go to some other place in search of love far away from me, and while thou dost not leave me, may thou be damned by the power of the incarcerating black magic."

---

133. Translator's note: Ave Maria and Gloria Patri.

134. Translator's note: A genus of the *Verbenaceae* family.

135. Translator's note: literally "root of a thousand-men", *Aristolochia gigantea*, also called Brazilian Dutchman's Pipe or Giant Pelican Flower.

136. Translator's note: This possibly refers to *Mastruço, Coronopus didymus*, a common name for the Lesser swine-cress, but I am somewhat unsure of this.

After eight days, one should make an egg omelet with the rest of this ointment and some lamb meat and feed it to a dog with a black sign on its head. As soon as he finishes eating, hit this dog with a ram's horn that needs to be burned on both sides, until the dog yelps three times. Then release the dog and throw the horn at it while saying these words:

"Let (NN) run from me, always as swiftly as that."

XVIII

The meeting of St. Cyprian with a sorceress who was performing the sorcery of the snakeskin wrongly, and how he corrected her

St. Cyprian, while returning home from a Christmas party, and not being able to cross some fields as a consequence of a river flood, was forced to take shelter in a natural tunnel, and spend the night there.

He wrapped himself in a thick cloak and nested in the safest crevice of that cave.

Near midnight he heard footsteps and noticed a dim light. Fearing that these were evildoers he further coiled himself, holding a sharp rock. Shortly after he heard in that great cave a cavernous voice saying the following:

"Oh magician Cyprian, my king of sorcerers, for thee I come here with four torches and beg thee to aid me in winning my lovesick client's prize."

The saint was about to get up, so as to interrogate who thus spoke, but he was forced to back down when he heard these words:

"Oh Lucifer, oh mighty governor of the Country of Fire, rise from the flames, come to me, enter this cave where I come every night and aid my work of consoling unhappy wives!"

After this, that underground was filled with a terrible smelling smoke.

The saint marched towards the voice and saw an old woman with long uncombed hair in the front of her head and clearly shaven in the back.

"What art thou doing here woman, and who is this Cyprian thou just now evoked?"

"He was a sorcerer who recently converted to the Christian faith and had the gift to operate all that was his will, with the aid of Satan."

"But why dost thou call upon him now?"

"I wanted to ask him for a recommendation to the Devil, so as he will aid me in a working on which my fortune and the tranquility of a wealthy lady depends."

"And who is this lady?" asked the saint.

"She is the daughter of the count of Erverardo of Saboril, married to the grand-duke of Terrara, who has mistreated her greatly because of another lady in court he greatly adores. The daughter of the duke promised me a *rasa*[137] of gold if I unbind her husband from his lover's arms."

"What fuel is that, so suffocating and with such a terrible smell?" asked the saint.

"It is snakeskin with flower of Paterson's Curse[138] and heather[139] root, which I am burning in the name of Satan to fumigate the clothes of the duke, to see if I can separate him from that woman. This magic was always successful when my mother practiced it under these same roofs, which no man's hand took part in making. My mother untied with it all manner of girls from noblemen to kings, but I have done it six times, and the duke just mistreats his wife more and more."

"That is because thou did not use the main ingredient, for thy mother did not reveal it to thee."

"Tell me what this ingredient is, by the God of the idolaters."

"Thou art a pagan? Dost thou profess the law of the barbarians?"

"I do."

"In that case I shall not teach thee this secret. And thou can be sure that thou will never save this woman from her martyrdom."

The poor sorceress started crying and fell abandoned onto a pile of tree branches some shepherds had brought there.

The saint helped her up with great care, and, after cleaning and tidying her dress, told her:

"Wert thou capable of doing this to me if I had fallen at thy feet?"

"No!" responded the sorceress, "for I believe thou art not of my law, and we only love our own and have the obligation of doing evil onto the children of other religions."

"This is because thy law is evil! Thy religion is the waste of all others!"

The *Bruxa* began to tremble, convulse and foam at the mouth, as if taken by hydrophobia.

St. Cyprian covered her with his cloak and continued:

"And here is the proof. May Our Lord Jesus Christ forgive me for taking myself as an example. I aid thee because my religion, which is the Christian one, says that all are children of the same Omnipotent God, and we should not inquire about the beliefs of our suffering brothers."

"Blessed be it, that religion, but I cannot follow it, for my own would condemn me to hunger and abandonment; for I am fed by the gentilic high priests."

"And what is the problem with that? If I manage to assure thee a means of sustenance, dost thou wish to convert?"

---

137. Translator's note: an old unit of measure, equivalent to an *alqueire*.

138. Translator's note: *Echium plantagineum*, also called Purple Viper's Bugloss.

139. Translator's note: plants of the *Ericaceae* family, mainly the *Erica* and *Calluna* genus.

"Yes! But how shall thou achieve my happiness, being as poor as thy clothes indicate?"

"How!? Did thou not tell me that the daughter of the count of Erverardo would give thee a *rasa* of gold if thou restituted her husband's love?"

"I did, however..."

"Tomorrow, at the ninth hour, meet me in the Christian temple, for I will present thee to Presbyter Eugene, so as he may give thee the lustral waters, and then I will give thee the secret that makes this magic infallible."

"But who art thee?"

"I am Cyprian, the former sorcerer, for, as soon as I felt the waters of baptism upon my body, I could no longer use magic; but since this is for a good purpose, and I can gather one more soul to Christianity, I will tell thee the proper method of performing the sorcery thou hast tried in vain."

"Tell me, lord, tell me!"

"Wait. Only tomorrow, after thy name hast been written in the Christian book will thou know it. Be at peace and I will wait for thee there."

And the saint went out into the darkness of night, in the direction of Eugene's house to tell him what had happened.

The next morning, waiting in Church with the presbyter, he saw the *Bruxa* enter, who immediately ran to kiss the priest's feet.

She was then baptized and, at the end of the ceremony, Cyprian called her and gave her a square scroll where the following orison was written:

Make the sign of the Cross ✠ three times.

"Oh pregnant snake, by God who created thee, I skin thee, by the Virgin I bury thee, by her beloved Son I burn thy skin in four pots of fused clay. With flower of Paterson's Curse I wed thee, with heather root I ignite thee, and with sabean resin[140] I bind thee, and by making this white magic six times, tear thee from the arms of that treacherous lover (NN) and with this sabean resin I fumigate thee, taken today from the temple of Christ. Amen."

As soon as the sorceress finished this orison, she went on her way to the palace of the grand-duke, a few leagues from the village. The very moment the duke put on his suit, fumigated by the *Bruxa*, he fell to the duchess' feet asking forgiveness for his lust. The very next day he tore out one of his lover's eyes and despised her.

---

140. Translator's note: I haven't been able to determine exactly what this incense is, or even if this is simply referring to the ancient inhabitants of the South of Arabian Peninsula (modern Yemen), the ancient Arabic sect of the Sabeans or even the Sabians of Harran. Should it be the first then the incense should either be frankincense or myrrh, as these were two of the most lucrative trading goods of the Sabaen people.

The count's daughter immediately ordered that a *rasa* of gold coins be given to the *Bruxa* and took her as her private aid.

XIX

Recipe for women to get rid of men they no longer wish to put up with

When a lady is bored with a man and wishes to get rid of him without any scandal or exposing herself to his revenge, she needs to do nothing else but the following:

First of all, she should make herself untidy with her body, not combing her hair or washing herself, and also she should not have any carnal interest when he challenges her for vulgar actions. As soon as she does this, place twelve ant eggs and two hot chilies inside a hole in a red squill[141] and place this inside a clay pan, very well shut, and place it over a fire. The woman should go to bed, and as soon as the individual in question is asleep, she should uncover the pan slightly, and, returning to bed, she should pass her right arm over the man's chest and say the following words in her mind:

"In the name of the prince of Hells, unto whom I make a testament of my soul, I banish thee, with red squill, chilies and ant eggs, so as thy figure may be put far away from me, for thou bothers me as much as the cross bothers the angel of darkness."

XX

Method of continuing the previous magic

In the following night and in the next eleven days in a row, one should repeat this practice and also sprinkle chili powder on the side of the bed where the man in question usually sleeps, which will produce such affliction that he will become scared of that house and abandon it.

IMPORTANT PREVENTION

Some men will sometimes become suspicious of the itch and the suffocation caused by the smoke of the previous preparation, and ask the woman to sleep on his side of the bed. In this case one should be prepared and wash her body

---

141. Translator's note: *Drimia maritime, Urginea maritima, Urginea scilla* or *Scilla maritime,* also commonly known as squill and sea onion.

with celery water and male *roquette*[142], which will prevent her from feeling the slightest inconvenience.

Try and see the fine result you will achieve.

XXI

Infallible recipe so as women do not have children

There are various recipes to avoid that women have children; the following one is, however, infallible, and many people used it under the advice of a poor woman who St. Cyprian, touched by her ill fortune, revealed it to, under the utmost secrecy.

Her gossiping however made her be charged as a *Bruxa* and burned by Diocletian.

Later this recipe was abandoned, for its efficiency is such that it was thought to be the work of the Devil.

.

. .

One afternoon, while Cyprian was going to his home, he saw a poor woman surrounded by five children, having another on her back and another one in her arms.

Cyprian approached her and said:

"To where dost thou take all those children, woman? Thou probably stole them!"

"Steal them my lord?!... Should I have nothing else to do, when every year I birth two more! Oh, my lord, poor as I am, for my husband works the fields and earns meagerly, imagine the problems I have in feeding all these children, not even counting the ones still to come!"

Cyprian, touched by her story, asked her:

"And dost thou wish to have any more children?"

"I, my lord, not even the ones I have now..." and, taking back her words, "Now, since they are here, poor things, let them be raised; but I would gladly give a few years of my life so as not to have any more."

They then came to a place from where they could see the sea in all its extension.

Upon arriving there Cyprian, said:

"I will teach thee a recipe so as not to have any more children, but avoid revealing it, for that may be fatal to thee."

"I will keep an absolute secret," she promised.

---

142. Translator's note: *Eruca sativa*, also known as rocket, rucola, rugula, or arugula. I do not really understand what is meant by the adjective "male".

Cyprian smiled, for he remembered how much a secret is worth in the mouth of a woman, and continued.

"If thou dost not keep it a secret, the problem will be thine," and, pointing at some rocks, continued, "Dost thou see those shells over there?"

"I do," said the woman.

"And by those shells, what dost thou see?"

"Sponges, my lord."

"Well then, pick one of them up, clean it of that gelatinous substance, let it dry and beat it, so as to remove any sand it may have, and, when thou wishes to copulate, make it moist in some water, squeeze it, and put it compressed inside thy vagina, conserving it there during the whole act of coitus."

The poor woman, in her joy, was about to retire without thanking Cyprian, when he called her back.

"I did not yet tell thee the size that the sponge should have, for this is the most important part."

"This is true," said the woman with sadness.

"I could punish thee for thy lack of gratitude, for thou wert about to retire without thanking me; but I wish to be indulgent. The sponge should have this size."

And he drew in the sand, with a wand he carried in his hand, a circle.

It was the size of the woman's palm.

XXII

Another recipe so as not to have children

Procure a portion of corn that has been chewed or bitten by a mule, and put this in a glass vase with a little of that animal's fur, taken from the tail, close to the body.

Next place over this the following:

- Alcohol, 150 grams
- Cypress apple powder, 26 grams
- Red holly flowers, 50 grams

Cover the vase well, and when the woman is about to enter coitus, uncover it and smell it three times, saying:

"Oh cursed mule, for having wanted to kill the Divine Redeemer on the cliff of Bethlehem when he was born, thou wert condemned to never bear fruit in thy womb, may thy saliva in this jar defend me from becoming a mother."

To obtain the corn bitten by a mule, you should grease her teeth, so as it will slip from her mouth and fall back into the manger.

This recipe is easy and it always gives good results.

XXIII

Method of operating abortions

When, in the first month, a woman's blood tribute does not come and she is suspicious that she is pregnant, she should place her feet in very hot water, the hottest she can bear, that the abortion will happen by itself, with her monthly tribute soon to follow.

XXIV

Sorcery of the sweet cake to do harm

This recipe is not well known, however, many people have used it with excellent results.

Whoever takes a wheat flour cake and places it under their armpit for seven days, very well tucked in so to absorb plenty of sweat, and then feeds it to any person, will get her to do anything one may desire: Love, money and even the forgiveness of any crime.

We do not advise our reader to perform it though, for Saint Albertus Minor says that, after the person who has eaten the cake dies, she will appear at the late hours of the night to whoever gave it to her, with such insistence that it may even cause their death.

XXV

Recipe to heat up cold women

When a man feels passion for a woman and she is starting to lose interest in him, he must do the following:

- Cork oak root, 20 grams
- Wild *sarganha*[143] seeds, a handful

---

143. Translator's note: In the old Livraria Ecónomica version there is some contradictory information, as at this point this herb is referred to as being wild salva, *Phlomis lychnitis*, and in the orison to follow it is refered as *sarganha*, *Helianthemum*

- Chest hair with their roots, 24
- Peanut flour, 30 grams
- Cantharides, 1
- Hazelnuts, 4

Grind all of this and mix it well, until you make a ball, then, leave it under the night sky for three nights, making sure it doesn't rain on it or that it gets wet from the morning dew. After this time, open a hole in the mattress of your bed while saying:

"By the wounds of Christ and by the love I give (NN) I hide thee, cork oak, bonded with *sarganha*, with threads of the chest, peanuts, cantharid and hazel fruits; I desire, by the virtue of Cyprian, that this woman becomes connected to me, through love and flesh."

After this is done, very rarely will the woman not begin to look at the man with more fire and love.

This recipe is equally good to increase the enthusiasm of wives who are cold in their intimate contact with their husbands.

XXVI

The power of the viper head to do either good or evil

Acquire a viper head and, after it is dried, attach it to a cane, an umbrella or a piece of horn and carry it with you. Thus armed you will be able to perform many things, both for good and for evil.

For example: if you wish that some entrepreneurial does not bear good results, say the following: "Viper, to do evil I call on thee." If you wish it to go well say the following: "Viper, to do good I call upon thy power."

If you wish for an enemy to beg you for mercy, this is the means to do so. All you need to do is call upon the aid of the viper and whisper to it: "Viper, order (NN) to come here with humility." And that person will appear with soft words asking for forgiveness. If it becomes necessary for you to ask for the help from someone you are not in good favor with, say these words: "Viper, through paths without cliffs send me (NN), here to my aid, or condemn him to suffer jealousy for the rest of his life."

For a proper success it is important that everything be said with your thoughts on God and that no one know of your secret; otherwise it will lose all its magic.

---

olyssoides. So as to keep consistency I have chosen to place *sarganha* in both points.

XXVII

Magic of the pregnant rabbit hanged from the ceiling

Take a young female rabbit, which hasn't yet been with any male rabbit, and hang it, tied by the ears, on the ceiling of your house for six hours, while saying:

"Should thou not die, (NN), thou shall be mine, by the power of Lucifer, and all the demons of Hell."

If during that time the rabbit doesn't die then it is appropriate for this magic, and one should immediately have it be covered by a male rabbit that has a black spot somewhere on its back.

After 36 hours, kill the rabbit and, upon opening its belly while it is still warm, remove the ovarians of that generation and put them inside the egg of a wild duck, through a hole made on the side it was fertilized (this you can search for with the aid of a candle).

Wrap the egg with a silk tissue covered with gum arabic[144] and place it under a roosting chicken.

When the other chicks are born that egg should remain in one piece but with a yellowish color; one should take it and place it inside a glass vase with a cypress wood cover and tied shut with wire.

The person who possesses this egg will achieve everything in love. A man will dominate every woman he wishes, and a woman every man, however, the owner of this talisman will never be able to possess a virgin.

It is necessary to pick up the egg very carefully, for if it breaks the person who has made it will be assaulted by a great regret over their indiscretion.

When an individual wishes to cause a great harm to another, he may execute his vengeance by sending him the egg. We do not advise this however, for the person may get their revenge, but their businesses will generally not fare well.

XXVIII

The powerful magic ring

Every person who wishes to be idolized their whole life by people of the opposite gender to their own should do the following sorcery, which is attributed to St. Cyprian:

Buy a ring with a small shiny jewel, have it removed and feed it to a crow, at the stroke of midnight, put the ring on your pinky finger and keep it there until the crow expels the jewel through his natural excretion. As soon as this happens, have the jewel put back into the ring and place it on your left hand finger while saying:

---

144. Translator's note: Also known as acacia gum, chaar gund, char goond, or meska.

"By the power of God and by all the power thou and all thy jewel brothers have, that thou achieve everything in the world, for thy power is greater than that of gold, I ask thee to make me achieve all I wish regarding love. Amen. P. N. A. M. S. R.[145]"

As was said, whoever carries this ring, being a man, and knowing how to present himself, will marry the woman he most desires, and will be able to possess even others that may awaken carnal desires in him. Being a woman, she will achieve the same ends; but we cannot advise this use, should they want to be respectable women, for this talisman makes its wearer very lustful.

These are the instructions of the *Grimoire*.

XXIX

Method of knowing if an absent person is faithful

Dig a hole in the earth, about two feet deep. Place inside this hole, kneaded into dough, the following: 30 pounds of sulfur, an equal portion of iron powder and the necessary amount of water. Over this mass place a picture of the absent person, wrapped in leather. If one does not have a picture or portrait then a piece of paper with the person's name written on it should be sufficient. After this is done cover the hole with the same earth you dug up, while saying:

"Cyprian, by thy magical knowledge and saintly virtue, make it so as I learn if (NN) is faithful to me."

After fifteen hours the earth will form a small volcano, which will begin to expel flames and ashes. If the picture of the person is respected by the fire it is because she is faithful; if it is attacked by the flames this person is bonded by love.

If the picture stays within the earth, it is because this person is bound by strong love ties; if the picture is thrown out of the ground to a short distance, it is because this person is trying to break free from her prison; if it is thrown to a large distance, it is because this person, having broken all bonds, is on her way back to unite herself with whomever is calling her.

XXX

Ingenious way of knowing who are
the people who wish you harm

Should on any occasion any person feel a great itch on the palm of their

---

145. Translator's note: Pater Nostri, Ave Maria and Salve Regina.

right hand, to know if this is due to someone wanting them harm, and also, who is talking against them at that time, rub the itching part four times on a crucifix, saying the following orison while kneeling:

"By God, by the Virgin
By all which is holy,
This enchantment be broken
With rock salt;"

Throw a few rough grains of salt into a fire and, while it is crackling, keep on saying:

"For I know not
Why any living creature
Would wish me harm."[146]

Make the sign of the Cross ✠ three times and throw some grains of red aniline into the fire.

The person who has bad-mouthed you and wishes you harm shall appear before you within 24 hours, with as many red spots as grains of aniline you threw into the fire, and thus, you will know who your enemy is and you may then avoid him.

---

146. Translator's note: In the original Portuguese it should be noted that this short orison rhymes, as such it should be transcribed in its original form.

Por Deus, pela Virgem,
Por tudo que há de santo,
Se quebre o encanto
Com pedras de sal;

Não sei o motivo
Por que haja algum vivo
Que assim me quer mal.

Also, the original book has the following note:

In this new edition of this book we were able to correct this verse, which was unreadable in the original scroll, which has given rise to many incorrect editions.

ART OF DIVINING THE FUTURE

BY

THE PALM OF THE HAND

LINES OF THE HAND

1 - Ring of Venus.
2 - Heart line.
3 - Head line.
4 - Health line.
5 - Fatality line.
6 - Life line.
7 - Triple bracelet.

EXPLANATION OF THE LINES

1 - RING OF VENUS - Being visible it means love and happiness; broken it means fickle love.

2 - HEART LINE - When it is whole and doubled it means inheritance; single and without breaks means a happy and long life; broken means a slight heartlessness.

3 - HEAD LINE - Straight and long means great intelligence; with breaks it means a character for scientific inventions.

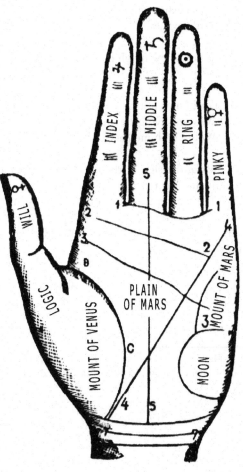

4 - HEALTH LINE - If whole it means health; broken means sickness.

5 - FATALITY LINE - If long it means an unexpected fortune; when ending in the heart line it means a wealthy marriage.

6 - LIFE LINE - Check on the next section for the method of determining the duration of one's life.

7 - TRIPLE BRACELET - When the three lines are well separated each of them signifies 30 years of existence.

METHOD OF KNOWING THE DURATION OF ONE'S LIFE

One must divide, as in the example, the life line into 10 equal parts or degrees, starting from the line of Saturn, perpendicular to the middle finger.

Each one of these degrees represents 10 years of life.

The place where the life line completely ends reveals the amount of years one has to live.

If the life line, while ending, turns towards the center of the hand, this is a sign of good health.

DESIGNATION OF THE FINGERS

Thumb – Finger of *Venus*.
Index – Finger of *Jupiter*.
Middle – Finger of *Saturn*.
Ring – Finger of *Apollo*.
Pinky – Finger of *Mercury*.

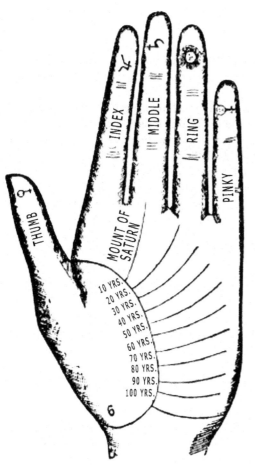

ALCHEMY

OR

THE ART OF MAKING GOLD

Cecilio Rodigenio, in his book *Crimini Falsi*, mentioned the following, regarding the fabrication of pure gold:

Such seems undeniable, that it is possible to make gold, with human and diabolical artifice, as the alchemists profess; for whoever knows how to recognize and unite the simple ingredients, applying in the appropriate proportion *Activa passicivis*, without a doubt will create gold of good quality and other such materials of worth, better even than those taken from the bowels of the Earth.

Furthermore, there is no shortage of true and faithful books that prove this resolution.

I myself have met, not long ago, a Frenchman, a poor man but extremely wise, who had invented the method of creating a certain water, with which he could separate gold from silver or bronze, and maybe this was the water used in Milan and in other places to unbind metals.

I believe piously in these preparations, for João André, wise canonist and my master, mentions that Arnaldus of Villa Nova had fabricated some gold ingots, which he showed in the Pope's court in Rome, so as they could examine them and see if they were pure and fine or false and merely apparent.

Ramon Llull was never persuaded that such an art existed, and after arguing with Arnaldus, he was convinced that this experiment would break itself down by the following morning.

This was executed, and the evidence not only convinced Ramon as made him apply himself to this profession, becoming in it so famous that he fabricated many gold coins in a fortress in London, becoming known as *Nobili Raymundi*.

I am much more inclined to believe in this art, for Bernard Trevisan did manage, after a long practice, to make gold through the art of alchemy, and Guillermo Aragosio, well versed in Philosophy and Medicine, visited Hector Ausonius, a famous doctor, in Venice, who showed him three rings of pure gold made by a botanist from Trevigi.

Aragosio decided to speak with this man, and sought him in Trevigi.

The botanist informed him that a Frenchman, whom he had housed for a few months, had given him certain powders to make gold, and that, seeing as he esteemed to a greater amount the public good than personal gain, he went to Venice to denounce him to the Republic; however, upon returning to Trevigi, he did not find the Frenchman, but from that day on, every night, a great ghost would appear to him to torture and call him a fool.

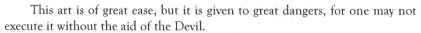

This art is of great ease, but it is given to great dangers, for one may not execute it without the aid of the Devil.

In the *Demonomania* one may read that the companions of the famous alchemist Constantine, not being able to learn the secret with which their master created gold, requested the Devil to teach it to them.

The Devil appeared to them and said:

"Take these powders and make a deed of thy souls to me, if thou wishes to be rich."

And he gave them some powders I will shortly reveal to the reader.

After they all signed the deeds to their souls, they began working and made a great number of gold ingots.

One of them, however, when he found himself rich, repented having sold his soul to Lucifer and went to confess himself. The priest who confessed him banished the spirit of darkness in such a way as it made him drop the deed at his feet.

When he returned home and went to search for his gold he could not find it; but his other companions did come in his aid by giving him part of their belongings.

This action made the other alchemists also wish to confess, and so they did; but to prevent the Devil from taking their gold, they tied the ingots to a cross and sprinkled them with holy water.

In this way they managed to fool the Devil and assure the happiness of their families.

The powders which the alchemists used for the fabrication of gold, those made by the Devil, contained two metals: *argento vivo* or mercury and Resch powders. This mixture, when placed in a boiler, creates the purest gold, being mixed with a quarter part of copper.

This is, however, dangerous for two reasons; the first is the pact with the Devil, and the second is the fraud of using this gold for the minting of money, for such is only permitted by the State.

THE SORCERESS OF ÉVORA

OR

THE STORY OF THE FOREVER-BRIDE

**Taken from a manuscript
written by Amador Patrício dated in Salvaterra on 23
of April of 1614**

The *Mouros* of Évora lived happily with their King Praxadopel, as also did the Christians on account of the good rule of this good king.

Many great things did King Praxadopel do for the good of his city and its surroundings, such as ordering the construction of a castle of which today we can still see the ruins, and is called the Castelo Giraldo.

While the initial excavation for the foundations of this castle were being made, the grave of Montemuro was found and also a complete house, buried under the ground, six *varas* in length and four in width. This was the lair in which *Bruxa* Lagarrona made her diabolical sorceries.

In the middle of this house was a hole with the height of a man. The inside wall of this hole was painted with lizards, snakes and reptiles. On the outside edge, circling it, there were four stone toads, very naturally made, and between these toads some figures of little boys, each with the height of half a cubit. In their hands they held a bunch of reeds with which they threatened the toads. In one of the corners of this house was the figure of a monster, which from the head to the waist was like a man, and from the waist down was a like coiled serpent. In one other corner there was a turtle, and on it a raven with a bat in his beak, as if eating it. In the other two corners there were two female figures, one sleeping and the other awake; the awake one had in her left hand, grabbing it by the hair, the head of a man, and at her feet a mongrel dog with an open mouth, as if wanting to take the head, but the woman's other hand prevented him from doing so.

The sleeping one had in one of her hands an owl and in the other a hawk with opened wings, as if wanting to attack the owl. Throughout the walls there were paintings of snails, slugs, frogs, wasps, bumblebees, scarabs, beetles, and other small critters.

The floor was tiled and near the hole was a large rock with an inscription, saying the following:

Whoever is first in opening up this ditch
Will see great things never before witnessed;
Dig forth so as thou may resist
To the great terror with hard chest.

Do not fear, do not fear, do not show terror,
To the deep go, enter through the center,
For all thou may see, much more will be inside
A thing of great worth is hidden.

Thou shall find the success yet to come
In coming times when Portugal
Shall once again have a royal banner
Of hard and victorious people.[147]

They tried to remove the rock to see what else was inside, as the sign indicated, but this they could not do on account of its great weight; and, by digging around it they found the grave of Montemuro with his skull and bones, completely rotten, and also some old books, too decayed to be read; by writing down all of these things, was this information stored in the memory of the city library, where, after the Christians conquered it, were found many great manuscripts of astrologists regarding these enchantments. It was by filling all of this with strong foundations that the castle known today as Giraldo was made.

Not far away from this place, King Alvado had a farm where he had a grave prepared for when he died.

---

147. Translator's note: This small poem should be observed in its original language:

Quem for o primeiro que abrir esta cova
Verá grandes coisas jamais nunca vistas;
Cava por diante para que resistas
Ao grande temor com peito de prova.

Não temas, não temas, não mostres temor,
No fundo te mete, entra pelo centro,
Que quanto mais vires, muito mais lá dentro
Está escondida coisa de valor.

Acharás sucessos que hão-de acontecer
Em tempos vindouros em que Portugal
Tornará a ter o pendão real
De gente esforçada que sabe vencer.

On this farm there lived a man called Faust, who had a most beautiful daughter, with which a *Mouro* astrologer and magician, called Matacabel, fell deeply in love, and, kidnapping her, took her to a house outside of the city, where a *Moura* called Lagarrona, also a magician and beautiful, lived. This *Moura* had a son called Candabul, who, seeing this Christian girl, immediately fell in love with her, and as such, kept her from Matacabel. Perceiving this situation, Matacabel decided to take her away from Candabul, which caused him to lose his life, as Candabul, while awaiting for him in a hiding place, killed Matacabel, having him buried in the place nowadays called Matacabelo.

The law of the land, having known of this case, went in search of Candabul to arrest him, but his mother Lagarrona turned him invisible and in this way convinced the officers of the law that he was away. Lagarrona had known, by means of her enchantments, that her son would disappear over the love of a Christian, and, thinking this to be the one she had in her power, decided to make her a *Moura*, so as her son could marry her. The girl, however, said to Candabul that she would only be content if she saw her parents, something which Candabul accepted, accompanying her to her house and promising to come back to retrieve her.

Her parents were greatly pleased to see their daughter and decided to immediately marry her before Candabul returned, who, by learning of this, told his mother Lagarrona, who made certain sorcerous preparations which she gave to Candabul, who then went on his way invisible to the Christian home.

He arrived too late, as the girl was already married, placing then those sorceries under the pillows of the newlyweds, where they slept. Candabul then also placed certain materials in the clothes of the groom, who, as he got dressed was immediately struck down with sickness, losing his speech, and, even though all of the neighbors tried to help him with medicine, he was gradually consumed and died within 24 hours.

The parents of the bride were greatly saddened and decided to marry her again, to which Candabul responded by doing the same as he did to the first husband once again; and, having their daughter marry yet another time, Candabul did the same again.

These Christians no longer knew what to do to marry their daughter and insure her happiness, and as such, sent a message to the sorceress' son so as he would come get her back, for they had no other remedy, as this was not only killing the grooms, but also causing great losses to those Christians' farm.

In the meantime, they informed the law to come to their home in order to arrest Candabul for the traitorous death of Matacabel, which was indeed performed to the great relief of the Christians, who were very worried. They then married their daughter to a Christian called Fabrício, a wealthy man with a farm not far away from there; and, as the people from that place had called the girl the *Sempre Noiva*[148], for having been married four times in such a short time, that place become known as the Sempre Noiva, as is still known to this day.

Candabul was sentenced to be hanged and quartered, for the killing of Matacabel. Learning of this, Lagarrona placed her magic and sorcery to release him.

That night, in the prison, many dark shadows enveloped in fire appeared, wanting to break the building apart, to the point of making the guards want to abandon their post, but, upon informing the *alcaides*[149] they become suspicious that this was the work of the prisoner's mother; for they saw many armed giants and wild animals.

They then tied the hands and feet of the prisoner and took him out to fulfill his sentence; but, as they arrived at the gallows, the sky roared with great thunder and lightning, frightening everyone present, and immediately after there came such dark clouds that enveloped everyone and they could not see each other. The earth split open and some dark shadows emerged, flying through the air, carrying snakes in their hands with which they fustigated all the present. Then, after a great noise and earthquake, the sky became clear again.

Immediately the executioners rushed to deal with the criminal and wrapped the noose around his neck, hanging him. As they were preparing to cut him up, they saw that he had turned into a donkey, to the great amazement of all those present, becoming obvious that this was the work of Lagarrona, for they saw the criminal escape, running away throughout the fields.

When Lagarrona saw her son, she sent him off, enchanted as he was, to the Sempre Noiva, to where Fabrício lived with his wife, while she made the preparations to disenchant him and take possession of Fabrício's wife.

The law rushed after Lagarrona, so she would give them her son or fulfill the sentence herself; but, upon finding her door very well closed they had to force their way in and break it down, which she did not hear for she was so immersed in her sorcery.

When the officers of the law entered, the *Bruxa* was standing, with her left hand raised and with her right hand waving in the air, as if writing something. In front of her was a mirror where she gazed upon herself; above this mirror was the open hand of a man, which slowly closed itself, and, whenever it was completely closed, she would bang her foot on the ground and once again it would open.

On the floor was painted a *signo-saimão*, and in the middle of it was a pole reaching up to the ceiling. At the base of this pole were two rats, holding it up,

---

148. Translator's note: Forever Bride.

149. Translator's note: from the Arabic   , leader. This was a title used during the *Reconquista* to designate a local military leader appointed by the king. It is used still today in Spain to designate a city mayor.

217

for it was supporting a great beam from which a stone with a hole in the middle, like a millstone, was hanging. The beam would lower and rise very slowly and when it was down the *Bruxa* would put her head in the hole, and, while saying certain word, a bat would appear and fly around the house and the beam would then rise. As Lagarrona would make her sorcery with her hands and feet, once again the stone would lower, and saying her words with her head in the hole, once again a bat would fly into the house.

These words being said by the sorceress, so claim Gulpódio, Dicánio, Zurmio and other such ancient authors were the following:

Olenta in pus, nigalao, negabus. Oleolapaô merrinhaô, merrinhao , nhâo, nhân, nhâo!

When first the officers saw her, there were two bats in the house, and, while they waited to see how she performed her magic, two more entered. Not wanting to wait any longer they then entered to arrest her, and this was in such a way that the rats holding up the pole ran away, dropping it and making the beam and the great stone fall in its wake, hitting Lagarrona on the head and killing her, breaking all her enchantments.

The law then hanged her there, where she remained to rot, for that was her house, and from that day that place become known as Lagarrona; taking the name of this sorceress, and as time went by it changed into what it is called today: Lagardona.

The sorceries the *Bruxa* was performing to disenchant her son Candabul were left unfinished, and as such he remained enchanted in the Sempre Noiva, and still today he is there, for one can still sometimes hear loud bangs on the houses of the Sempre Noiva, where Fabício lived for many peaceful years with his wife and three children, of which the youngest, called Rodrigo, King Alvado of Évora took as a gardener on his farm.

PROOF OF FACT

While concluding the reprint of this book we heard from the newspapers of the neighboring kingdom that near Moscoso a poor farmer named Simon Ariza found, near an olive tree, an important treasure buried, mostly made up of women's belongings: jewels, precious gems, etc. Moved by curiosity we consulted this book, in the section that refers to treasures and enchantments, and we found treasure 150, which gives us reason to believe it to be the same treasure as Simon Ariza found:

150. We have the inheritance of Moura Trebinka in the outskirts of Moscoso. It is in the flood lands to the North, near a small olive tree and a male chestnut tree.

The treasure was evaluated at many millions of *duros*. Just a single necklace that Arzila donated to the city museum, by advice of an archeologist, was evaluated at 30.000 *duros*.

THE EDITOR.

COMMENTARIES

to

THE BOOK

OF

SAINT CYPRIAN

THE SORCERER'S TREASURE

Explanation of the Comments

As stated in the Introduction, what follows are extensive comments on the content of *The Book of Saint Cyprian*, being that the inclusion of these comments was the only way I found to make a translation of this book viable and fair.

This is the exposition of how I have come to personally understand *The Book of Saint Cyprian*, and, as such, they can range from the strictly academic, the magically inclined, or the purely personal and emotional.

Even if during my daily life I pride myself in having an academically oriented mind, given my proximity to *The Book*, this was a path I found impossible to follow here. Even if I did try to remain somber and sober, *The Book* always moved my writing out of my comfort zone and into an emotional state.

I am conscious that many times I will perhaps expose myself too much (if not too much, at least more than I would like), or maybe seem like a fool to your surely judgmental eyes, dear reader, but beyond themselves, these comments are my testament and testimony of love to History, Culture, this *Book* and also to You, who chose to pick it up.

The comments follow the same linear layout of *The Book*, meaning that they are divided into the same three books as the original grimoire, and these are divided into the same various sections and points as these books also are.

The comments are then given on a point-by-point basis, in the same order as in *The Book* (occasionally a few non-consecutive points might be commented together, but these will always be labeled with their correct position in *The Book*), with very little instances of a comment on a general concept of *The Book* or on a whole section.

Many of the various comments are, in themselves, divided into various points. These different points are meant to indicate several different aspects that I thought necessary to expose and which are not linearly related, which means that one comment on one point of *The Book* might actually consist of several comments on the same point.

Following most of these comments I have also inserted a list of sources used in their elaboration. These are meant to assist the interested reader in further exploring any particular concept referred to in that comment by offering a reduced and selected bibliography.

Beyond my own original material, as explained in the Introduction, inserted here are those comments made by Enediel Shaiah in his own version of *The Book* (*El Libro Magno de San Cipriano*). In the instances that these feature, they will always follow an indication such as "comment by Enediel Shaiah", with the occurrence of a few instances where I found it necessary to also comment on these comments.

Finally, given the direct mention of the works of Jeronimo Cortez Valenciano in the body of *The Book*, I have collected a few entries from his seventeenth century books which relate significantly to the content of *The Book*.

This has seemed to me to be an author many times overlooked in the history of Iberian and South American folk traditions and magic, and beyond the love of completion, I also hope in this way to offer another lead into what is actually a fundamental player in the whole Ibero-Afro-American magical worldview. Just as with the Enediel Shaiah material, a specific mention to these entries will always precede them in the comments.

BOOK ONE

THE FIRST PART OF *The Book of St. Cyprian* (curiously titled *"Book of St. Cyprian"*), presents itself as probably the most fundamental of the whole tome. Even though one may argue about its organization, it does deliver a coherent and complete system of healing and exorcism through prayers and orisons. Every necessary aspect is covered and every instruction is provided.

However, the most remarkable aspects of this whole system might pass unnoticed or unappreciated to the majority of the general public. *The Book of St. Cyprian* is deeply rooted and located in Northwestern Iberian culture; it is both modeled out of it and, reciprocally, models it.

It is natural that, regarding healing and exorcism, one doesn't need to dally for long; this is a common practice across cultures (particularly Christian, as is logical), and apart from small specific details, the symbolism used is purely biblical, meaning that it is transcultural and generally accessible.

CHAPTER II

1. The open hours refer to particular moments in the day where the borders between the world of the living and the dead are most tenuous and spirits and demons are freer to roam the Earth, a concept similar to the "open body" presented a little further down the book (a body which is particularly vulnerable to the influence and occupation by spirits). These hours, as can be seen, are described in *The Book of St. Cyprian* as the four extreme moments of the daily trajectory of the Sun: Midnight, Sunrise, Midday, and Sunset.

These moments are usually marked even today in some rural churches by a particular bell ring, with the purpose of reminding the faithful to pray at these delicate times. Besides these four, and also depending on the time of the liturgical calendar, several other particular times may be marked for various purposes (regional and national variations do occur), but usually those going into the night, particularly the 21:00 bell ring, the *toque das almas* (ring of the souls), are the ones reserved for the souls of the departed (see the comment on Chapter V, page 239).

Traditionally the prayers of the Trinities consist of: at Sunrise, three Hail Marys, meant to remind the faithful of the annunciation of the Archangel Gabriel to the Virgin Mary, and, at Sunset, a *terço*, one third of a full Rosary. Being that the Rosary consists of fifteen mysteries, with one Mystery consisting of ten Hail Marys (counted on the small beads) and one Our Father (counted on the large beads), which usually can take up more than an hour to pray, the *terço* is merely composed of five Mysteries.

The Book of St. Cyprian, however, places very different prayers with a very specific purpose at these times. Given the place where these prayers present themselves in *The Book*, I do believe these are meant to be practiced by the priest/exorcists on a daily basis so as he may be spiritually fit and protected in order to perform the orisons and exorcisms to follow.

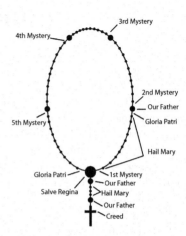

TRADITIONAL CATHOLIC *TERÇO*

2. Looking into the traditional Portuguese folklore of the open hours, it is at these times that we find most forms of monstrous apparitions and otherworldly visitations. In the Azores, Midday is the hour of the *Encantados*, beings stuck between worlds (see the commentaries on Chapter VII, page 257), such as the *Entreaberto*[150] (Half-Open); in Vila Nova de Anços this is the time of the *Rosemunhos* (whirlwinds), duelers of the crossroads, and to the North the *Secular das Nuvens* or *Escolarão das Nuvens* (Secular or Scholar of the Clouds, being that *Escoler* is the name given in Galicia to a necromancer) and also the *Homem das Sete Dentaduras* (Man of Seven Dentures).

In the Algarve, Sunset is the time of the *Pretinho do Barrete Vermelho*[151] (Black Boy with a Red Cap). From Sunset to Sunrise or from Sunset to Midnight is the time when the *Lobisomens*[152] (werewolves) run their *fado* (see footnotes 173 and 174). Midnight is the hour of the *Velha da Égua Branca*[153] (Old woman with a White Mare) and the *Homem do Chapeu de Ferro*[154] (Man with the Iron Hat).

---

150. This type of *Encantado* can be recognized by having a burning ember on his back, which they do their best to hide. These are a strange type of aggressive treasure spirit, which will call its victim and incite them to dig for treasure, killing them if they obey him. One should always insist that the spirit dig himself, and after the treasure is revealed one still needs to cast three drops of blood on it so it will not turn to coal.

151. This is said to be the Devil's youngest son who greatly disobeys his father by being a gentle friend of the good souls.

152. Also traditionally called *lâbushóme, lâbushómem, lâbishómem, labishome, lubishómem, lubishóme* and, don't get too excited, according to traditional lore these most commonly turn into donkeys and horses.

153. This specter is said to have been a woman who refused a loaf of bread to Jesus Christ who appeared to her disguised as a beggar. Upon her death her soul did not enter salvation and as such she now roams the fields on a white mare, producing horrible noises and releasing oxen from their pens. She carries with her a bread carving knife, wears a white bonnet with numerous red ribbons resembling infernal lightning.

154. This is one of the most fearful figures of Portuguese folklore. The *Homem do*

3. Logically, these hours need not only be feared, as, given their nature they have been traditionally elected as the most favorable for the performance of specific sorceries and maleficas. Teófilo Braga gives the following example:

> Should you wish to reconcile with your lover, prick a lemon
> with a needle, while saying the following three days in a row
> at the hour of the Trinities[155]:

> *Just as I prick this lemon,*
> *I thus prick thy heart;*
> *so as thou may not eat,*
> *nor drink,*
> *nor sleep, nor rest,*
> *while thou dost not come to speak with me.*

And Vasconcelos offers the following:

> When a girl wishes for a boy to come see her, she should
> say the following three times at the hour of the Trinities,
> banging her foot on the ground each time:

> *(NN) thou shall not eat, nor drink, nor sleep, nor write, nor rest, if*
> *thou dost not come to see me.*

4. Finally it should be noted that more recent editions of *The Book of St. Cyprian* offer alternative orisons for the Trinities and Midnight. These are as follows:

FOR THE TRINITIES

The Holy Trinity
Accompanies me my whole life,
Let it always keep me,
And have mercy upon my soul;

Chapeu de Ferro is a gigantic bronze colored figure, with a gaping fire-breathing mouth, lurking along roadsides, under olive and fig trees. He appears on consecutive nights, once accompanied by a black pig, once by a deer whose antlers reach the highest towers and once by a black rooster, all of which are forms of the Devil who constantly torments him. Besides his random murdering habit, he has the power to stop thunders and storms, but equally to destroy the whole world, and is said to have been one of the soldiers who tortured Christ. Even if he is fearful, he flees at the mere sight of the *Velha da Égua Branca*.

155. In this particular case, I believe this is only meant to be done at 6 a.m.

Oh Eternal Father aid me,
Oh Son bless me;
Oh Holy Spirit touch me
Protection, honor and virtue;
Never let pride envy me,
Instead of evil let there be good
Holy Trinity
Accompany me always. *Amen.*

FOR MIDNIGHT

Oh angel of my guard,
In this hour of terror,
Free me from terrible visions
Of the terrifying Devil;
Let God make my soul alert
From the dangers of temptation,
Away from me all bad dreams
And the oppressions of the heart.
Oh angel of my guard,
Ask the Virgin Mother on my behalf
To keep me from danger
While I live. *Amen.*

5. Enediel Shaiah further adds the following comment:

> Let the reader forgive us for having preserved the unruly
> form of this poetic monstrosity, for, in formulas of magical
> power, which ever they may be, it is an essential precept not
> to change even a single letter in their great inaccuracies; this
> we are forced to do by motives of an esoteric nature.
>
> We also understand that our readers may find it strange
> to see orisons of a perfectly orthodox character in a text of
> magic, being that the Church's formal condemnation of
> all practices which even hint at a goetic origin is very well
> known. These are typically reserved for the use of a selected
> few, such as exorcists, which, as we all know, not everyone
> can become; but in truth, all we need to do is open the
> most common of religious prayer books to see that all of
> these are in fact true treasure troves of magical conjurations,
> with such prayers having no real difference from those of
> the grimoires, as far as their structure, implementation and
> virtues go.

In a 1902 edition of the *Devocionario: manual, arreglado por algunos Padres de la Compañia de Jesús* printed in Bilbao with all the necessary licenses, we have on page 173 the following orison to ask for health on behalf of a sick person:

Almighty and Eternal God, eternal health of all believers; benevolently accept these prayers we make for these, Thy sick servants, on behalf of which we implore for Thy mercy's aid, so as, when our health returns, may we deliver our actions of gratitude in Thy Church. By our Lord Jesus Christ. Amen.

Very similar are these words to Saint Blaise (page 167):

Most Holy bishop and martyr Saint Blaise, who, upon death was given by the Lord the grace of aiding those who in their illness and suffocations invoke thy name. I beg thee to intercede with the Lord to free me from (this ailment I am suffering), that my tongue and my throat so frequently utter the sweetest names of Jesus and Mary, and never have my lips been contaminated with any words which oppose the Holy law of God, but instead they deserve to eternally sing the praises and divine mercies for centuries without end in Heaven. Amen.

On page 168 there is another orison to Saint Roch asking to free one from the plague and all epidemics, as well as their consequences, for this saint has superhuman power over all kinds of contagion; but in this book there is one far more eloquent prayer from the magical standpoint, the Pact of the Sacred Heart on page 118, which ends on page 121, having the following advertence: This is an easy and simple way for people who do not have much time to pray to accumulate many merits for eternity and attract for themselves, and for the whole world, a great deal of graces and benedictions. All one needs to do is pray this orison once or several times a day and renew the intention of repeating it whenever time is at hand.

The 'method of honoring the saint of the month' (page 170), is of a great esoteric significance and its details are reminiscent of many magical methods, both ancient and modern.

Certainly that the wise are not oblivious of the many points where esoterism and the orthodoxy of the Catholic religion meet, and those who enjoy such studies will find many useful things in the writings of Eliphas Levi (Constant).

6. For completion's sake we should mention that the *Devocionario* mentioned by Enediel Shaiah is actually a most remarkable piece of religious literature, with prayers and orisons for a great diversity of purposes, saints, and afflictions. Every time I read it I am struck by the infinite and plainly open possibilities it presents for any number of magical saintly works. It slams open the door for a proper Catholic hijack.

Given Enediel's reluctance in transcribing the orisons of Saint Roch[156], the Pact of the Sacred Heart and the honoring of the saint of the month, they are as follows.

ORISON TO SAINT ROCH

Glorious Saint, who by thy great charity with the poor and sick earned that the Lord give thee superhuman power over all kinds of contagion and epidemic, promising to hear our supplications when these are offered on behalf of those ailing ones, I beg thee for thy protection to those who are struck by the epidemic God sends to our lands, so as thou may free us from the plague and the dire consequences carried by this punishment from heaven. Plead for the forgiveness of those who are its victims, appear before the judgment of God, and by the remembrance of thy merits ask that their guilt and faults be forgiven. For those who have not endured the grieving punishment of God, save them from it by thy merciful mediation. Oh glorious Saint, make it so as the divine will be made unto me, that, should it be my fate, I be struck by disease, and receive it as a gift from heaven, and, should I be cured of it, may I give graces to God for such a unique blessing; and above all, aid me in loving God and the world so as I may enjoy its glory with thee. Amen.

The Pact with the Heart of Jesus is indeed a most remarkable orison, with vast applicability in several religious contexts well beyond the purely Catholic (colorful Caribbean *Espiritismos* cross my mind). The comments on chapter V (page 239) deal extensively with the Souls in Purgatory mentioned in this orison and, as such, these will not be discussed here.

My God, how many times has my heart ached, passing in front of any Church or any cross, or being tempted, or finding any person coming or going, working or resting, I promise to offer the intentions (as many times as there are instants in a day, as there are grains of sand in the earth and atoms in the air) of the merits of Our Lord Jesus Christ,

---

156. Interestingly both St. Roch and St. Blaise are associated with the Orisha Obaluwaye.

St. Blaise – February 3ᴿᴰ – One should note that this saint is called upon to deal with issues of the throat, which casts some light onto the orison presented in the *Devocionario*.

St. Roch – August 16ᵀᴴ – The symbolism and iconography of St. Roch should be particularly appreciated as in his traditional biography the healing dog, not falling too far from his psychopomp role, is the agent which leads Count Gothard to meet the saint and become his acolyte.

His fasting, penitence, and painful passion, His adorable blood, His humiliations and His death; all the Masses which have been celebrated and will be celebrated, the merits of the Holiest Virgin, the work of the Apostles, the blood of the martyrs, the purity of the virgins, the austerities of the penitents, the orisons of the Holy Church; in a single word, all the great works that have been practiced and will be practiced with the purpose of achieving the forgiveness of my sins, and those of my relatives, friends and enemies, of the infidels, heretics, Jews and bad Christians; my conversion and that of all sinners that are today and shall be; the exaltation of the Church and the fulfillment of Thy adorable will, on earth as in heaven; the acquisition of all the virtues, and particularly this one... the rest of the souls in Purgatory, particularly the loneliest of them, on whose behalf I wish to earn all the indulgences conceded to all good works which I may perform during this day; and finally, the grace of a good death.

I wish to further thank yet once more on my own behalf, and on that of my relatives, and of all men who have been, are and shall be until the end of the world; all the graces which Thou hast given me, be them known or unknown to me; all the natural and supernatural gifts which thou have given me, and all those thou gives me every day, and gives me for the rest of my life, and not only to me, but to all past, present and future men. I also desire to thank the kindness with which thou hast awaited for my penitence, and hast so many times forgiven me and all other miserable sinners.

In a single word, it is my intention to make whatever life I have left into a continuous act of expiation, thankful actions, adoration, supplication, and above all, a continuous act of love.

I wish I could, my God, mend in this way all of my lost time, and pay Thee back all the glory which Thou hast been deprived until now.

METHOD OF HONORING THE SAINT OF THE MONTH:

1 – Before distributing the *cedulas*[157] on the last day of the month say the following orison:

Appoint to me, Lord, the Saint who since eternity Thou hast established for this month, so as he may be my special mediator with Thee, and protect me from all evil, and assist me in the hour of my death.

2 – Take the *cedula*, and read, if you can, the life of the Saint; taking careful notice of the particular virtue which is indicated on the card as the one of that Saint, and the intention, according to the same card, one should have during that month. Place the *cedula* near your crucifix, or the devotionary, or in any other place one may easily see it, so as you may be continuously reminded of the virtue and the intention specified on it.

---

157. A kind of prayer card referring to a particular saint.

3 - On the Saint's feast day one should perform some special offering in his honor, such as performing communion, some form of mortification, etc...

4 - Every day, at a particular time, or whenever it is convenient for you, honor the Saint with the following titles:

Oh Saint (NN)
Guest of the month,
Friend for eternity,
Preacher of truth,
Zealot of perfection,
Who seeks my salvation,
Who tells me to be virtuous,
Who illuminates my understanding,
Who sets my heart ablaze,
Powerful patron,
Loving Father,
Vigilant shepherd,
Who motivates my work,
Who calms my tongue when speaking,
Who speaks in silence,
Light which illuminates all good works,
Captain who incites the battle,
Counselor in troubled times,
Who comforts me in cowardice and depression,
Who consoles me in bitterness,
Who reprehends my faults,
Who aids the fallen in abandoning sin,
Defender against the enemy,
Mediator with God,
Who pleads for the forgiveness of guilt
Who intercedes in the achievement of grace,
Model and example of this pilgrimage,
Protector in agony,
Companion in glory.

ORISON

Oh Saint (NN), I, miserable sinner, trusting in thy merits, come to thee with all my heart and affection to humbly beg thee to be my patron and protector, so as in this way I manage to faithfully exercise the virtue of (name the virtue) which by thy example I have aimed to achieve this month, for the greater glory of God, in honor of thy name; and to achieve the intention of (name the intention) which hast been specifically given to me.

SOURCES

Devocionario - Manual arreglado por algunos padres de la Compañía de Jesús, Imp. Del
Corazon de Jesus, Bilbao, 1889, (digital edition).
J. Leite de Vasconcelos: *Annuario para o Estudo das Tradições Populares Portuguezas*,
Livraria Portuense de Clavel & C.ª, Porto, 1882.
J. Leite de Vasconcelos: *Tradições Populares de Portugal* – Bibliotheca Ethnographica
Portugueza, Livraria Portuense de Clavel & C.ª, Porto, 1882.
Nicholaj de Mattos Frisvold: *Exu & the Quimbanda of Night and Fire*, Scarlet
Imprint, 2012.
Teófilo Braga: *O Povo Português nos seus Costumes, Crenças e Tradições*, Vol. II,
Publicações Dom Quixote, Lisboa, 1994.

CHAPTER III

1. One may find this chapter to be a strange addition and, in truth,
practically obsolete, seeing as a full report of St. Cyprian's life is already given
immediately at the beginning of the book. While some may consider this to
be simply a bad collage of material, as the fluidity of this book allows for such
events to happen, I believe that this is an essential element of this first part.

The story of St. Cyprian and Justina, extracted from the *Flos Sanctorum*,
is meant to give context to *The Book* as a whole, and it serves its purpose
adequately. However, the summary of St. Cyprian's life, as given in Chapter III,
appears to be presented so as to give power and authority to the orisons which
follow. One should note that up to this point the name of St. Cyprian has not
been mentioned in this part of *The Book*, as such, one must establish and define
St. Cyprian as a power to be respected and feared, if we are to call upon him to
aid us in banishing sickness.

One should seriously ponder, if planning to perform these rituals, if this
summary of St. Cyprian's life should actually be recited as preamble to the
healing rituals that are about to follow. Such would actually fit quite well in the
tradition of healing magic worldwide, where the magician/healer narrates the
history of the ailment in question, acquiring power over it and thus the ability to
defeat it. In this case, the ailment is the Devil and his sorceries, and by narrating
the life of St. Cyprian one narrates the method of defeating the Devil and the
said sorceries, further enhanced by the summoning of St. Cyprian, the master
of the creation and destruction of magic. The unique ending to this text should
further underline this, as it describes in quite heterodox terms (when compared
to the narrative of the *Flos Sanctorum*) the final whereabouts of Cyprian's magic,
in a "poor house" where he called "all of the Devil's crafts into." This is a ruin,
a place outside of the contact of the common folk, a space outside of society.

2. Enediel Shaiah does have one comment to add, but we should take into
consideration that this comment is mostly made due to the fact that in his own

version of *The Book of St. Cyprian* (*Libro Magno de San Cipriano*), the original *Flos Sanctorum* narrative is not presented:

> In the *Flos Sanctorum* there are a few more details regarding Saint Cyprian's last days that should be mentioned. Eusebius here is given the role of a counselor which in the book is given to Saint Gregory, who, by the way, seems to have played no such role, but rather he freed Cyprian from Hell, at least judging from the *Flos Sanctorum*.
>
> "In the meantime the grace of Jesus Christ forced his freedom, for he had become lord of his heart. Cyprian had, thus, to endure hard battles against the enemies of his soul, but the God of Justina, who he always evoked, constantly conceded to him the necessary aid to be at all times victorious."
>
> It was also Eusebius who presented the converted Cyprian to the Christian congregation, at whose meetings he was instructed on all aspects of this new doctrine.
>
> Knowing of his fame and of the great prestige of Justina, Emperor Diocletian, who at the time was in Nicomedia, had both of them arrested and taken to the presence of Eutolmius, prefect of Phoenicia. Being taken to Nicomedia they were sentenced to death, achieving the honor of martyrdom on the date of 26th of September. Their bodies were carefully collected by their brothers of faith and taken to Rome, where they were secretly buried by a very devout woman in her own home. In the time of Constantine the Great their bodies were transported to the basilica of St. John Lateran. At least this is how the mentioned collection of biographies tells it.

Chapter IV

1. The "Act of Contrition" mentioned in this series of orisons is a particular type of prayer meant to express sincere and complete remorse for one's sins. It should not be confused with Confession, which is an act of atonement, and, in that sense, is joyful. To be contrite is to feel the crushing weight of one's faults and to be put in a state of profound humility and receptiveness towards the Divine. As a concept it is one of the fundamental bases of all of Christianity.

Given that this might be a complicated state to be achieved by many practicing magicians and sorcerers, those who at least have turned a cold back either on Christianity or on the concept of sin (these are not mandatorily associated), when performing these exorcisms try to at least focus on the emotional state it is supposed to bring. No religion or denomination has a monopoly over the concept of goodness, and it is always possible to find regret in not being as good as one should be or could be.

Thankfully, to aid us in this complicated step, over time a large number of contrition prayers have been written, and it should be possible to find one which does appeal to you, even if you have to change a few words in it. Being that there is no point in transcribing these, we still offer here the one given in the Jesuit *Devocionario* mentioned above by Enediel Shaiah:

> My Lord Jesus Christ, true God and Man, my Creator and Redeemer: for being Thou who Thou art, and because I love Thee over all things, my heart weighs on me for having ever offended Thee; I firmly intend to never again sin, and steer clear of all situations which might offend Thee; to confess myself, and do the penitence which might be imposed upon me; I offer Thee my life, accomplishments and works as satisfaction for all my sins, and I trust in Thy kindness and infinite mercy of forgiving them by virtue of Thy precious blood, passion and death, and in Thy grace to correct me, and aid me in persevering in Thy holy service until the end of my life. Amen.

2. Enediel Shaiah has this to add to the orison of St. Cyprian:

> There is no point in the readers of the *Libro Magno de San Cipriano* trying to understand the significance of these and other orisons and conjuring formulas and the reason behind the fact that some strange combinations of words aren't used for the sole purpose of their explicit meaning. The esoteric tradition greatly consecrates those formulas which come to us magically charged by the fervor of those who have used them in the past. Regarding the value and structures of conjurations, in the commentaries to our edition of the *Red Dragon*, we said the following:
>
> The banishment formulas against malignant influences are of an extremely ancient use and have an exoteric and esoteric origin which we should distinguish.
>
> The first was determined by the most ancient religions, in which man would personify nature and meteorological phenomenon as deities, be them beneficial or adverse, benevolent or fearful, to whom he could pray by means of a particular orison to achieve protection and divert the heavenly wrath. These prayers eventually crystallized into

ritualistic forms consecrated by tradition, receiving the prestige given to all things of great antiquity.

The evolution of religion gradually refined these cults. First we had the idea of multiple gods, then that of a single God developed in the mind of our ancestors with the growing notion of a spiritual reality infinitely greater than the initial primitive religious conceptions; but as man increasingly felt himself dependent on the divine will, orisons acquired a much greater prestige, and supplications expressed by the act of prayer and other exterior cultic practices constituted, and will always constitute, the base on which every religious practice is built.

Being God, in the monotheistic creeds, the All Mighty Father of humanity, it is obvious that the believer should resort to Him in his tribulations, and if that belief admits the existence of the Devil, it is obvious that to him are attributed all evils and that one should resort to God to counteract the power of the king of the abyss.

Initially, supplication for divine intervention is done by fervent prayer, in a non-ritualized form; but as a prayer is done in this way and is perceived as effective, immediately it crystallizes into ritual with the passing generations, constantly surrounded by the loving respect of the faithful who do not dare to change or alter a single letter in it, this by fear that it will lose its magical power. This is how we find these rituals today, and so powerful is this character of invariability that, in Catholicism, we find the use of Latin, a language which no one speaks today, but it is nonetheless seen as a desecration to change it into the language spoken by the believers. In such a way is faith based on this assumed efficiency that it may almost be said to be specific to these combinations of words, which many times the person using them, even if belonging to the clergy, is uttering something whose significance is completely unknown to him, or, should he actually understand them, this is only in a very imperfect way; nonetheless their effectiveness is never doubted for a single instant, as long as they are said exactly as they are described.

Esoterically, that is, for the initiated, the origin is different and surely much more important from the magical standpoint. The secret science has always held as undeniable fact that articulated sounds, words, have a powerful effect on the astral, both by their vibratory power and by the empowerment of the intelligent force of thoughts, of which they are the vehicle. As a consequence, words can be, and are, magical forces which the initiated has at his disposal and combines according to their phonetical value and the effect he wishes to produce, and he thus recognizes the efficiency the believers of the various religions have in invoking with such orisons, awarding their powerful magical effect to the voices which compose it and not to the direct intervention of the divine to which men are praying.

There are magical orisons whose significance would cause the greatest trouble and difficulty to the most intelligent translator. There are words of invocation and conjure of which there is no way of knowing from which language they originate and, however, an occultist will never recommend that these should be changed or modified in such a way as to make them comprehensible, for it is assured that these antigrammatical barbaric terms are a set of well proved magical sounds, which should be implemented just as they are without any thought about significance.

Some contemporary occultists have dedicated themselves to observing the effects of sound and words on individuals under hypnotic trance and in the astral plane, taking advantage of the visionary capabilities of certain subjects, either awake or asleep. The results are that, apart from the creative and destructive power of thoughts, words and the sounds of syllables and letters have a characteristic effect in the invisible regions and in people who are in the position to be affected by their influence. This experimentally demonstrates the existence, or at least the possibility, of conjuring formulas and the terror that every nation in the world feels regarding curses, and also that exorcisms cause certain effects on neurotic and unbalanced people, in those who believe themselves possessed and bewitched, and all those who suppose themselves victims of a supernatural and evil influence, although, as is stated in the *Red Dragon* (La Editorial Irradiación, translated and commented by Enediel Shaiah), one should not pay too much attention to the diabolical disturbances which so greatly troubled our forefathers.

Chapter V

1. Sidetracking all of the content of this part of *The Book*, there is one particular and extremely relevant aspect of this system where we must dally.

As can be observed time and time again, there is an almost obsessive preoccupation in this section with "the good Spirits". This is actually a fundamental aspect of the Galician and North Portuguese culture, commonly known as the *Almas Penadas*, Pining, or Languishing Souls (sometimes erroneously translated as Lost Souls), a particular type of ghost, directly related to the Catholic concept of Purgatory.

The lore about these apparitions is not in itself obscure or mysterious; these are the souls of the departed who experienced a *má morte*, a bad death, usually characterized by either having left unfinished businesses in the corporeal world, having experienced an exceedingly violent death or having lived less than virtuous lives which do not permit them to enter a state of grace in the afterlife or a restful death.

The belief in such specters is generalized (or at least was) and they came to occupy a central aspect in the religious preoccupations of the common folk in these Northern regions. Certainly the Church, no matter how much it tries, can never erase culture, as, in one way or another, culture is immortal, and this set of lore presents itself today as a resurgence of a classical cult of the dead, vividly colored by Christian ideals. The beautiful and flamboyant cults of the dead in South America still owe something to these hardy mountainfolk and their constant and obsessive preoccupation with the afterlife and the tragedy of not achieving rest upon death.

As the belief goes, out of the three places a soul may find itself upon death only Purgatory is temporary. Heaven is the final resting place of the blessed and faithful, Hell is the fiery pit for the sinners and unrepented. Purgatory is left for all those in between.

From the Catholic Catechism:

> 1030 All who die in God's grace and friendship, but still imperfectly purified, are indeed assured of their eternal salvation; but after death they undergo purification, so as to achieve the holiness necessary to enter the joy of heaven.

> 1031 The Church gives the name Purgatory to this final purification of the elect, which is entirely different from the punishment of the damned. The Church formulated her doctrine of faith on Purgatory especially at the Councils of Florence and Trent. The tradition of the Church, by reference to certain texts of Scripture, speaks of a cleansing fire:

"As for certain lesser faults, we must believe that, before the Final Judgment, there is a purifying fire. He who is truth says that whoever utters blasphemy against the Holy Spirit will be pardoned neither in this age nor in the age to come. From this sentence we understand that certain offenses can be forgiven in this age, but certain others in the age to come."

1032 This teaching is also based on the practice of prayer for the dead, already mentioned in Sacred Scripture: "Therefore [Judas Maccabeus] made atonement for the dead, that they might be delivered from their sin." From the beginning the Church has honored the memory of the dead and offered prayers in suffrage for them, above all the Eucharistic sacrifice, so that, thus purified, they may attain the beatific vision of God. The Church also commends almsgiving, indulgences, and works of penance undertaken on behalf of the dead:

"Let us help and commemorate them. If Job's sons were purified by their father's sacrifice, why would we doubt that our offerings for the dead bring them some consolation? Let us not hesitate to help those who have died and to offer our prayers for them."

Given that perfect faithfulness and Sainthood is a rare thing, and that rarer than a Saint is a person completely devoid of virtues, Purgatory presents itself as the most likely destination for the large majority of all deceased. One can then understand how this concept came to gain such relevance in the rural mind and develop itself as its own liturgy, barely under the control of the priesthood.

As one comes to accept that the dead populate Purgatory in large numbers, and that this is a place of atonement, it becomes a small leap to consider that souls might transit from this place into the world as part of that atonement. In some form of logic this actually makes a lot of sense, as Purgatory is more than just a place; rather, it is a state of existence. It would be thus unjust for the judging Divine to keep souls from actively correcting their mistakes while in it. As such, they are permitted to wander out of this Neither-Neither state and into the world of the living, where all action takes place.

The Christian element then takes hold as a touching sympathy for the dead and the pining souls that constantly need relief, which can be given through good thoughts and prayers from the living. Since one is allowed to pray for the dead, and this prayer relieves their suffering, one cannot ever hope to be considered a good Christian if one does not perform this prayer. It is quite the same as having an unlimited amount of food at home and still refusing to give any of it to the hungry constantly knocking at your door (from the Catholic Catechism: "*1498 Through indulgences the faithful can obtain the remission of temporal punishment resulting from sin for themselves and also for the souls in Purgatory*").

It is precisely this cultural aspect and struggle that this section of *The Book of St. Cyprian* so exemplarily covers, offering methods of identifying such souls, the proper techniques to help them find their relief and end their torment, while at the same time sternly condemning all those who attack such souls who only seek succor with the living.

And, of course, there is also some *quid pro quo* in all this: as you pray for the relief of the dead, and consequently free them from their pining state and open the doors of Heaven, so is this action by itself an exercise of charity and goodness, opening the gates of Heaven for you upon your own death. The souls themselves, being liberated by this method, upon arriving in Heaven, will intercede on your behalf with the Saints, who then intercede with God, acting as proper mediators between the Earthly and Heavenly planes (if you are a good Christian towards the dead, expect the dead to be good Christians towards you). In *The Book of St. Cyprian* this is strongly reinforced with the suggestion that every spirit one may save in this manner will become bonded to us, and further aid us in all aspects of life, allowing the exorcist to build up a spiritual network and acquire powerful and grateful familiars.

This is then precisely one of the origins of the wider cult of the *Anima Sola*, the Lonely Soul, observed in many traditional Catholic countries, but particularly remarkable in Santeria and Voodoo. In the same typical but somewhat more magical fashion, in exchange for your prayer and sponsorship, Anima Sola performs certain works for and on behalf of a practitioner.

An interesting element regarding the Anima Sola, only present in Afro-Caribbean religions (where she can also be seen as a guise of Elegua), is the creation of a kind of trinity of lesser but extremely effective spirits with Anima Sola, the Intranquil Spirit and the Dominant Spirit. But these begin to fall already too much outside of the European concept of the lonely souls, as in these Afro-Caribbean cults the Anima Sola is used in very aggressive and tormenting magic, not at all coherent with the typical Portuguese *Alma Penada* behavior (even if they are naturally tormentors of the living, like *The Book of St. Cyprian* describes, this is merely a fatality of their state).

Indeed back to Iberia, a particularly remarkable piece of lore regarding this entity can be found in Galicia (where it is named Ánima Soa), where a prayer exists to have this soul act as a spiritual alarm clock, waking you up at your desired time by saying the following prayer:

"*Oh soul! The loneliest and most abandoned soul of Purgatory! I feel thy pain, I feel compassion upon hearing thy moaning and suffering, abandoned in this hard penitence, and I wish to relieve thy suffering and longing by offering thee all the good* and decent works I may perform during my life, and all the pains I have endured, endure now and will endure in this life, so as thy faults may be paid to God and He may give thee His grace, and I hope that thou will do me the great help of requesting that His light clear my judgment so as I may follow His law, loving Him above all things and my fellow man like unto myself, so as in that way I may deserve His divine majesty and infinite mercy and salvation. Amen."

This should then be followed by five Our Fathers and one Hail Mary.

As the observant and informed reader may notice, this is actually the same prayer presented on most Anima Sola prayer cards, be them from Europe or from the Americas, being that these usually have a small addition before the main prayer, consisting of the following:

CATHOLIC DEVOTIONAL CARD REPRESENTING THE SALVATION FROM PURGATORY BY INTERCESSION OF THE VIRGIN MARY.

"Soul of mine, Soul of peace and war, Soul of the Sea and War, I desire that all I am missing or have lost be returned to me or found."

Given this fact, it seems that this orison may be used for a great variety of purposes, all depending on the intention of the practitioner.

Interestingly, the Ánima Soa in Galicia, as in many other places, is not regarded as a single individual soul, but rather the loneliest soul in Purgatory, the one with the least people to pray for it and release it from its suffering bonds. This makes Anima Sola a title rather than a name, an intelligent system of insuring that eventually every soul in Purgatory will be prayed for in accordance to the services/ atonements it provides.

COMMON ANIMA SOLA PRAYER CARD

In this same vein we find a particular procedure, taken from the Inquisition process of one Maria Ortega (1637), for the contact of this same versatile entity:

Close to midnight prepare an altar with two lit candles, a loaf of bread, and a jar of wine, below a fiery panel of Purgatory and the figure of the crucified Christ. After praying eighteen full rosaries three nights in a row, for the most needy of souls, this soul will appear to you and answer anything you may ask of her.

(See also the commentary to points VIII and IX of the "Mysteries of Sorcery" section, page 343.)

2. Of course besides these there are numerous other orisons and prayers to the dead and the souls in Northern Portugal and Galicia, even with particular festivities and semi-liturgical rituals (in all aspects these are religious rituals colored by Christian symbols and formality, but the priesthood has little to do with them) around the 1st and the 2nd of November, the day of all Saints and the day of the faithful dead respectively (November being *par excellence* the month of the dead). These are usually organized and upheld by specialized semi-secular brotherhoods called *irmandades* or *confrarias das almas*, responsible for the gathering of alms and prayers.

Examples of such festivities and rituals, which place great emphasis on open charity and full community involvement for the relief of the saintly ancestors (as all ancestors are saints), are the *Pau das Almas* (Wood of the Souls), a gigantic bonfire held in the center of a village, the *Lenha das Almas* or *Lenha dos Santos* (Wood for the Souls or Wood for the Saints), an auction of fire wood with the aim of gathering funds for the ordering of prayers and the maintenance of the festivities for the dead, or the *Pão das Almas* (Bread of the Dead), the first bread of each baking batch, which acts as relief for the dead by substituting the flames of punishment by the holy and purified flames used to create the sustenance of the living (never forget that bread is a most sacred and holy food). Other examples of feeding the dead are also abundant, like in the Minho region, where after Christmas supper it is advisable to leave food out with clean cutlery until the next morning, so as the dead may come and take their fill.

Accompanying these events and celebrations even orthodox religious practice frequently suffers a shift from the usual saints directly to the dead, as these are now the receptacle of all prayers, promises, and devotions. This translates itself, in all aspects, as widespread pact-making, deal-making, and commerce with the dead.

Even when abandoning the North and its most impressive cult of the souls, the whole Portuguese countryside is flooded with constant reminders of the ever present and needy dead, as every roadside and crossroad is dotted with small chapels and niches, commonly known as *alminhas*, reminding all travelers to offer a prayer to the souls.

It then becomes clear how French Kardecism would very well fit into this system, with all its notions of spirit elevation and communication, and later give rise to remarkable cults such as Umbanda and Quimbanda in Brazil. The Portuguese/Galician influence on Afro-Brazilian religions is many times overlooked in favor of an Afro-centric one, but the mark is obviously there. One must not forget that a large part of the Portuguese immigrants to Brazil in the XVIIth and XVIIIth centuries were exactly from the North, and these ideas were vividly carried with them.

3. Further developing the topic of *má morte*, this is in truth the whole basis of Iberian folklore: the disturbance of the natural flow of life and death. All supernatural activity arises either from *má morte*, which creates lost and pining souls, or from evil enchantments which violently pull individuals out of the natural continuum of life and death, turning them into *Encantados* (like *Mouras*, see the commentaries on chapter VII, page 257), a state of neither living nor dying. Nonetheless, according to the local lore, the general rule and motivation of most supernatural entities in this area is to actually terminate their supernatural state and achieve a proper death. And it is the living's responsibility and obligation, as Christians, to help relieve their suffering and aid them in achieving their final rest, even if sometimes this may assume anti-Christian aspects.

It is the particularities behind the *má morte* which determine the nature of the supernatural entity being dealt with, as this traumatic experience may deform the souls of the dead into a variety of *Duendes* (*Trasgos*/*Trasgus*[158], for example, are the souls of unbaptized children, a bad death). These are usually regarded as extremely wild entities, barely recognizable as having once been human spirits, nearly impossible to handle and appease (in case you're thinking of trying to have one join your spiritual posse), but, keeping with the motif, it is nonetheless forbidden to exorcise them, for this would throw them into Purgatory or into an even darker place, causing them further suffering. This is further reinforced by the notion that if such an entity is disturbing you it is highly likely that it is somehow related to you, making it an even graver sin to bring them any form of harm. In these cases the only alternative is to conform yourself with the situation and put up with them as you would a relative you don't particularly care for.

4. Catholic prayers to the Souls:

1) *Terço* for the souls. This is most appropriately prayed in the month of the Souls, November, using a regular rosary.

On every large bead say: "*My God, I believe in Thee for Thou art Truth itself; I await in Thee for Thou art faithful to Thy promises; I love Thee for Thou art infinitely good and gentle.*"

---

158. A name possibly related to the Latin *transgredi*, to transgress, or to Tatar.

On every small bead say: "*Merciful Jesus, give them eternal rest.*"

Instead of the Glory (after ten small beads and one big bead): "*Jesus have mercy!*"

On the three beads near the cross: "*Jesus, do not allow me to die without receiving the last rites.*"

2) Novena for the Souls (if possible this should be prayed in front of a crucifix).

Offering

Most high Lord, I offer Thee these prayers in union with the merits of Thy only born Son and my Lord, Jesus Christ, to whom I ask to receive them as payment and satisfaction for my guilt and sins. Confirming what Saint Gregory and the other Pontiffs have conceded to those who pray in front of the image of the Crucified Jesus, it is my will that all that I may come to earn be applied to the Souls in Purgatory, this in the priority which is most divinely pleasing to Thee.

Day one
My Lord Jesus Christ, I worship Thee on the Cross, bearing the crown of thorns on Thy holy head; I plead to Thee that that most noble Cross be the shield which will release me from the ministers of Thy violence. Amen.
Our Father and Hail Mary.

Day two
My Lord Jesus Christ, I worship Thee on the Cross, hurting and covered in wounds, where Thou wert given vinegar and gall to drink: I plead to Thee that those blessed wounds be the remedy and the health of my soul. Amen.
Our Father and Hail Mary.

Day three
My Lord Jesus Christ, by the sufferings Thou suffered for me, a miserable sinner, on the Cross, mainly on that most holy hour when Thy soul left Thy body: I plead to Thee to have mercy on my soul when it leaves the tent, which is my body, and take it to the eternal life.
Our Father and Hail Mary.

Day four
My Lord Jesus Christ, I worship Thee in the Sepulcher, anointed with myrrh and scented balms: I plead to Thee that Thy precious death be my blissful life. Amen.
Our Father and Hail Mary.

Day Five

My Lord Jesus Christ, I worship Thee going down to Limbo, to free the souls of those who wait for Thy desired arrival: I plead to Thee to release my soul from all prisons.
Our Father and Hail Mary.

Day Six

My Lord Jesus Christ, I worship Thee rising among the dead, rising full of glory up to Heaven and sitting on the right side of Thy Eternal Father: I plead to Thee to make me deserving of accompanying Thee to that glory and enjoy Thy blessed vision. Amen.
Our Father and Hail Mary.

Day Seven

My Lord Jesus Christ, blessed shepherd, keep the just in grace, convert the sinners, be merciful to all the faithful and favor with Thy holy love this miserable sinner. Amen.
Our Father and Hail Mary.

Day eight

My Lord Jesus Christ, I worship Thee in Thy coming on the Final Judgment, calling all the just unto Heaven and condemning the sinners to Hell: I plead to Thee that Thy painful Passion may free us from that guilt and take us to eternal life.
Our Father and Hail Mary.

Day nine

Oh beloved Father, I offer Thee the innocent death of Thy beloved Son and the love of his Divine Heart, by all the guilt and penalties I, sinner, have deserved on account of my faults. I plead to Thee also for all my relatives and friends, living and dead: have mercy on all of us. Amen.
Our Father and Hail Mary.

Final Petition

My Lord Jesus Christ, who so admirably revealed the mystery of Thy holiest Passion to Thy blessed servant St. Gregory, I plead to Thee to allow me to reach the remission of my sins, which the venerable Pontiff with his Apostolic Authority freely gives to all those who truly repent their sins and meditate on Thy Passion. Thou who lives and reigns through the centuries of centuries. Amen.

2) From the Jesuit *Devocionario* mentioned by Enediel Shaiah (see pages 229-230):

My Lord Jesus Christ, King of glory, release from the sentence of Purgatory the souls of all the faithful dead;

free them from that lake of harm and pain; free them from the claws of the lion, so as they may not be confounded in the abyss, nor cast them into the darkness, but rather let the Prince of the Angels, Saint Michael, guide them to the house of that eternal light, which Thou promised to Abraham and his descendents. To Thee we offer, Lord, supplications and sacrifices of praise; receive them for the souls who we commemorate; bring them from death to life. Amen.

5. Traditional prayers for the Souls (not necessarily non-Catholic):

1) *Oh God, who wields such mercy and is always willing to forgive, humbly do we ask that Thou feel compassion for the souls of the faithful dead buried in the cemetery.*

Do not give them, Thy servants, to the power of the enemy, neither forget them forever; but order the Angels to receive and guide them to the eternal motherland, Paradise. And since they, in their earthly life, had such trust in Thy mercy, do not permit that they suffer in the mansion of the dead, but, contrarily, turn their hopes into reality, by entering them into the eternal bliss.

V. *Let the souls of all the faithful dead, by the mercy of God, reach their peace.*
R. *Amen.*
V. *Give them, Lord, eternal rest.*
R. *Amen.*
V. *May they rest in peace.*
R. *Amen.*

2) *Oh Mary, Mother of Mercy, I deposit in Thy hands, on behalf of the souls in Purgatory, all my good works, also all other works which might be done on my behalf during my life, my death and after my death, I give myself completely to the compassion of Thy Maternal Heart, Amen.*

3) *Oh Father of all mercy, have pity on the good souls of Purgatory*

Oh merciful Redeemer of the world, Jesus Christ, free the souls in Purgatory from their torment.

Holy Spirit, God of all love, free the souls of the faithful dead from their great sentences.

Virgin Mary, full of grace, Mother of mercy, give unto the souls forgiveness and mercy.

All the Angels, visit them and console them in their prison!

All the Saint and Blessed of Heaven, pray for the souls in Purgatory who suffer so dearly.

Humble Thyselves all before the throne of God, asking for their forgiveness.

Oh God, answer the pleas of Thy Saints and free the souls who suffer so dearly in the fire of Purgatory.

I cry out with them to Thee, Lord: look with gentleness unto Purgatory, and remember Thy mercy and pity.

Oh! How terrible are the flames of Purgatory! How cruel the pains those souls suffer!

By the Passion and Death of Jesus Christ, have mercy on them, oh Father of mercy, oh God of all consolation!

I offer Thee, for the purification of the souls of the faithful dead, the tears of Jesus, and for the relief of their penitence and pains I offer Thee the most precious Blood of Thy divine Son.

I offer Thee, for the expiation of their guilt, the torments which Jesus suffered on the cross, and for the forgiveness of their sins, all the horrors the same Jesus suffered in his Agony.

I offer Thee, for their freedom, all the saintly Masses and the sacred Body and the precious Blood of Our Lord Jesus Christ, which is present on our altars.

Oh my God, Father of mercy, accept with kindness these offering, and save the souls in Purgatory, by the love of the Holiest Mary, and above all by the love of Jesus Christ, Thy divine Son, Our Lord. Amen.

Give them, Lord, eternal rest,
Among the splendours of perpetual light.
May they rest in peace. Amen.

The following are chants and calls for prayer, usually sung by *confrarias* during processions in preparation for or during the appropriate festivities for the dead, in particular on the 26th of November. Usually these chants had to be sung and heard in seven parishes, typically in high places, crossroads, or at cemetery gates. Particularities regarding these are abundant, with some traditions indicating that each line should be said with a single breath.

1) From Covões (district of Coimbra).

Blessed and praised, praised be the sacred death and passion of Our Lord Jesus Christ.

Christian faithful, Christian faithful. Let us remember the souls who are pining in Purgatory with an "Our Father" and a "Hail Mary".

Let it be for the love of God.

Let us pray another "Our Father" and another "Hail Mary" for those riding the waves of the sea and may the Lord guide them to good port.

Let it be for the love of God.

2) From Gafanha da Nazaré (district of Aveiro).

Let us kneel on the ground
We are not the first

In our company comes
Jesus Christ the true

Tormented by pain
And continuously suffering
Thus are the saintly souls
In Purgatory burning

3) Awake faithful Christian, from that slumber
God is knocking at thy door, and thou sleeps and snores.
Thou sleeps and snores, in the turpitude of sin
Be careful should thou awake, buried in hell
Buried in hell, I shall not awake
Our Virgin Lady, will keep us
Our Virgin Lady, accept these steps
For we are begging, for the needy souls
At the Door of the Saintly Souls, God is knocking every hour
And the souls asked him, my Lord what dost thou wish for now?
For thou to leave the world, and go on into glory
In the company of God, take us in good time
Oh my God oh my Lord, oh Jesus, those who find themselves
In the company of the Angels, and the Virgin Mary
The tabernacle is open, and God is already inside
Let us worship, let us worship Jesus Christ the Redeemer
Oh what beautiful tabernacle, all golden
Let us worship, let us worship, the Divine King of Glory
Oh what bountiful tabernacle, such proper gold
Where Jesus Christ was, for nine months encased
Blessed and praised be, the Holiest Trinity
For they came to the world for us, oh Virgin of Mercy
Oh Virgin of Mercy, devotion forces us
To pray for the Saintly Souls, to pray with joy
Men, women and children, people listening
Give the alms thou can, for the souls in Purgatory
As Lazarus asks thee, do not give them lands
Give them crumbs, growing on thy tables
Those possessions thou have, share them in life
Thou may find them in glory, when thou also depart
We shall all die, only God knows where we will go
The Souls of Purgatory we should remember
Who tormented with pain, are still suffering
Thus are the Souls of Purgatory burning
Give alms if thou can, if thou give them with devotion

For thy mothers, thy sons, thy fathers are there
Those alms thou give, do not think we spend them
It is for masses for the souls, this is our devotion
Let us kneel on the ground, we are not the first
In our company comes Jesus Christ the true
Jesus Christ the true and only Lord
Save our souls when they leave this world
Oh blessed Saintly Souls ask Our Lord
For this orison is in thy praise
Let it be in thy praise, and also of the Virgin Mary
For the Souls an Our Father, for them a Hail Mary
(All kneel and pray an Our Father and one Hail Mary)
Thou who gave alms, have given them with devotion
From the Angels thou will have thy prize, in Heaven salvation
Blessed be the Souls, who are in Purgatory
Our Virgin Lady, accept our prayer.

4) From Castanheira de Pera (district of Leiria), this one is usually prayed during a procession between Coentral and Lugarinhos.

The souls of Purgatory
Asked us to come here
So thou may give us alms
To free them from the fire
The tabernacle is open
The Lord is already inside
We may now worship
The Divine Sacrament (bis)
It is good for us to remember
That we shall all perish
Only God knows our destiny
Shall we achieve Glory
Or Purgatory to pine
Oh my God, oh my Lord
The worry weighs so much
And I am not ready
To accompany him
Where he goes so beautiful
So golden as he goes
Gold so well arranged
Where the Good Jesus was
Nine consecrated months
Let us kneel on the ground

We are not the first
Let Jesus Christ pass
Jesus Christ the true
To the door of the Saintly Souls
God knocks there at every hour
So say it the Blessed Souls
Oh my God, what dost thou wish now?
I wish for thee to leave the world
We shall go into the Glory
Oh my God, oh my Lord
There are those who find themselves there
In the company of the Angels
With the Virgin Mary
Blessed and prayed be
The Holy Trinity
Those who come into the world for us
Virgin Mother of Mercy (bis)
Devotion forces us
Let us pray for the Saintly Souls
Let us pray with joy
Jesus Christ the true
Goes in our procession
Accompanied by the pains
Of continuous suffering
Thus are the Saintly Souls
In Purgatory burning
Sinner do not fall
In the pit of sin
Thou might wake in the morning
Buried in Hell
As for that
I gain passion and kindness
In the sole consideration
That the grave is soon to come
Thy relatives are already
In the eternity
Calling to us the living
Have mercy on us (bis)
Have compassion on us
We are in Purgatory
We are in the darkness
Come women and children
All these people listening

Give alms if thou can
To the Souls of Purgatory
The Souls of Purgatory
Do not ask thee for land
They ask only for the crumbs
Growing on thy tables
These possessions thou own
Used to belong to us
Now the only thing of worth
Are thy Our Fathers
We have no use for money
Nor the most beautiful pearls
Only the alms
Of the merciful folk
The merciful folk
Awaiting for Glory
Thou will achieve a great grace
If thou thus remember
If thou hears the mass
Leave all thou art doing and go to it
Our Lady is listening
Jesus Christ is near it
When they say "Holy, holy"
God comes down to the earth
Oh souls ask God
And also the Virgin Mary
To accept our steps
Be it night or day
To remedy the Saintly Souls
They are in thy praise (bis)
Also for the Virgin Mary
For the Souls an Our Father
For them a Hail Mary
Here I am at thy door
Singing the prayer
Come and give us alms
Or may God forgive thee
These alms thou give us
Do not think they are for us
It is for mass, it is for the Souls
This is our devotion
These alms thou art giving
With what devotion art thou giving them?

Thy children are there,
Thy mothers and thy fathers
These alms thou art giving
If thou give them with devotion
In the Earth thou will have the prize
In glory the salvation.

4. Comentary by Enediel Shaiah on the *"Useful orison to heal all sickness"*:

> In the next footnote we will analyze the possibility of Saint
> Cyprian having said such things. Apart from this question,
> to which we give very little merit, in the last words of this
> orison it is easily seen the ultimate proof that this author
> knows very well of the prodigious effects of a firm belief,
> the marvels of self-suggestion and the magnetic magical
> power of words in their most powerful form: prayer (see
> *Magnetismo Personal o Psiquico*, by H. Durville; *El Magnitismo
> Personal o Arte de triunfar en la Vida*, by Garcia Ruy Perez,
> and *Curso de Magnetismo Personal del Imperio sobre si mismos*,
> by Turnbull, published by Editorial Escribano, Ortuño, 4,
> Hotel. – Puente de Vallecas. – Madrid).

SOURCES

Alexandre Parafita: *A Mitologia dos Mouros – Lendas, Mitos, Serpentes, Tesouros*, Edições Gailivro, Canelas, 2006.

Alexandre Parafita: *O Maravilhoso Popular – Lendas, Contos, Mitos*, Plátano Editora, Lisboa, 2000.

António Pinelo Tiza: *Inverno Mágico – Ritos e Místerios Transmontanos*, Ésquilo Edições e Multimédia, Lisboa, 2004.

Daniela Buono Calainho: *Jambocousses e Gangazambes: Feiticeiros Negros em Portugal*, Afro-Ásia, 25-26 (2001) p.141.

Devoção às Almas do Pugatorio, Editorial Missões, Cucujães, 2010.

Donald Warren, Jr.: *Portuguese Roots of Brazilian Spiritism*, Luso-Brazilian review, Vol. 5 (1968) p.3.

J. Leite de Vasconcelos: *Tradições Populares de Portugal – Bibliotheca Ethnographica Portugueza*, Livraria Portuense de Clavel & C.ª, Porto, 1882.

Jaime Lopes Dias, *Crenças e Superstições da Beira*, Alma Azul, Coimbra, 2002.

José Diogo Ribeiro: *Turquel Folklórico, Revista Lusitana*, Vol. XX (1917) p.54.

Manuel J. Gandra: *Portugal Sobrenatural – Deuses, Demónios, Seres Míticos, Heterodoxos, Marginados, Operações, Lugares Mágicos e Iconografia da Tradição Lusíada* – Vol. I, Ésquilo Edições e Multimédia, Lisboa, 2007.

Michel Giacometi – *Filmografia Completa* – 01,RTP Edições, 2010.

Nicholaj de Mattos Frisvold: *Pomba Gira & the Quimbanda of Mbúmba Nzila*, Scarlet Imprint, 2011.

Rezai Pelas Almas do Purgatório, PAULUS Editora, Porto, 2011.

Teixeira de Aragão: *Diabruras Santidades e Profecias*, Vega, Lisboa, 1994.

Various authors: *Conjure Codex - A compendium of invocation, evocation and conjuration*, Volume I, Issue I, Hadean Press, 2011.

Xoán R. Cuba, Antonio Reigosa, Xosé Miranda: *Dicionario dos seres Míticos Galegos*, Edicións Xerais de Galicia, Huertas, 2008.

CHAPTER VI

1. Commentary by Enediel Shaiah:

As the reader may notice, the various sections which compose *El Libro Magno de San Cipriano* do not pretend to have been actually written by this famous martyr of the church, but rather to be a repertoire of magical procedures attributed to this repented sorcerer, which are further complemented by information taken from other various sources by many distinguished authors. The authentic *Book of Saint Cyprian* which we here reproduce, is not (and neither does it try to be) much more than a compilation of formulas, procedures and traditions, which constitute a not always harmonious set, graced by a prestigious denomination which serves as its title and consecrated badge among the catalogued grimoires of the occultism library.

We insist on this point, repeating what we have said in the preliminary warning, so as no one falls into deplorable confusions regarding our claim of reproducing the authentic book, for this authenticity does not mean that it was written by Saint Cyprian, but merely that this is a copy of the famous book which received such extraordinary praise in the eyes of those most competent in magical workings, both by the blind faith it inspires in many regions of the Iberian Peninsula, particularly the Galician and Lusitanian, and by the sheer difficulty in finding this material.

Furthermore, there is a lack of foundation to the various references, both in this as in other books, to an original manuscript written by the Saint himself, so much so as Alfred Maury, in the remarkable critical historical study *La Magie et l'Astrologie*, mentions in the second footnote of page 147 the following: One may find on this subject the legend of St. Cyprian the magician, which confided to his confessor the practices in which he was engaged before his conversion (Bolland, Aet, Sanctor. 26 Septemb. pag. 233 et suiv). It should not be necessary to mention that, should there actually exist an original book, this author would never say that we should consult the words legend places in this martyr's mouth, while referring to what seems to be the collection of the lives of Saints written by the Bolandists.

Anyway, the faith which has indeed been deposited in the magical book we now reproduce is such, and particularly in the disenchantment of treasures, that, in Galicia, this belief is so deeply rooted to the point that reading it and performing the rites in it has on more than one occasion actually made priests fall to the condemnation of the authorities (Jesús Rodriguez López. 'Ligeros apuntes sobre las Supersticiones de Galicia'). The *Ciprianillo* (which in the current edition is placed together with other sections of the *Libro Magno*, making in this way a complete edition), a book not in any way less exalted by tradition, is presented to us with no less confidence than that which it inspires among the Galician peasants, as the great poet Curros Enriquez writes. And since this work has forced us to include the fearful verses (if you can call them verses) of the second chapter, we thus take our revenge by including the beautiful poetry of this illustrious Galician poet.

This is a follows:

Contame, Xan, que che pasa
Pra, dempois d'haber Mercado
Casa e hortas
Vender hortas, vender casa
Y andar oxe atravesado
¿Pol-as portas?

Hay quen di que non sei cando
Non sei quen falouche a orella
Cousa estrana
D'un libro de contrabando
Escrito na vella fala
Castellana.
Entr-as follas revesgadas
D'ese libro, dánse seña
De tesouros
E riquezas enterradas

Pe dos rios e das brañas
Pol-os mouros.

Pra co libro fagueres
Traballache cal ferido
D'unha espora;
Fuche rico antes do seres
Mais agora qu'otes lido
Que es agora?

¡Pobre Xan que desengaño!
Cantas terras rexistrache
Cos teus ollos,
Rexistrachelas en vano
O tesouro que'atopaches
¡Foi de piollos!

———————

Tell me, Xan, what has happened
For, after having had the market
House and farms
To sell the farms, sell the house
And today you are
Begging at people's doors?

Someone told you I know not when
I know not who spoke in your ear
Such a strange thing
Of a contraband book
Written in the old tongue
Of Castile

Among the old pages
Of that book, there are the secret words
Of treasures
And riches buried
Near rivers and brushes
By the *Mouros*
To get this book
You worked until you bled
With a spike;
You were rich before

But now that you have read it
What are you now?

Poor Xan what a disappointment!
How many lands did you register
With your eyes,
Registered in vain
The treasure you found
Was but lice!

2. This poem mentioned by Enediel Shaiah is called O *Ciprianillo*, being that *Ciprianillo* is the common name given to *The Book of St. Cyprian* in Galicia. It was originally published in the book *Aires da miña terra* by the mentioned poet, Curros Enríquez, in 1880. The poem is actually much longer, and it tells the tale of Xan de Deza, an archetypical Galician man who gets rid of all his possessions to acquire a *Ciprianillo* and is consequently thrown into misery. The poem is quite aggressive with *The Book* as it urges both temporal and ecclesiastic authorities to ban it.

However, the situation it describes was actually a very real problem in XIXth century Galicia, with shady editions of *The Book* being smuggled into that region and sold to farmers for more than unreasonable amounts.

This was also the same motivation behind the publication of the book *Brujos y astrólogos de la Inquisicion de Galicia* by Bernardo Barreiro in 1885, which included in it a full "*Book of St. Cyprian*" as a lengthy appendix, which was actually a Spanish translation of the *Grand Grimoire*. This choice was not in itself absurd, as this is another grimoire with significant magical treasure connections and, in all honesty, one of the early commercially available *Books of Saint Cyprian* was indeed just a Spanish edition of the *Grand Grimoire*.

Anyway, this book by Bernardo Barreiro was intended to be published as a cheap edition to prevent farmers from squandering all their possession on the purchase of a *Book*.

SOURCES

Bernardo Barreiro: *Brujos y astrólogos de la Inquisicion de Galicia y el libro de San Cipriano*, Extramuros Edición, S.L., Sevilla, 2010.

CHAPTER VII

1. The current ritual and subsequent list of treasures are possibly the most fundamental part of *The Book of St. Cyprian*. From my analysis and meditation upon this book, this has come to reveal itself as the core, the very heart of the mystery of it.

Of course this is a fairly common kind of ritual in grimoires, with an extraordinary ancient tradition, but nowadays, many times, considered a mere curiosity, rarely taken seriously. Records regarding these kinds of magical treasure hunting abound in all nations, continents and ages, and generally these are always "long in the effecting, and bringing thereof to pass, and to be a piece of tedious & tiresome practice"[159].

At its core The Book of St. Cyprian has always been intrinsically linked with treasure hunting, and Northern Iberia has always been a land of treasure hunters. Here we find the Roteiros de Tesouros, Treasure Guides, a quality of books solely devoted to listing the locations of such buried treasures. Among these the Millonario de San Ciprián, an early commercially available proto-Book of St. Cyprian which consisted entirely of a list of treasures and their proper method of disenchantment, should be highlighted for its historical significance. This booklet, however remarkable, should not be taken too seriously (not without a good dose of humor at least) as many locations, inscriptions, and incantations are merely anagrams of such pearls as "This is the last test of my stupidity and human misery".

In the traditional sense such magical books have always been a part of the folklore of the Atlantic rim of Iberia; in Galicia you have the legends of the Libros de ler e desler, Books of reading and unreading, said to be used by priests to banish Bruxas, Nubeiros (cloud spirits, creators of thunder and storms, related to the Secular das Nuvens and Escolarão das Nuvens mentioned above) and to disenchant treasures. By reading them in the proper direction they produce one effect, if you read them in reverse they produce the opposite effect.

Furthermore, the actual Book has always had other uses and functions in wider folk treasure hunting traditions besides those specified in its content. Teófilo Braga mentions one such tradition from the Minho in which The Book is used for the creation of two rabdomantic wands (see Enediel Shaiah's addition on point VII of the "Occult Powers" section, page 303). This details that on St. John's day[160] one should cut two wands from a holly bush, two decimeters in length, the moment the Sun reveals its first rays. While one is cutting the wands, the liturgy[161] of St. Cyprian should be read from The Book (I assume this is the ritual in The Book... or perhaps a lost section of a lost Book). Afterwards you extract the medulla and fill the wands with mercury, cover the tips with leather caps similar to thimbles and cover the length of the wands with braided straps as a whip. These wands can then be used indefinitely and to do so one must go to the place where treasure is thought to exist, and, while a priest reads from The Book of St. Cyprian (I think you can probably just ask a friend), by balancing the

---

159. David Rankine: The Book of Treasure Spirits – A grimoire of magical conjurations to reveal treasure and catch thieves by invoking spirits, fallen angles, demons and fairies, Avalonia, London, 2009.

160. He does mention day, not eve or night.

161. The actual word is ofício.

wands horizontally on your thumbs, you slowly start walking and as soon as they turn towards the earth it means that you are in the presence of metal. You may then draw a circle on the ground, so as all may take refuge inside it, and while the priest reads the liturgy of St. Cyprian you may dig for the treasure.

Vasconcelos also mentions a similar tradition meant to force the Devil to fetch a treasure.

> Firstly it is necessary to acquire *The Book*. Then you must acquire an olive tree branch, which you may accomplish by climbing one of these trees and as soon as the first rays of the Sun break over the horizon, cut the branch using a sickle, having then the branch blessed by a priest. On the day you wish to perform the operation, you must gather the priest and two other people, who must carry lit candles during the whole rite. On that night, which should be immensely dark, all should go the selected location around midnight, draw a circle on the ground using the branch and kneel inside it. The priest, who should be wearing his stole and surplice, may at this time begin the prayer, which will cause great waves of fire to burst from all sides but never cross the circle, all sorts of creatures and phantoms will appear and finally Lucifer will ask the attendants – "What wish thee?" – and you should answer – "I wish for the treasure which lays in such place" – Lucifer may then start placing more questions and doubts regarding the delivery of the treasure but all must stay strong and insist on it, for he will forcibly deliver the treasure. After the treasure is delivered it is then necessary to make another banishment orison which is called the *imposta*, which will make all return to the state it was in before the beginning of the operation and when all is done you may go home and divide the treasure.

Again, it is not really explained in which part of the ritual *The Book* is supposed to enter, but most likely it is in the orisons to summon/banish the Devil and also in the location of the treasure one gives the Devil.

2. But the actual ritual in question is worthy of a little more attention.

In the current Portuguese book it usually features twice, or is mentioned twice; in the first part of *The Book* regarding the disenchantment of 148 treasures from Porto de D. Gazua, referring to Northern Portugal, and in the third part of *The Book*, referring to 174 treasures from Galicia. The rare Spanish editions which do possess this ritual usually only have the one referring to Galicia, as this actual section appears to be a genuine Portuguese product in the continuum of *Books of St. Cyprian*, which did flow into Spain in the 1905 edition of Enediel Shaiah in a selective form. Similarly, of all the Brazilian editions I have consulted only two possess such a ritual and treasure list, which in truth is understandable, not only for the lack of interest that a list of Iberian geographical places would have for a Brazilian treasure hunter, but for other cultural reasons we will explore in due time. However, in Maria Helena Farelli's[162] version of the book and one other by the publisher Pallas (which also possesses the disenchantment ritual in an incomplete form) we can also find a list of 26 extra treasures, being that these are spread all throughout the world and not just Portugal and Galicia.

Approaching now the ritual itself, certain aspects of it should be put into perspective, first and foremost, the protection "Triangle".

Regarding the word "AGLA" we shouldn't dally too much. It is, as is widely known, the notarikon of *Atah Gibor Le-olam Adonai* or *Athah gabor leolah, adonai*, frequently used as a divine name. However, the presence of four AGLAs in the "triangle" does cause some suspicion. The number four will automatically invoke in the attentive reader the idea of the four elements or four directions, but should this be the case, it is indeed strange that this is the only divine name used, as one would expect different names for different elements/directions. But, alas, this is mostly a mystery and not so much a riddle.

On the "triangle" itself some may choose to see in there a unicursal hexagram, but, if we are to take that approach (which is quite legitimate), one thing must be taken into consideration. From the usual description of the unicursal hexagram, from the Golden Dawn system, it *"symbolizes the presidency of the Sun and the Moon over the four elements united in and proceeding from the Spirit"*. This is of course displayed as follows:

The major difference with the current sigil of protection is that, since it is inscribed in a rectangle, the Sun and the Moon lose their presidency and are now on equal footing with the elements. The line which now crosses the sigil

---

162. Leader of the Temple of Gipsy Magic.

vertically may then indicate that very same thing; just as with the elements, the Sun and the Moon now bear a direct connection with the Spirit. However, this hypothesis is seriously weakened by the hexagram being inscribed in a rectangle and not a square, the form of stability and equilibrium. Furthermore, in the current disposition, the diagonal lines connecting the elements to the Spirit are indeed longer than the verticals, uniting the Sun and the Moon. As such, one may even consider that, in fact, the elements are actually presiding over the sigil, making it an absolute opposite of a Golden Dawn unicursal hexagram.

This idea may have its serious merits if we let the presence of the four four-letter AGLAs capture our imagination, making it, probably, a strongly elemental sigil, which, strangely, diminishes its possible sexual symbolism. But, independently of what we choose to see, this hypothesis clearly breaks the possibility of inscribing this sigil of protection in the Qabalistic scheme of the Tree of Life.

One other interpretation of this sigil may arise if we take some liberties with the writings of Andrew D. Chumbley, as this sigil does resemble some expressions of the Sigillum Azoëtia, whose tapestry of intercrossing lines illustrates the Sabbatic Grimoire *Azoëtia*. This hypothesis is, to say the least, remarkable and, should it be so, it suggests that *The Book of St. Cyprian*, as a grimoire of sorcery, is somehow related to the Sabbatic Craft of Essex, most probably through an immaterial link, making them, consequently, part of the same magical current. But this discussion is best reserved for actual initiates into the Sabbatic Craft.

If we now abandon such conjecturing and fall back into the roots of Portuguese folklore and symbolism we may find a similar sigil being used in this territory for quite some time. Traditionally this is a particular form of what is called a *sino-saimão dubrado*[163], a doubled sign of Solomon. This symbol, however, cannot be equated with the unicursal hexagram, as the vertical line which crosses through its middle is indeed a fundamental aspect and cannot be removed without altering the significance of the sigil (and in truth it does not alter its unicursality), as eight appears to be the dominating number among the *sino-saimão dubrados*. The sigil itself bears no particular or special significance; it is merely a traditional sign of protection against sorcery, Witchcraft, and the Devil. Of the forms that the *sino-saimão dubrado* may take, this one is, however, the least common, being more frequent the ones that follow:

---

163. Traditionally, an individual specialized in sigil work and writing is called a *Carago* or *Caraju*, and his sigils are called *Carântulas*. These should not be confused with *Siglas Poveiras*.

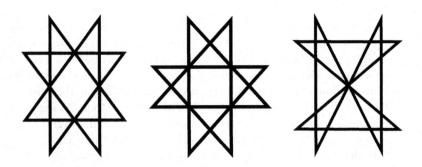

The number of crosses around our sigil does also appear to be flexible, as a version with merely six of them has been observed by Leite de Vasconcelos, three at the top and three at the bottom. In these dealings numbers are always important, and the six may aid some aspiring occult treasure hunters to make a greater Kabbalistic sense of the sigil, although overcharging the solar symbolism here may actually be counterproductive, both for the reasons already mentioned and those still to follow.

An alternative to this sigil is also given in Enediel Shaiah's *Libro Magno*, but this is actually just the circle of protection from the *Grand Grimoire*. How this circle came to feature in the St. Cyprian current is actually quite simple, as one of the early commercial editions of the *Book of St. Cyprian* was actually just the Spanish translation of the *Grand Grimoire* (as mentioned previously) and, as such, occasionally certain chapters and sections from this book emerge somewhat unexpectedly along the various editions. In the case of the Enediel Shaiah edition in particular, it is originally provided in the text of the *Libro Magno* in a chapter which is actually just a direct collage of the *Grand Grimoire*. Later in the book, in the treasure disenchantment section, instead of the "triangle" it is simply said that the conjurer and his companions should always be inside "the circle". It should be further noted that this same circle of protection is also given in the Sulfurino Book[164].

The second aspect that should be noted is a particular sentence in the Second Banishment, immediately following the initial Latin – the sentence *o Senhor seja comigo e com todos nós. Amén*. This sentence is in Portuguese and it simply reads, "*May the Lord be with me and with all of us. Amen*" and the reason why I did not translate it is quite simple. This is actually a detail which is practically impossible to perceive in Portuguese editions of *The Book*, but upon analyzing Spanish editions one may notice that this sentence always remains in Portuguese. If this was a mere distraction by the original translator or a deliberate choice is for each one to decide, but it nonetheless stands there between the liturgical and the vernacular almost to make the transition between one and the

---

164. A heartfelt thanks to Félix Castro Vicente, once again, for calling my attention to this.

other, and for that reason I did not translate it nor do I think it should ever be translated if one wishes to perform this ritual[165].

3. Some might be naturally put off by the exaggerated Christian tone of this ritual and by this general undefined "Devil" being banished.

In truth, treasure finding throughout Europe is usually associated with the Devil for a number of reasons, ranging from our pagan roots to standard Christian ethics. The Devil, as an underworld power, has natural claim over the riches of the earth, and a buried treasure is naturally property of the Devil. Moreover, approaching the issue from a Christian perspective, wealth is meant to be earned from your own hard and honest work, and such buried treasures promote an easy way into wealth which cannot have its roots anywhere else besides the Devil. In the purely dualistic perception of religiousness, in a Christian Catholic environment, when you are not in league with the Church/Jesus you must be in league with the Devil.

Of course, if such perception of the divine offends you, you may chose to place yourself outside of this forced duality and try to work yourself around the ritual without all that "Jesus," but I for one think that a great deal of richness is lost in this process. And in all truth such offense need not apply in this case.

If we manage to work in the proper cultural context we can see that all such sharpness of concepts is easily smoothed. The Devil in Iberia is not a linear character (much to the Church's distress), particularly in the Northwestern regions (Galicia and Northern Portugal). Evil is not an attribute of the Devil here, rather cunning is. If we look at the rich mythical corpus of the Devil we find him mostly as the anti-hero, the trickster, a force of change, worthy of respect and even honors. He is mostly a powerful chthonic tutelary spirit, or a monstrous agglomeration of wild natural elements, acting as balance keeper and even law giver, dangerous, no doubt, but not inherently evil. Examples can even be found in The Book of St. Cyprian, in small notes and paragraphs which add flavor and context to certain sorceries, in the dialogues of Cyprian and the Devil, and more remarkably in the tale of Victor Siderol, with the Devil being not only a keeper but also a dispenser of wealth, frequently advising Siderol to be charitable and less ambitious.

But one may still consider all the Jesus in this ritual to be exaggerated[166], but that is merely the natural response in a Christian society to all of the Devil involved here, either implicitly or explicitly. Of course it may even be that the

---

165. There are many possible reasons and ramifications based on this issue of a sentence in Portuguese standing between the liturgical and the vernacular, but such exposition is not the objective of the current study.

166. I've heard people complain about having to call out to Jesus or any other Christian characters in many of these grimoire rituals, however, I have never heard anyone complain about having to call out to the Beast or having to face the Boleskine house during Thelemic rituals.

ritual is as it is just as a cover to keep the priesthood from frowning over it even more, and actually you don't need to banish the Devil so aggressively as this ritual indicates. Victor Siderol's dealings with the Devil were always courteous (more from the Devil's side, who always appears generous and loyal, than from Siderol's, who is always a doubtful prick willing to go back on his deal at the slightest hint of difficulties) and if this ritual also comes as a follow up to his story then maybe it can be taken as an example.

So, to sum up, if all this bothers you, then maybe you can smooth out your Jesus together with your Devil, or drop the Jesus if you think him unnecessary, or even just be a democrat about it and get rid of them both altogether. But know that if you adequately juggle these concepts you may be able to find yourself in that cultural Northwestern Iberian goldilocks point where you need not deny the Jesus to be a friend of the Devil, or vice versa, and that is where, I believe, this ritual is meant to operate. For you see, you need two sides here, you need the "Jesus"[167] and the "Devil". This is a complex Neither-Neither fluidic travel between states.

4. One final issue now brings us to the core of the matter: the *Mouros* mentioned in the second banishment.

Mouros and *Mouras* have already been mentioned within this book a few times, and when dealing with *The Book of St. Cyprian* in a conscious way it is nearly impossible not to mention them. This is unfortunately not an easy topic; it stands at a unique crossroad of history and folklore, a far-reaching mythical complex which cannot be explained quickly[168].

This is the crucial point which makes it evident how *The Book of St. Cyprian* is imbued and deeply intertwined with Iberian folklore. This book here goes well beyond its physical existence; it becomes an idea, a black box concept of all mystery and magical operations. This may come to explain why transporting this book outside of the Ibero-American cultural context in fact reduces it, and it may also come to explain why this book can never be responsibly translated just as it is. It is not about translating words, it's about translating ideas, concepts, and culture.

Mouras and *Mouros* (also *Moiras*, or *Moros*, in Castilian), or, more accurately, *Mouras Encantadas* and *Mouros Encantados*, stand as the most relevant figures in Portuguese folklore. These are, logically, also strongly present in the various regions of Spain, but it is in Portugal that they came to inhabit a truly dominant

---

167. Some may think that Jesus is given too much credit here and that I should have written "God" and the "Devil". From this Northwestern Iberian point of view the counter-balance of the Devil cannot be God, for the Devil is an entity always close and ready to intervene in the mundane lives of men, either by his own initiative or by evocation. God on the other hand is too distant from the world; the only one even remotely capable of the interaction the Devil has with humanity is Jesus... alternatively some Saint or Angel of respectable power.

168. Before there was South-American syncretism, there was Iberian syncretism.

role in the rural folklore, taking up the "niche" of most other mythical figures. Whereas all along the Spanish nations you have *Hadas* and *Fadas*, *Xanas* and *Janas*, in Portugal you mostly just have *Mouras*[169].

From a, let's call it, pseudo-historical perspective, the *Mouras* originate from the Ummayad occupation of Iberia, or more precisely from the Christian *Reconquista*, as "Moura" and "Mouro" are simply the feminine and masculine Portuguese words for Moor. Legends say that as the Moorish peoples were being driven out of Al-Andalus at the tips of Christian spears, some left their treasures behind, buried, and, as the powerful sorcerers that they were, enchanted them together with their beautiful daughters meant to act as their guardians[170]. These treasures, it is said, they hoped to once again recover when, from the shores of North Africa, the Muslim armies would take back Iberia from Christian rule. Hence their daughters became the *Mouras Encantadas*, Enchanted Moors.

Stepping now into more complicated waters, we have that, arising from the *Reconquista* and the exacerbated duality and tension between Christian and Muslim populations in the medieval Iberian context, in the collective mind of the young warring nations, the abstract Moor became associated with the concept of the "Other". This concept, in due time, became an amalgamation of all that which was not Christian, not "Us", expanding well beyond the mere Muslim. As such, in the rural imagination, the *Moura* and *Mouro* became the great concept on which to drop any unexplained unnatural phenomenon. Standing stones, dolmens, Iron and Bronze Age ruins, remnants and echoes of Roman and native pagan cults[171], all things which in the landscape evoked another time, another people, all streamed into this umbrella concept, feeding it like rivers to the Ocean. All that was not "Us", was *Mouro*.

As with Irish fairy lore, *Mouros* became the underworld inhabitants of old *castros*[172], caves, ruined temples, fountains, creeks, dolmens, and wild and inaccessible places. These places of the dead became the places of the *Mouras*, known today as the Rock of the *Moura*, the Cave of the *Moura*, the House of the *Moura*, and so on throughout the whole of Iberia, entrances to the *Mourama* (*Mourindade* in Galician), a place of imprecise location, whether underground or somewhere in a distant Muslim country, the Iberian *sídhe*, the underground realm of the dead. They became the strange and the ancient, irradiating the glamour and the fear of the alien and exotic.

---

169. This is logically not a general statement. The Algarve can boast quite a healthy mythical body of *Jans*.

170. One of the earliest accounts of buried treasures in Galicia appears in the *Liber Sancti Jacobi*, also called *Codex Calixtinus*, a XIIth century guide for the Santiago pilgrim. One passage reads: "the moors hid their possessions under the earth and escaped".

171. In certain regions *Mouro* is also a synonym for pagan or for someone who is not baptized.

172. A Bronze age Northern Iberian fortified settlement.

Together with this, old fragments of folklore were assimilated into this concept: fairies, nymphs and other small gods all became *Mouras*, as these now have an extremely strong connection to springs, creeks, and natural or ruined water basins, suggesting ancient water cults. Furthermore the very name of "Moura" or "Moira" may suggest a Greek connection with the *Moirae*, weavers of the fates[173] of humans. As we have them now, *Mouras* are then this strange and complex nexus of times and cultures.

Although their mythical corpus is insanely vast, all along Iberia it does present clear lines of coherence, but each case is a mystery to be resolved. There are *Mouras* who guard treasures, *Mouras* who weave, *Mouras* who are the builders of ancient structures, eponymic *Mouras* and so on infinitely[174]. This has led to much confusion, as many *Moura* classification systems have been put forward by folklorists such as Leite de Vasconcelos, Consigliery Pedroso, the Baçal Abboth, Teófilo Braga, Martins Sarmento, Ataíde de Oliveira and countless others. These have always been flawed as they may take diversity into account but never unity.

Making a small detour: for too long has Portugal's understanding of its deeper self been a prisoner of the brilliance of such remarkable men. The work of all these XIXth and early XXth century folklorists is without a doubt invaluable, but the reverence and untouchable holiness it has been elevated to until this day has for too long muddied our vision of ourselves. Well beyond the merely academic sphere, I have seen the difficulties and dead ends clinging to the works

---

173. "Fate" will lead us to another crucial concept in Portuguese and Galician folklore, the *fado*. This, beyond the delicate and beautiful music from Coimbra and Lisbon, is the typical word for all earthly tragedy. All have a *fado* to follow, and none can escape it; our existences and lives are our *fados*. The folkloric connections here are extremely rich, as to be *fadado*, fated, may also mean to be under the influence of a *fada*, a fairy. Like humans, all mythical and folkloric figures have their *fado*, their tragically obligatory trajectories, be them *Bruxas*, *Trasgos* or *Mouras*, all have their *fado*, their pining, for an enchantment or a curse is a *fado*.

174. Occasionally some take on certain attributes similar to *Peeiras*, also called *Lobeiras*. These are a particular kind of *Bruxa*, a wolf shepherdess, the *fado* of the seventh daughter of a couple which has only had daughters, who is not baptized Benta or Custódia and whose godmother is not one of her older sisters. This is the female counterpart of a *lobisomem*, a werewolf, the seventh son of a couple which has only had sons, who is not baptized Bento or Custódio and whose godfather is not one of his older brothers (many variations exist). The fado of a *lobisomem* is to, on the nights he is to transform (not necessarily into a wolf), run seven counties, seven churches, seven border towns and so on. For this reason they are usually called *Corredores*, Runners, because they very literally run their *fado*. Curiously, a particular Brazilian piece of lore does state that in order to become a *lobisomem* one needs to go to a crossroad where an animal (usually a donkey) has rolled around in the dirt. He should then also roll around in that dirt while reciting a certain passage from *The Book of St. Cyprian*. From my investigations I have not been able to determine which passage exactly this refers to... but there are people out there who know.

of Leite de Vasconcelos has led certain attempts at a Portuguese or Lusitanian pagan reconstructionism.

Lusitanian ethnology, anthropology, and mythology (good Lord the mythology!) does not end with Vasconcelos (as all of us, a tragic child of his time), it merely begins.

Gladly new winds are now blowing in the academic sphere; the rest of us just need to realize that.

Focusing on the concept of *Encantada* or *Encantado*, this is a complex and far-reaching idea, as there is a whole Iberian-American lore on "The Enchanted Ones" which goes well beyond the *Mouras*. From (ironically) Leite de Vasconcelos, *Encantados* are "beings forced by an occult supernatural force to live in a certain state and place, as if numb or asleep, while a certain circumstance does not break their enchantment, occasionally, one other circumstance will double their enchantment"[175].

A very similar concept exists in the *Encantado* cults of Brazil, such as *Pajelança*, *Terecô*, *Jarê*, *Catimbó*, *Jurema*, or *Encantaria*. In these, the concept of the *Encantado* is a syncretic fusion of Portuguese, of which the *Moura* is the paradigmatic example, and native lore and practices. The *Encantados* are people which did not die, but instead *encantaram*, passing into an invisible world, from which they may return to manifest themselves in the bodies of their devoted initiates. These are not spirits but in fact humans of flesh and blood who, due to their *encanto*, can manifest themselves as men, animals, or incorporate into other humans.

From this perspective the Brazilian *Encantado* is a much more fluidic and dynamic concept than the Portuguese, as more and more *Encantados* can come into existence, since in fact, anyone can in theory become an *Encantado*, while in Portugal the *Encantado* is always something of extreme remote existence.

In the particular case of the *Mouras*, as part of their enchantment, and similarly to the some Brazilian accounts, mainly from the Amazon region, they may present themselves under the form of an animal, almost always a monstrous serpent (occasionally having the detail of being covered in fur, displaying a long and great mane, or even of being golden). Some authors[176] see in this a distant echo of *Ophiussa* and the ancient serpent cults of the *Saephe* and *Dragani*, the People of the Serpent and the People of the Dragon, described by Rufus Avienus Festus. While I personally prefer to take my Greek and Roman historians with a grain of salt, I do also believe that this is the appropriate stand to have if you wish to place yourself in an Iberian based *Encantado* cult.

---

175   J. Leite de Vasconcelos: *Opúsculos – Volume V – Etnologia*, Imprensa Nacional de Lisboa, Lisboa, 1938.

176. Dalila Pereira da Costa is the paradigmatic example of this, although she also relates *Mouras* with primordial Great-Mother cults quite intensely... as she does everything.

A remarkable and significant peculiarity of the Serpent *Moura* is its usual method of disenchantment (in Iberia the objective and *raison d'être* of an *Encantado* is to break its enchantment), consisting of letting the serpent coil itself around your body and kissing it, so as she can suck your baptismal oils. The sexual connotation here is quite obvious and significant, further exemplified by the habit of certain *Mouras*, mainly in Galicia, to kidnap and eat small children, the fruit of the loins[177].

If we compare the *Mouros* (masculine) with the *Mouras* (feminine) we can also find many striking differences deserving of attention. *Mouras* always present themselves as seductive and beautiful beyond reason, fair skinned and blonde, casually delighting in all the sanctioned social norms of traditional rural society. Their description places them in an ambiguous position, as the most desired and simultaneously as the most unobtainable of women. Still, they are always regarded with compassion and pity.

The *Mouro's* description on the other hand is closer to their North African namesake, being described with dark skin and dark hair, or sometimes just plain black-skinned (there is an interesting dynamism here between the solar symbolism of Gold and the black skin of the *Mouro* which does not exist with the *Moura*). These are presented as fierce warriors and guardians, sometimes even described as giants made of precious metals, or just plainly as demons. Occasionally, and falling into place with the *Mouro* as a treasure guardian, these can be described as dwarves, under the name *Marochinho* or *Mouro Anano* (Galician). These striking differences between *Mouras* and *Mouros* may suggest that these should actually be treated as distinct entities, two different agglomerates which merely share a name. I, on the other hand, believe that these differences are not contradictory, but merely complementary. The *Mouros* may have a more Gnomic function and quality, and the *Mouras* a clear Nymph association, but they both serve the same purpose and occupy the same space in the rural Iberian mind.

Going back to the pseudo-historical perspective, the *Mouros* are said to have been mighty warriors, left behind to be disenchanted when once again the Muslim armies came to conquer Iberia and, as such, contrary to the *Mouras*, who are mostly involuntary victims of evil sorcerers, the *Mouros* are always regarded with scorn.

Compared to *Moura* legends and folktales, the number of *Mouro* legends is extremely reduced and, as you would expect, as the sexual theme is a constant in these, they usually revolve around young women heroines, whereas *Moura* legends usually revolve around young male heroes.

Mouros, keeping with this theme, are frequently enchanted in the form of bulls, wild boars, other rough wild beasts, or even just as grotesque monsters. The bull is a particularly interesting form, as this animal, besides being the

---

177. This may eventually tie them in even further with *Bruxas*, as these are said to feed on the blood of children during the night.

great totemic beast of the Iberian peoples, has also significant connections to some Brazilian *Encantados* such as Légua Boji[178], leader of the *Codó* or *Mata de Codó* Family, or King Sebastian[179], leader of the *Lençol* Family, occasionally

---

178. Aê Seu Légua Condeinha
Ô Légua Boji Buá (bis)
Junta areia na terra Seu Légua
Areia do mar (bis)

Aê Sir Légua Condeinha
Ô Légua Boji Buá (bis)
Gather the sand in the land Sir Légua
Sand from the sea (bis)

Seu Légua tem doze bois
Na Ilha do Maranhão
Vendeu sua boiada
Foi embora para o sertão (bis)

Sir Légua has twelve oxen
In the Island of Maranhão
He sold his ox herd
He left for the sertão (bis)

Boi, boi, boi, Seu Légua
Tira tamanca do boi Seu Légua (bis)

Ox, ox, ox, Sir Légua
Take the tamanca off the ox Sir Légua (bis)

Seu Légua quando chega
Vem fazendo confusão
Arranca tamanca do boi, Seu Légua
Lugar de peso é no chão (bis)
Aê do Codó, aê do Codó
Seu pai é rei do Codó
Aê, aê lá no Codó

When Sir Légua arrives
He brings a ruckus with him
Tear the tamanca from the ox, Sir Légua
The place of such weight is on the floor (bis)
Aê of Codó, aê of Codó
Your father is the king of Codó
Aê, aê in the Codó

(*ponto cantado* taken from Reginaldo Prandi (org.): Encantaria Brasileira – O *Livro dos Mestres, Caboclos e Encantados*, Pallas Editora, Rio de Janeiro, 2004)

179. In the Luso-Brazilian context, King Sebastian, the Hidden One, is the ultimate *Encantado*, representing not just the lost Portuguese king but a lost and decayed world and society. Although there is abundant Portuguese local lore on how one may become an *Encantado*, Sebastian is probably the only historically locatable person to be accepted into these ranks in the Portuguese context.

The disenchantment of the Christ-like Sebastian is equivalent with a second coming, the advent of a golden age of justice and peace, the Fifth Empire of Nebuchadnezzar's dream or Joachim de Fiore's Age of the Holy Spirit. This has taken extremely impressive aspects in the ill-fated Sebastianist movements of the Brazilian Northeast such as the rebellion of Canudos and the bloodthirsty cult of Pedra Bonita, where an attempt to disenchant King Sebastian and his treasure was made by bathing a particular rock formation with the blood of countless innocents.

His legend and associated symbolism is vast and complex, as far-reaching as the legends of Atlantis or the Hidden Island, where the king slumbers and awaits, and has been fed by figures such as Fernando Pessoa, Camões or countless nameless prophets and madmen from both sides of the Atlantic. His myth crosses cultures and social ranks as the always hopeful better tomorrow.

Rei Sebastião, Rei Sebastião
No balanço do mar aé (bis)
Ele é pai de terreiro (bis)

King Sebastian, King Sebastian
In the rocking of the sea aé (bis)
He is the father of the terreiro (bis)

mentioned as riding a half red half white bull on the beach of Lençol.

Lingering on the Brazilian perspective, *Mouras* and *Mouros* would have even more parallelism with the *Encantado* Family of Turquia (Turkey), lead by Father Turquia, Dom João de Barabaia[180], also called Ferrabraz, a great *Mouro* king said to have fought the Christians. These are warrior *Encantados*, connected to the mythical narratives of the Crusades and sometimes considered as Islamized *voduns*.

Of the *Mouras'* treasures something might also be added. As is usual with many other European fey folktales, these may come in the form of golden tools or combs, objects of a real and practical utility. Alternatively the treasures may

Dentro da guna real aé (bis)	In the royal guna aé (bis)
Chamei na praia, ninguém me atendeu	I called out at the beach, no one answered
Tornei a chamar, ninguém deu atenção (bis)	I called again, no one paid attention (bis)
Chamei na praia, praia do Lençol	I called out at the beach, beach of Lençol
Que é pertencente ao Rei Sebastião (bis)	Which belongs to King Sebastian (bis)
Rei, Rei, Rei Sebastião (bis)	King, King, King Sebastian (bis)
Quem desencantar Lençol	Whoever disenchants Lençol
Põe abaixo o Maranhão (bis)	Takes down the Maranhão (bis)
Rei, Rei, Rei da caridade (bis)	King, King, King of charity (bis)
Ele vem pedindo esmolas	He comes asking for alms
Não é por necessidade (bis)	Not out of necessity (bis)
Rei Sebastião, guerreiro militar (bis)	King Sebastian, military warrior (bis)
Ê Xapanã ele é pai de terreiro	Ê Xapanã he is the father of the terreiro
Ele é guerreiro	He is a warrior
Dentro da guna real (bis)	In the royal guna (bis)

(*ponto cantado* taken from Reginaldo Prandi (org.): *Encantaria Brasileira – O Livro dos Mestres*, Caboclos e Encantados, Pallas Editora, Rio de Janeiro, 2004)

The typical themes of the Sebastianist myth are easily identifiable in his *ponto cantado*: 1) his undisputed authority as the true king, the last true divinely appointed king of Portugal and Brazil, making all other forms of government since him mere caretakers or usurpers; 2) the shift in social norms which his return is meant to operate, bringing down the Maranhão as a symbol of the establishment; 3) Sebastian as the king of beggars and fools, inaugurating the kingdom of equality and freedom; 4) Sebastian as the fierce warrior;

180. Fala vodum Seu João de Barabaia   It is the vodum Sir João da Barabaia who speaks
      Prenderam o turco nosso Rei da Barabaia   They have arrested our King of Barabaia
      Vodum chorou no romper do dia   Vodum cried at the break of day

(*ponto cantado* taken from Reginaldo Prandi (org.): *Encantaria Brasileira – O Livro dos Mestres*, *Caboclos e Encantados*, Pallas Editora, Rio de Janeiro, 2004)

come disguised as something of little value. A common folktale motif is the story of a young man who is approached by a *Moura* who in exchange for a small favor, a gift of saltless bread or a portion of milk, gives the youth a concealed package, telling him to not open it until he gets home. The simple request is usually not followed and the package reveals to only contain lumps of coal. Another common treasure disguise is the fig, which upon disenchantment turns into a gold nugget or doubloon. The fig here is extremely significant by its sexual symbolism and for being the fruit of the Devil's tree.

The connection and relation between *Mouros* and the Devil should also at this point be obvious; the *Mouros*, as outsiders, radical others and opposers to the social and Christian norm, are figures which very easily align with the Devil. The sensual, anti-moral and tempting *Moura*, the promise of easy wealth and buried treasures, the anti-Christian warrior *Mouro* are all elements from the Devil's realm.

If we are now to focus particularly on the extensive mythical corpus of *Mouras* and their treasures, two main lines may be distinguished. The most common is the treasure and commerce with a *Mouras* as an apparently random event: a youth is tending to his normal life, either working or traveling, and is approached by a *Moura* with promises of treasure and love in exchange for a simple, even if satanic, favor which would break her enchantment. The second type is of much greater interest for us: the resorting to *The Book of St. Cyprian*.

The Book of St. Cyprian appears time and time again in the *Moura* legends as the utmost, certain method of treasure disenchantment. *The Book* has managed to imbue itself beautifully into this mythical continuum, which can actually be traced to the most remote antiquity of Iberia. Even if it is nothing more than a fancy product of the XVIIIth or XIXth century, by this virtue it has claimed its own glamour and ancientness by its solid ties with *Mouras* and their treasures.

Still, each legend is its own case and there is no universal rule on how this book needs to be used in order to perform the disenchantment. From my research, never is an exact section of the book mentioned, merely "*a passage from The Book of St. Cyprian*", followed by some detail such as "*it should be read in Latin*", or even "*it should be read from the back to the beginning*". But one thing is a constant: that the book must be read without flaws, absolutely without flaws, word for word, otherwise disaster will strike.

From what I can gather, this mysterious passage should be the disenchantment ritual examined above, as no other part of the book seems to have even the slightest connection to treasure hunting. The introduction to the list of treasures from Galicia in part three of *The Book* actually seems very clear about it: *All treasures and enchantments of the ancient kingdom of Galicia were deposited by the Mouros and the Romans in underground lairs. A greatest number of them, according to this scroll, are in short distance from fountains and springs that conserve their abundant flow even during the harshest of summers.* So it would stand to reason that this ritual would be a genuinely Iberian way to establish commerce with *Encantados*.

But what are the implications of this? From a, let's call it, modern perspective, removing our minds from the promise of easy material fortune, this ritual, inserted in its proper cultural and folkloric context, suggests itself as one of the transcendence of duality, and as such, the *Moura's* treasure acquires some very interesting aspects. Placing the *Mouras* as the radically *other*, the remote and distant ancestor, all that was before, their treasure becomes a whole other thing, and they themselves something completely different and distinct from any other treasure spirit. This treasure might just be knowledge of absolute ancientness, resurging from the underground regions of the psyche, latent and repressed there by the dawn of the rational and normative mind. If you are an Iberian or of Iberian descent, then it may even come from the body itself, from the blood of all ancient peoples which crossed this land back to the most remote of times at the dawn of civilization (a resurgent atavism), all agglomerated into the mighty *Mouro* and the ophidic *Moura*, under the tutelage of the Devil, the ruler of all otherness.

The geographical places described in *The Book of St. Cyprian*, as the spots to seek out treasure, should then be seen as power points, where the energies of ancient humans and ancient spirits can be awakened. Under this perspective, one may probably try to perform a disenchantment ritual in any other place of appropriate energy and ancientness in order to release the spirits and elementals who slumber there or in that part of our raw subconsciousness which was waking mind in such remote times.

This may very well be the lycanthropic connection with *The Book of St. Cyprian* mentioned in some Brazilian legends (and practiced in some dark corners of Iberia, see footnote 174): taking us to the rim of human consciousness and beyond, to the invocation of our ancient beastly selves at the crossroad where animals rest.

Having stated the above, a great new problem comes into play. Returning to the *Moura* mythical corpus, particularly the folktales that mention *The Book of St. Cyprian*, one thing seems to be a constant. As is usually the case in these dealing with elementals or fey folk, there is always a strict code of conduct which needs to be followed if we hope to be successful. In the particular case of the *Mouras* it is the absolute prohibition of mentioning, carrying, or performing any Christian action. Calling upon the name of God, crossing yourself, the presence of holy water or even the use of the Seal of Solomon is reason enough for the whole ritual to fail catastrophically. By looking back at the ritual in question we can see that it does nothing else but resort to Christian symbols, a great and absolutely incompatible contradiction, even if we have already smoothed out our Jesus and our Devil.

If we expand our view of the *Moura* lore once again we can trace two other attitudes towards disenchantment: one aims to bring the treasure to the user and the other the user to the treasure – towards the *Moura* in particular, and one needs to keep the Devil in mind at this point. These two attitudes translate as follows: the Christianization of the *Moura*, bringing her into the light and norm of society, into a Christian state, or the diabolization of yourself through the assumption of anti-Christian attitudes, joining the *Moura* in her outsider state. By gathering those folktales where disenchantment does in fact happen, these actually fall into the second category: the *Moura* is disenchanted if the disenchanter cares not about the treasure or the prohibitive norms of society and, instead, decides to embrace the *Moura* as she is; it is and shall always be all about the woman. The ritual in *The Book of St. Cyprian*, as we have it today, has the opposite orientation, aggressively banishing anything that stands between the disenchanter and the bringing of the treasure to the light of day.

This then suggests that if one chooses to disenchant a *Moura* and her treasure using *The Book* he should maybe consider revising the ritual, which in turn will invalidate the absolute certainty of disenchantment... a complicated issue I am yet to resolve.

5. Returning back to the actual book being commented, the list of treasures itself is also not such an easy riddle to crack.

Although I have many times tried to locate all of them on a map, I've had very little success in doing so. Some locations, like *Castelo do Mau Vizinho* (with seven treasures attributed to it), are very easy to find, as they are quite famous *castros* or other forms of ancient ruins, but a great deal of them remain elusive. There might be a number of reasons for this, namely that the names given here may not be the "official" ones, but rather local nicknames; the references might have been purposely obscured, which, as described above, is actually a common practice in some proto *Books of St. Cyprian*, either for mystification purposes or so as to protect the treasure sites themselves, or, these places may simply be made up.

Among the treasures presented here, two of them do deserve particular attention, treasures 14 and 135, as these two refer to "living things". Although I cannot at this time exactly say what these "living things" are meant to signify, they should be carefully noted. These are treasures of the *Mouros*, and as *Encantados* they are in a perpetual state of suspended animation until their enchantment is broken. In theory each of these treasures should belong to a different *Mouro* or group of *Mouros*, which is underlined by the use of the word *haver/aver* in the original language, which can be roughly translated as "belonging". In traditional terms an *haver* is the name given to a treasure which is kept by a *Mouro*, and in the current list we have thirty-six references to *haveres* (treasures 6, 19, 24, 25, 26, 27, 28, 29, 31, 42, 43, 49, 53, 55, 58, 59, 61, 62, 69, 72, 76, 78, 82, 85, 92, 96, 100, 101, 104, 123, 124, 128, 129, 133, 134 and 135). You should know that, unfortunately, I could not effectively translate this nuance when dealing with this list of treasures, but still, these are the only two treasures with which one must take care not to disturb the actual *Mouro*.

This indication to "*not kill*" may bring a new light into *The Book of St. Cyprian*. Even if it presents itself as a Christian book, and the disenchantment rituals almost group the *Mouros* with the Devil, this particular care of not killing may appear strange. *Mouros* and their treasures aren't really distinct entities; they are one and the same thing. Given the lengthy explanation above, as a general rule, should you chose to disenchant a *Mouro* treasure, independent of which one, I strongly advise you to NEVER KILL WHAT YOU FIND STILL ALIVE. However (as nothing about this issue is simple), there are some pieces of lore about particular treasures, not presented in *The Book*, which do require some killing, usually of a bull, a wild boar or a giant serpent, but this is meant merely as a test of courage placed by the *Mouro* in question.

Should you take up the mantle of magical treasure hunter in Iberia, be sure to always check the local lore, as, don't forget, alternative tests of courage might be to just kiss or actually let yourself be rent by these beasts.

6. The D. Caprina mentioned in treasure 58 might be a reference to the Portuguese legend of "The Lady of the Goat Foot," as the word *Caprina* is an adjective to describe something as goat-like (there is something of the Brazilian Exu here). This is a Melusine type of legend with an extraordinarily rich demonic and anti-Christian symbolism and connotation, and, given its brevity it should be analyzed in full:

THE LEGEND OF THE LADY OF THE GOAT FOOT

D. Diogo Lopes, a noble Lord of Biscay, was hunting on his dominions one day when he was surprised by a beautiful singing lady. He immediately offered her his heart, his lands and his servants in exchange for her hand. The lady accepted but imposed on this arrangement the single condition that he should never again bless himself (cross himself). Later, upon arriving at his castle, D. Diogo realized that the lady had a forked foot like that of a goat.

The two lived happily for many years and had two children: Inigo Guerra (War) and Dona Sol (Lady Sun). One day, after a good hunt, D. Diogo decided to reward his great hound with a large bone, but his wife's black *podenga* (a Portuguese dog bred with extremely ancient origins, small but wiry) killed the hound with a single bite in order to take this piece of boar. Surprised by such violence, D. Diogo blessed himself and immediately the Lady of the Goat Foot shouted and began to rise in the air together with her daughter Dona Sol, both exiting through a window, never to be seen again.

After that D. Diogo went to confess himself and he was told that, due to his actions, he was excommunicated, and his penitence for this was to wage war on the *Mouros* for as many years as he had lived in sin, ending up in captivity in Toledo on this account.

Without knowing how to rescue his father, D. Inigo decided to search for his mother who, according to some, had become a *fada* and, according to others, a Pining Soul.

The Lady of the Goat Foot decided to help her son, giving him an onager, a kind of wild horse, which transported him to Toledo. There the onager opened the gates of D. Diogo's cell with a back kick and father and son rode off. Along the way, they passed by a stone crucifix which made the animal immediately stop. The voice of the Lady of the Goat Foot was heard across the sky, instructing the onager to avoid the cross. Upon hearing that voice after so many years, and not knowing of the agreement between his son and his former wife, D. Diogo blessed himself, which made the onager throw them off the saddle and the earth tremble and crack open, revealing the fires of Hell, swallowing up the animal. With fright father and son both fainted.

D. Diogo, in the few years he still lived became a pious man, going to mass every day and confessing himself every week. D. Inigo on the other hand never again entered a church and it was believed that he had a pact with the Devil, for, from that day on, he never lost a single battle.

SOURCES

Aleister Crowley: Magick: Liber Aba: Book 4, Weiser Books, York Beach Maine, 2000.

Alexandre Parafita: A Mitologia dos Mouros – Lendas, Mitos, Serpentes, Tesouros, Edições Gailivro, Canelas, 2006.

Alexandre Parafita: O Maravilhoso Popular – Lendas, Contos, Mitos, Plátano Editora, Lisboa, 2000.

António Quadros: Poesia e Filosofia do Mito Sebastianista, Guimarães Editores, Lisboa, 2001.

Dalila L. Pereira da Costa: Corografia Sagrada, Lello & Irmão Editores, Porto, 1993.

Dalila L. Pereira da Costa: Da Serpente à Imaculada, Lello & Irmão Editores, Porto, 1984.

Dalila L. Pereira da Costa: Dos Mundos Contíguos, Lello Editores, Porto, 1999.

David Beth: Voudon Gnosis, Fulgur Limited, London, 2010.

David Rankine: The Book of Treasure Spirits – A grimoire of magical conjurations to reveal treasure and catch thieves by invoking spirits, fallen angles, demons and fairies, Avalonia, London, 2009.

Donald Warren, Jr: Portuguese Roots of Brazilian Spiritism, Luso-Brazilian Review, 5 (1968) p.3.

Francisco Martins Sarmento: A Mourama, Revista Guimarães, 100 (1990) p.343.

Francisco Martins Sarmento: A propósito dos "Roteiros de Tesouros," Revista Guimarães, vol V (1888), p.5.

Gabriela Morais, Fernanda Frazão: Portugal, mundo dos mortos e das mouras encantadas, Vol. I, Apenas Livros, Lisboa, 2010.

Gabriela Morais, Fernanda Frazão: Portugal, mundo dos mortos e das mouras encantadas, Vol. II, Apenas Livros, Lisboa, 2010.

Gabriela Morais, Fernanda Frazão: Portugal, mundo dos mortos e das mouras *encantadas*, Vol. III, Apenas Livros, Lisboa, 2010.

Jake Stratton-Kent: *Geosophia – The Argo of Magic*, Scarlet Imprint, 2010.

Jake Stratton-Kent: *The True Grimoire*, Scarlet Imprint, 2009.

Jennifer Larson: *Greek Nymphs – Myth, Cult, Lore*, Oxford University Press, New York, 2001.

Jerusa Pires Ferreira: *O Livro de São Cipriano: Uma Legenda de Massas*, Editora Perspectiva, São Paulo, 1992.

J. Leite de Vasconcelos: *Opúsculos – Volume V – Etnologia*, Imprensa Nacional de Lisboa, Lisboa, 1938.

J. Leite de Vasconcelos: *Opúsculos – Volume VII – Etnologia*, Imprensa Nacional de Lisboa, Lisboa, 1938.

J. Leite de Vasconcelos: *Tradições Populares de Portugal – Bibliotheca Ethnographica Portugueza*, Livraria Portuense de Clavel & C.ª, Porto, 1882.

José Diogo Ribeiro: *Turquel Folklórico*, Revista Lusitana, Vol. XX (1917) p.54.

José Leite de Vasconcelos: *Signum Salomonis; A Figa; A Barba em Portugal – Estudo de Etnografia Comparativa*, Publicações Dom Quixote, Lisboa, 1996.

Kenneth Grant: *Aleister Crowley & the Hidden God*, Samuel Weiser, New York, 1974.

Kenneth Grant: *The Magical Revival*, Starfire Publishing Limited, London, 2010.

Maria Helena Farelli: *A Bruxa de Évora*, Pallas Editora, Rio de Janeiro, 2006.

Mundicarmo Ferreti: *Encantados e Encantarias no Foclore Brasileiro*, VI Seminário de Ações Integradas em Foclore, São Paulo, 2008.

Nicholaj de Mattos Frisvold: *Exu & the Quimbanda of Night and Fire*, Scarlet Imprint, 2012.

Nicholaj de Mattos Frisvold: *Pomba Gira & the Quimbanda of Mbúmba Nzila*, Scarlet Imprint, 2011.

Pinharanda Gomes: *História da Filosofia Portuguesa – A Filosofia Arábigo-Portuguesa*, Guimarães Editores, Lisboa, 1991.

Reginaldo Prandi (org.): *Encantaria Brasileira – O Livro dos Mestres, Caboclos e Encantados*, Pallas Editora, Rio de Janeiro, 2004.

Samuel Liddell MacGregor Mathers (trad.), Aleister Crowley: *The Goetia – The lesser Key of Solomon the King*, Weiser Book, San Francisco, 1997.

Teófilo Braga: *O Povo Português nos seus Costumes, Crenças e Tradições*, Vol. II, Publicações Dom Quixote, Lisboa, 1994.

Various authors: *Actas da 1ª Xornada de Literatura oral – Afigura do demo na literatura de tradición oral*, Asociación de Escritores en Lingua Galega, 2005.

Various authors: *Conjure Codex – A compendium of invocation, evocation and conjuration*, Volume I, Issue I, Hadean Press, 2011.

Xoán R. Cuba, Antonio Reigosa, Xosé Miranda: *Dicionario dos seres Míticos Galegos*, Edicións Xerais de Galicia, Huertas, 2008.

The final chapters in this section of the book are solely dedicated to divination. One cannot help but wonder about their origin as they appear to have been written with a clearly different attitude than the rest of the chapters. While the former carry an honest and faithful tone, these next two at times seem quite satirical.

Interestingly, if we analyze this introduction to the Cartomancy system we may be able to roughly locate the elaboration of this section in time. The reference to Friedrich Schiller (1758-1805) places this text no later than the XVIIIth century, but it is most likely younger than this.

1. The Cartomancy system presented here is one of three presented in the whole of *The Book of St. Cyprian*. There are actually four sections on Cartomancy in *The Book*, being that two of them present the same system: the current one and the one in Part II. The difference between these is that while the second one plainly presents the reading instructions, while providing examples, the current one does this as a kind of (ironic) narration. Also, both of them present different prayers to recite during the reading. Nonetheless, one might just regard them as different examples of working with this system, which, truth be said, is not the simplest one ever developed. These two sections could probably be put together in an edited book with no loss in content and I am quite surprised this hasn't been done yet.

2. Regarding the system itself, should you be confused with the instructions at this point, a reading should go as follows:

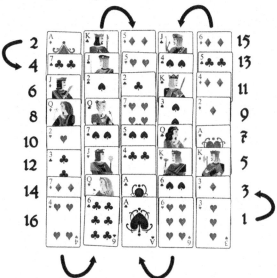

Given that in both the current example and in the one to follow in the next section of *The Book* there are no figure cards in the middle column, making up what is referred to as a "novelty", I assume that, should a "novelty" not occur, the reading should simply terminate with the middle card of the middle column.

The "novelty" procedure is also not particularly clear. The column of 21 cards shouldn't be a problem, but the remaining 8 cards, placed in a cross, should probably go something as follows, even though I don't really know in which order one is supposed to cast them down:

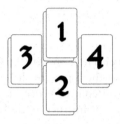

One further question that remains is if this "novelty" event, and its particular procedure, is only valid in the middle column, or if it may actually be valid in any other. Unfortunately no further clarifications are given.

2. Commentary by Enediel Shaiah:

> It should be observed that this interpretation will never be merely capricious, this if the cartomancer isn't just a practical joker, and if there is a good understanding of the full extension of the significance of the cards, so as to mold the answer according to the intended question. The most well known Tarots are: *Tarot Egipcio*, of 78 cards; *Tarot Italiano*, of 78 cards; *Tarot Sacerdotal*, with 22 major trumps; *Tarot Adivinatorio of Papus*, of 78 cards; *Gran Etteilla*, with 78 cards; *Juego de Mlle. Lenormand*, 54 cards; *Pequeño Etteilla*, 32 cards; *Libro del destino*, 32 cards; *Sibila de los salones*, 52 cards, and many others made available by La Editorial Escribano.

Chapter IX

1. Of the astrology section one cannot really make too much of a commentary, except that it is not at all remarkable. It seems just as valid and legitimate as any other system presented in any women's fluff magazine.

However, I cannot help but be slightly mystified by its introductory text. It clearly goes from talking about Quiromancy (a section on Quiromancy is present in the final sections of *The Book*) to Astrology without any justification, being that the term *buena dicha* refers particularly to Gipsy palm reading, meaning something like "good fortune" or "good bliss".

2. Lengthy addition by Enediel Shaiah:

> The previous information regarding star signs does not come from the quiromantic art, and, as it is very much certain that it is from this science that the revelations of the *buena dicha* are based, in no way can this provide predictions regarding the months of one's birth.
>
> Similar revelations recognize as their cause the same principals in which judiciary astrology is founded upon, which is a complete system of prediction based on the calculation and mathematical operations necessary to assemble an individual's horoscope; it also offers another simpler system, even if not as accurate, according to the astrologers, which requires the information of the day, month and hour of birth of the consultant and also the place where he was born. With this data you may assemble a zodiac, meaning, that which relates to the month and the planetaries, which arises from the influence of the planets on the day and hour and determine which sign dominates which region of the earth. By gathering all this information, a general idea of the character and condition of a specific person is achieved, and, since it does not seem to us to be inappropriate to teach this procedure, since the *Libro Magno* does touch upon this subject, we complement the above information with the following instructions taken from Cortés and other such authors:

ZODIAC INFLUENCES

Aquarius – This sign is dominant from the 21st of January to the 18th of February; belonging to it are the nations of Aragon, Saxony, Ethiopia, Dalmatia, Arabia, Piedmont and India and in particular the cities of Constancia, Jerusalem, Urbino, Pavia, Monferrato, Zamora, Medina, Palencia and Seville (in part). A man who is born under the influence of this sign will be average in height, well-spoken, secretive, kind-hearted and joyful in all that he undertakes; it should be noted that he is prone to be struck by iron, he will always be in danger if he is in water and he will be inclined to travel to foreign lands, where he will fare better than in his native one. Should he return, he shall return rich and prosperous and should keep himself from great bothers, for this will cause him much harm. A great illness will threaten his life before the age of thirty; if he survives it he should, according to his nature, reach fifty-eight years of age.

A woman will be very spirited and should she ever be in danger, she will never lose that which she has managed to achieve in life; one should still note the danger of water, that from her middle age onward she will not fare much better than before, and that before her thirty-eighth birthday she will suffer from two great illnesses: the first when she is twenty-four and the second when she is thirty-five; she should, according to her nature, live up to eighty years.

Pisces – This sign is dominant from the 19th of February to the 20th of March and to it belong the nations of Ireland, Normandy, Portugal, Libya, Sicily, Pamphylia and Persia and in particular the cities of Cologne, Venice, Regensburg and Alexandria, Orense, Santiago and Seville (in part). A man born under this sign will be a fond of seeing other lands, traveling by water and will have a great affection for food, which may cause him to have an unhealthy life, this if his planet does not aid him in this condition. He will be a man of few words and inclined to leave his homeland. He should suffer a great illness when he is fifteen and thirty-eight, and should he survive them he should reach sixty-five years of age.

A woman will suffer from ailments relating to the eyes and will be very honest and merciful; she will have a great deal of children. She should keep away from fire and any iron with a sharp edge, during her whole life she will be in danger of dying by fire during the hours of the afternoon and early evening and of being indivertibly injured by her recklessness or by that of someone close to her. She shall suffer from three ailments, one at the age of twelve, the other at twenty-one and the last at thirty. The limit of her life is at the age of fifty-nine years.

Aries – This sign dominates from the 21st of March to the 19th of April; belonging to it are the nations of England, France, Germany and Poland and in particular the cities of Florence, Naples, Batavia, Venice, Kracow, Sumala, Pergamon, Zaragoza, Tortosa and Valladolid. A man born under this sign will be ingenious, prudent, but not too cautious, of a noble character and somewhat talkative. He will have temper outbursts, which will become evident by his habit of talking alone or to himself, revealing in this way, without noticing it, his most intimate musings and thoughts, being this the reason why he will think himself betrayed by his friends with whom he trusted his secrets, when it is actually his own fault that this information reached the ears of ill-intended people, all because of his love of talking. He will never be too rich or too poor, he will be a good friend, his old age shall not be guaranteed by any inheritance or greed, but rather by the generosity of some other person who is good in business affairs; but, before this is to happen, he will suffer many misfortunes, setbacks and difficulties. On some occasion he will be bitten by a four-legged animal and receive a wound from a blade. He will suffer many illnesses, but above all there will be a very serious one that will leave him at the edge of death when he is twenty years old; he has a great probability of surviving it, and should this happen he shall live until he is seventy-five.

A woman will be outspoken, of a good appearance, very impressive and irritable. Between seven and twelve years she will suffer from a serious illness; should she marry she will soon become a widow and promises, according to her nature, to live for forty-nine years, in which she will experience great losses, which she will overcome by her dexterity and industrious nature, without ever enjoying her triumph, for this will only come a few months before her death.

Taurus – This sign dominates from the 20th of April to the 20th of May. To it belong the nations of Persia, Switzerland, Asia Minor, Egypt (in part), Armenia (in part) and Cypress and particularly the cities of Messina, Capua, Salerno, Bologna, Sena, Verona, Ancona, Trier, Parma, Mantua, Palermo, Girona, Toro, Badajoz, Astorga and Jaén.

A man born under this sign will be cocky, presumptuous and haughty; he will be easily distinguishable by the desire to abandon his home and travel to strange lands. In these he will find a matrimony which will give him a good position and large tracts of land, and from this point of view this marriage will be a great success; should he marry in his country he will never have the advantages which luck offers him with a woman of a different nation. Should he enter into business, he will not fare too well; but he will earn his own, especially if he goes into those of a commercial nature, although money will never be abundant, for his vanity and the desire to be admired will give rise to expenses not proportional to his possessions. He should avoid all contact with women which are not his own and he should be very prudent with this, both before and after he gets married, and if he gets married he could possibly become a widower soon, for his fate bears the danger of a violent death related to a woman. Should he travel by sea, the first trip will open the path to his desired land; but all other trips might be dangerous and fatal; he should stay away from every brawl where any blades are drawn, equally taking care to never carry these with him. He shall be, at some time, bitten by a dog. He shall go through three illnesses; one at the age of ten, another at the age of twenty and another at the age of forty, and should he survive he can expect a life free from disease, enjoying good health until the age of seventy years, the maximum length of his life.

A woman will be curious, careful and with a decided character, equally dominated, as the man, by the desire to see distant lands. She will have many children; she will suffer some illnesses, but not too serious, at the age of sixteen and thirty-three, and, should she survive a fall from a high place, which will happen between her forty and forty-six birthday, her life can go up to sixty years.

Gemini - This sign dominates from the 21st of March to the 21st of June. To it correspond the nations of Hyrcania, Cyrenaica, Marmarica, Egypt (in part) and Armenia (in part) and in particular the cities of Trento, Sète, Vita, Pau, Nuremberg, Brussels, Lyon, Magnesia, Sigüenza, Murviedo (Sagunto), Cordoba and Talavera.

A man born under this sign will be distinguished by his generosity and good sentiments. The gentleness of his character and the beauty of his soul will make him fare badly in his own country, and he will seek an environment with a purer morality and justice, but disappointments will make him a constant wanderer and on at least one occasion he will find himself persecuted over his scrupulous cultivation of chivalry and truth. After this, his life will enter a period of calm and he will obtain prestige and wealth; water is a danger for him and he will encounter a rabid dog. It will be extremely convenient for him not to expose himself to the injuries of fire arms, or to walking in high places or bridges. He will suffer from some sickness in the first half of his life, which should come to the age of sixty-eight.

A woman will be greatly esteemed, with a tranquil and formal character and will be an excellent family woman. She will suffer great heartbreaks and some illnesses and should live to be sixty-two years.

Cancer – This sign dominates from the 22nd of June to the 21st of July. To it belong the nations of Numidia, Holland, Norway, Zeeland, Bithynia, Burgundy, Scotland, Rhodes, Lydia, Ethiopia, Africa and Phrygia in general and in particular the cities of Constantinople, Milan, Pisa, Luca, Venice, Tunis, Geneva, Santiago of Galicia, Lisbon, Granada and Barcelona.

A man born under this sign will be valorous, with a respectable stature, reserved, humble and joyful; he should go thought a few labors over legal disputes of which he will not be defending his own interests, his fate seems to draw him to become a lawyer, prosecutor or something of that sort; he will be distinguished by spending all he saves. He will be in constant danger from water, iron and fire; he will suffer from some sickness and may come to live up to seventy years.

A woman will be diligent and hard-working, always prone to getting angry and just as equally prone to regaining her calm once again, her great quality will be gratitude. She will suffer a few concerns related to her children and the rest of her family. She will have a large succession and is in danger of falling from high places. At some time she will find expensive things which were hidden, but these will not have a great value. Her health will be good and she may live up to seventy-five years.

Leo – This sign is dominant from the 22nd of July to the 23rd of August. It has influence over the nations of Sicily (in part), Arabia (in part), Bohemia, the coast of the Red Sea (both banks), Chaldea, Italy, Greece, Turkey, Pontus, the Alps and Macedonia and in particular the cities of Rome, Ravenna, Cremona, Ulma, Cretón, Damascus, Prague, Murcia and Leon.

A man born under the influence of this sign will be enthusiastic, haughty, hard working and handsome. It should be noted that he will also be as arrogant as cheeky and eloquent; if he gives himself to study he will become extremely instructed, a wise man. He will reach high dignities and will perform important jobs and is sure to make many voyages. Marriage will give him even more fortune. On some occasion he will be seriously injured by a blade and on many occasions his businesses will give him great honors and enjoyments. He will suffer from various illnesses (one of which, when he is forty, will be very serious) and if he gets rid of them he should live to be seventy-one years old.

A woman will be beautiful, with a solid mood and worthy of being feared; but she will, nonetheless, be distinguished by her religiousness, without being a prude, and her charitable character. She will possess a considerable fortune. Her ailments will be related to the stomach and blood, and she should live to be seventy-one years.

Virgo – This sign dominates from the 22nd of August to the 22nd of September. It exerts its influence over the nations of Greece (in part), Persia (in part), Syria, Mesopotamia, Sicily (in part), Rhodes (in part) and Candia (an island to the South east of Greece) and particularly over the cities of Pavia, Paris, Ferrara, Toulouse, Poreč, Corinth, Lleida, Toledo, Avila and Algeciras.

A man born under this sign will be honorable, chaste and of a noble condition. It should be noted that he will also be thorough and careful with his affairs, and he will obtain a position of charge or leadership. He will have a shameful and somewhat uncertain temper and regarding wealth he will be poor on account of bad fortune, for he will not approach these issues in the most convenient ways. He will suffer from a few illnesses when he is in his thirties, and, according to his nature, he will live to be eighty-four.

A woman will be shy, hard-working and given to devotion. In her life she will never enjoy good health. She is in danger of falling from some high place, she will experience a serious illness when she is around thirty, and may come to be seventy-seven.

Libra – This sign dominates from the 23rd of September to the 23rd of October. It has influence over the nations of Austria, Bactria and Syria (in part) and in particular over the cities of Plasencia, Lodi, Regio, Parma, Ghent, Vienna, Burgos, Almeria and Salamanca.

A man born under this sign will be honorable and venturous in everything which he may take on. He will travel to foreign lands, where he will fare much better that in his own and will become a person, given his discretion, from which one may receive good advice. He will suffer from some ailments around the age of six, eighteen, and thirty-five, and should he survive them he should live until seventy-seven.

A woman will be joyful and with a sensitive and frank attitude. On some occasion she will suffer some injury in her feet. She will suffer some ailments of little importance but it is possible that her fondness of travel may cause a few issues of relative importance. She will live, according to her nature, until the age of sixty-six.

Scorpio – This sign dominates from the 24th of October to the 22nd of November. It exerts influence over the nations of Scotland and over all the coast in general, Syria (in part), Mauritania, Gaetuli, Cappadocia, and Judea and particularly over the cities of Messina, Padua, Aquileia, Valencia, Xátiva, Segovia, Tudela, Prague, Málaga and Burgos.

A man born under this sign will have bad habits, he will be a traitor, lustful, opinionated and with an inclination for robbery. His words will be deceitful given the fairness and softness he will be able to impart in them. His inclinations will take him to many other countries, which, much like anywhere else, his subtlety and cunning will prevent anyone from ever knowing the depths of his thoughts. He will never become wealthy, but he will never be poor. He is in great danger of suffering an injury by a rock or blade. His illnesses will be located mostly in the stomach and genital area, and he may be able to reach the age of sixty-one years.

A woman will be sociable and with a strong and terrible temper. Her life will be in danger from wounds made by blades, of which she will always conserve the scars. She will suffer from serious stomach pain. She will go through many dangerous and difficult situations and she will know serious heartache, which will not be able to diminish her characteristic impetuosity and bravery. As a general rule her health will suffer from strong stomach pain and a weak constitution, but nonetheless she may come to live for seventy-two years.

Sagittarius – This sign dominates from the 23rd of November to the 20th of December. Its influence is active in the nations of Arabia Felix, Slavonia, Dalmatia, Etruria and Liguria (in part) and the cities of Malta, Avignon, Jerusalem, Asti, Milan, Jaén, Calahorra and Medinaceli.

A man born under this sign will be self-conscious, affable, honest and will not have any shortage of good luck; he will travel the sea, which will earn him great wealth; he is in danger of being injured by a four-legged animal, and the sicknesses which will most greatly affect him will be when he is seven, eighteen and twenty-eight years old. If he survives them he will reach sixty-seven years of age.

A woman will be shy and meditative. She will have wealth and many children. She will suffer from three noteworthy ailments in her life, among others of little importance and will reach the age of fifty-seven years.

Capricorn – This sign dominates from the 21st of December to the 20th of January. It has dominion over the nations of Macedonia, Barbary, Portugal, Albania, Moscovy, Tracia, Croatia, India and Slavonia and particularly over the cities of Verona, Forli, Savoy, Florence, Constantinople, Tortosa, Soria and Carmona.

A man who is born under this sign will be valorous, a lover of the warrior life and will not be joyful. He will suffer from some setbacks in his luck and wealth, which will easily take him to seek other horizons in distant lands, but he will not find better luck in these and will return home greatly disappointed. His health will suffer from frequent setbacks but he will nonetheless be able to live until the age of seventy-seven years.

A woman will be of a vicious condition and her fate pushes her, although not fatally, to a life of vice. She will have influence over two men of whom she will be the cause of disgrace. She will suffer from a few ailments of little concern. If she manages to escape her indicated fate she will come to enjoy the high consideration of honorable people, but it will still be obvious that she does not see life in the same way as those with a good soul, and for this reason she will never enjoy the affection of anyone. She will live, according to her nature, to the age of sixty-six.

In the previous information one must observe a few issues, so as it does not give rise to wrong interpretations. One must not forget that, according to astrologers both ancient and modern, each of these general influences is modified by all others which have an impact on the character of each person; this meaning that their value is far from absolute or fatal, depending on all other circumstances, which complete or modify them.

Regarding the various places of the Earth over which each sign has influence, we have used many names from ancient geography which are given by several authors, for it seemed to us that this would not be an obstacle and would avoid greater difficulties.

Not all texts agree on this, which we may call the vulgar interpretation of the astrological influences; consequently, and sticking to the *Pronósticos* of Gerónimo Cortés as our base, we have complemented this information with some other extracted from other books, both older and younger.

The most correct application of the zodiac prognosis consists of implementing that information which corresponds to the day, hour and year of birth to the consultant.

To obtain the hour one must count every hour passed since the rise of the sun to the moment of birth, and for every two hours one should count one sign, starting from the one which corresponds to the days of that month, such as, for example, if the person was born on the 4th of August, at one p.m., we shall count eight hours since dawn, and being this in the sign of Leo, we count the next three: Virgo, Libra and Sagittarius, which, by being the fourth, is the one we are seeking.

To obtain the year we take the number and we reduce it in the simplest form by Theosophical reduction, so as it gives us a number equal to or smaller than 12, which is the number of the totality of the signs of the zodiac. Let us suppose that the proposed year is 1907, which, by summing the number will be, one plus nine, ten; ten plus seven, seventeen; this is composed by the numbers one and seven, which reduces to eight: now we find the eighth sign, starting from Aries, which gives us Scorpio.

But we have also said that the zodiac signs should be combined with the planetary ones, so as we may obtain a full prognosis, which will save you the troubles of, should you not want an absolute precision in the astrological details of the problem you are looking into, learning how to make a full horoscope, as the masters of this initiatic science teach.

The planetary influences arise from the seven heavenly bodies, the Sun, the Moon, Mercury, Venus, Mars, Jupiter and Saturn.

The days of the week are subjected to the following influences:

Sunday	Sun
Monday	Moon
Tuesday	Mars
Wednesday	Mercury
Thursday	Jupiter
Friday	Venus
Saturday	Saturn

In each one of these their twenty-four hours are divided into twelve day hours, which one should count from one p.m. until twelve at night, and twelve night hours, which are counted from one a.m. until midday. As a general rule the day hours receive influence from the Sun and the night hours from the Moon. Each one of these hours belongs to one of the seven astrological planets, taking into consideration that for each day the first and eighth day hour and the third and tenth night hour correspond to their planet, this by making an adjustment in the order in which they are placed, which is the following: Sun, Venus, Mercury, Moon, Saturn, Jupiter and Mars. As such, the hours of Sunday are as follows.

Day hours:

1st Sun; 2nd Venus; 3rd Mercury; 4th Moon; 5th Saturn; 6th Jupiter; 7th Mars; 8th Sun; 9th Venus; 10 Mercury; 11th Moon; 12th Saturn.

Night hours:

1st Jupiter; 2nd Mars; 3rd Sun; 4th Venus; 5th Mercury; 6th Moon; 7th Saturn; 8th Jupiter; 9th Mars; 10th Sun; 11th Venus; 12th Mercury.

The conjunction of the astrological signs on certain days and hours determines the existence of certain fatidic moments of the year, which were determined by the knowledge of the Chaldean Mages and the Masters of Hermetic wisdom in the form we shall see, organized according to the day and followed by the moment in which all actions taken and all births will be accompanied by the most unfortunate luck.

Fatidic moments:

1st of January	11 p.m.
25th of January	6 p.m.
4th of February	8 p.m.
20th of February	10 p.m.
1st of March	4 p.m.
28th of March	10 p.m.
18th of April	8 a.m.
20th of April	11 p.m.
3rd of May	6 p.m.
15th of May	10 p.m.
10th of July	6 p.m.
16th of July	4 p.m.
13th of June	11 p.m.
22nd of June	11 p.m.
23rd of June	11 p.m.
1st of August	1 p.m.
20th of August	7 p.m.
31st of August	7 p.m.
1st of September	3 p.m.
21st of September	4 p.m.
3rd of October	8 p.m.
22nd of October	9 p.m.
5th of November	8 p.m.
28th of November	5 p.m.
7th of December	1 p.m.
22nd of December	9 p.m.

The direct influence of the planets on the destiny and condition of human beings may be both favorable and adverse in the following way:

Sun

Favorable influence: It makes people honest, good, merciful and chaste; it concedes science and the love for honor acquired through work, it is associated with the magnanimity of thoughts and actions, just as the love for one's family.

Adverse influence: It determines those qualities directly opposed to the ones above.

Moon

Favorable influence: It makes men famous by virtue of an unexpected act of fate.

Adverse influence: It determines vanity, narrowness of mind, lack of intelligence, fickle spirit and a feverish activity without objective or good results.

Mercury

Favorable influence: Provides one with a clear intelligence, fit for the study of any subject, with a serene judgment, making one a clear and deep observer of nature and also a very good inventor, skillful and eloquent in his reasoning and words.

Adverse influence: Makes people inconstant, blabber-mouths, forgetful, boastful and sly.

Mars

Favorable influence: It grants robustness and physical strength, the love of governing and the ease of obtaining it.

Adverse influence: It determines the joy of bloodshed, the sanguinary spirit and cruelty and all aptitudes which make a man into a tyrant, an executioner and a bandit.

Venus

Favorable influence: It grants sweetness of character and a generous soul, filled with sentiments of love and charity.

Adverse influence: This makes people effeminate, cheaters, weak of character, cowards, unscrupulous, of variable whims, false friends and inconstant in their love.

Jupiter

Favorable influence: It determines all sentiments of generosity, nobility, valor, faithfulness, modesty, love for justice and work and grants extraordinary aptitudes for all great endeavors.

Adverse influence: It determines those qualities directly opposed to the ones above.

Saturn

Favorable influence: It grants great depths and tireless love for study, the desire for isolation in solitude, patience, calmness, perseverance, great frankness and valor in one's own actions, and perfect indifference regarding all good any other person may achieve without the slightest hint of disgust or envy.

Adverse influence: it defines deep sadness, constant pessimism, bad intentions, envy, detachment from everything and everyone, the dissimulation of the constant and insane thoughts of treachery and the indolence over the pains of others.

The gathering of all the information regarding the instant of birth, from the precise hour to the year, will form a set which will sometimes be harmonious (those cases when the reading of the horoscope does not offer the slightest difficulty) and other times contradictory, indicating a clash and opposition of influences. On those occasions the interpretation needs to seek the results of neutralizations of those characteristics which will dominate over common characters in the competing prognosis.

There exists other more perfect and delicate methods of determining an astrological reading. One of these, being extremely sensitive, consists in seeking out in astrological tables of months, days, and hours, the signs corresponding to the moment of birth of the person in question, and the determination of which planets were in their period of greatest brightness on that particular moment. Further, by adding the information of the phase the Moon, one has enough data to perform quite a complete prediction. Another method consists in dividing the visible sky above the place of birth into five parts. East, West, North, South and the Zenith (vertical), or, the dominating, and by knowing that North marks the evil influences, South the good, East the ones in the first half of one's life and West those in the second half, and the vertical those dominating one's fate, one may read the meaning of each part.

Astrology is an initiatic science, which, by admitting to the influence of the planets and other celestial bodies in the successes of the life and luck of the beings inhabiting the surface of the Earth, occupies itself with finding the significance of the sidereal aspects in all moments of human existence, particularly that of birth, so as to deduce the happiness and tribulation awaiting each man.

In the most remote times of the Chaldean civilization and the druidic initiations, astrological knowledge had reached a progress almost universally recognized by all wise men. Astrology and Astronomy were one and the same thing, having at their base the study of physical and mathematical truths; but, the Astronomy of that time not only studied that which we may call the purely scientific aspect of this matter, but also sought its relations with the universal life and its influence on the problems of organic existence, preserving this knowledge in the initiatic schools, which only allowed for the free distribution of the purely astronomical part of their teachings, keeping all the Astrological secrets and the study of meteorological predictions of that time hidden in those priestly colleges. In the druidic schools it is well known that Astrology was cultivated with even greater dedication than in Chaldea and Egypt. Today we know of some of the astrological predictions which were made in ancient Gallia which came to pass exactly point by point, and more concretely, it is also known that the Roman wars and the victorious expedition of Julius Cesar had actually been predicted; all of this revealed by the astrological methods used by the druids.

Arriving at a field where one may analyze concrete evidences, we proclaim that the influence of the heavenly bodies is not something without its reason. Nowadays, for example, the connection between solar spots and great magnetic storms which have been observed here on Earth is known as a fact. That the solar spots are directly responsible for the mentioned storms, may or may not be confirmed; but it is without a doubt that these storms faithfully follow the variability of the Sun, regarding its spots. Furthermore, the amount of these spots, which seems to be subjected, in their number and disposition, to, approximately, an eleven year cycle, corresponds to the variations in the yearly average temperature, and this is thoroughly proven, and as such, variations have an effect over all phenomena of terrestrial life. We could then establish here an astrological principle for future predictions, whose information had been gathered by pure observation, and all of this without having given one single step outside of a scientific model. The influence of the Moon is another such case where there is no room for illusion, as anyone living in the countryside may very well observe: all its phases correspond to certain phenomenon of growth and well or ill-being of animals and plants which no one would be foolish to deny. We ourselves have had ample opportunity to observe such things. Does this mean that the Moon effectively is the cause of such events? One does not need to go so far in order for the coincidences described, regarding the movements of our satellite and the mentioned phenomena, give rise to something which may enable one to perform astrological predictions. The Sun, as we very well know, along the year travels across the twelve signs of the zodiac, and to each of them corresponds a certain amount of time during which all organic creatures experience the various stages of this periodic movement. Would it be laughable that, without any further preconception regarding its true origin, one would say that to the influence of Libra, Scorpio, etc., etc., would correspond a determined variation in nature and its creatures? We are once again in the terrain of Astrology.

One could still make an objection to the astrological knowledge of the initiated, on account of the disagreement resulting from the divisions these make of the heavens and the celestial bodies, and those made by the glorious conquests of Astronomy.

In the remote antiquity of the Chaldeans and Egyptians, both these ways of considering the starry sky were one single science, and it seems without reason that at that time the mages and priests were solely occupied with astrological calculations while ignoring the true system of the universe.

Nothing could be further from the truth. From the most remote of eras, of which we have any chronological information, there has always existed an exact idea of the movement of the celestial bodies, the measurement of time has been performed with an astounding precision and the celestial phenomena were calculated in the most precise way. These days, all these things are a part of the most essential exoteric knowledge of initiation, and just as there used to be a secret doctrine of Astronomy, as well as many other things, there was also a public one, in which was taught that which was more convenient to the powerful priestly castes of those civilizations and in which the facts were disfigured to the desires of the initiated under the veils of allegory and theogonic symbolism whose key was received from those masters, after swearing the most solemn and terrible oaths.

The veil of the secret science, however, does not always remain thick and closed; there is a time when a temple will allow for the initiation of laymen, of those who are outside of the priestly caste and condition, in which it is revealed, given some restrictions, in a more or less complete way, this acquired knowledge. Pythagoras was one of those who learned many things in an Egyptian initiatic temple, including the real system of planetary movements, the roundness of the Earth, the central position of the Sun, father and origin of all cosmic and organic life in the sidereal bodies which rotate around it, etc., etc. These teachings he did not transmit to all his students, for he divided them, as is known, into two classes, the public and the secret, or, the true Pythagoreans. One of them, Philolaus, actually made the secret teachings of his master public, surely breaking his oath of silence, so as to defend the spherical shape of the Earth and the theory of its movements and those of the remaining planets around the Sun.

Modern investigation has discovered that these same astrological truths were found among the Chaldeans, as well as the Egyptians, the Hindus and the druids. The Hebrews were also quite well versed in this subject, without a doubt thanks to Moses, who had received this knowledge from the Egyptians, and nowhere in the Bible does this seem to be disproven. One other purer and more respectable testimony of this is the cabalistic tradition, which demonstrates that the ideas of the *chosen people* were very different between their initiated and their more lowly classes. In China it is unknown when the study of astrological phenomena began; but what is known is that in extremely ancient times there was already a well established body of astrological schools, and that there was even an execution over a failed eclipse prediction. From this information we may have some idea of the progress of astrology in the Heavenly Empire, when the sidereal moments were studied with this exactness.

Occultists often call for the impartial criticism regarding the identities, knowledge and opinions found in the most distinct nations of antiquity to prove the following: 1st that there has always existed a hidden doctrine professed by the initiates of the whole world; 2nd that that secret doctrine is Occultism.

Regarding Astronomy, they say that they had and will always have the full knowledge of scientific truth, something which, as has been seen, science has proven; the same, they say, shall happen one day with the rest of their knowledge, and that these days they only reveal but a small part of it, for the greater part would not be believed nor esteemed by what it represents to man.

They say that the worlds are not as it is believed, that they are colossal balls of rocky materials on whose surface life reigns, but that they are beings, who, like man, have a body, a vital fluid which circulates in them, an idea-producing brain and even a soul, named the *planetary soul*. Let us examine how. The rocky mass of the world is its armor, its *bones*; the sedimentary and formation masses its *muscles* and its other *tissues*; the metallic veins, the nervous network of the planet; its underground waters the venous system; the intense evaporation of its oceans and surface its breathing; vegetation its coverings, its fur; the animals its nervous cells; man the cells of intellectual life; The gathering of tendencies and desires of all organic creatures are its intuitive and lower life and the collectivity of the thoughts of the human race, its intellectual life, its soul.

And how does this method of considering the celestial bodies apply to one in a state of ignition (the Sun for example) and one without air, water or life, as seems to be the case of the Moon? With sensitivity. Celestial bodies are born, they live and they die and, just like men, they go through many phases and periods. The Sun is a celestial body in its first stages of formation, still in its embryonic stage, and the Moon has been a *cadaver* for many centuries. Further on, our satellite will crumble into pieces, and when it reaches the aerolythic state, it will disappear as dust into the bosom of the cosmos, just as a body is dissolved by the bosom of the earth.

Just as a man is, at the same time, a complete organism, a human being, and a nervous cell of the creature "Earth", so is this also part of another larger organism: the solar system. In this individuality the brain is represented by the Sun.

It may shock that now we say that the Sun is the center of intellectual life when previously we said that it was a organism in an embryonic state; meaning, the less fit state for thought and reasoning; but if we think of the way in which occultists regard the generative process, during which the soul molds the body in the womb of its mother, much like a man builds his house, we may see how the Sun may be the seat of intelligence and reason of this organic *planetary system* without the slightest inconvenience.

But what about this soul of the Sun, what is it then?

It is the soul or intellectual activity formed by the immense sum of human souls of all the planets, whose last residence is the solar body, after much transmigration, when their progress no longer requires them to have a material body more or less dense.

The Sun is also part of another more elevated organic system, and as such do occultists arrive at the Grand Whole, whose organism is the Universe, whose intelligence is the sum of the intelligences and whose soul is the *universal soul*, or, in a single word, God.

Let as make one final objection. One could argue that nothing was actually mentioned regarding the influence of the unnamed planets: Uranus and Neptune, for example. Indeed, this influence exists, as the influence of the asteroids also exists (which astrologically are equivalent to the presence of another planet); but its determination is not necessary to the construction of a horoscope, nor does their influence originate any particular tendencies that need to be specified. Those of the last two planets are the same as Saturn and their influence can only strengthen this one, and that of the asteroids results in the same influence as Mars. Regarding other satellites, we know that their effect merely contributes to the one of the planet at the center of their rotation.

3. It should be noted that the Gerónimo Cortés who Enediel Shaiah was

quoting is the same Jeronimo Cortez Valenciano who is mentioned in *The Book of St. Cyprian*, and that the book *Pronósticos* he mentions is the *O Non Plus Ultra Do Lunario, e Pronostico Perpetuo, Geral e Particular para Todos os Reinos e Provincias*.

Analyzing the original material and the one given by Enediel Shaiah, should we have consulted similar editions, we can at least say that he took some liberties with it.

SOURCES

J. Leite de Vasconcelos: *Opúsculos – Volume VII – Etnologia*, Imprensa Nacional de Lisboa, Lisboa, 1938.

Jeronimo Cortez Valenciano: *O Non Plus Ultra Do Lunario, e Pronostico Perpetuo, Geral e Particular para Todos os Reinos e Provincias*, Lisboa, 1857 (digital edition).

Occult Powers

Cartomancy, Orisons, and Banishments

Point II

1. Interestingly, Teixeira de Aragão also describes these same categories of the tormented as being part of the official church doctrine on the Devil and his victims. Further still he adds the "energumen", the "demoniac" and the "vexed", not presented in *The Book*. One other name he drops is *arrimadiço*, which I honestly have no idea how to translate. This last one he defines as the name given when the Devil or a demon appears in the form of an animal.

2. Commentaries by Enediel Shaiah:

> In the work *Heaven and Hell* by Allan Kardec, our readers may find the interpretation which spiritism assigns to the concepts of angels and demons.

> In *The Book on Mediums*, by Allan Kardec, and in the *Collection of Spiritist Prayers*, one may find the procedures to avoid and get rid of obsession.

SOURCES

Teixeira de Aragão: *Diabruras Santidades e Profecias*, Vega, Lisboa, 1994.

Point III

1. The Coscinomancy ritual presented in this part, in itself, is not particularly remarkable. As with all Coscinomancy it does not fall far from the usual tradition. However, this whole part of *The Book*, which focuses greatly on divination, does touch again and again on the more widespread Iberian Cyprian oral traditions.

When compared to other traditional St. Cyprian divination methods, which frequently rely on a very specific verse-like incantation describing a hypothetical seven year journey performed by St. Cyprian somewhere after his repentance (as in the Cartomancy system presented in point V, page 302), this one presents a very obscure and coded sequence of words.

This incantation however, is presented again further down in *The Book* as part of the creation of a love elixir, made from the hair of two black cats ("Another magic of the black cat", point III of the "True Treasure of Black and White Magic or the Secret of Sorcery", Book II). Seeing as it is used for such different objectives this does not seem to be a specialized incantation, most likely having distant roots in Iberian or Portuguese oral Cyprian traditions.

2. As far as Coscinomancy goes, J. Leite de Vasconcelos mentions one such ritual which calls directly upon St. Cyprian:

> To ascertain what exactly this operation consisted of, I subjected myself to it once, in this region (Alto-Minho) in the house of a woman of virtue, to whom I asked if I was ever getting married. The woman told me to sit in a chair; then she sieved some ash through a sieve and drew upon it with her finger a figure as such:

> Which she erroneously called *sino-samão*. Taking the sieve, she placed inside it, on its rim, a rosary, a closed scissor and a vintém[181] (instead of a vintém any other coin will do: made of copper, silver, etc.), on the outside, also on the rim, a second closed scissor; around which she tied another rosary. To the sieve thus arranged it is said to be mounted. Next she sat before me, blessed herself and said the following prayer three times, while at the same time we both held the sieve by the scissor, each one by their own finger, which was thus hanging over the *sino-saimão*:

> St. Cyprian, dearest[182] St. Cyprian,
> Sorcerer, dearest sorcerer,
> Donkey's ears[183],

---

181. The name of an old Portuguese coin.

182. This is a semi-free translation. The original Portuguese goes S. *Cipriano*, S. *Ciprianinho*, being that "Ciprianinho" is merely a diminutive for "Cipriano", either indicating actual physical smallness or a term of endearment. I have chosen the latter.

183. This is an expression I have tried to grapple with many times; it is usually present in a number of songs and nursery rhymes. One such goes as follows:

Dlim dlão	Dlim dlão
Cabeça de cão	Dog's head
Orelhas de burro	Donkey's ears
Não tem coração	Does not have a heart

Thou spoke with the Devil at midnight
Tell me now what I am seeking:

If this man is to be married, turn to him;
if not turn to me.

The sorceress imprinted a rotational motion on the sieve and it ended up turning towards me, she then added that I was either married or about to get married. Both assertions were wrong. – To this whole operation it is given the name of casting the sieve. – And from the method the *benzedeira*[184] operated I concluded that she faithfully believed in the efficiency of the operation, which was put into practice according to every prescribed rule; she was not, in this case, an impostor, but rather a trusting *benzedeira*.

(...)

The walls of the house of this sorceress to which I refer were completely covered with saints, while on her table she had a *figa*, a metal *sino-saimão*, a ten *réis* coin from Brazil with an armillary sphere and a rosary with a few jet beads – all of these are objects with a pagan character.

It should be noted that, as Vasconcelos himself hints, the figure meant to be drawn on the ash by the *benzedeira* in question was an armillary sphere. The confusion between this image and the *sino-saimão* arises from pure and simple force of habit, as early divination methods and certain Portuguese amulets resorted to coins featuring a *sino-saimão*, a pentagram, frequently originating from North African Islamic countries. As the armillary sphere became part of the Portuguese royal coat of arms (which can still today be seen on the Portuguese flag) and began to be imprinted onto the empire's currency, this symbol took up the attributes of the *sino-saimão*, as these coins began to be used for the same purposes as the ones with the proper *sino-saimão* (as was observed on the *benzedeira*'s tabletop by Vasconcelos). Also, regarding the *figa* and the traditional magical use of jet, see the commentaries to point XVI of the "Mysteries of Sorcery" section of Book II, page 350.

Besides rhyming I really cannot make heads or tails of it. In the current incantation it appears to serve the purpose of rhyming with *procuro*: seeking.

184. Literally a "blesser", a specific kind of folk healer who works mainly through prayers and blessings, what is usually referred to as *ensalmos*. This has traditionally been the most widely accepted kind of folk magic, with some of these, in Medieval times, being considered as legitimate doctors or physicians (see Annex I).

3. One other orison with great similarities to the above incantation is also reported by Leite de Vasconcelos, also for the purpose of divination, which, falling in line with what was discussed above regarding traditional St. Cyprian invocations, refers to Cyprian's seven year journey:

> My St. Cyprian
> My dearest St. Cyprian,
> My sorcerer
> My dearest sorcerer,
> In the sea thou roamed,
> Eleven virgins did thou find,
> With them did thou speak,
> Thou ate and thou drank;
> Thy luck[185] thou threw in,
> Better did thou take it out:
> Tell me now mine
> To know if I am to be married

Apart from mentioning that this orison is from Guimarães, Vasconcelos offers no other information regarding it, by which I think it may be safe to assume that one may use this orison for whatever divination methods may come to mind, adding an extra Cyprianic flavor to your personal practices. Also, it seems to me that final line can be substituted with any other question one may want to ask the Saint, as really there seems to be no poetical reason, neither metrics nor rhyme, why it should be kept.

Yet another similar one goes:

> St. Cyprian,
> Seven years the sea thou roamed,
> To learn news of thy lady
> Seven lucks thou threw in...
> Thy luck thou took out right...
> I ask thee now my dearest miraculous saint,
> That thou discover this for me.

SOURCES

J. Leite de Vasconcelos: *Opúsculos – Volume V – Etnologia*, Imprensa Nacional de Lisboa, Lisboa, 1938.

José Leite de Vasconcelos: *Signum Salomonis, A Figa, A barba em Portugal – Estudos*

---

185. Luck isn't exactly the correct translation here; *sorte* can also refer to fate, or destiny – anything in life which might have a random outcome.

de Etnografia Comparativa, Publicações Dom Quixote, Lisboa, 1996.

J. Leite de Vasconcelos: *Tradições populares de Portugal*, Livraria Portuense de Clavel & C.ª Editores, 1882.

Teixeira de Aragão: *Diabruras Santidades e Profecias*, Vega, Lisboa, 1994.

POINT V

1. This second section on Cartomancy, although apparently presenting the same system as before, does deserve some careful considerations.

The information presented in this section is of the greatest importance not only for an aspiring Cyprianic diviner, but for all avid scholars. Should you have an ample knowledge of traditional Cyprian practices, this chapter of *The Book* gives you the keys to finally comprehend a whole lot of these apparently disparate traditions.

It is here presented the extremely heterodox account of Cyprian's seven-year trip as described in various divination rituals and incantations. This account, it must be noted, is in all aspects incompatible with the accepted account of Cyprian's life as presented in the *Flos Sanctorum*, and yet, one does indeed need to accept it in order for a great deal of traditional St. Cyprian practices to actually make sense.

Of further remarkableness in this section is the proper way of preparing and consecrating the cards used for this Cartomancy system, something completely absent from the previous account and without a doubt, precious and fundamental.

2. Commentary by Enediel Shaiah:

> We shouldn't need to mention that the cards detailed in this explanation could not possibly have been used by St. Cyprian, the sole reason of this being that they did not exist during his lifetime. There is no doubt that before the French card suits there existed the Spanish suits, the one with the four suits of *oros*, *copas*, *espadas* and *bastos*. In the same way the Egyptian tarots precede the Spanish; as such, it is in no way possible that the system of Spanish suits was known at the time of St. Cyprian (see the entry Cartomancy, in the *Dicionario de Ciencias Ocultas* by the publisher Escribano).

Regarding the small story narrating the origins of this system of divination Enediel Shaiah adds the following:

> There is a tendency, which extends well into the towns of Portugal and in Spain to much of Galicia, Asturias, Leon, etc., to, curiously, remove the diabolic character previously

attributed to cartomancy, which is what distinguishes it in other parts of Spain and Europe, to the point where it is actually common, in this kind of operation, to perform an evocation of the Devil.

Indeed, modern Witches commonly receive their consultants in a room free from meddlesome curiosity and covered by black veils (when it is prepared with proper goetic luxury). At the center of the room there is usually a small table covered by a green cloth which covers it entirely and is completely decorated by black cabalistic figures; over this there are three black candleholders with three green candles and in front, drawn on the wall, one will see the seal of Solomon, formed by two purple triangles. The Witch sits the consultant on the side of the table opposing her own and begins the session by evoking the infernal powers while lighting the candles. When closing the session she banishes these spirits and puts out the candles, while saying certain words which should be said in the presence of the consultant.

POINT VII

1. The "Occult Power or Secret of the Hazel Wand" section is quite a mystery and, plainly speaking, it is nothing more than a magical cock tease. One can always go ahead and make the most diverse considerations about it, as hazel wands are surely more than common in the grimoire tradition.

If we analyze the text two contradictory interpretations may come from it, independently of the language used. The first being that the magic of the hazel wand is not given for it is an object of the Devil, used in communication with demons, reinforcing the grimoire connection (see the *Grimorium Verum*, for example). The second being that indeed the magic is not given out of genuine fear by the author and that in fact this magic has nothing of the Devil's power.

2. Enediel Shaiah has the following to add:

We of course cannot begin to even guess at which terrible Arcanum this text refers to.

The mysterious applications mentioned regarding this hazel wand are completely unknown to us; but for what it might be worth, we shall describe the magic implementations of its rabdomantic power and also as a symbolic instrument of the magus in his operations.

In the occult sciences, rabdomantic wand is the name given to a small forked branch which, being held by the hands of he who wishes to use it, will lean and indicate the place where the metals or materials one is searching for are buried.

This wand should be made of hazel wood, cut when it is still young and fresh and containing a large amount of medulla. It should also be prepared so as to have the shape of a fork and it should be cut during sunrise. According to various authors, it is convenient to cut it on the very same day one wishes to use it, for in this way it will produce the most efficient results, and that to mold it and trim its leaves one should use the same knife used to cut it.

It also happens that all of those using rabdomantic wands do not use them in the same way, nor do they give them the same shapes. Straight as an arrow or as twisted as any regular walking stick is enough for some men; nonetheless, the majority seems to prefer this forked shape, for it seems to them to be the most efficient and the most convenient.

As it is assumed that the user's hands communicate some kind of virtue to the wand, one can easily arrive at the conclusion that, by placing one on each extreme of the branch, the feeling or sensitivity gathered in the tip of the branch would no doubt be doubled. Furthermore, this is a much more comfortable and simple disposition, which allows for the hazel fork to very easily mark with its tip that which is sought.

One may also make it with the tip pointing downwards or pointing upwards, as with its tip straight, parallel to the horizon.

When one uses it with the tip facing down its movements will have the tendency to point up; if it is pointing in the opposite direction it will move towards the ground and if it points forward it will oscillate indistinctly between these two directions.

Some do not hold the wand with both their hands, but rather they merely balance it on one of them, which is held open in front of them.

To discover underground waterbeds it is necessary to use a forked branch, be it hazel or any other class of tree, approximately one foot long, and as thick as a finger, so as the wind does not move it by itself; one then balances it on one's hand, making its movements as free as possible, so as when one may pass over a buried treasure the wand will rotate in that direction, and one may take note of the spot.

The best way to discover treasure, it is said, consists of carrying over one's palm a straight wand, resembling any other ordinary one.

This way of carrying the wand is certainly meant to enable one to disregard the suspicions that the movements given to it might be the effect of some other force besides the hand holding it. Apparently this motive has given rise to a different method used in Germany. One takes a straight wooden stick, completely free of wood knots, and cuts it into two parts; in the extreme of one of these parts one makes a hole, sharpening the other part, so as it may fit into this hole made in the first one.

Arranged in this way one holds it with the tips of two fingers, between which it will rotate as soon as one passes over anything metallic.

Father Delbegne, a Dominican, claims that he has seen near Braine-la-Courte, between Mons and Brussels, a young man who, in order to discover a vein of buried ore, would sink a wand into the ground, which would then move when this same individual touched it, should it be over the said mine.

Lastly, there are those who also use four forked wands simultaneously, believing that in this way they have the greater advantage, should there be several treasures in the area they are searching, that each of the hands will point to a different location where one should dig.

Vhier assures us that in order to discover treasure by means of a rabdomantic wand, it is necessary to, at the same time, recite the *Psalm De profundis... Credo videre bona Domini in terra vivemtium.* Bodin advises something similar. Some carve on their wands mysterious figures; others draw over them a cross and in a certain place in Paris there existed four extremely ancient wands on which were written the names Balthazar, Caspar, Melchior (the names of the three wise men, who, according to the Christian legend, worshiped Jesus in the manger) without a doubt to invoke these three men, who are famed for having offered great treasures to the Child God.

Having been the object of many controversies, and given the scope of many known feats of charlatanism, there have been individuals who, taking advantage of the ease with which many people allow themselves to fall into error, so as to prove that the qualities of his wand were due to causes and effects of magic and the action of superstitious practices, such as giving oneself to Satan, Lucifer, etc., have added to the use of the rabdomantic stick invocations where they mix the sacred and the profane. After these one conjures up a kind of demon, which appears that very instant to follow the orders of the invoker.

In this way the divination wand has become an infernal wand and natural magic has been converted into black magic (*Red Dragon*. Escribano publishing).

Rabdomancy, by itself, is a divination method which is practiced with a stick or branch from a tree. It is extremely ancient. Ezekiel and Hosea mention it as an already remote and purely superstitious thing, and reprehended the Hebrew people who allowed themselves to be seduced by such ways of predicting the future used by the idolaters. Indeed, among the Assyrians, the ancient Tartars, the Phoenicians and the nations of Greece, rabdomantic divination was a widespread practice, much like many other divining methods.

To obtain a revelation from Rabdomancy, it is most frequent to display the divining wand in the following way: Remove its leaves only from one side throughout all its longitude, this when cutting it from the tree, which cannot be done by any other cutting object besides a consecrated dagger made of rock. To perform this operation it is necessary to wait until the first moment of dawn, when the Sun is rising on the horizon and is only half visible. Should there be any clouds or if in that instant any mist should rise, blocking in any way the golden splendor of the celestial king, then this magical operation has to be postponed until circumstances are more appropriate.

After the branch is naked on one side, it should be wrapped in a red cloth on which certain names of great magical power are written and it should be carried in this way to the place selected to perform the operation. Then the operator should face East, evoke the tutelary genies of that section of the world and throw the stick into the air up to a considerable height. If this falls with the side naked of leaves facing up this is the most fortunate of omens, especially if, after repeating the operation, the same result should happen again. Should the branch fall in the opposite position, then this is a terrible prediction for the thing or event to which this divination is directed.

The divinatory wand, also called rabdomantic for its purpose (divination and revelation) and its method of use (as stick or branch), falling exactly inside the etymological meaning of this designation, is merely a variety of the forms and uses of the classical scepter or magical wand used by the magician in all his operations, and considered one of the most universal and ancient symbols of initiatic power. The priests of the Orient and across the whole nation of classical initiation, India, always carry with them a wand adorned in a variety of ways, being as a badge of their hierarchy and priestly condition. The Episcopal crosier of the Christian priesthood has absolutely no other origin; the royal scepters, symbols of power, are a consequence of having the significance of the wand gradually identifying the significant itself, for, when the positive interpretation of this symbol was lost, much like the priestly condition in Asia, the traditional respect of the common folk, their ancient submission to all those who were depositories of initiatic knowledge, symbolized by the wand or staff, the pure symbol of the most remote occultism, was then converted into the expression of hierarchy, of power, of the external life of societies. From the idea of superiority represented by the scepters of kings, comes the costume of the leadership batons of civil and military authorities, and finally, the very cane we all use, is a social badge which, in our time, substitutes the knight's sword or the short sword, carried by the wealthy classes of the beginning of the XIX century in most nations. And this is indeed how the most skeptical opponents of occultism leave their houses every day, carrying in their hands the most remote magical symbol, whose significance, almost forgotten today, was given in the mystery of the ancient initiations, where it was attributed to the Neophyte in order to grant him the power and ability for the exercise and implementation of the Magical arts.

Although there is no little evidence of the use of rabdomantic wands in the time before Santiago Aymar, as can be seen in the work by Del Rio "Disquisitiones mágicae", it is certain that in the year of 1692 practically no one would give credit to such a thing.

The prodigies performed by Aymar awoke the curiosity in people and in a short time the miraculous properties of the rabdomantic wand obtained a great success and an indescribable fame. In the beginning the wand gained reputation as a discoverer of thieves and evildoers, to whose proximity it would start to move in the hands of the one carrying it so as to reveal the presence of the individual in question; these were its first known services, those given to police officers gifted with marvelous insight; but it was soon detected that with equal ease this would reveal the place where there would be a hidden spring, a metallic vein, or a hidden treasure. Similar faculties rose regarding the merits of the hazel stick and once this was accepted by the general public there came the effort to seek an explanation for them. And here began the divergence of opinions.

Father Lebren and none other than the wise Mallebranche, credited, very logically, the Devil for this prodigy, an easy thing to say in their time. Other less preoccupied people sought to find a more natural hypothesis and found in Physics their explanation, by admitting the influence of underground electricity over the hazel wood. Not long ago Tormey intended to prove the veracity of this phenomenon by means of magnetism and Ritter, a professor in Munich, a wise man of recognized prestige, pointed towards galvanic phenomena so as to establish an explanation and abjure the belief and virtue of the wand, this not many years before he died. As the same Aymar mentions, sometimes it is necessary to say that we are wrong, so as not to stress those people who absolutely deny the possibility of rabdomantic prodigies.

It is very difficult to explain, using the theory of organic and underground electric emanations, the many marvels that are said to be executable by means of this wand. Not only the cited Aymar, but also many others, used it to discover sorceries; and there was also a curious application by the bishop Morienne that consisted of using it to distinguish a true relic from a false one. In the year of 1700 a priest from Tolosa became a celebrity for discovering with this wand what any person, which was not in his presence, was doing and what was happening, had happened or was going to happen. Lastly, in the hands of some people, it further demonstrates a great virtue in discovering those who were ill, and, above all, the leprous, no matter how well they hide this sad and fearful disease.

The preparation of the rabdomantic wand is described in the *Gran Libro Mágico* in the following way: At the rise of the Sun in the Orient, grab a virgin branch of wild hazel with your left hand and cut it with your right with three strokes, while saying: "I cut thee in the name of Elohim, Metatron, Adonai and Semiphoras so as thou may follow me, etcetera, etc."

In other grimoires it is said that this should be done with the trunk of a young tree one or two years old, without any knots, either of hazel, laurel or almond. It should be cut with a newly exorcised knife, either made of iron or silver, during a full Moon Wednesday and at the planetary hour of Mercury. One should say what we have indicated above while cutting it, and it should also be necessary to engrave on its bark the symbols of Mercury and the Moon, as also some crosses on both its extremities and, in the middle, the three magical words we have mentioned when discussing the magical wand. It should be two palms in length and as thick as a finger and that, for its use, besides the indications we have already given in this text, one should consider the following points:

1st If one wishes to know if it is water that the wand is detecting he should wrap it in a piece of wet fabric, if the movement persists then there is no doubt that it is detecting a waterbed.

2nd If one is searching for metals or coins, then he should fix on the tip of the wand a coin or a piece of metal, and it is also convenient not to carry anything metal with you, neither on your clothes or your shoes, not even the tiny nails sometimes used to attach the soles on shoes, so it will be convenient to have some footwear stitched merely with some hemp strings, without any other material to support it.

3rd When one is searching for hidden money or an object made of gold or silver, and wishes to know the depth at which it is buried, he should take two branches of hazel which have two young shoots each, which, much like the original trunk, should be one year old. Once these wands are cut, in such a way as they resemble the letter Y, one then picks them up by their trunks, one with each hand (after consecrating them) and should then walk around the indicated place observing the movements of these two rabdomantic devices. If they cross each other with the upper or lower shoot, it can be deduced if the treasure is either buried at a great depth or if it is close to the surface.

4th When the treasure is hidden in an enchanted place or protected by magical formulas, it is necessary to nullify this obstacle with ceremonies and ritual procedures which resort to conjurations inside a magical circle.

The wand or scepter of the magician is one of the most ancient instruments mentioned in all operations of a theurgical or goetic nature and its use is not limited to only drawing a circle on the ground, inside which the evoker places himself so as to be protected from all danger caused by the invisible potencies he is calling forth. This by virtue of the mighty signs and evocations he uses, which are obeyed by the evoked forces with much greater haste than any of us will ever obey any authority presenting a leadership baton. This is assured by the masters of Occultism.

For the magical wand to have all this efficiency it is essential that it is prepared in the correct fashion and adequately consecrated. It should be made of hazel wood and it should be a shoot which was born that very year; it should be cut on the first Wednesday of the Moon, between eleven and twelve at night, while pronouncing these words and making the indicated signs of the cross over it. *Agla* ✠ *On* ✠ *Tetragrammaton* ✠ *Abraxas per dominum nostrum* ✠ *fiat- Deus luxunus* ✠ *in tenebris-trinus* ✠.

The knife used should be new, having engraved on one of its sides "*Vade retro Sathan!*" and on the other, between two five pointed stars "*Ammbarghemethomp*", which, as it seems, in a magical language means: The potencies obey me.

Once the hazel wand is cut it is consecrated by making three crosses in the air while facing North and by writing on its bark with an awl (which should never have been used before for any other thing) in the upper part *Agla* ✠; in the middle *On* ✠ and on the other extreme *Tetragrammaton* ✠ and one should say the following while doing this: *Conuro te cito mihi obedidiere. Venias per Deum virum* ✠ *per Deum verum* ✠ *per Deum Sanctum* ✠.

Other times a branch of almond or hazel is selected, which should be perfectly straight. This should be cut with a single stroke at the moment when flowers begin to open at the first light of dawn. Then one drills a hole throughout the whole of its length and encases inside this branch a rod of magnetized steel, whose points should display, one of them, a polyhedral prism of seven sides and the other a triangular prism. In the center of the wand one should fit two rings, one of zinc and one of copper, and from this area to the extremities, one should paint the wood silver, up to the side of the triangular prism, and gold up to the seven-sided prism.

The consecration lasts seven days, starting in a new Moon. The words, signs and ceremonies we have already mentioned.

The magical wand may also be made from some other wood (although the usually preferred is hazel) if one places on this seven rings of the seven initiatic metals, meaning, lead, iron, gold, copper, a mix of mercury and tin, tin and silver, and placing the rings in this same order and placing on each extreme of the wand a steel ball, positively magnetized on one side and negatively on the other.

The Indian mages implement other simpler wands; one of these is a bamboo shoot with seven knots, without any signs or letters. Its consecration is also not difficult. The initiate goes out into the night alone, seeking the shoot which best suits him, cutting it in no special way, and sticks it in the ground in front of him while saying his mantras, a kind of magical orison appropriate for the occasion, reaching out with his hand towards it so as to magnetize it. After this he may use this rod whenever he wishes and these are said to have a greatly proven science and power in all which refers to the area of occultism dealing with conjuration and evocation.

Some ancient occultists used as a magical wand a conveniently consecrated arrow and in Tartary, even today, their evokers and respected diviners use a small spear for the same effect as magicians use their scepters.

Point IX

1. The exact instruction on how to perform this operation mentions something called *pedra d'ara*, which can be translated as an altar stone. This is in fact a small movable square on a Catholic altar, but such will not be discussed here at length; see the commentary on point XXIV of the "Mysteries of Sorcery" section, Book II, page 362.

2. There seems to be a call for freethinking and personal morality in this rather inconspicuous point that to me doesn't seem to be solely valid in the applications one may give to this enchanted money. It is a most curious point.

Point X

1. The Orison of the Custodian Angel is an extremely widespread orison, going far beyond the Portuguese borders, with variations beyond counting. Besides this name it is otherwise popularly referred to as the orison of Saint Cyprian or as "The Twelve Words Said and Returned".

The influence and fame of this orison and its variations cannot be overlooked, as, according to Teófilo Braga, their widespread use caused them to be outlawed in the XVIth century and references to them can be found in a number of Inquisition processes as an effective method to banish and exorcise demons. Other references further mention that these orisons may even be used for the disenchantment of *Mouros* and their treasures (see commentaries to Chapter VII of the "*Book of St. Cyprian*" section, page 257).

I personally struggle with the thought that a better translation of this angel's name, given the very particular context in which he is presented in *The Book*, aiding Cyprian in dealing with some *Bruxas* by offering him his orison, would perhaps be Guardian Angel, as in Cyprian's actual Holy Guardian Angel, but these are merely personal musings...

2. Other traditional variations of this orison are as follows:

From Foz-do-Douro (Porto):

"Simon my friend."
"Simon yes, thy friend not."
"Of the twelve words
      Said and returned
      Tell me the first."
"The first is the house of Jerusalem,
      Where Our Lord Jesus Christ
      Died for us, amen."
"Simon, etc.
      Tell me the two."
"The two are the two tablets of Moses
      Where Our Lord Jesus Christ
      Placed His Holy feet."
"Simon, etc.
      Tell me the three."
"The three are the three persons
      Of the Holiest Trinity."
"Simon, etc.
      Tell me the four."
"The four are the four evangelists."
"Simon, etc.
      Tell me the five."
"The five are the five wounds
      Of Our Lord Jesus Christ."
"Simon, etc.
      Tell me the six."
"The six are the six holy candles."

"Simon, etc.

Tell me the seven."

"The seven are the seven sacraments."

"Simon, etc.

Tell me the eight."

"The eight are the eight beatitudes."

"Simon, etc.

Tell me the nine."

"The nine are the nine months."

"Simon, etc.

Tell me the ten."

"The ten are the ten commandments."

"Simon, etc.

Tell me the eleven."

"The eleven are the eleven thousand virgins."

"Simon, etc.

Tell me the twelve."

"The twelve are the twelve apostles.

> Twelve rays has the Sun,
> Twelve rays has the Moon;
> Blast away from here Devil,
> This soul is mine, not thine."

From Trovões (bishopric of Coimbra):

"Custodian, my friend, tell me the one."

"Custodian yes, thy friend not; one I shall tell thee."

"The one is the Holy House of Jerusalem, where Jesus Christ was born and died for us, amen!"

"Custodian, my friend, tell me the two."

"Custodian yes, thy friend not, the two I shall tell thee. The two are the two tablets of Moses, where Jesus Christ placed his Holiest feet."

"Custodian, etc."

"The three are the three persons of the Holiest Trinity, Father, Son and Holy Spirit."

"Custodian, etc."

"The four are the four last things of Man[186]."

"Custodian, etc."

---

186. The four last things refer to Death, Judgment, Hell and Glory. These are the four concepts a man should keep in his mind and constantly meditate upon to keep himself from sinning.

"The five are the five wounds of Christ."
"Custodian, etc."
"The six are the six holy candles."
"Custodian, etc."
"The seven are the seven Sacraments."
"Custodian, etc."
"The eight are the eight beatitudes."
"Custodian, etc."
"The nine are the nine temples of the Holiest Trinity."
"Custodian, etc."
"The ten are the ten commandments."
"Custodian, etc."
"The eleven are the eleven thousand virgins."
"Custodian, etc."
"The twelve are the twelve apostles."
"Custodian, my friend, tell me the thirteen."
"Custodian yes, thy friend not; the thirteen I shall tell thee.

> Four quarters has the Moon,
> Nine rays has the Sun.
> Be blasted, devils and she-devils![187]
> For this soul is not thine."

This previous orison is meant to be said always at midnight (an open hour), and can convert an unwise man in the hour of his death.

From Vila Nova de Gaia (district of Porto):

"Custodian, friend!"
"Custodian yes, but not friend."
"Dost thou wish for salvation?"
"Yes, indeed, I do."
"Then tell me the first."
"The first is the priest."
"Custodian, friend!"
"Custodian yes, but not friend."
"Dost thou wish for salvation?"
"Yes, indeed, I do."
"Then tell me the two."
"The two are the two tablets of Moses.

---

187. The Portuguese original is *diabos* and *diabas*, the masculine and feminine form of Devil... I admit that what I came up with isn't the most elegant translation.

– And the first is the priest.
    Etc."
"Then tell me the three."
"The three are the three prophets.
    Etc."
"Then tell me the four."
"The four are the four patriarchs.
    Etc."
"Then tell me the five."
"The five are the five wounds.
    Etc."
"Then tell me the six."
"The six are the six holy candles.
    Etc."
"Then tell me the seven."
"The seven are the seven psalms.
    Etc."
"Then tell me the eight."
"The eight are the eight holy bodies.
    Etc."
"Then tell me the nine."
"The nine are the nine choirs of angels.
    Etc."
"Then tell me the ten."
"The ten are the Ten Commandments.
    Etc."
"Then tell me the eleven."
"Eleven are the eleven thousand virgins.
    Etc."
"Then tell me the twelve."

> "Twelve rays has the Sun
> And twelve rays has the Moon.
> Be blasted over there Devil
> That this soul is not thine"

When one says this orison a devil is blasted in Hell.

The following is meant to be recited to those who are dying. From Idanha-a-Nova and Monforte da Beira (district of Castelo Branco). This particular one also comes with the indication that whoever prays it must at all costs not make a single mistake, and he should also not start praying anything else without finishing it:

"Angel Christopher, my friend..."

"Christopher yes, thy friend not."

"Dost thou wish for salvation?"

"Yes, Lord, I do."

"Tell me the thirteen words said and retuned."

"The first is the Holy House of Jerusalem where Our Lord Jesus Christ died for us, amen."

"Angel Christopher, my friend..."

"Christopher yes, thy friend not."

"Thou told me one, tell now two."

"The two are the two tablets of Moses where Our Lord Jesus Christ placed his divine feet, the first is the Holy House of Jerusalem where Our Lord Jesus Christ died for us, amen."

"Angel Christopher, my friend..."

"Christopher yes, thy friend not."

"Thou told me two, now tell me three"

"The three are the three persons of the Holiest Trinity, the two etc..."

"Angel Christopher etc..."

"Thou told me three, now tell me four."

"The four are the four Evangelists, the three etc..."

"Angel Christopher etc..."

"Thou told me four, now tell me five."

"The five are the five Wounds of Our Lord Jesus Christ, the four etc..."

"Angel Christopher etc..."

"Thou told me five, now tell me six."

"The six are the six blessed Candles that appeared in Bethlehem and returned in Jerusalem, the five etc..."

"Angel Christopher etc..."

"Thou told me six, now tell me seven."

"The seven are the seven Sacraments, the six etc..."

"Angel Christopher etc..."

"Thou told me seven, now tell me eight."

"The eight are the eight thousand Choirs of angels, the seven etc..."

"Angel Christopher etc..."

"Thou told me eight, now tell me nine."

"The nine are the nine months the Baby was carried in his Holiest Virgin mother's womb, the eight etc..."

"Angel Christopher etc..."

"Thou told me nine, now tell me ten."

"The ten are the Ten Commandments, the nine etc..."

"Angel Christopher etc..."

"Thou told me ten, now tell me eleven."

"The eleven are the eleven thousand Virgins, the ten etc..."

"Angel Christopher etc..."

"Thou told me eleven, now tell me twelve."

"The twelve are the twelve Apostles who accompanied Our Lord Jesus Christ, the eleven etc..."

"Angel Christopher etc..."

"Thou told me twelve, now tell me thirteen."

"The thirteen are the thirteen rays carried by the Sun and the thirteen rays carried by the Moon; blast from here Devil that this soul in not thine."

From Santana da Comeada (Sertã, district of Castelo Branco):

"Custodian my friend."

"Friend of God, but thine enemy."

"Tell me then the thirteen words said and returned."

Custodian said:

"I shall tell thee, I shall tell thee for I know them well."

"Then tell me the first."

"The first is the Holy House of Jerusalem where Christ was born and died for our good."

"The two?"

"The two, are the two tablets of Moses, where Our Lord Jesus Christ placed his divine feet."

"And the three?"

"The three are the three people of the Holiest Trinity."

"And the four?"

"The four are the four Evangelists."

"And the five?"

"The five are the five wounds."

"And the six?"

"The six are the six blessed candles."

"And the seven?"

"The seven are the seven sacraments."

"And the eight?"

"The eight are the eight blessings."

"And the nine?"

"The nine are the nine months the Holiest Mary carried Jesus in her womb."

"And the ten?"

"The ten are the Ten Commandments."

"And the eleven?"

"The eleven are the eleven thousand virgins."

"And the twelve?"

"The twelve are the twelve Apostles."

"And the thirteen?"

"The thirteen I will not tell you. Thirteen rays carries the Sun, thirteen rays carries the Moon, blast, Devil, go out into the street, that this soul belongs to God, not thee."

Given the variability and flexibility of these orisons these are extremely vulnerable to contaminations from other similar numerical formulas. A good example of this is the addition of the four lines starting with "Twelve rays has the sun", which is actually a part of the orison of St. Custodian. Other examples are also plainly visible as the characters in the orison vary quite dramatically.

Now, given these examples, and looking back at the version presented in *The Book*, one can very well assume that the numeration behind each of the Custodian Angel's lines is actually meant to be read out loud. Other traditional instructions also indicate that at every new number you are supposed to repeat every previous number before that one (hence being called "twelve words said and returned"), as also appears to be suggested in a few of the examples above. Should you fail to do this you are at risk of falling under the Devil's influence, which is what most likely is meant by the cryptic instruction of *"should you want to use it for evil it is necessary that you not finish it"*. Furthermore, according to tradition, anyone who is named Custodian must recite the whole orison should any section of it be said in front of him (this is great at parties).

Further worldwide variations exist in Spain, Germany, Greece, and even Kirgizstan, and this great number may even be multiplied manyfold if we add all those incantations (for the magical character of this orison should be quite obvious by now) with a similar structure. The following folktale, called "The twelve truths", is a good example originating from Benquerença (note that in the original Portuguese this whole narrative rhymes... I am afraid I wasn't able to recreate this in my translation):

The Devil one day came to a shepherd who was having his dinner and said to him:

"May I bless thee." (instead of "God bless thee")

"Not now, for I am eating" answered the shepherd.

"What art thou eating?" asked the Devil.

"*Chincharões*[188], here on the frying pan."

"Can I have one?"

"No, for they might burn thee."

"I shall blow on them then."

"Just for that I will not give them to thee."

"Dost thou know that thy wife went to the goat herd?"

"Because surely she knew where it was."

---

188. A fried meat dish, similar to pork rinds.

"She took one of thy goats."

"Because surely she found it in the herd."

"She made a good dinner out of it, and didn't save any of it for thee."

"Because surely she did not remember me."

The shepherd finished his dinner and went to wash himself. But all the fountains were dry, for the Devil had dried them all. With no water he urinated on his hands and washed himself.

The Devil, greatly admired and irritated, said:

"I banish thee, creature of the mountain, that thou hast a fountain near thy cock! Since thou art so smart tell me then, if thou can, the twelve truths. Tell me one."

The shepherd, armed with the sign of the cross, responded rapidly:

"I'll tell you the one.

The nail was made for the finger."

"Tell me the two."

"The gloves were made for the hands."

"Tell me the three."

"From pine was pitch made."

"Tell me the four."

"The shoe was made for the foot."

"Tell me the six."

"Good wine drink the kings."

"Tell me the seven."

"The serpent is harder than a kern."

"Tell me the eight."

"From good wheat you make good biscuit."

"Tell me the nine."

"There is no kid without a goat."

"Tell me the ten."

"There are no sheep without feet."

"Tell me the eleven."

"There is no metal harder than bronze."

"Tell me the twelve."

"The twelve I will not tell thee. Seven rays caries the Sun, the same carries the Moon, blast thee Devil, that this soul is not thine."

The Devil shouted and disappeared.

SOURCES

F. Adolpho Coelho: Notas e Parallelos Folkloricos – II As doze palavras retornadas, Revista Lusitana, Vol, I (1889) p.246.

J. Leite de Vasconcelos: Tradições Populares de Portugal – Bibliotheca Ethnographica Portugueza, Livraria Portuense de Clavel & C.ª, Porto, 1882.

Jaime Lopes Dias: *Crenças e Superstições da Beira*, Alma Azul, Coimbra, 2002.

Teixeira de Aragão: *Diabruras Santidades e Profecias*, Vega, Lisboa, 1994.

Teófilo Braga: *O Povo Português nos seus Costumes, Crenças e Tradições*, Vol. II, Publicações Dom Quixote, Lisboa, 1994.

Points XIV & XV

1. This is once again a paradigmatic example of one of the curious peculiarities of *The Book of St. Cyprian*: the introduction of a narrative (much like the previous section "An Episode of St. Cyprian's Life"). This, as explained in the Introduction, is something quite common in *The Book*, and it is usually used to provide context for a specific orison, prayer, sorcery, or recipe. This time, not very well disguised in this story, one can actually extract a complete system for the evocation of Lucifer into visible appearance. This evocation follows in the line of classical Solomonic magic evocations, coercing the spirit in question to appear to the magician under threat of torture or by the power of some divine names. The tools employed here for this task are simply the *boleante* rod and the ram horn chain (which can be substituted by some priestly artifacts).

Personally I think this ritual may be very easily complemented with some other more usual goetic tools, such as a circle and a triangle (although the evocation does mention the distance at which Lucifer is supposed to manifest) but this should, of course, be up to the individual practitioner. One should also question whether this same evocation may be used to call upon any other spirit other than Lucifer simply by changing the name being called out.

Now, given the nature of the *boleante* rod, this whole ritual seems to be oriented toward the purpose of obtaining the services of the Devil without having to make a pact/deal with him, and to this end it simply resorts to force, taming him into submission with pure and simple violence (although I don't personally see how, morally, this is any less damaging to your immortal soul).

2. I for one cannot help but be troubled, time and time again, by the way the Devil/Lucifer is treated in this book. In all his interactions (in other such narratives) the Devil presents himself mostly as completely and utterly honest (he does lie a few times, but only when fearing that one of his pacts might be in danger of being broken); he is a being of a perfect and unblemished character. And yet, time and time again, all his good will, honesty and fairness is persistently repaid with trickery, lies, torture, and pain.

Dearest reader, this book is offering you the methods and tools to summon and torture the Devil, but please, do abstain yourself from unnecessary violence and cruelty. And please do be careful; this is Lucifer we are talking about.

3. Enediel Shaiah adds the following to the use of the name "Adonis" in this evocation:

This texts presents the name "Adonis"; but given the orthodox character of this conjure, and the attributes of the power it invokes, it seems to us that this has nothing to do with the mythological figure of the beautiful son of Cinyras and Myrrha, being that this is likely to be a confusion with the Hebrew term Adonai, which is one of the names of God, meaning Lord (See *Diccionario de Ciencias ocultas*, Escribano publishing).

This same author also offers a small drawing regarding the placement of the nails in the *boleante* rod, although, analyzing the instructions in *The Book*, his diagram does not seem to be correct:

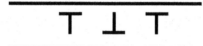

Still, one cannot help but find the instruction in *The Book* quite confusing. My best interpretation is that the nails should be nailed across the rod, making it then important that the rod has a diameter larger than one centimeter (the length of the nails) so as to prevent their tips from coming out on the other side.

ORISON OF THE JUST JUDGE

1. THERE ARE SEVERAL DOCUMENTS MENTIONING THE USE of a written orison of the Just Judge as a part of a *bolsa de mandinga*. Although I cannot be sure that this was the same orison of the Just Judge as given in *The Book of St. Cyprian*, this is indeed the exact kind of ingredient to be included in such a talisman.

2. Commentary by Enediel Shaiah:

> This evocation is most curious, particularly regarding the following comment on the text: "'Although this orison in not of St. Cyprian, we publish it nonetheless for it is extremely miraculous." Observing its odd structure, its illogical and incongruent combinations of words, in which one may actually detect an archaic cadency and phonetic rhythm, we can see that we have a magnificent sample of what magical formulas are meant to be like, which must be respected due to motives already explained in a previous note. A curious detail in this formula is the evocation of the supreme protection of the great theurgical prodigy, not only to combat the disgrace of life's missteps, or to free the body

from the threat of an enemy, but also to avoid falling into the hands of justice, which, apparently, in all ages has been such a calamity that it is necessary to call upon a miracle to free oneself from it.

SOURCES

Vanicléia Silva Santos: *As Bolsas de Mandinga no Espaço Atlântico: Seculo XVIII*, Universidade de São Paulo, São Paulo, 2008 (PhD thesis).

NEW TREATY OF CARTOMANCY

1. THE SECOND SYSTEM OF CARTOMANCY presented in this second part of *The Book* is in all much simpler than the previous one; however its usefulness does still seem limited to the most mundane female concerns. As with the previous system, and the one to follow, it appears to be specialized in marriage preoccupations. Nonetheless, as Enediel Shaiah mentioned in his own comments to the first Cartomancy system presented, one should have a *"good understanding of the full extension of the significance of the cards"*, and this means being able to scrape off the merely superficial banality of these significances.

Analyzing the information provided, there are a few points which are not entirely clear. Even if the significances of single cards are given for those between the Ace and the Seven of each suit, one does notice that the Sixes are also present and meant to be used when one starts reading multiple card combinations. The case is probably that the Sixes do not have individual meaning, but only in combination with other cards.

2. Commentary by Enediel Shaiah (justifiably trying to make a profit):

> See the *Diccionario de Ciencias ocultas*, by Enediel Shaiah, published by Escribano, where it is explained, in the chapter entitled Cartomancy, the origin of the different card suits, the methods of casting them and their meanings. This publisher also possesses a catalogue of works on Cartomancy and a wide range of Tarot decks.

BOOK TWO

TRUE TREASURE OF BLACK AND WHITE MAGIC

OR

SECRETS OF SORCERY

THE CROSS OF ST. BARTHOLOMEW AND ST. CYPRIAN

1. THE USE OF CYPRESS IN ANY TALISMAN should always be regarded with interest, as this is usually considered a sinister tree, whose wood, if used in any house, will emanate illness and disease. This however is likely just to further underline the power of this tree, which is probably re-aligned by the consecration instruction for the cross.

2. The mention of St. Cyprian in this entry seems to be spurious, as in the incantation/consecration of the cross St. Cyprian is not at all mentioned. Nonetheless a talisman by the name of "Cross of St. Cyprian" is quite well known and quite easily obtainable in any esoteric bazaar in Portugal or Brazil. You can find these in any variety of shades, in combinations of black and white, more or less polished, more or less ornamented, more or less detailed, but it is always a cross within another cross.

This same cross is also meant to be accompanied by the following orison, which is supposed to be prayed daily:

I who carry thy Cross,
The Cross of St. Cyprian
That hast the virtue of banishing
Wickedness and the evil of black sorcery,
I beg thee to defend me
From curses, night and day...
Only thee, lord of magic,
Who, by the grace of the divine,
Wert converted to Jesus,
Could give a Cross
Such power and mystery
Which, by its interception,
Neither graveyard dirt,
Neither dog giblets,
Neither hedgehog entrails
Neither black bugs, neither salt

Nor any other sorcery
Will be able to harm us!
Amen.

3. Focusing on St. Bartholomew, he is a most respectable saint in Portuguese or Iberian saintly magic, being also associated with the Orisha Oxumaré.

Not long ago his feast day (24th of August) was still marked by the gathering of possessed and bewitched people at his consecrated churches hoping to be freed from their torment by his most miraculous blessing and exorcism, this being also a very good day to take a blessed sea bath (of an uneven number of waves). The brilliant Camilo Castelo Branco described one of these occasions in the following way:

> I was not actually surprised by the great number of possessed women I saw in the feast of St. Bartholomew in Cavês. Of the usurped lordship over some of these, I must admit, I was indeed envious of the foul beast! These were some impressive girls from the Barroso, scarlet and vigorous as the matriarchs of the human race; iron wrists, flaming eyes, and shaped like such ancient beauties that I was taken by the idea that the Devil does not go for the skinny types, and as such, roams these mountains in search of bodies which are powerful enough to receive him. I am glad he does.
>
> (...)
>
> But retuning to the story, most impressive meaty girls were those possessed I saw in the church of Cavês, in 1842. How long has it been... In those days, even girls with an evil spirit seemed fine to me.
>
> On the 24th of August, in the village called Cavês, whose bridge over the Tâmega borders, to the North, the two provinces of Minho and Trás-os-Montes, the feast of St. Bartholomew is celebrated, a saint which is most bothersome to Satan. From many miles around dozens of possessed people come here. One should note that it is very rare to see a man among those who has been taken by the Devil. Women, it seems, who already face so many difficulties in life, have also to bear the bitterness of being visited by infernal spirits, a unique case, in my perspective, in which the mentioned spirits show themselves to be spirited.
>
> I returned there the following year, armed with figas, to keep away the bad airs, and other such talismans greatly refractory to the Devil.

(…)

I went straight to the church to observe St. Bartholomew's fight with the Devil. This was my main concern.

When I got there I simply saw five possessed women, pinned down by fifty mighty arms from the Barroso, while the saint, of a respectable size and made of stone, was carried from the head of one of those energumen to the next. The Devil rabidly flayed in them when the miraculous granite weighed down upon their heads. And the priest would also raise his angry voice, unforgivably insulting the enemy of the human race, forcing him to hide his defeat in the deeps of Hell. The released girls would then fall onto their crying mothers' arms, regaining their strength little by little, when they finally went up to the saint's altar to place their vow and go around the church on their knees.

I was later told that a few weeks after this all of those girls ended up marrying those individuals which their Devils had previously declared to them.

What strange jobs the Devil takes up sometimes!… but still, this is the greatest use I have found for him.

Besides these rituals, there is also the belief that during his feast day the Devil, which this saint keeps imprisoned, is let loose on the world for one or two hours, which makes this an extremely fateful day and underlines the importance of honoring St. Bartholomew on it.

Still, examining the fine details of the typical northern cult of St. Bartholomew, such as is present in Esposende (Mar) where he is honored as São Bartolomeu-do-Mar (St. Bartholomew-of-the-Sea), hints that this is one of the few genuinely masculine and virile rural Portuguese saints (with most others being either beardless youths or decrepit old men). This, and his traditional cult and celebrations, consisting of the offering and consumption of black animal meat (particularly that of young chickens),

ST. BARTHOLOMEW – AUGUST 24TH

may actually point out that in this context St. Bartholomew and the Devil, at their core, might actually be one and the same character.

Orison to St. Bartholomew:

Glorious St. Bartholomew, sublime model of virtue and pure vessel of the Lord's grace, Protect this thy servant who humbly kneels at thy feet and begs thee to have the kindness to request on my behalf to the throne of the Lord.

St. Bartholomew, use all thy resources to protect me from the dangers which surround me every day! Cast thy protecting shield around me and keep me from my own selfishness and from my indifference towards God and my neighbors.

St. Bartholomew, inspire me to imitate thee in all my actions. Shed over me thy graces so as I may serve and see Christ in all other men and work for thy greater glory.

Graciously obtain for me the favors and graces of God for I greatly need them in my miseries and afflictions of life. I invoke thy powerful intercession here, trusting in the hope that thou shall hear my orisons and shall obtain for me this special grace and favor which I claim from thy power and fraternal kindness, and with all my soul I beg thee to concede to me the grace (mention the grace you desire), and also the grace of the salvation of my soul so as I may live and die as a son of God, reaching the kindness of thy love and eternal happiness.

Orison to St. Bartholomew against nightmares:

St. Bartholomew told me
To lay down and sleep
Without fearing the sea or wave
Neither the man of evil shadow
Nor the wicked pesadelo
Who has a hole in his hand
And a crooked nail

4. Comment by Enediel Shaiah:

> In some villages of Galicia, Asturias and the Santander Mountain, it is customary to have over your chest, hanging by the neck and under your clothes, a print of St. Bartholomew, which has on its back a doubled armed cross. For a long time we have kept, as a rare curiosity, a scapular (we are unaware of its origin) having an image of St. Bartholomew on one side and on the other side that of St. Cyprian, and on the dark fabric which corresponds to the back of the wearer, one may also observe a simple red and blue cross, made with two small pieces of colored fabric.

SOURCES

Camilo Castelo Branco: *Noites de Lamego*, (digital edition).

J. Leite de Vasconcelos: *Tradições Populares de Portugal – Bibliotheca Ethnographica Portugueza*, Livraria Portuense de Clavel & C.ª, Porto, 1882.

José Diogo Ribeiro: *Turquel Folklórico*, Revista Lusitana, Vol. XX (1917) p.54.

Moisés Espírito Santo: *A Religião Popular Portuguesa*, Assírio & Alvim, Lisboa, 1990.

Teixeira de Aragão: *Diabruras Santidades e Profecias*, Vega, Lisboa, 1994.

Teófilo Braga: *O Povo Português nos seus Costumes, Crenças e Tradições*, Vol. II, Publicações Dom Quixote, Lisboa, 1994.

POINTS I AND II

On a superficial level, both these sorceries may appear to be extremely similar, bearing many resemblances to other very common grimoire and folk magic sorceries. While at first glance both of them appear to be instructions for the creation of invisibility charms, if we take a closer look at them we see that the cat bone charm is actually something quite more mysterious, as its power simply appears to be to put you in any place you wish without being seen.

This whole issue is complicated even further if we analyze the narratives of Clotilde, Adelaide and Elvira (respectively points XIII of this same section and IX and X of the "Mysteries of Sorcery" section, pages 343 & 344), where Cyprian uses a magical fava in order to travel great distances and enter whatever places he wishes, being that it wouldn't be unreasonable to assume that this fava is the same as the one mentioned in point I. However, the powers described in these narratives do seem to be much more akin to the cat bone charm than the fava. In these mentioned narratives we can see that this charm enables Cyprian not only to enter places unseen, but also gives him power of flight, which he uses to dispose of the unnamed sorceress in the Elvira story. Indeed this doesn't seem to be a mystery that can be resolved by scholarship alone.

All we can further derive from these two sorceries is the nature of their power: both of these rely on the sacrifice of a black cat, a stealthy animal, very appropriate for entering places without being seen.

POINT III

On this point we once again find a particular incantation which is to be found three times in the whole of *The Book*: in the Coscinomancy ritual on the "Occult Powers" section in Book I, the current black cat love scent, and further down in the Clotilde narrative (point XIII of this same section). If we analyze the context in which it is used in all of these we cannot trace any particular area of influence or action, as one is used for divination, another for a love sorcery, and the other as a reversal for the destructive action of Cyprian's familiar devil (see the commentaries to points V and VI of this same section).

About this sorcery itself, it should indeed be noted as remarkable for the sheer creepiness and date-rape-like attitude it actually suggests. Not that this is in any way rare in this book, but somehow it seems less reprehensible if you, while bewitching someone, do not say anything about it and just let the magic work by itself. To actually go out of your way to lie and trick someone into falling for your sorceries just seems inelegant.

Don't kid yourself – if you use this as suggested you're a lowly piece of shit.

Points V & VI

Similar to sorceries I and II above, these two points have many troublesome common points.

Indeed in several of the narratives presented in *The Book*, a tiny familiar devil of truly fearful power is frequently mentioned as one of Cyprian's most feared and effective weapons, able to raze armies and destroy entire nations, all with a single word from its master.

However, once again there seems to be some confusion about which one of these two devils the stories refer to. We can clearly see in the Clotilde narrative (point XIII of this same section) that this devil is kept in a silver tube, and, looking at the instructions on the creation and maintenance of the two devils, we have that one should be kept in an ivory or boxwood tube (V) and the other in a silver box (VI). The one used by Cyprian seems to be a mix of both these instructions.

Still, given the nature and moral of these narratives I think it is fairly safe to assume that the devil in question is the one mentioned in point VI. Also, looking at their instructions one can tell that the devils made from cat's eyes are meant for more mundane and monetary issues, while the one which actually involves the pact is meant for a wide range of activities (as mentioned: all the desires of life).

Point VIII

1. The fern seed sorcery presents itself as one of the most powerful in this section, with the added warning that this is indeed a divine power and should be used and respected as such. It may seem contradictory that after the two first warnings about their proper use are given, the author goes on to explain how to charm a girl (or boy) with them. It must be noted, if one analyzes the many love philters, scents, and talismans in *The Book*, that love sorceries are not regarded as being in any way evil. True, from a Judeo-Christian perspective, these may be considered as an attempt against free will, but the idea *The Book* transmits is that love is never evil, and it quite clearly disregards any judgment on pre-marital or lustful sex. Love and sex, for the sake of love and sex, are never bad intentions.

2. This procedure is actually an elaboration on a pre-existing folk magic practice common throughout Europe; in Portugal it is frequently called the *feito* or *feitelha*, as reported by Teófilo Braga. Keeping in line with the theme, this author very simply states that fern seeds caught on St. John's Eve will make their owner be loved, without any of the additional safety precautions or proper instructions given in *The Book*. Teófilo Braga further states that this is a derivation of ancient satyr cults of the Fatuus or Fatuellus, although his association is not particularly clear to me.

Vasconcelos' report on this same tradition seems to be more in line with *The Book*. According to him, on St. John's Eve, the Devil and his shades gather around the fern to dance (a clear fey connection here I believe), and at the stroke of midnight the Devil shakes the fern so as to release its magical seeds. A person wanting to acquire these seeds should then place a sheet under the fern and take refuge inside a *sino-saimão*, as *The Book* indicates, being that in the Galician version of the ritual the *sino-saimão* is meant to be drawn on the sheet.

This then sheds a different light on these seeds as, according to this tradition, these seeds are probably tools the Devil expects to gather for himself during the said night for his own devilish designs, and one then needs to interfere in his plans in order to acquire some of them. It would then be reasonable to assume that the *sino-saimão* should really be drawn on the sheet so as to prevent the Devil from acquiring the seeds which fall inside it (as the Galician tradition claims), but honestly, better be on the safe side and draw two of them.

Regarding this tradition there are also interesting folk songs from around the Douro that directly allude to it:

Meu amor não vás a Avintes,	My love do not go to Avintes,
Nem p'ra lá tomes o jeito;	Nor take up a life there;
Olha que as moças de lá	Know that the girls there
Trazem a semente do feito.	Have the seed of the *feito*

SOURCES

J. Leite de Vasconcelos: *Annuario para o Estudo das Tradições Populares Portuguezas*, Livraria Portuense de Clavel & C.ª, Porto, 1882.

J. Leite de Vasconcelos: *Tradições Populares de Portugal – Bibliotheca Ethnographica Portugueza*, Livraria Portuense de Clavel & C.ª, Porto, 1882.

Teófilo Braga: *O Povo Português nos seus Costumes, Crenças e Tradições*, Vol. II, Publicações Dom Quixote, Lisboa, 1994.

POINT IX

Again, this is a traditional practice. Vasconcelos also mentions a similar one meant to enable one to marry their beloved. The details are somewhat sketchy, being that the only information given is that one should take a four-leaf clover caught on St. John's morning and place it under an altar's *pedra d'ara* (see the commentary on point XXIV of the "Mysteries of Sorcery" section, page 362).

SOURCES

J. Leite de Vasconcelos: *Tradições Populares de Portugal – Bibliotheca Ethnographica Portugueza*, Livraria Portuense de Clavel & C.ª, Porto, 1882.

POINT X

The logic behind this second rag doll sorcery may appear complicated. At first glance the idea which might be transmitted is that this is a powerful baneful magic, which, in order to enact harm upon its target, will take equal toll on the caster, as the nails are meant to go through both dolls. However, the information given in the "Declaration" may point in a different direction.

One doll is obviously meant to be the caster and the other the victim, and the caster should be placed in contact with the victim in a position of power, as if *"wanting to kill him"*, probably by strangulation. In that way one should perhaps consider that the nails going through both dolls aren't really going through them both, but rather they should be thought of as being projected from the caster doll into the victim. This then mandates that the nails should be put firstly through the caster doll, so as they come out of its body as weapons or harmful mental projection, and into the victim doll.

A fundamental part of magic is belief and, given the alternative, this seems like a good thing to believe in. But be careful, although you are using dolls, this magic is by no means impersonal; you are establishing a powerful bond between you and your victim.

POINTS XI & XII

1. There is an important aspect to be underlined in both black dog sorceries in this section, as well as all the other black dog sorceries in the rest of *The Book*. In none of them is there the specific instruction to actually kill a black dog, rather, the only instruction given is to perform the sorcery *"when the dog is dead"*. This is quite contrary to the previous black cat sorceries, for example, where you have the specific instruction to kill the animal in question. There is a great difference to be noted here, as actively killing an animal in this way and for these purposes means to take its life force as energy for the sorcery in question – a sacrifice, a forceful appropriation of its life.

Under this perspective it would be reasonable to assume that what is being suggested here is that a black dog is the most appropriate familiar for a Cyprianic sorcerer, for, according to St. Cyprian, *"a black dog has great magical power*". Then, upon the death of your most faithful magical companion, he can further assist you by providing the, quite literal, raw materials for new tools of the Art, one of which is even meant to help you acquire another dog.

Should this be the case then you really do not need to forcibly take the dog's life and energy for any sorcery, for your dog will gladly give it to you. A most fitting and loving use for its remains.

2. Valenciano offers these two dog-related natural secrets, which seem to be very close to the two sorceries presented in *The Book*:

Secret of the dog's heart

Baptista Aranda writes in one of his books that whoever carries with him the heart of a dog needs not fear other dogs, for they will flee from whoever carries this. This same author also says that ants will flee from the heart of a bird called hoopoe.

Secret of the dog's eye

Baptista Porta writes in his book of secrets that whoever carries with him the eye of a black dog will cause that no other dog will bark at him; this is because the said eye releases such a glamour and scent, which dogs immediately feel due to their great sense of smell, that not only do they not dare to bark but they will also not bother you in any way.

3. Addition by Enediel Shaiah:

In all that was just transcribed, as well as in many other sorceries still to come, one cannot exclusively follow and believe their exoteric significance, for these speak of such impossible things that one would never be able to take for certain their experimental merit. Nonetheless, tradition seems to perpetuate these sorceries to the point where any grimoire of any time period which one may read does still contains these formulas, expressed exactly in the same words in all of them. From this perspective these make up a document of traditional magical teachings, which imbues them with a degree of authenticity worthy of our attention.

The criticism of the profane, when placed before the difficulty of not being able to extract anything certain from these formulas, will gladly take the opportunity to depreciate them, mocking the old times when these were given magical importance and also those who still today respect them to a certain degree.

The initiated, however, may not disregard them for two reasons, an esoteric one and an exoteric one. From the point of view of the first of these, in all grimoire formulas, no matter how absurd, he knows that there is always a fundament of truth in them, more or less corrupted, and he should make the effort to seek out this fundament which is at the base of any superstition; for this procedure in truth is not at all illogical. We have seen, for example, that according to a certain recipe of St. Cyprian, there is a certain bone in the head of a black cat that can make a person who places it between their teeth invisible; it is a proven fact that many other grimoires include this same procedure and at the same time it is also an undisputed fact that under no circumstance could anyone convince himself, no matter how strong his faith, that a cat's bone or any other talismanic object recommended, will produce the impossible feat of invisibility. How is it possible then that this superstition manages to perpetuate itself? How can a formula which at first glance clearly demonstrate its uselessness pass from one generation to the next? There should be only one way: if it possesses a fundament, a base made up by certain facts whose existence is hiding among the thick veils of purely superstitious interpretation, which could then supply us with some basis to understand the reason why these formulas persist in the grimoires.

Let us apply this method of analysis to the current case. We observe that, firstly, this formula indicates that an individual place himself in front of a mirror, gazing into his own image while putting the cat bones in his mouth, one by one and, knowledgeable as we are about the wonders of self-suggestion and self-hypnosis, it will be a short leap to realize that the individual will hypnotize himself by one of the most direct and efficient means possible (a mirror). If this person lacks hypnotic impressibility, this experiment will merely become one of the many which do not produce results; but if he is sensitive to his own ocular irradiation, reflected back by the mirror, it will not take long until he falls into a fascinated state, or even into a deep sleep; let us also observe that these fascinated people do not think themselves to be sleeping, in such a way that, when asked if they are asleep, they decidedly respond "no", and in this state of sleep, self-suggestion is intensely developed, causing the individual to see his own image disappear.

Arriving here we can surely comprehend how this is a natural and purely hypnotic event, but there is a second part to it which corresponds to the territory of magical experimentation.

Every state of nervous imbalance offers an occasion for the astral body to project itself outside of its organism, in ways which may produce some perfectly proven phenomena, among which we can name remote vision and double sight. Well then, the fascination we have referred to in our example is more than sufficient reason to cause an astral projection, by which the individual sees himself being transported to other places, where he is, naturally, invisible, being able to recall exactly what he observed in them afterwards. And this is how the famous recipe of the bone of a black cat may have been able to survive thus far, by generating phenomena of hypnotic fascination and astral projection, which are attributed to the influence of some superstitious magic, a very different interpretation from the true one, that which is professed by the initiates of occultism.

But the *Libro Magno* also mentions certain methods of harming people and magically capturing their will, methods which belong to the procedures of bewitching, and in these the popular tradition is actually closer to reality than the opinion of other non-preoccupied people. A grimoire of which we have recently published the first Spanish commented edition deals with this subject in a way which seems to us deserving of being reproduced, it goes as follows:

METHOD OF PRACTICING BEWITCHMENT

Whenever you hear of Witches and their malefic arts, I advise you, reader, that you do not give this any credit whatsoever, for with confidence do I say to you that the great majority of bewitchers have so far been nothing more than charlatans, regular knaves or stark mad, however, do not laugh at the possibility of bewitchment, for I sincerely hope that you will never find yourself targeted by such a malefica.

Not all bewitchment has the objective of causing harm; some are meant to magically cure a persistent illness, and others to capture the affection of a certain person for another. Nonetheless, these are used by Witches, sometimes to produce harm on a person or their possessions, and to do this they may use different methods, which I will not reveal to you in detail, believing that it is sufficient, and safer, that I merely talk of them. I am referring to the bewitchment by the use of a wax figure.

Let us see what the wise Paracelsus teaches regarding this issue, he who possessed the whole of the magician's science since the most remote antiquity.

> "Already do you know that, according to the will of a spirit in battle with another spirit, if one is to cover with earth and stones a wax figure made in the image of any man, that this man will begin to feel restless and tormented in the area of his body where the stones were piled and he shall not rest while this figure is not unburied. Do know that if a leg is torn from this image that the man in question will feel the same pain as he would have felt with a fracture, and the same is true for needles and other kinds of wounds one may inflict upon this figure... If one is to paint a figure on a wall, made in the likeness of a certain person, it is certain that any blow or wound one may inflict upon this painted figure will be equally received by the indicated person." (*De entesipiritum.* Cap, VII and IX).

The only remedy for breaking this kind of malefica, according to those well learned in these issues, is the *desembrujamiento*[189]. To go about doing this, should you know where the figure in question is buried, one should go to it and the person being targeted should throw the figure into a fire himself. If one doesn't know the bewitcher neither the class, place and moment in which this malefica was made, one should resort to orisons and unbewitching religious practices, as well as pilgrimages to sacred sites, churches and chapels, those which have a well documented fame for protecting one from the invisible attacks of all sorts of bewitchments.

I repeat, reader, do not give credit to any evil power,

---

189. Unbewitching... too many prefixes for the English language.

for many people take advantage of this, sometimes to reap benefit from the fear simple folk have of Witches so as to fill their own pockets, and other times simply for their fraudulent desire to distinguish themselves in any way, even under the threat of eventually falling into the severe hands of the judges when they least expect; but do not forget that bewitchment is possible, and that spite is its greatest resource, and that in this field, the persecutions of a hateful woman are the most infernal malefica attributed to the skills of the goetic magician.

Let us now see our comment:

The belief placed in the possibility of bewitchment is ancient and universal. The Egyptian rituals, referring to the beliefs maintained by that ancient and powerful civilization, mention this and not as a new and debatable thing; the same can be found in the texts of Vedic India; and in a small tablet from the Royal Library of Nineveh, Assyriologists have decoded its cuneiform script to contain twenty-eight formulas for banishing evil spirits, disgraces and illnesses, similarly to a litany, among which one can read: "He who makes the image, he who enchants it, the evildoing face, the evildoing eyes, the evildoing tongue, the evildoing lips, the evildoing word. - Spirit of Heaven awake. Spirit of the Earth awake." In Greece we find an abundance of references and information; let us say what Plato said. "There exist two classes of malefica whose exact distinction is not easy to make. One comprises of those made from one body to the other, without any other implements which are not natural. The other, which is made by virtue of a certain enchantment prestige called binding, is used to persuade the masses that there exist certain people who are capable of causing harm by the already mentioned procedures, and this has indeed a most terrible power. It is not always a trivial thing to determine in what to believe regarding a certain point, and anyway, it will always be difficult to persuade all others of this. As such, it is a waste of time to try and convince a certain quality of worried people that they should not be concerned about wax figures placed under their doorsteps, paths, or under the tombs of their ancestors..." (*Leyes-libros* XI).

When missionaries visited China, several regions of the Americas, Africa and Oceania, they found in all of these places similar beliefs, making it possible for one to say that, in the whole world, equally among the most civilized and the most savage and barbaric nation, Witchcraft persists at the foundation of all belief and opinions. Nowadays bewitchment is still practiced, and furthermore, it is being discussed, from a scientific perspective, in the most cultured nations of Europe and America. Regarding the events of the past XIXth century, we shall mention such remarkable cases as the one which happened in the parish house of Cydeville (of which there is a judicial testimony containing declarations from over thirty people of several classes and backgrounds), the no less spectacular one of the coalman Lerible of Paris, which preoccupied the press of those day for a considerable time.

Not many years ago a priest died in France of an extremely rare and unknown illness, who happened to dabble in magic, and on his final hour he declared that he had fallen under a bewitchment, and that he knew very well the person who had caused this... The reader will certainly understand that lies in the hour of one's death are something which certainly does not happen, and at least we can admit that this dying man firmly believed in what he was saying. Modern investigators, basing themselves on the curious phenomenon of sensitive exteriorization, have been trying to explain bewitchment. One of these has performed notable and rigorously proven experiments in Paris, and has concluded the following: "My work proves that this agent, this special nervous influx (the fluid of sensitivity), under regular circumstances, does not come outside of the border of the skin on one's body, meaning, the outmost extreme of the nervous filaments; but some people, under the influence of particular procedures, can project this outside of themselves through their pores... so as to form a kind of atmosphere capable of transmitting to the brain the same impressions from the contacts it experiences... It has also been observed that: 1st certain substances can absorb this agent and re-emit it, in a similar way as we have with a phosphorescent body; 2nd that if such a substance is placed for enough time close to an individual whose sensitivity is exteriorized, it will become charged with it, in a quantity proportional to the time and the intention of the subject, in such a way as the charged substance will convert itself into a field, more or less extended, capable of transmitting to the subject's brain, the impressions it receives. From all this one may gather that if by an action of intensity i the radios of the sensitivity field of the subject is r and that of the substance is **r'**, the individual will receive the mechanical actions of an intensity equal to **i**, exerted over the charged substance or over any point of this substance's field of sensitivity, while between the substance and the subject there is a distance of less than **r** plus **r'**, and if this distance is greater than this, there is no possibility of transmission, at least while the contact between these exteriorized sensitive atmospheres **r** and **r'** is not reestablished..." (De Rochas).

By reason of prudence we will not be any clearer; but what was said is more than enough to call the attention of those true friends of knowledge to the surprising phenomenon of bewitching.

We have also said that there exists another reason of an exoteric nature for the conservation of the incoherent and fantastical integrity of grimoire formulas. This is mainly meant to conserve the superstitious practices of a traditional nature, which reveal to us the magical ideas of bygone times; as these may be considered relatively important documents of the history of occultism.

Considering the content of the grimoire in this way, these acquire an importance which justifies the care taken by competent researchers in seeking to differentiate the authentic editions from the many apocryphal ones, which do exist of those more renowned books, and it is here that we must make clear our desire to unbury from forgetfulness and forgery the three texts which are considered to be originals of the famous grimoire of Saint Cyprian, the Sorcerer.

Point XIII

The story of Clotilde is indeed a complicated one if you want to place it in a continuum of Cyprian's life, as it is stated that it happened in the year of 1009, and furthermore, in it Cyprian deals and converses with Satan as his close friend and ally while at the same time claiming to be a bishop.

There seems to be something else to be disclosed in this narrative, besides the given orison, that I have not been able to understand. There seems to be an unusual amount of detail regarding numbers, times, and dates. Most of these stories are vague at best, being that they are likely to have been gathered from oral folk stories regarding Cyprian and predating *The Book*. As such, all this detail seems exaggerated and at least suspicious.

Here there is also the mention of the silver tube containing a devil and the most complete version of the strange recurring incantation in *The Book*.

Mysteries of Sorcery

Extracted from a manuscript of black magic that is thought to be from the time of the Mouros

1. The reference in this section's title to the time of the Mouros is more than significant. As previously explained (see the commentary to Chapter VII of the "Book of St. Cyprian," Book I), the Mouros refer to a mixed historical and folkloric concept, the crossing between the vague historical memory of the Umayyad occupation of Iberia between the VIIIth and XIIth century and echoes of fairy lore and ancient pagan cults.

They translate to the idea of All Otherness, but in the current case it may go even a little beyond that, as the idea here is that the sorceries to follow are of the most remote ancientness, for in the minds of the rural folk, the Mouros are all that existed before Us – all that remained, either physically or mentally, from unidentified Bronze and Iron Age tribes, Romans, barbaric Christian kingdoms and Muslim occupiers. These are the eternally mysterious, wise and powerful people, masters of all sorcery and enchantment.

2. The short sentence mentioning the current whereabouts of this manuscript might have something else to add.

Évora is currently a pearl of a city in the heart of the scorching plains of the Alentejo, famous for its Roman temple, deep in the old Mouro territory. The name of this city comes from the Celtic root ebora/ebura, yew tree, in the same way as York, in northern England, used to be called Eboracum/Eburacum by the Romans. But should we take some liberties with this name, Évora can also relate to the Arabic Yeborath, يعبره, which was actually the name of Évora during the Umayyad occupation of the Iberian Peninsula. This word means "crossed", which may simply be a reference to the crossroads, making this a scroll of crossroads magic.

And of course this can also be directly related to the mentioned Bruxa (Witch) or Feiticeira (Sorceress) of Évora (see the commentary to "The Sorceress of Évora or the Story of the Forever Bride, the last section of Book III, page 414), many times mentioned in other books as being one of Cyprian's masters (although the mentioned section does make up quite a large text in the current book, the association of the Bruxa de Évora and St. Cyprian seems to be later than this book). All this points to many interesting suggestions, which only gain a satisfyingly solid body when we step out of the Iberian context and into the wider South American magical world where the lore of the Bruxa de Évora (either as a Pomba Gira or as herself) is much more substantial.

Point I

The first sorcery of this section is, without a doubt, the most spectacular sorcery ever! One does not need to be an experienced Magician, Witch, or

Sorcerer to immediately understand the ground-breaking efficiency of these most occult proceedings described here.

These methods are so effective that I will even go further and suggest that some of the sorceresses reading this book try out this great and hidden mystery without that whole dog marrow and needle case business. Or, madness of madness, try undertaking this dark malefica even if you think your beloved is not cheating on you, for you may be surprised.

Indeed the whole procedure is based on dosing your significant other with sweet tasting aphrodisiacs and constantly and ruthlessly bombarding him with love, affection, understanding and sexual suggestion.

Ah! The *Mouros* were a most magical, remarkable and advanced people.

Points IV & V

1. Sorcery IV is the repetition of sorcery VII of the "Occult Powers" section, as is indeed declared the first time it is disclosed. Analyzing both sorceries, one can tell that the first version is extremely more detailed regarding the actual method of producing the magical powder, while the second version, as is indicated, transmits the knowledge behind the magic of this same powder.

2. Again this is a most profound Arcanum of sorcery rescued from the shadows of the most remote antiquity.

To procure the love of your preferred gender has been a magician's concern since times immemorial, with many great and powerful demon princes being recruited and called upon for this most daunting task, as can be seen in many and ancient and renowned grimoires. *The Book of St. Cyprian* however takes a radically different approach.

My fellow occultists, should you want the attention of someone you find pleasant here is what you should do: 1) learn something about this person and change your behavior and attitude into something they might find enjoyable and interesting; 2) get yourself some decent clothes, nothing fancy, just something that looks clean; 3) wash the fuck up! Besides your black dog (who is too good for you anyway), nobody likes your stink; 4) keep up these practices of proper hygiene, giving this person some attention and making yourself into somebody they might like for about six months and you might just get lucky... if you still feel uncertain, here's some animal cruelty and opium hosh posh you can also try.

If that still doesn't work, ladies, give the man some cake, a warm delicious beverage and try cooking some warm meals for him once in a while... with plenty of pheromones.

3. What a world it would be if the secrets of both these sorceries, together with sorcery I, were known to all men and women. A world filled with sweet chocolate and coffee, properly dressed people, exuding nothing but the freshness of soap, shampoo and perfume... and opium.

4. The procedure used to prepare the eggs in sorcery V has many parallels with other folk practices using this same food. Typically a woman wanting to captivate a man would rub an egg all over her body while saying the following grammatically challenged incantation: "*egg I pass to whom eats thee my love kills him for love of me*".

SOURCES

Juliana Torres Rodrigues Pereira: *Feitiçaria no Arcebispado de Braga: denúncias a Ana do Frada à Visitação Inquisitorial de 1565*, Cadernos de Pesquisa do CDHIS 24 (2011) p.587.

Point VII

Saint Barbara (born in Nicomedia, the same city where Cyprian died), as should be known to most readers, is one of the great saints of folk Catholicism (with a powerful popular devotion) and many African-inspired religions, being associated with the Orisha Iansan in Afro-Brazilian syncretism.

In Portugal she is frequently associated with Saint Jerome, these two being the favored protectors against lightning, with Saint Gregory also having some devotion and a few similar prayers.

Her popularity and widespread devotion provides for an abundance of easily obtainable material on this saint, and as such, we further offer service in providing a few traditional Portuguese and Brazilian prayers and orisons to the lightning Saints.

"*Oh St. Barbara, who art stronger than the fortress towers and the violence of hurricanes, make it so as lightning will not strike me, thunder not frighten me and the roar of the cannons not shake my courage and bravery. Be always by my side so as I may face, with my head risen and with a serene face, all the tempests and battles of my life: (make your request) so as, winning every battle, with the conscience of having fulfilled my duty, I may thank thee, my protector, and offer Graces to God, creator of Heaven, Earth, and Nature; this same God who hast the power to dominate the fury of storms and calm the cruelty of wars. Amen. Saint Barbara, pray for us.*"

St. Barbara – December 4ᵀᴴ

Pray three Our Fathers, three Hail Marys and three Gloria Patri.

The following "Evocation of Saint Barbara", from Viseu, is an orison with a great number of variables from all across the country (and also attributed to many other saints), many of them featuring Saints Jerome and Gregory:

Saint Barbara rose,
Her holy hands she washed,
Her shoes she put on her feet,
To the path she took.
In the middle of the path
Jesus Christ she found.
Jesus Christ said to her:
"Saint Barbara, where dost thou go?"
"I shall go with thee Lord."
"With me thou shall not go."
In this land thou shall stay
To cast away these thunderstorms
To where there exists nothing
Neither fig trees
Neither Christian souls
Nor curls of wool.

Orisons to cast away thunderstorms, from Beja:

1) Blessed Saint Barbara
In the Sky it is written
In the Earth it is destined
Saint Jerome and Saint Barbara,
And all the angels in Heaven,
Accompany our souls.

2) The virgin Saint Barbara
Dressed and put on her shoes,
On the path of the Lord she walked
The Lord she did find
And he asked her:
"Where dost thou go, oh Barbara?"
"Oh! Lord, I am going to Heaven
To take apart the thunderstorm
That thou hast armed there."
"Go then, Barbara!
And place it far beyond the mount,
Where there is neither bread nor wine,

Nor baby's breath,
Nor olive branch,
Nor rocks of salt
Nor anything which it may harm"

3) Generous Saint Barbara
She was lost and was found,
To the scarf of Jesus Christ she was tied.
Those with devotion
Who read this orison
Will be free from Hell
And from the danger of thunder.
A thunderstorm formed
I hid under a trovisco
I called for Saint Barbara.
Jesus Christ came to me.
I heard the thunderstorm
I hid under a trovisco
I called for Saint Barbara
Saint Francis came to me

From Guarda:

St. Jerome, St. Barbara
godly saints,
strong saints,
Miserere nobis!

St. Jerome, St. Barbara
free us from lightning
and sudden deaths
do not let us die
without the true confession

SOURCES

J. Leite de Vasconcelos: *Tradições Populares de Portugal – Bibliotheca Ethnographica Portugueza*, Livraria Portuense de Clavel & C.ª, Porto, 1882.
Jaime Lopes Dias, *Crenças e Superstições da Beira*, Alma Azul, Coimbra, 2002.
José Augusto M. Mourão: *A oração a Santa Bárbara (semiótica da acção, semiótica da manipulação), Revista Lusitana – Nova Série, n.º 3*, Lisboa, Instituto Nacional de Investigação Científica, 1982-1983, p. 22.

Points VIII & IX

1. This is one of two particularly remarkable oils presented in *The Book*. The method of producing it is actually quite easy and common in certain areas and with certain wine producers; simply, instead of olive oil one fills the bottle with wine or some strong spirit to give it a special fruity taste.

2. Regarding the oil in particular, comparing it with the following one (sorcery X), and the narratives which illustrate them, both can be used to paralyze through astonishment, although this one does seem to possess further much more interesting virtues than the following one. Property number three seems the most interesting of them all, relating once again to the traditional cult of the souls in Purgatory, but this time with a much more magical and authoritarian nature over the said souls. The processes of enlisting the souls' aid is also similar to the one described in sorcery XXXIII of this same section, to be commented in due time.

However, it is worth noting that this third property only allows you to speak with the souls in question (contrary to the already mentioned sorcery XXXIII which does suggest that one may force the souls to take concrete action in the material world), meaning that it is, by definition, a necromancy rite, meant for divination and acquisition of knowledge. One other such divination rite (which does not require you to go to a cemetery) is also mentioned by Teófilo Braga, which can be found in the Inquisition process of Luis de la Penha, suggesting that many such practices were commonplace in traditional Portuguese sorcery. Coming into line with the more "tamed" aspects of the traditional Portuguese cult of the dead, this one enlists the aid of the souls through the offering of large amounts of prayers, meant to alleviate their suffering and promote their spiritual ascension. It is as follows:

Stand in front of a wax taper for one hour and say the following three times:

God is light, light is God,
Resquiescant in pace
For the Faithful of God

Next pray thirty-three Creeds, thirty-three Hail Marys and thirty-three Our Fathers and after this say the following:

Saintly lonely soul
to this world may thou be returned
and by God may thou be unbanished

By that desire, ardor and fervor,
That thou hast in seeing God Our Lord,

I ask thee to come speak with me,
And tell me what thou knows;
And these prayers I now here pray
I shall not give nor offer to thee
Until thou comes to speak with me;
And should thou come to speak with me I shall give thee
All I have prayed
And all that thou may ask

Repeat this every night until a soul appears to speak with you.

3. There might be something to meditate about in the fact that the following story of Cyprian and Adelaide is mentioned as having happened in Carthage. Quite possibly there is some kind of confusion here between Cyprian of Antioch and Cyprian of Carthage, although this is really not the case in most of *The Book*, where both Cyprians are regarded as quite different and distinct people, like, for example, the story of Cyprian and Barnaby (point XXVI of this same section).

One other strange and suspicious point in this story is the fact that in Cyprian's conversation with Adelaide he is mentioned as a saint, although, when questioned, he claims to worship *"the God Lucifer of Hell"*.

4. Five minutes... it seems that not even all the Devil's sorcery and magical art can make you last longer.

SOURCES

Teófilo Braga: O Povo Português nos seus Costumes, Crenças e Tradições, Vol. II, Publicações Dom Quixote, 1994, Lisboa.

Point X

1. The most relevant aspects regarding the magical objects used by Cyprian in this narrative have been commented in points I and II and V and IV of the "True Treasure of Black and White Magic" section, pages 327 & 328).

2. Analyzing this narrative in itself, it should be noted that it once again features the king of Persia, who previously had been introduced as the father of Clotilde. This may then make it easier to understand why the king already knew of Cyprian when the unnamed sorceress approached him and, more importantly, why he really wouldn't mind to see him dead.

The identity of the unnamed sorceress in this narrative, however, is without a doubt the most interesting thing about the whole story. And if nothing else, it at least tells us that Lucifer plays favorites with his children.

Of further notice, as far as the narrative goes, is the fate described for Elvira: a rich palace. Given all the wickedness displayed by Cyprian in this narrative, one must admit that this does display some degree of genuine love and admiration on his part – something very rare in all these Cyprian narratives.

3. Given the clear connection between Valenciano's work and *The Book of St. Cyprian*, the use of rosemary incense in this narrative may require some additional analysis. As, according to this author, there appears to be a direct antithesis between rosemary and the effects of poisonous animals, which is interesting seeing that it is due to an oil made from poisonous animals that Cyprian ends up defeating the protective incense used by the sorceress. Valenciano has the following to add on rosemary:

> Rosemary will keep all poisonous animals away, and its smoke is good for all plague and contagious ailment.
>
> (...)
>
> Those homes which, by being dark and damp, are usually not healthy, by being fumigated with rosemary, shall become sound and dry.
>
> (...)
>
> Dioscorides and Arnaldo say that boiled rosemary has the same effect as theriac has against poison. They also add that wherever there is any rosemary, no poisonous animals or venomous spiders will be able to live.

Related to this general use, other traditions mention that rosemary incense might be used to counteract the shingles, which in any case, was thought to be caused by contact with certain poisonous animals.

Further on rosemary incense, Vasconcelos offer the following prayer for a purifying fumigation:

> Our Virgin Lady
> By Egypt she passed;
> With a branch of rosemary
> Her divine son through the smoke she passed;
> May this creature became as clean
> As her Son became.
> In honor of St. Sylvester
> For he on these things
> Is the divine master.

Teófilo Braga also offers that, besides these properties, rosemary incense is also traditionally used against lightning and the plant itself is a good protector against sorcery.

4. There is an extremely relevant point made in the very last sentence of this narrative. This is the mention that all these magical properties of apparently

completely ordinary materials (be they olive oil, or lowly insects) were discovered by the Devil. What this may indicate is that this magic is not in itself diabolical, as being discovered by the Devil is not the same as being made, invented, or created by the Devil. As such, these may be considered as mere natural secrets, the natural magic of things whose knowledge the Devil acquired at one point or another (as the saying goes: The Devil isn't wise because he is the Devil, but because he is old). This point was actually also made in the previous grape oil recipe and is once again hinted at in the lengthy narrative of Victor Siderol, where the Devil mentions the Cabala of the *Mouros* as an acquired knowledge and not something he created or devised (given the antiquity that is traditionally attributed to the *Mouros*, it might actually be possible that these can be considered as being older than the Devil).

This gives us, as is the truly traditional notion, a much more interesting perspective on the Devil than any Christian theology might ever reach: the notion that the Devil is but another player in this world, just like any of us. The big difference is that he is one who has been playing for a very long time, long enough to challenge the creator of the game himself. Hence, as a folk figure, the Devil is always present, always hearing, always listening and ready to leap into action in the world of men at the sound of a single word, his cue onto the board. He is readily accessible, eager to play and be played with by the spirit of man.

This is partly what I believe the objective of *The Book* is: to prevent one from being a mere pawn in the game, but rather, by revealing the tricks discovered by the greatest of all players, the Devil, to make one into an active participant in the game.

Honest pacts and deals can only be made between beings with some form of mutual respect and equality; this states the difference between acquiring a companion, a teacher, or a taskmaster (don't get me wrong, sometimes a taskmaster is really what is required), and *The Book* levels out the plane so as friendship, not submission, may be sought.

In truth this is the very nature of St. Cyprian's tale in the *Flos Sanctorum* and these other smaller narratives, the alliance and friendship between Cyprian and the Devil which allows them to speak on an equal footing with one another, this to the point of having Cyprian eventually, and unilaterally, banish the Devil from his life.

5. Finally, still clinging to this last sentence, in it is also justified the very existence of not only this book, but also of all other books attributed to Cyprian, be they the old handwritten *Cyprianus* of Scandinavia (see Annex II) or the fresh new editions still being written in Brazil and South America, for Cyprian has spread these secrets *"throughout the world"*, and it will take the whole world to put them together.

SOURCES

J. Leite de Vasconcelos: *Tradições Populares de Portugal – Bibliotheca Ethnographica Portugueza*, Livraria Portuense de Clavel & C.ª, Porto, 1882.
José Diogo Ribeiro: *Turquel Folklórico, Revista Lusitana*, Vol. XX (1917) p.54.

Teófilo Braga: O *Povo Português nos seus Costumes, Crenças e Tradições*, Vol. II, Publicações Dom Quixote, 1994, Lisboa.

Points XI, XII, XIII, XIV, XV, XVIII, XIX & XX

1. These are the greatest group of toad sorceries presented in *The Book*, a type of practice, which, as is shown, has great relevance in the whole system.

The basis behind this particular discipline is very simply explained in point XI: toads are the infernal sustenance; they somehow have the property to nourish and feed infernal spirits. This occult power then gives them the magical quality of being the perfect simulacrum or magical symbolical representation of any one person you wish to target, as long as you appropriately identify the said toad with something belonging to the person being targeted.

The exact nature of how this magic works may be hard to determine, however. It could be that the toad has truly in itself a quality which enables this magic to target your victim, a natural magical quality, or, it could also be that these effects are produced by the unseen mediation of infernal spirits attracted by the offering of the toad being used, a goetic quality (for lack of a better word). But this question should be left for the skilled visionary mage.

2. Still, it is also openly admitted in *The Book* that the sorceries listed here are but examples. The demonstration of this can be seen in sorceries XIV and XVIII which, apart from being generally confusing, are indeed meant to have exactly the same effect even though they present completely distinct methodologies. It is thus suggested that, resorting to this hidden quality of toads, using the appropriate lines and ribbons, the appropriate symbols, the appropriate torture, and resorting to these points as basic guidelines, one may perform whatever bewitching may come to mind, as the limit becomes your imagination (and cruelty – do not try to fool yourself). In fact, one can make a whole school of magic just based on this small piece of lore.

As with many other sorceries in *The Book*, it is logical that besides these examples there are many (MANY) more Portuguese procedures using this animal (Teófilo Braga mentions the example of feeding a toad some bitten bread with needles so as the person who originally bit the bread will begin to waste away), as toad sorcery is in fact one of the great legendary qualities of the traditional craft, with lore spanning all continents and ages. But again, most of these rely on some unseen property of this animal to sympathetically affect one's desired target without ever offering any explanation regarding it.

3. Also, besides using toads in the described methods, one should seriously consider the idea of using them in other forms of infernal and diabolical magic as offerings for the spirits involved, at least if you choose to place yourself in the Cyprianic current. This should in fact be, if *The Book* is to be believed, the most suitable offering for all the denizens of Hell, the ultimate infernal food.

There might also be something related to this same suggestion in point

III of this same section, as a toad powder is prepared for the attraction and direction of a spirit of a dead relative. This is indeed a complicated point to settle, as, should this system be consistent, this would place this dead relative in Hell, while traditionally dead relatives are placed in Purgatory, and, as can be observed in a few sorceries throughout the book, the appropriate offerings to these are actually just prayers.

6. There is a peculiarity in point XIV which should not go unnoticed: the calling upon of the limp/lame Devil. I'll admit my relative ignorance regarding all the attributes of this curious character, although I do see something of the Brazilian Exu in all of this. This designation, of course, is in some contexts a nickname for Asmodeus, although Bethencourt, quoting Marcelin Défourneaux, does seem to suggest that his name is actually Renfa, a lesser vice demon.

Nonetheless this is a relatively frequent entity to resort to as is illustrated by the following "true" story by Teixeira de Aragão that relates his visit to a *Bruxa* in his young age:

> As she ended her speech, she placed her glasses on her forehead and changing tone said: "Let us get down to business. What you gentlemen need is the unfailing sorcery to salt the door of your loved ones: this needs to be done on three consecutive nights, and that evil woman's heart will completely turn to tenderness. There is no indifferences or levity that can resist. It is yet to fail... do try it if you wish to enjoy a happy love life... for this orison each one should pay according to their generosity."
>
> We threw in her lap two new cruzados, the currency of the time, and said as a duo: "Let that orison come."
>
> The old woman looked with a blaze at the payment and collected it with eagerness, and with a somewhat trembling voice said: "Now write what I will dictate to you."
>
> We opened our notebooks and transcribed what that wench dictated, which enables us to now offer this prodigious orison to all unfortunate lovers:
>
> *The door of (NN) I come to salt, for my good, not my ill, so as to the husband, lover or boyfriend who wishes to enter, such a river, such an ocean, such a war and such disunion may rise as with Fierabras and his brother: this (throw a handful of salt) is for Caiaphas; this other (throw another handful of salt) is for Pilate; this one (third handful of salt) is for Herod and the limp Devil, may he tighten the garrote and make it snap, and may she never rest until she comes to the door when I pass and with me talk; all that she may know she will say, all she may have she will give me, all men she will abandon and only me will she love.*

(Also see point XXXIX in the "Mysteries of Sorcery" section and its corresponding commentary.)

5. Valenciano describes the following uses and instructions for toad/frog powder:

A much necessary secret to stop bleedings

Occasionally a wound will bleed so much that those who do not have access to medicine will be drained out and gone in an instant, and this is not only due to wounds, but also from nose bleeds, medical bleedings or by regular blood flows which are natural in women. To avoid these dangers Master Constantino writes, and this is further confirmed by Master Pedro Logredo, that one should apply roasted frog powder on the bleeding area and it will immediately hold its flow. One of these masters also says that, should a woman or man bring these strong powders with them, in contact with their bodies, they should not fear, for they will never die from bleeding, even if they will still bleed a regular amount.

How to prepare the frog powder

Put the number you so wish of live frogs in a new pan, covered and sealed so as no breath may come out of it. Place the pan over some fire or red embers until the frogs are completely roasted and after grinding them you shall finely sieve them and thus you may use this powder on those occasions we have mentioned, and one should also note that these have the virtue of mending open veins.

SOURCES

Andrew D. Chumbley: *The Leaper Between – An Historical Study of the Toad-bone Amulet; Its Form, Functions and Praxis in Popular Magic*, Three Hands Press, Lammastide, 2012.

J. Leite de Vasconcelos: *Tradições Populares de Portugal – Bibliotheca Ethnographica Portugueza*, Livraria Portuense de Clavel & C.ª, Porto, 1882.

José Diogo Ribeiro: *Turquel Folklórico, Revista Lusitana*, Vol. XX (1917) p.54.

Teixeira de Aragão: *Diabruras Santidades e Profecias*, Vega, Lisboa, 1994.

Teófilo Braga: *O Povo Português nos seus Costumes, Crenças e Tradições*, Vol. II, Publicações Dom Quixote, 1994, Lisboa.

Point XVI

1. Of the *figa* a number of things should be said – not, however, on what it is or what it is for, by itself, as this is one of the most universal magical signs and talismanic objects in the world.

The Portuguese ethnographer José L. de Vasconcelos very concisely describes it as such (while avoiding the sexual symbolism):

> The figa is a magical gesture which is made by closing your hand with your thumb emerging from between the index and middle finger. This gesture is imitated in figures of jet, coral, bone, etc., that one superstitiously keeps in his home or carries as an amulet.
>
> (...)
>
> Not only does it avoid the *quebranto*[190], which may be produced by the evil eye and by words of excessive praise, but it is also a gesture of offense and contempt towards something or someone, and it is a counter measure against curses (...)

In the Portuguese context, as a gesture (which should be made with the left hand), it can be used both as a curse and as protection. As a curse this sign should be concealed from its target, either behind your back or under some form of clothing or cloth. Such precaution is not mandatory when one means to protect oneself or others with it (see the commentary to point XXXIX, page 378).

The protective character of the *figa*, in the traditional Christian context, can sometimes be associated with the fact that one crosses the thumb with the index finger while making it, representing in this way a cross, being that in some regions, when one is instructed to "make a cross", what is actually implied is a *figa*. This might be a good lead for the more anti-Christian inclined readers, should they feel disgust in crossing themselves, to include a Pagan tone in some of the sorceries and orisons in this and other books (although I do not personally advise this). One other alternative to the magical character of the *figa* as a gesture is that it actually draws a *sino-saimão* with the lines of one's

Sino-Saimão as drawn by the figa

---

190. The *quebranto*, which may be translated as the "breaking", is a set of symptoms frequently associated with the evil eye: headaches, tiredness, general indisposition and the happening of unfortunate events. One should not be confused with the other, not all evil eye causes *quebranto* and not all *quebranto* is caused by evil eye.

hand and fingers, acquiring all the protective characteristics of this symbol in traditional lore.

As a talisman against the evil eye, sorcery, the Devil, or general badness, it can be worn like any regular pendant: on the wrist, neck or shoulder. It is also commonly used to adorn working animals, especially if still young, to keep the *quebranto* away.

The most common and recommended material for these is indeed jet, the most virtuous one originating from the Asturias (other common materials are silver, ivory, coral, and horn), with folklore saying that this material is so remarkable that it would rather shatter than let any evil pass by it. Teófilo Braga mentions, in the Inquisition process of Ana Martins (1694), a certain blessing/banishing that relies solely on jet beads:

> After a blessing draw circles with the beads around the head
> of the person being treated, while saying the following:

> > *By the power of God*
> > *of St. Peter and St. Paul*
> > *and all the Saints*
> > *may they free thee from thy ailment;*
> > *I banish thee*
> > *to the island of Sulfur*
> > *and to the curdled sea*
> > *for as many years*
> > *as grains there are*
> > *in an alqueire*
> > *of millet*
> > *for I am the benzedeira*
> > *the lady and the healer...*

> One may also add the following:

> > *I break the air of the fig tree*
> > *The air of the opening and closing of the door*
> > *The air of the roosting chicken*
> > *The air of the house's dust*

2. Tragically the Portuguese arsenal of traditional talismans is tremendously repetitive, meaning that while there is quite an abundance of them, they are meant for a very small amount of uses. This, of course, unless you consecrate them appropriately, as *The Book* exemplifies.

Should you feel like this is something you might be interested in I further offer a list of some Portuguese talismans.

i) For the protection of children:

Half Moon – These can be attached to the strings tying the diapers of newly born infants. When they are three or four months old this talisman can be placed around their necks by a string of silk or cotton. They should be made either from silver or copper coins or from *aroeira*[191], usually by the godfather of the child. It is effective against the *quebranto*, evil eye and *luadas*[192].

Figa – Already discussed, but it should be noted that although it is greatly used for the protection of children, it is also popular with adults.

Sino-Saimão – This should go without saying. It is usually made of silver or coral and it is effective against Witchcraft, *quebranto* and the evil eye.

Heart – Made of silver or coral. Good against the evil eye and general pain.

Wolf's tooth – An actual wolf's tooth, fixed to a silver base. Good against tooth problems.

Valenciano also says the following regarding the virtues of wolves' teeth as amulets for working animals and beasts of burden:

A secret for the rest of beasts walking on paths

Pliny writes that by taking the largest teeth of a wolf, and
tying them around the necks of your horses, these will not
be hurt nor become too tired due to their traveling.

Other animals whose teeth are also used as talismans for this same purpose are sharks and sea lions.

Small ring – Made of silver, with the same attributes as the previous.

Cornicho – A small object shaped like a horn, made from either real horn or jet, with the same virtues as the previous.

Gopher's hand – The left hand of a gopher, fixed to a silver base. Against the *quebranto* and *luadas*.

---

191. A common name given to trees from the *Anacardiaceae* family, particularly the *Pistacia lentiscus*.
192. Literally "moonings", a harmful lunar influence.

Jaw of a hedgehog – The lower jaw bone of a hedgehog. These are usually put in a small bag of chintz and worn around the neck. Used so as teeth may be born without pain.

Coins with holes – Just regular coins, either of silver or copper, where one makes a hole. Good against the *quebranto* and *luadas*.

There is also one coin amulet in particular which may be used by adults to counteract migraines. To acquire this you must ask a beggar for a coin "for the love of God", making a hole in it and putting it around your neck.

Triton (sea shell) – Small enough so as to be carried by the neck. Good against the evil eye.

Key – Made of silver, has the virtue of healing aphthas.

Goat horn – The tip of a goat horn, fixed to a tin base. The production of this amulet is quite complicated as it should only be made from a goat horn one did not search for, but merely found by accident, either on a Tuesday or Friday, and one should kick the horn twice before picking it up. Useful against the evil eye.

Lavender pouch – A simple chintz pouch with lavender, meant for those children who have trouble keeping milk down.

II) For lactating issues:

Milk bead – An agate bead of a milkfish blue tone. Meant to make a woman's milk production abundant. It should be worn by the neck on a white string.

Jet bead – Against the *luadas*.

Leituario – An amulet consisting of a moss agate bead fixed to a silver base and hanging on a scarlet string. Used to preserve the milk of wet nurses.

Fig tree rosary – A rosary made from small sprouts of a fig tree, worn around the neck. It is meant to dry the breasts of a woman who wears it when she wishes to stop breastfeeding. The idea is that the milk dries in the same proportion as the sprouts dry on the string.

III) Against diseases and several ailments:

Clotting stone – An agate stone with a wire or silver ring crossing it and hung on a string, usually sculpted like a fruit. As the name indicates it is used against bleedings.

Nails – The horseshoe nails from the front right hoof of a horse that carries the image of St. Jorge in the procession of the Corpus Christi. These are carried in a silk pouch and are effective against epileptic fits.

Fava ring – A silver ring with a yellow stone shaped like a dry fava. It is carried on the ring or pinky finger and it is used against migraines.

Hardhead's eye ring – A silver ring with a bone taken from the head of a hardhead[193] (a fish). It is used for the same purpose as the one above.

Stomach stone – A circular object with two holes made from turtle shell. It is carried by the neck and is effective against stomach pain.

Oleander rosary – A rosary made from pieces of sprouts of oleander[194] and used around the neck. Good against erysipelas.

Mercury tube – A small tube of silver containing mercury which is carried by the neck. Used against erysipelas.

Sea horse – A dried sea horse, either carried by the neck or in one's pocket inside a box. Good against erysipelas.

Tooth bug – The description of this one is very vague, it is simply described as the chrysalis of an insect which can be found by the creeks. It is carried on a silk pouch around the neck.

Speck stone – A small stone the size of a lentil meant for the extraction of specks and sand from one's eye. I have not been able to determine exactly what stone this is supposed to be but these might actually be made from the shells of sea snails.

Pedra d'ara – A fragment of altar stone carried in a pouch and hung by the neck. A good protector against sorcery (see commentary on point XXIV, page 362).

Lion's nail – The curved nail of a lion fixed to a silver base and carried by the neck. Used against fevers.

Sezões **critter** – A beetle or bumblebee which is put inside a pouch and worn around the neck, being activated by praying an Our Father and a Hail Mary for St. Cornelius. Used against intermittent and periodical fevers.

---

193. *Sciaenidae* family.

194. *Nerium oleander*. I feel like I should warn you that this is a significantly toxic plant.

Quartan critter - A tube with a live lizard inside which must be caught without being searched for. This is used against a particular kind of fever which comes every three or four days, a common symptom of malaria. The theory states that as the lizard withers and dies, so does the disease.

Cagado[195] - A small turtle placed inside a chintz pouch and carried around the neck. Like the previous one it is believed that liver spots will disappear in the same proportion as the turtle withers and dies.

Garlic clove - This is carried either in a pouch by the neck or in one's pocket. Proper against sorcery and insect bites.

Three-ridged walnut - A regular walnut that instead of the characteristic two ridges along its length has three. A home where such an amulet is kept under one's pillow is free from sorcery.

Rue - Bundles of rue, hung from the ceiling or over doors to keep epidemics and general evil away. It may also be carried in a neck pouch to free one from sorcery. When one is traveling and passes by some rue it is most convenient to smell it. A folk song goes as follows:

> *Whoever passes by a patch of rue*
> *And does not smell it,*
> *If he had little health, with less he was left.*

Lightning stone - Contrary to what may be assumed these are not actually lightning stones, as in stones which are the result of lightning hitting the earth, but rather pre-historical hand axes which have the virtue of protecting a house from lightning strike. Nonetheless, it is (or at least was) the general belief that these stones were actually lightning which had hit the ground.

Ox, ram, goat or deer horn - These, placed on top of small poles or sticks, which are then placed around a section of farmland, are meant to drive away malefic influences (for this same purpose one may stick a frog on a reed and place it in a field). Also, when an animal is struck by the shingles, one should put these poles around its pasture.

Mule horseshoe - This is self-explanatory and it is used for the same as the previous one. Sometimes there is the additional indication that this should be the left horseshoe and in this case it may be used for such diverse purposes as avoiding lightning.

---

195. Common name for turtle of the *Chelidae* family.

Dog bone - A pouch of dog bones which is put around the neck of an animal which has been struck by mange.

Pig's tooth - The tooth of a pig used for procreation (not castrated), fixed to a tin or brass base. Used against the evil eye and to protect working animals from evil spirits.

Church tabernacle key - As with most liturgical objects, this has the ability to keep the Devil away. Occasionally keys like this may be also used to dry a woman's milk after there is no more need for breastfeeding. In this case it should be put around the neck, but hanging over one's back.

Antler of a *vaca-loura* - The large antlers of stag beetles, attached to a silver base, and wore on the shoulder, under the clothes. These are greatly effective against sorcery and bad airs.

Apart from these, there is also the logical use of pouches with an assortment of virtuous objects and herbs, the descendents of the old *bolsas de mandinga*, similar to modern mojo bags. These, as explained previously, contain in them the strongest and most relevant syncretic forms of Afro-Iberian Magic. Currently, however, there is not much to discuss about them, as these can be assembled by anyone with enough traditional botanical/geological knowledge, as these pouches usually don't seem to follow any closed recipe or ritual procedure for their construction.

Among all the talismans described above, the *figa* is particularly associated with the *sino-saimão*, the half or crescent moon and the wolf's tooth (sometimes this can be referred to as a horn), forming a composite talisman called *cambulhada*, *cambada* or *arrebiques* (this is the general name for any assortment of talismans, being that the particular assortment described here can, in some regions, actually be given the name *sino-saimão*).

EXAMPLES OF PORTUGUESE TRADITIONAL TALISMANS: A FIGA AND CORNICHO, A SINO-SAIMÃO, A
CRESCENT MOON, A HEART WITH A CROSS, A COMPOSITE MOON WITH THE ENGRAVING OF A KEY,
SINO-SAIMÃO AND FIGA, A COMPOSITE KEY WITH A CRESCENT MOON, SINO-SAIMÃO AND FIGA AND
A CAMBULHADA OF A CROSS, CRESCENT MOON, TWO COINS, TWO RELIGIOUS MEDALS AND FIGA

(Images taken from José Leite de Vasconcelos: *Signum Salomonis, A Figa, A barba em
Portugal* – Estudos de Etnografia Comparativa and J. Leite de Vasconcelos: *Opúsculos* –
Volume V – Etnologia)

3. Of Saint Lucia, like the previous case of Saint Barbara, one could fill a book.

The remarkable thing about her involvement in the current point should be mostly due to the fact that Lucia, according to her canonical lore and popular cult, is mostly associated with vision, which, we should keep in mind, has double meaning as physical and spiritual vision. This may actually be the direct association of this saint with this talisman, as it is clearly instructed that the user should not be blinded by ambition. Lucia probably enters here so as to keep the gambler's eyes unclouded by greed and open enough to know when it's time to cash in and go home.

Also, there is one other connection between Lucia and Cyprian, as they were contemporaries and both of them were killed by Diocletian's persecution.

Traditional orisons to Saint Lucia:

I) *Oh Saint Lucia you preferred to have thy eyes gouged and torn than deny thy faith and soil thy soul; and God, with an extraordinary miracle, gave thee two new eyes, healthy and perfect to reward thy virtue and faith, and made thee the protector against illnesses of the eyes, I plead to thee to protect my sight and heal my eyes.*

Oh Saint Lucia, protect the light of my eyes so as I may witness the beauty of creation, the light of the Sun, the colors of the flowers, the smile of children.

Protect also the eye of my soul, the faith through which I may know my God, understand His teachings, recognize His love and never be lost on the path leading to thee, Saint Lucia, thou art in the company of the angels and saints.

Saint Lucia, protect my eyes and preserve my faith.

Amen.

St. Lucia – September 13th

II) *Oh Saint Lucia thou preferred to have thy eyes gouged and torn than deny thy faith.*

Oh Saint Lucia the pain of having thy eyes torn was not greater than the one of denying Jesus. And, as an extraordinary miracle He gave thee new eyes, healthy and perfect, to reward thee for thy virtue and thy faith.

Protector from the illnesses of the eyes, I plead to thee...

(make your request)

So as thou may protect my sight and heal the illnesses of my eyes.

Oh Saint Lucia protect the light of my eyes, so as I may see the beauty of creation, the light of the Sun, the color of the flowers, the smiling of children. Protect also the eyes of my soul, of my faith, through which I can see my God and learn His teachings so as I may learn with thee and always refer to thee.
Saint Lucia protect my eyes and preserve my faith.
Saint Lucia protect my eyes and preserve my faith.
Saint Lucia give me light and discernment.
Saint Lucia give me light and discernment.
Saint Lucia pray for us.
Amen.

iii) An oldschool *benzedeira* healing with St. Lucia:

To cure the mist of the eyes (cataracts) take three olive tree leaves and place them at a cross between the thumb and index fingers of your left hand, while making crosses with the right over the face of the sick person and say:

Lady Saint Lucia,
Had three daughters;
One kneaded
The other tended,
The other burned the fire,
If thou art a carnicão[196]
Aid thee St. John
If thou art cabrita[197]
Aid thee St. Rita
If thou art mist
Aid thee the Lord of the Mountain.

SOURCES

A Thomaz Pires: *Miscellanea III, Revista Lusitana vol.3* (1895) p.366.
J. Leite de Vasconcelos: *Opúsculos – Volume V – Etnologia, Imprensa Nacional de Lisboa*, Lisboa, 1938.
J. Leite de Vasconcelos: *Tradições Populares de Portugal – Bibliotheca Ethnographica Portugueza*, Livraria Portuense de Clavel & C.ª, Porto, 1882.
José Diogo Ribeiro: *Turquel Folklórico, Revista Lusitana*, Vol. XX (1917) p.54.
José Leite de Vasconcelos: *Signum Salomonis, A Figa, A barba em Portugal – Estudos de Etnografia Comparativa*, Publicações Dom Quixote, Lisboa, 1996.

---

196. A kind of fungus rash.

197. I am somewhat unsure if this can simply be translated as a "young goat" or if this refers to the folk name of some disease I am not familiar with.

Teixeira de Aragão: *Diabruras Santidades e Profecias*, Vega, Lisboa, 1994.

Teófilo Braga: *O Povo Português nos seus Costumes, Crenças e Tradições*, Vol. II, Publicações Dom Quixote, 1994, Lisboa.

Victorino d' Almada: *Elementos para um dicionário de Geographia e Historia Portugueza - Concelho d'Elvas e extinctos de Barbacena*, Villa-Boím e Villa Fernando - Tomo Primeiro, 1888, Elvas, (digital edition).

POINT XVII

1. The *raison d'être* of this sorcery might elude some readers. This particular point refers to and tackles directly one of the most crucial concerns of the Portuguese rural folk: emigration.

Since the sixteenth century, and the unexplainable emergence ("invention" is a more appropriate word) a few centuries earlier of a worldwide empire, the vast richness of the world has had a profound impact on the Portuguese rural mind.

As the empire crumbled (today we are still trying to dig our way up from the debris) Portugal changed from a nation of navigators to a nation of emigrants, still seeking, as if children, the lost lands of Prester John or the tree of the *patacas*.

This idea of emigrating in search of wealth has, in certain areas of the country, become a cultural trait. One has the desire to go out into the world, as the Fool of every legend, seeking the mysterious Indies or the lands of Vera Cruz, to once again return home a wealthy and mighty king. This is precisely what this sorcery addresses: the fear of not returning home and instead wasting away in a faraway land with the sickness of Ceuta.

One may agree or disagree with it (I personally take the words of the Jesuit António Vieira to heart, "*a small place to be born, the whole world to die in*"), but this sorcery addresses more concerns and preoccupations of a collective people than a whole library of grimoires.

2. Nonetheless, analyzing the instruction one can easily understand its mechanics, being that it basically means to direct sexual energy into the work to be done, probably calling on Saint Lucia so as not to lose sight of the ultimate goal: wealth, the return home, and happiness.

POINT XXI

1. The presence of this narrative in *The Book* is, to say the least, strange. Some details presented are strikingly different from either the historical event or Plato's account of it.

Although this story is used to introduce this same strange magical ring, there is little point to it as the description of the ring is admittedly incomplete, although it is obvious that it follows the description given by Eliphas Lévi in *Dogme et Rituel de la Haute Magie*.

2. The reference of an unnamed Portuguese sorcerer seems to be the most unusual detail in this point, and it would indeed tie this narrative to the context of Portuguese sorcery and Witchcraft, thus justifying its presence in *The Book*. We, however, should be cautious of what we choose to believe.

3. As a side note, the man Gyges finds bears resemblance to some of the spirits of the first book of the *Lemegeton*, maybe Foras (although without a horse), Asmodai or Balan, alternatively, due to his "herculean form", Bathin, although invisibility is not a gift he is credited to bestow.

SOURCES

Éliphas Lévi: *Transcendental Magic – Its Doctrine and Ritual*, Martino Publishing, Mansfield Center, 2011.

Point **XXII**

As with many other instructions in *The Book*, this is also an elaboration of a traditional Iberian practice. Teófilo Braga simply states that, by placing a pillow over the chest of anyone who is dreaming, one can make him answer any questions asked.

Teófilo Braga: *O Povo Português nos seus Costumes, Crenças e Tradições*, Vol. II, Publicações Dom Quixote, Lisboa, 1994.

Point **XXIII**

Teófilo Braga mentioned one other similar recipe involving the picking of holly on St. John's Eve. This simply states that by sprinkling this plant with wine, and taking it into one's home after midnight, it will attract fortune to its owner. Vasconcelos adds the following folk song/incantation used on such occasions:

Azevinho, meu menino,	Holly, my boy,
Aqui te venho colher,	Here I come to pick thee,
Para que me dês fortuna	So as thou gives me fortune
No comprar e no vender,	In all I buy and sell,
E em todos os negócios	And in all business
Em que me eu meter.	In which I enter.

Of course the collection of herbs on St. John's Eve is by no means a rare thing, either for divination (usually for matters of the heart) or as general ingredients for the most diverse magical practices. Nonetheless, holly, elderberry, fennel and rosemary, appropriately caught on this night, are said to be excellent talismans against lightning.

SOURCES

J. Leite de Vasconcelos: *Tradições Populares de Portugal – Bibliotheca Ethnographica Portugueza*, Livraria Portuense de Clavel & C.ª, Porto, 1882.

Teófilo Braga: *O Povo Português nos seus Costumes, Crenças e Tradições*, Vol. II, Publicações Dom Quixote, Lisboa, 1994.

POINT XXIV

In this particular recipe there is an ingredient which should be highlighted.

Pedra de Ara, also *Pedra d'ara* or *Pedra d'era*, translated as "altar stone", is one of the most common and remarkable magical/talismanic components in the Iberian sorcerer's arsenal; it is a thing in itself and not just merely an ingredient (although it is many times this too).

In the proper Catholic liturgical ritual, this is a small stone square attached to the actual altar, where the relics of a saint may be kept, and upon which the mass is performed.

Standing on its own, the traditional uses of the *pedra d'ara*, or fragments from it, can be seen to be very similar to many others attributed to a number of many other objects and products described in *The Book*, namely, to bind or unbind lovers, mostly by men seeking women. Its method of usage is usually just a simple touch, which would cause the victim to follow the caster regardless of their own will. The following incantation is indicated as a means to activate this virtue:

> *God save thee pedra d'ara*
> *That in the sea thou wert created;*
> *Such as the Bishop or Archbishop*
> *Cannot say mass without thee,*
> *May also thee (NN)*
> *Not be able to part from me.*

Other qualities of *pedra d'ara* are common, such as the tradition which claims that a woman who takes a *pedra d'ara* from an altar, or places her hand on it, will never bear children.

Remarkably, this concept became a major nexus in the XVIIIth century Afro-Portuguese magical syncretism, bridging into the Yoruba concept of *Edoun Ara*, commonly called lightning stones, carriers of the *axé* of the Orisha Xangô. From their original Yoruba significance, these can be thought of as emanations of Xangô, and once acquired should be kept on an altar upon which appropriate sacrifices are made. The association of both these concepts should be almost immediate and intuitive, both in linguistic terms and in methodology. This syncretism can be remarkably observed in some XVIIIth century reports on the ingredients of a *bolsa de mandinga*, which mention that some of these, which included a lightning stone, had to be kept under a Catholic altar stone for a certain period of time so as mass would be given over them and impart them with divine power, the same power which gives the *pedra d'ara* its virtues.

SOURCES

Didier Lahon: *Inquisição, pacto com o dêmonio e "magia" africana em Lisboa no século XVIII*, Topoi, v.5,n.8, jan-jun. 2004, pp.9-77.
J. Leite de Vasconcelos: *Tradições Populares de Portugal – Bibliotheca Ethnographica Portugueza*, Livraria Portuense de Clavel & C.ª, Porto, 1882.
Teófilo Braga: *O Povo Português nos seus Costumes, Crenças e Tradições*, Vol. II, Publicações Dom Quixote, Lisboa, 1994.

Points XXV & XXXV

1. At first glance both these sorceries seem to be meant for exactly the same purpose. Apart from slight application details the end result of both is to create a needle with an extremely powerful and versatile power of bewitching. However, if we take our time in analyzing them we can see very distinct differences.

These are related to the type of power to which they resort. Naturally, sorcery XXV works by resorting to the power of the dead; this is directly invoked in the needle's creation process and in the incantation used for bewitching. The second needle resorts to, I suppose, natural magic, by the virtue a needle and thread acquires by passing them through the eyes of a bat, blinding and possibly killing it (which then constitutes a sacrifice).

The original Portuguese employed in these two sorceries does not make it clear if the stitches are to be made in a cross or if these are simply cross stitches, but given the fact that sorcery XXV indicates that to enchant someone you should make three stitches, it seems unlikely that you are supposed to make them as a cross.

Also, should we allow ourselves to be concerned with historical accuracy, then the idea of St. Cyprian describing a sorcery discovered in the XIIth century might be problematic.

2. Teófilo Braga also mentions the dead man needle as an elaboration of a preexisting folk sorcery, and interestingly, Vasconcelos mentions a similar process as these, but using a snake instead of a bat, with the resulting needle having the same attributes as these two sorceries.

SOURCES

J. Leite de Vasconcelos: *Tradições Populares de Portugal – Bibliotheca Ethnographica Portugueza*, Livraria Portuense de Clavel & C.ª, Porto, 1882.

Teófilo Braga: *O Povo Português nos seus Costumes, Crenças e Tradições*, Vol. II, Publicações Dom Quixote, Lisboa, 1994.

POINT XXVI

1. Interestingly these same instructions given by the shepherd Barnaby can also be found in Valenciano's *"Fysiognomia e Varios Segredos da Naturesa"*, and, according to this same author, this was taken from yet another unidentified book. His version:

NATURAL SECRET WHICH SEEMS MORE MIRACULOUS THAN NATURAL

> In a certain handbook I have found this secret, which I did not have the opportunity to test, and I give it here for someone with curiosity who might want to try it. This secret is, in Summer time, when the swallows are doing their nesting, one should observe when one of them has laid all of its eggs, and with the utmost care and vigilance take these eggs, in such a way as to not be seen neither by their father nor mother, and put them in a small pan of boiling water, so as they will be boiled almost instantly and lose their living color. In that same instant take them out and place them back in their nest, and, as the swallows will not know of this unfortunate event, they will go on caring for them, and upon seeing that the eggs do not hatch in their due time, these same swallows will think that this is their own fault and will immediately seek a herb, which they recognize by natural instinct, and they place it on top of the eggs. This herb has the virtue and efficiency to once again generate them, and by having this herb on top of them will these eggs return to their previous state shortly and generate new swallows. This is indeed a most noteworthy thing, should it be true. And the same author also says that this herb has many other virtues and he noted them in his book. Should this all be true then I do not doubt that this herb has many virtues, and these are surely great.

2. Teófilo Braga mentions a very similar concept to this swallow herb, existent in certain regions of Spain. This, instead of a herb, is described as a stone, and to obtain it one should locate a swallow's nest, with their hatchlings already born, and blind them. Upon seeing their blind babies, the swallows will fetch a stone with the virtue of healing every illness of the eyes, leaving it in the nest and curing its offspring. One then needs only to take this stone.

Teófilo Braga: *O Povo Português nos seus Costumes, Crenças e Tradições*, Vol. II, Publicações Dom Quixote, Lisboa, 1994.

Point XXVIII

This long list of days may present some problems for the avid practitioner. First of all, although the original indication is that these days aren't suitable for the performance of "good" sorceries, further down there is the reference that apparently all sorceries performed on these days will not achieve their proper end, indifferently of their orientation. Either way, the total amount of days presented are 123 (Jan - 18; Feb - 13; Mar - 9; Apr - 10; May - 10; Jun - 8; Jul - 11; Aug - 8; Sep - 8; Oct - 10; Nov - 10; Dec - 8), roughly one third of the year.

Among these days we find the 24th of June, St. John's Eve, a very specific night mentioned several times in *The Book* as the one to be used for very specific workings. How serious this list should be taken is probably best left to the individual practitioner.

Also, I don't think that there is any point in analyzing in depth all the days presented here as anyone will be able to find any relevant significance he may wish for any of them.

Point XXIX

1. This sorcery is common to many regions of the world. In Portugal it logically exists outside of the scope of *The Book*, being usually used by young women wanting to discover the job of their future husbands by the configuration the egg may take up during this same night, with some of these shapes having taken up a particular interpretation, such as a coffin, announcing death, a church, announcing a marriage, or a boat, announcing a trip to Brazil (see the comment on Point XVII in this same section, page 360).

2. The three saints mentioned in this simple sorcery are what in Portugal we refer to as the *santos populares*, the popular saints. All of their feast days, and nights, fall relatively close together and are, logically, part of the same Summer Solstice festival complex, of which the bonfires of St. John's Eve are without a doubt the crown jewel.

All of these enjoy wide and enthusiastic devotion by thousands of followers in Portugal, having developed at times into their own semi-organized cults and association. On their cults and devotion on a worldwide scale we should not dally, as St. Anthony and his syncretism with the Orixa Eshu (together with St. Jorge) would, by itself, fill more than a few books.

3. Focusing on the Portuguese case, St. Anthony's cult and festivities are the strongest in Lisbon, the city where the saint was actually born. The characteristics

of this cult deviate rather significantly from its Catholic aspects, as St. Anthony, commonly referred to as Sant'Antoninho (St. Tony), is commonly evoked and dealt with as an ever-present and accessible entity, a companion or a loving old friend, always in one's mind and heart ready to be called on for any difficulty or any matter of the immediate world, with particular emphasis, of course, on matters of the heart (a position he shares most notably with St. Gonçalo de Amarante, matchmaker of old women, St. John, St. Cyprian, St. Mark [see point XXXII], and the *Corpus Christi*) and lost objects.

St. John, apart from the countless rural semi-pagan bonfire festivities, is greatly celebrated in Porto, where St. John's Eve is marked with fireworks, hot air balloons, the curious tradition of festival participants hitting each other on the head with leeks (the plant), branches of citron or lemon tree or, more recently, plastic hammers – all this besides the bonfires of course.

St. Peter does not hold a particular bastion as the other two, but as the patron of fishermen his cult is strong in many coastal cities, being particularly dramatic and unique in Póvoa do Varzim. In this context, he is also regarded as one of the few unambiguously masculine saints of Portuguese folk magic (bearded and energetic), similar to St. Bartholomew. As the protector of fishermen, his is the rare circumstance in Portuguese folk religion where a Patriarchal power is summoned as protection against a dangerous and devouring Mother (the raging ocean), which in its turn might have some connection to the very apocryphal figure of St. Peter's Mother, Marta, who is described in some instances as "the greatest devil (fem.) in Hell, carrier of the broth for the hanged".

The symbolism of the two keys he carries is also slightly changed here, being that one is the key to Heaven (gold) and the other the key to the seas (black), revealing his male and potentially emasculating power.

4. Of these three, St. Anthony plays the greatest role in traditional sorcery and practical devotion, presenting himself as both the sober superior theological master and doctor of the Church and also as the easygoing saint, cheeky and devil-ridden, chasing girls to steal some kisses, breaking their water vases and putting them back together with spit, the saint to inspire young men towards all which is worthwhile in life.

It is his aspect as the saint of young men which helps to cement his devotion by young girls eager to find a suitor and resolve marriage issues. Traditionally this can be worked by typical "torturing of the saint", either placing his statue upside down (occasionally under water, which may also be used to ask the saint for rain), hanging it in a well, breaking it or by stealing his removable baby Jesus, or occasionally his hand, while he does not fulfill his task of bringing forth one of his protégés.

This particular aspect has led Teófilo Braga to attribute to the cult of St. Anthony a fiery and phallic component, as the baby Jesus he always carries can be thought of as the sacred fire made man. This may be further expressed by some extremely crude phallic folk songs about this saint common all across

Portugal (similar songs also exist regarding St. John) and his fame as a woman chaser and cheeky tormenter.

Besides these he is also commonly petitioned to calm storms, particularly tornadoes and whirlwinds, which are thought to be aspects of the Devil.

The following prayer to St. Anthony, from the Jesuit *Devocionario*, is a good example of a more creative and spiritually inclined type of Saint Anthony working. Much like the previous example of St. Lucia, where we must keep in mind that "sight" may have many meanings, here the recovery of lost things is again a flexible concept:

> *God and Lord of all Dominions, to whose power are subjected all human and angelic creatures, who conceded to Thy beloved servant Saint Anthony the privilege of having his devotees find their lost things, I give Thee infinite graces by the great favors Thou hast given this glorious Saint, and I ask Thee that by his intercession may Thou grant my soul celestial light and efficiency to dominate and restrain my unruly appetites, so as to follow Thy divine inspirations; may I never lose the precious gem of Thy grace and if by some disgrace I may come to lose it, may I once again find it. Amen.*

St. Anthony prayer to ask for protection:

Saint Anthony rose,
Through paths and roads he roamed,
Our Lady he did find,
She asked him:
"To where dost thou go Anthony?"
"To get thy Saint, I am going."
"Thou, Anthony, shall go
And on the earth thou shall stay,
My body thou shall keep
From the evil wolf and the evil she wolf,
From the evil dog and the evil bitch,
From the evil man and the evil woman
And from all evil that there may be,
May I never have any loss
Nor damage nor injury.
In praise of the Virgin Mary"
One Our Father and one Hail Mary

Response to St. Anthony:

Saint Anthony rose,
His shoe he put on,
His staff he took up,
His path he walked
Jesus Christ he found.
Jesus Christ asked him:
"To where dost thou go Blessed Anthony?"
"Lord, with thee I shall go."
"With me thou shall not come,
in the earth thou shall stay
keeping what is lost
so as to its owner's hand it is returned.
In the name of God and the Virgin Mary
Our Father and Hail Mary."

This response should be said three times, after which the lost things shall be returned.

Second response:

If a miracle thou desires
Resort to Saint Anthony;
thou shall see the Devil flee
As well as the infernal temptations

The lost is found,
The hard prison is broken,
In the center of the hurricane
The rageful sea is calmed.

By his intercession
Plague, error and death flee,
The weak becomes strong
And the sick becomes healthy

The lost is found... (repetition)

All human ills
Are calmed, are cured,
Let those who saw him say it;
Let the padovani say it

The lost is found... (repetition)

Glory to the Father and the Son and the Holy Spirit
As in the beginning, let it be now and forever.
Amen.

The lost is found... (repetition)

V. Pray for us blessed Saint Anthony
R. So as we may be worthy of the promises of Christ.

The lost is found... (repetition)

Let us pray: Eternal and all mighty God, Thou wished for Thy people to find in Saint Anthony of Lisbon a great preacher of the gospel and a powerful intercessor. We concede to follow faithfully the principles of Christian Life, so as we may deserve to have him as a Protector in all adversity.
By Christ Our Lord,

Amen.

Apart from these more or less common prayers, one may also refer to St. Anthony in certain divination practices. One such, hailing from Lisbon, says that, on the night of St. Anthony, one should go out and pick some snake grass (*Equisetum*), taking it to your home afterwards. Should this plant flourish this is a sign of fortune, which is somewhat similar to the practice of throwing thistles into the St. John bonfires to see if they flourish in the flames, which, should they do so, means that yours is a reciprocated love.

One other interesting example may be found in the Inquisition process of Ana Martins (1694), as reported by Teófilo Braga, consisting of a Coscinomancy ritual for discovering a thief. One should open with the following prayer:

> *Miraculous Saint Anthony*
> *by the habit thou wore*
> *by the cord thou tied*
> *by the breviary thou prayed,*
> *by the cross thou took*
> *by the Lord thou raised*
> *by those three days*
> *in the garden of Jesus*
> *seeking thy breviary thou wert*
> *by the contact thou had with Jesus;*
> *which in thy arms he sat,*

by the great sermon
which in the city of Padua thou preached,
and the revelation
thou had when they took thy father
over seven false sentences,
and from them thou freed him,
while the people prayed a Hail Mary
and thy sermon thou finished,
I thus ask of thee father Saint Anthony
make what was taken reappear.

The following instructions are sketchy, but it is further mentioned that *"after this prayer she would cast lots on a sieve, by attaching an open scissor to its rim, and performed certain blessings and banishments to it, when the sieve turned two times in correspondence with one of the names she said, then this was the person responsible for the theft"*.

Valenciano offers the following advice regarding St. Anthony in his *Perpetual Lunarium*:

MOST HEALTHY ADVICE AND VERY MUCH WORTHY OF
BEING TAKEN TO HEART BY EVERY CHRISTIAN

Any time the celestial bodies determine that a stolen thing
or a runaway slave shall not be returned to you, and any
sickness shall be dangerous, prolonged or deadly, it is most
wise to resort to God and his saints; for it is most certain
that these can hold back the celestial influences and make
it so as lost and stolen things are found, as has been done so
many times by the Blessed Saint Anthony of Lisbon, of the
Order of St. Francis, to those who, with confidence, asked
him through the following verses, which the church prays in
honor of this same Saint. It goes as follows:

> Si quæris miracula,
> Mors, error, calamitas,
> Dæmon, lepra, fugiunt,
> Ægris surgunt sani.
> Cedunt mare, vincula,
> Mambra, resque perdillas,
> Petunt, & accipiunt
> Juvenes, & cani.
> Vers. Pereunt pericula,

Cessat & necessitas,
Narrent hi, qui sentiunt,
Dicant Paduani.
Gloria Patri &c. Cedunt &c.

And in truth I say, for the glory of God Our Lord, and praises to the glorious Saint, that many times I have found lost and stolen things by means of these verses. And believe me those who hear me, that it may take a long time to fulfill your request, but do not lose confidence, nor cease to recite this verse many times, for, should this be convenient, it is certain that you will not be denied. And I say convenient, for although it is true that we always know what we ask for, it is also true that God Our Lord knows even better what is convenient for us; and as such, he will sometimes give what we ask by the intercession of the Saints, and other times not, as it happened to a certain lady of the City of Valencia, who, being greatly afflicted by a cancer, made a novena to the Blessed St. Luis Beltrán, of the Dominican Order, praying to him with great devotion for her health. Upon finishing the novena she become well and healthy. Some days later, this lady heard a preacher in that city saying that many times labors, disgraces and illnesses were the reason for many Christians to earn Heaven. And upon hearing this, this lady decided to make another novena to the Blessed St. Luis Beltrán, praying that, should that illness he had taken from her be her reason to be awarded Heaven, then he should put it back; and finishing her petition her cancer returned and she died but a few days later, and most faithfully do we believe that she is now contemplating God in Heaven. These two miracles are confirmed by D. Miguel Espinola, Bishop of Morocco, and Canon of Valencia.

Returning to our Paduan verses, you will find it not only useful for the finding of lost and future things as also to relieve you of many and great labors and miseries, for it is of a most effective virtue; similarly to drive away the Devil, to prevent one from falling into error and calamity, to free one from death, leprosy and other ailments, by which the sick will recover their health and the needy their remedies. To these verses are also obedient the sea, the winds and storms; and those who are weakened and paralyzed in their limbs will be free and healthy by the devotion to these verses. And let us note a strange thing, which is that the Holy Mother

Church allows one to ask God for miracles using these verses, as the three first words claim: *Si quæris miracula*. All of this I just said, for those who are suffering from theft and other similar troubles, was to simply prevent these from having to resort to having Astrological figures drawn for them, for these will not give you any profits, but rather they are the cause of infamies, suspicions and heartbreaks, as the very Astronomers will tell you and experience shows, as I have witnessed a few times.

ST. JOHN THE BAPTIST - JUNE 24ᵀᴴ

GOOD TONY - JUNE 13ᵀᴴ

ST. PETER - JUNE 29ᵀᴴ

Francisco Bethencourt: *O Imaginário da Magia – Feiticeiras, Advinhos e Curandeiros em Portugal no século XVI*, Companhia das Letras, 2004, São Paulo.

J. Leite de Vasconcelos: *Annuario para o Estudo das Tradições Populares Portuguezas*, Livraria Portuense de Clavel & C.ª, Porto, 1882.

J. Leite de Vasconcelos: *Tradições Populares de Portugal – Bibliotheca Ethnographica Portugueza*, Livraria Portuense de Clavel & C.ª, Porto, 1882.

José Diogo Ribeiro: *Turquel Folklórico, Revista Lusitana*, Vol. XX (1917) p.54;

Mariana Gomes, Isabel Dâmaso Santos: *Tradição devocional de Santo António*, Centro de Tradições Populares Portuguesas "Professor Manuel Viegas Guerreiro," Universidade de Lisboa.

Moisés Espírito Santo: *A Religião Popular Portuguesa*, Assírio & Alvim, Lisboa, 1990.

Riollando Azzi; *O Casamento na sociedade colonial luso-brasileira – uma análise histórico-teológica*, Perspectiva Teológica, 24 (1992) 49.

Teófilo Braga: *O Povo Português nos seus Costumes, Crenças e Tradições*, Vol. II, Publicações Dom Quixote, Lisboa, 1994.

POINT XXXII

1. St. Manso is a complicated one to grasp.

Given the purely traditional (non-orthodox) nature of his cult, this "saint" may sometimes be confused, associated and amalgamated with St. Manços, a semi-legendary saint, considered to be the first bishop of Évora and Lisbon, and St. Amancio, which may refer to either St. Amantius of Como or St. Amand or Amandus. This may still be further complicated by the fact that both St. Manços and St. Amantius of Como feature in the rural Portuguese Catholic feast calendars, with St. Manços being celebrated on October 7th and St. Amancio on April 8th, revealing for both of them an active popular cult.

But in truth there isn't any actual St. Manso in any Christian denomination, meaning that this is a purely traditional devotion in both Portugal and Brazil, being that he is mostly called upon for aiding one in finding a spouse through his ability to tame an individual into submission.

St. Mark – April 25th

St. Manso as we have him now is in fact an aspect of the popular and rural cult of St. Mark (the evangelist), a Saint who by himself has a position of great respect in Portuguese Witchcraft and sorcery, much like St. Cyprian.

This division of St. Mark into St. Manso arises from the historical evolution of his Iberian cult, as he was traditionally called upon for the taming of wild bulls (being that in Iberia St. Mark is more commonly associated with the Bull than with the Lion) which later led to his association with the function of finding a lover/suitor. As this dual sphere of influence fell upon this single Saint (patron saint of beasts of burden and matchmaker), his cult and devotion divided into the twins Marco Manso (tamed/gentle) and Marco Bravo (wild/ brave), two powerful and complementary forces. They mark, capture and tame, be it beasts or hearts.

Regarding this dual aspect, there are actually a few books with their name in the Brazilian market (some of which share part of their content with *The Book of St. Cyprian*), in which these are described as being twin brothers, born in year 6 in Rome.

2. Marriage orisons to St. Manso and St. Mark usually follow the same line, calling upon their power of domination:

(NN), Saint Manso tame thee so as thou dost not eat, or drink, or sleep, or rest while thou art not my husband and faithful companion.

Thou will be restless while thou dost not recognize that I am the perfect person for thy life until the hour of thy death.

Perform this orison with a picture of your boyfriend in your hand.

After the orison place the picture under your mattress and only remove it after the request has been fulfilled.

The following is from the Inquisition process of Luiz de la Penha, as reported by Teófilo Braga:

I enchant thee,
And re-enchant thee,
And double enchant thee,
With all the enchanters,
And with the Holy House of David,
And with the consecrated wafer
If this is so. Alleluia, Alleluia!
St. Mark mark thee,
St. Manso tame thee;
The grace of God and the Holy Spirit slow thee.
The consecrated waver flesh thee;
When thou sees me

In me be remitted,
When thou dost not see me
For me moan and sob.

The St. Mark and St. Manso orisons on the other hand have a more diverse character:

Orison to St. Manso and St. Mark to free one from all evil:

In the name of the Father, the Son and the Holy Spirit
Saint Mark mark me, and Saint Manso tame me. Jesus Christ calm my heart and take away my bad blood, the holy wafer in me; and should my enemies have an evil heart, let them not have rage against me; as Saint Mark and Saint Manso went to the mount and in it were wild bull and gentle sheep and these they trapped and pacified in their homes, so let my enemies be trapped and pacified in their homes under my left foot; as the words of Saint Mark and Saint Manso are certain, I repeat:

"Son, ask what thou will, that thou shall be heard and, in whatever house I stop, if it has a guard dog, let him be gone and let nothing move against me, nor living nor dead, and knocking at the door with my left hand, I wish for it to immediately open."

Jesus Christ, Our Lord, came down from the Cross; just as Pilate, Herod and Caiaphas were the executioners of Christ, and he allowed all their tyrannies, just as Jesus Christ himself was praying in the garden and found himself surrounded by his enemies, he said: "Sursum corda", and all fell to the ground until he finished his Holy Prayer; just as the words of Jesus Christ may those of Saint Mark and Saint Manso calm the hearts of all evil spirited men, wild animals and all who wish oppose me, be them living or dead, be it in the soul or body, be them evil spirits, visible or invisible, I shall not be pursued by justice nor by my enemies who wish to harm me, in body or soul.

I shall live peacefully in my home; by the paths and roads I may cross, no living thing shall block me, rather, all shall aid me in everything I require.

With this Holiest Orison I will have the friendship of the whole world and all shall wish me well, and I shall not be bothered by anyone.[198]

SOURCES

Cruz de Caravanca, *Editora Pensamento-Cultrix*, São Paulo, 2011.

Didier Lahon: *Inquisição, pacto com o démonio e "magia" africana em Lisboa no século XVIII*, Topoi, v.5,n.8, jan-jun. 2004, pp.9-77.

J. Leite de Vasconcelos: *Annuario para o Estudo das Tradições Populares Portuguezas*, Livraria Portuense de Clavel & C.ª, Porto, 1882.

---

198. Anon.: *Cruz de Caravanca*, Editora Pensamento-Cultrix, São Paulo, 2011.

Maria Helena Farelli: *Antigo Livro de São Marcos e São Manso – Os Tesouros da Feitiçaria*, Pallas Editora, Rio de Janeiro, 2010.

Riollando Azzi; *O Casamento na sociedade colonial luso-brasileira – uma análise histórico-teológica*, Perspectiva Teológica, 24 (1992) 49.

Teófilo Braga: *O Povo Português nos seus Costumes, Crenças e Tradições*, Vol. II, Publicações Dom Quixote, Lisboa, 1994.

Point XXXIII

This procedure once again relates to the cult of the souls in Purgatory, bearing some resemblances to the third procedure of the grape oil mentioned in point VIII of this section. Both of these are an active and much more magical approach to the dead in Purgatory, but this one, however, has a much deeper folkloric significance than the previous one.

The mentioned Tuesday is by no means a mere accident, as this is considered to be one of the greatly nefarious days of the week (Thursday is also a dangerous day, being that in some regions this is the day when the *Lobisomens* roam the night and the *Bruxas* make their *sámbleia*). This day is *par excellence* used for the communication with spirits and demons by traditional Iberian sorcery, which does make it the most appropriate for the operation in question.

But what one is accomplishing with this sorcery is actually the organization and forcible jumpstart of a procession of the dead, what in the Asturias is called *La Güestia* and in Galicia the *Santa Compaña* (numerous regional variations on this name exist, like *Procissão das almas, Hoset, Estadinga, Avexón* or *Avisóns*).

The lore regarding this particular apparition is vast and it is usually considered an omen of death for all those who see it. Many legends tell the tale of night wanderers who come across the *Compaña* and are handed a candle so as to join in, usually when these get home they find that the candle they were given is actually a human bone, a most misfortunate and inconvenient talisman as it will attract death and the soul of the person it belongs to. This bone should be returned to its owner as soon as possible, which can be identified in the *Compaña* as the soul walking with a limp.

The typical characteristics of the Galician *Compaña* make it very much identifiable with this sorcery in particular, as traditionally it is always led by a living person carrying a cross or a pot of holy water, sometimes called the *Antaruxado*. This position is actually a type of curse, and it may be passed on to another living person who crosses the path of the *Compaña*. This process can be avoided by various methods: by drawing a circle on the ground and stepping inside it; lying on the ground facing down; having your hands occupied with something else; carrying some garlic with you or a *vaca-loura* (the beetle mentioned in the narrative of Cyprian and Barnaby, see the comment on Point XVI of this same section); or by opening your arms as a cross and saying the name of Jesus Christ, or responding to the *Compaña*: "*I already have a Cross*".

The procedure described here then places the operator voluntarily in the place of the *Antaruxado*, leading a procession of the dead and finishing it with an Our Father and a Hail Mary, the typical and traditional offerings for the relief of the souls in Purgatory. After giving this offering nine times (and probably having elevated some souls in the process) the souls then offer you a reward, similar to the operations of the Ánima Soa.

This is then a typical *quid pro quo* devotional act to the souls in Purgatory, even if a dangerous one.

SOURCES

J. Leite de Vasconcelos: *Tradições Populares de Portugal – Bibliotheca Ethnographica Portugueza*, Livraria Portuense de Clavel & C.ª, Porto, 1882.

José Diogo Ribeiro: Turquel Folklórico, Revista Lusitana, Vol. XX (1917) p.54.

Xoán R. Cuba, Antonio Reigosa, Xosé Miranda: *Dicionario dos seres Míticos Galegos*, Edicións Xerais de Galicia, Huertas, 2008.

Teófilo Braga: *O Povo Português nos seus Costumes, Crenças e Tradições*, Vol. II, Publicações Dom Quixote, Lisboa, 1994.

Point XXXVIII

1. The mentioned Abraham Zacuto is actually a very specific and well known historical character.

Abraham ben Samuel Zacut was a Sephardic Jew born in Salamanca in 1452, a great astronomer and remarkable Kabbalist. Due to the massive expulsion of the Jewish people from Spain in 1492, the skilled Zacuto found a place in the court of King John II of Portugal where he became Royal Astronomer and Historian, developing methods and astronomical tools fundamental for star-based navigation, such as an improved astrolabe, essential to the Portuguese Empire's growth. Later he would also flee Portugal on account of the Jewish forced conversion decree by King Manuel I, moving to Tunis, Jerusalem, and possibly Damascus.

His remarkable work, of which we should underline the *Perpetual Almanac* (*Tabulae tabularum Celestium motuum sive Almanach perpetuum*), although of possible Kabbalistic interpretation, is on all accounts of a sober and scientific nature, at least as this was understood in his time.

As with any remarkable, mysterious and gifted person (even more if Jewish), he has over the centuries attracted many legends and non-historical facts to his image, and the current point in *The Book of St. Cyprian* is one such event. To the best of my knowledge he was not a practitioner of Witchcraft... although he did write about it.

2. Comment by Enediel Shaiah:

Some of the recipes featured in this second part also appear in the *Heptamerón*, a supposed book of the Sorcerer Saint, and many of these, like some others appearing further down, may be also seen in the curious Portuguese edition entitled: *O Grande Libro de San Cipriano* and the two books *Tesoros del Hechicero* and *Magia Suprema*. In these books the reader may find many interesting things, accompanied by comments and interpretations as insightful as well written and full of magical wisdom.

The books mentioned by Enediel Shaiah are most likely the following: 1) the *Heptameron o elementos majicos*, a Spanish *Book of St. Cyprian*; 2) the main Portuguese version of *The Book of St. Cyprian*, which you are holding in your hands this very moment (it should be important to remember that although Enediel Shaiah's edition shares much of its content with this Portuguese version, it is still quite different from it); 3) the more extended version of the Sulfurino Book; 4) and finally the *La Magia Suprema – Negra, Roja e Infernal de los Caldeos y de los Egipcios*, a book claiming to be the continuation of the Sulfurino Book, but translated by some mysterious Doctor Moorne.

SOURCES

Teixeira de Aragão: *Diabruras Santidades e Profecias*, Vega, Lisboa, 1994.

POINT XXXIX

This point is actually part of a wider Portuguese superstition. It states that should you cross paths with either a hunchback, a man with a limp, a blind man, a cross-eyed man or a one-handed man, this before you have had anything to eat on that day, you are at risk of being cast an evil eye. This, naturally, and agreeing with *The Book*, is an involuntary circumstance and should not be blamed on the person casting it.

The specification of these types of physical deficiencies can actually be traced to the XVIIIth century Portuguese physician Fonseca Henriques, who defined these as deficiencies capable of casting "fascination", a kind of magical influence. The same is also true of certain qualities of *Bruxas* designated *mulheres de maus olhos*, women of bad eyes, involuntary casters of the evil eye.

The solution for these unfortunate encounters is generally to make a *figa* with your left hand, being that *The Book* offers a much more assured way of dispersing this negative influence.

One other typical method mentions that, upon seeing one of these characters, all one has to do is rub a copper coin on the sole of your shoe.

Other similar traditions say that, when meeting a person one feels might jinx us, make a *figa* with your left hand and say:

Leek has three leaves,
Oh cursed one do not jinx me!

It should also be noted that leek is by itself a talisman.

When meeting someone you do not care for make a *figa* with both your hands and say:

Villain, cursed villain,
When God came upon the earth, thou wert nothing!

This will cause the person to be suddenly struck by confusion, giving you enough time to go through a different path.

Similar to these, should you see a *Bruxa* and wish to avoid her, make a *figa* with your left hand and say the following three times:

Tôsca e môsca seramantôsca;
Saramago, mostarda e alho.[199]

And the *Bruxa* will immediately change direction.

One other curious superstition (even if unforgivably racist) states that it is extremely unfortunate for a white man to cross paths with a black man before lunch, with the same holding true for a white woman crossing paths with a black woman. Should this happen one should make a concealed *figa* at him and say the following:

God save thee creature!
May God give me as much fortune
As thou hast blackness!

On the other hand, should a white man or woman cross paths with a black person of the opposite gender, then this is sign of good luck (now... I just don't know if this holds true for a black person crossing paths with a white one).

SOURCES

José Diogo Ribeiro: *Turquel Folklórico, Revista Lusitana*, Vol. XX (1917) p.54.

---

199. Although there are some words in there which might be easily translated, the whole incantation does not seem to even try to make sense and it probably should remain in the original language.

José Leite de Vasconcelos: *Signum Salomonis, A Figa, A barba em Portugal – Estudos de Etnografia Comparativa*, Publicações Dom Quixote, Lisboa, 1996.

Teófilo Braga: *O Povo Português nos seus Costumes, Crenças e Tradições*, Vol. II, Publicações Dom Quixote, Lisboa, 1994.

ART OF DIVINING
THE
PASSIONS AND TENDENCIES OF PEOPLE
THROUGH THEIR SKULLS AND PHYSIOGNOMY

THIS TEXT BEARS LITTLE TO NO INTEREST to the general topic of Iberian folk magic and sorcery. Its value is then mostly historical and chronological, as it can give us clues about the time period in which this *Book of St. Cyprian* began to crystallize as a commercial object.

The original cranial theory of Franz Joseph Gall (1758-1828) came around 1800, but the term "phrenology" was actually coined by Johann Gaspar Spurzheim (1776-1832), both contemporaries of Friedrich Schiller (1759-1805), the only other chronologically relevant reference in the text so far.

Seeing as these names are all from the same time period, one can indeed speculate that their reference isn't just due to any particular predilection of the mysterious author of *The Book*, but that rather these were renowned and well discussed characters and theories at the time *The Book* was being compiled.

But however we wish to look at it, this is a nasty piece of writing.

CROSSED CARTOMANCY

1. THIS IS THE THIRD AND FINAL cartomancy system of *The Book of St. Cyprian*.

As an introductory text it presents a remarkable tale of how this system came to be and how it was preserved and presented today. This story is in part reminiscent of the second presentation of the first system, with St. Cyprian finding himself isolated and in need of information from the outside world.

The system itself seems much clearer than the previous ones, and it also demonstrates a great degree of freedom and adaptability to the various circumstances that might be presented to it. The only thing one may point to is an apparent confusion as to which cards should be placed face down or face up, with directly contradictory instructions being given on two different occasions. But honestly, analyzing the system as a whole, it actually ends up being quite irrelevant which cards are visible or not, unless you have a particular predilection for the surprise effect.

2. The consecration presented is different and much simpler from the one described for the first system, although they both seem to rely on passing the cards through the waves of the sea, a consecration method very common in this

grimoire (I should not need to go into much detail regarding the symbolism of the sea, especially if we are to accept the African influence which seems to have played its part in birthing this book as we know it today). This may still be a reminiscence of the small tale describing Cyprian's isolation at sea, which has its base in traditional folk and oral sources, so the two consecrations might actually be equivalent.

3. Still, the topic on which these cards are directly meant to divine is once again the unremarkable tragedy of marriage and betrayal. There must surely be something which can be done about this, as *The Book* does state that this system "*may be applied for the uncovering of any mystery; for one needs only to personify the cards with the names of people one assumes to take part in what he wished to know*". Once again, I do believe these systems need to be carefully revised, but, nonetheless, if they are presented here as we see them, then maybe this is something which is actually supposed to be worked out by the private practitioner.

THIRD AND LAST

BOOK OF ST. CYPRIAN

OR

THE TREASURES OF GALICIA

THE TITLE OF THE THIRD AND FINAL PART OF *The Book of St. Cyprian* should be intimately related with the lengthy narrative of Victor Siderol and its subsequent list of buried treasures, for if one is to analyze the rest of the content of this part, as we shall, we find it very far removed from the Galician landscape and its people.

GRIMOIRE OF ST. CYPRIAN

OR

THE PRODIGIES OF THE DEVIL

1. THIS SECTION OF *THE BOOK OF ST. CYPRIAN* has been briefly discussed elsewhere[200]. Still, its richness and depth does demand that we delay ourselves in its study once more, as similar to other sections, there might be something in the current one which may help to localize the original manuscript of *The Book* in time.

First and foremost, the mentioned Mr. Zalotte is an absolute mystery to me. One would assume that, should this character be as famous as the author claims, he would be fairly easy to track, but such has not been the case.

On a completely personal note, I do not believe in the story of this "much respected French book", this for the simple reason that the narrative of Victor Siderol is too perfect to have been collected elsewhere and simply glued together with the rest of *The Book* and its culture. This makes no sense.

2. As mentioned elsewhere, there is a great deal about traditional magical practices one can learn with this narrative, but this is never given as an immediate and obvious instruction to the reader. One requires some intelligence and sensitivity to be able to read this story appropriately, and for the reader to actually be successful in doing so it is necessary that he approach it from a completely opposite side as would be expected; that is, from a superficial perspective. For the only way that this magnificent seed of knowledge will sink its roots and bear fruits in the mind of the reader is if one is able to read it from the Devil's side.

---

200. Various authors: *Conjure Codex - A compendium of invocation, evocation and conjuration*, Volume 1, Issue 2, Hadean Press, 2011, p.78.

The Devil is the universal lawgiver, the wild civilizer, the engine of change and the axis of the whole narrative. As Siderol approaches the Devil, motivated by his baser instincts (greed, laziness and lust), it is the Devil who, with his patient instructions and teachings, sublimates Siderol's animalistic drives into honor, goodness, and love.

This is the true purpose of spirit work - elevation and education of the self into something of worth and use for humanity.

3. Ironically, what is probably the least interesting part in the whole narrative is the original ritual performed by Siderol to summon the Devil. But still, and this is where one may catch a small chronological clue, there is a remarkable similarity in the description of the events surrounding this ritual and a particular passage from Éliphas Lévi's *Dogme et Rituel de la Haute Magie*:

> For this science, said the crowd, there is nothing impossible, it commands the elements, knows the language of the stars and directs the planetary courses; <u>when it speaks, the moon falls blood-red from heaven</u>; the dead rise in their graves and mutter ominous words, as the night wind blows through their skulls.

And from *The Book of St. Cyprian*:

> The Earth shook, and, after this convulsion, <u>the Moon, covered in stains of blood, fell down rapidly over the crossroad of Neuilly</u>, and, as it rose back to its place, a great lord appeared on the outside of the circle, into which he could not enter by virtue of the words recited.

Still, it may be hard to say with certainty if the author of *The Book of St. Cyprian* took this idea directly from Lévi, which would place the book after 1855 (which is very reasonable), or if both are simply quoting a similar source.

3. Apart from all the explicit and implicit diabolism of this narrative, there are various other points in this story that do demand attention, and these are all connected with the sheer lack of judgment it presents. One must not forget that this book, even if put onto paper at a more recent date than other European grimoires, is still over one hundred years old. In that sense there is a tiny note in Chapter X that to me appears as groundbreaking: the apparent acceptance of homosexual love. This does go hand in hand with the other few love sorceries in the rest of *The Book*, which do appear to suggest that they may be used by both men and women to attract both men and women. This just further highlights the point of free love that *The Book* makes quite a number of times throughout its body.

4. Quite a number of places mentioned in this story can actually be quite easily found on a map. On the village of Court I have found nothing direct, the only similar location is Courtry to the Northeast of Paris, which is actually at a distance quite close to five leagues from this city (throughout time, in Portugal, leagues have been a variable distance of between 4 and 7 kilometers).

MAP DATA ©2014 GOOGLE

The Parisian streets of Saint Honoré (where Siderol initially finds housing and his copy of the *Grimoire of St. Cyprian*), Saint Martin (where he finds an ancient coin) and Saint Jacques (where he publishes the *Gaul Sorceror*) are easily spotted. Of course, one cannot be exactly sure if these are the same exact streets as the ones mentioned in this narrative, but their relative short distance from each other does seem to make sense with the story.

Also *Neuilly* can refer to a number of places around Paris, which, given the fact that I have not been able to accurately locate *Revolta* (which does not seem like proper French to me, so it may actually be a corruption of some other name) casts a great doubt on its actual location. Still given the proximity with the edge of Saint Honoré Street I am tempted to point to Neuilly-sur-Seine, a rich commune in the western suburbs of Paris.

MAP DATA ©2014 GOOGLE

Also, most places mentioned in Siderol's travels through Spain do exist, and although some of them do not follow the geographical indications given in the text, they follow a relatively logical trajectory on the map. Of all of them only Ababides seems to elude me.

MAP DATA ©2014 GOOGLE

5. Of course, one should also crosscheck all of the treasures mentioned in this story with the ones given in the next part of *The Book*, as both of these sections are obviously intimately related. Sobroso, Ababides, Baigreza, Guilhade, Outeirello, Foçára and Lañas should be respectively treasures 39, 56, 99, 138, 148, 149 and 158 (some differences in spelling are directly related to differences in Portuguese/Castilian orthography).

Of Mondim, Mondariz, Fraguedo, Infiesta, Carballo, Rubióz I could not find a direct correspondence, but these might possibly be treasures 21 (both Mondim, and Mondariz), 16 or 79, 83, 90, 113 respectively.

The mentioned treasures of Meirol, Taboeja, Hyga Buena, Pojeros, Budinhedo, Aranza, Guinza, Caritel, Celleros and Bórdem I was not able to adequately locate.

SOURCES

Éliphas Lévi: *Transcendental Magic – Its Doctrine and Ritual*, Martino Publishing, Mansfield Center, 2011.

Treasures of Galicia

1. This is the second list of treasures presented in *The Book*.

Although it may seem like a strange repetition, this list of treasures bears significant differences from the one presented in the first part of *The Book*.

There is a small passage in the "Important Explanation" which reads that the "*intelligent reader will be able to decipher*" certain sections of this list, which might be a hint that what we are actually facing here is nothing more than a huge riddle. Such an event is actually quite a common thing in Cyprianic literature, with, as explained earlier (see the commentaries to Chapter VII of the "*Book of St. Cyprian*" section, Book I), some early *Books* merely consisting of lists of treasures and their disenchanting methods, which were really nothing more than humorous riddles, plays on words and anagrams. If this is the case, then I am very much afraid that this aspect of *The Book* is all but lost when you translate it into any other language.

Also, supporting such a possibility is the very Portuguese used in these lines. I have read many texts with various degrees of ancientness and linguistic archaisms, but never have I come across such words and such expressions. I have tried my best to push through this maze of jumbled letters, confusing grammar, *non sequiturs* and contradictory meanings, but I am very much afraid that I was unable to accurately translate this list (whatever "accurate" may mean here). If ever I wavered in my resolution to translate this book, it was in this section.

Apart from this issue, this list of treasures, if we are to accept it as it is and not as it may be, is in all much more mysterious and suggestive than the previous one, for here we have many indications and suggestions which tie it firmly and directly with the *Encantado* lore of Iberia.

2. The historical characters mentioned in the introduction of this text are also problematic. True there was a King Ferdinand I of León and Castile, who died in 1065, and it is also true that he had a son called Garcia, King of Galicia and Portugal (not the current Portugal, but one other older Portugal), however, Guttierre de Altamira is a different story.

The only reference I have to such a nobleman is of Gutierre de Cárdenas, lord of the castle of Altamira, built in the XVth century. This is too late of a date to match the information given, and even if we look into the history of the Counts of Altamira, original lords of Altamira, this title was only created in 1455 by Henry IV of Castile. We thus have a serious discrepancy of dates here, although what might solve it is the fact that the castle of Altamira was built over a previous Almohad fortification from the XIIth or XIIIth century. This is still too late of a date, but at least it does tie the fortification to *Mouro* rule.

3. In case anybody is wondering about the "*Biblioteca Académica Peninsular Catalani*, of D. Gumerzindo Ruiz Castillejo y Moreno, shelf n°76-A", do know that people have checked and there is nothing there, neither scrolls nor library.

Relation of the Treasures and Enchantments

1. As a whole this list of treasures, not considering the riddle hypothesis previously discussed, presents itself as being much more suggestive, mysterious and magically oriented than the first one. In it we find a much greater amount of explicit *Encantados* and warriors, be them *Mouros* or strange metallic animals and beasts (treasures 9, 30, 32, 53, 55, 57, 59, 64, 76, 79, 95, 106, 123).

Of these treasures, 95 does deserve special mention as the theme of the enchanted sow with piglets is wide and far-reaching, solidly crossing from Portugal to the Brazilian *porca dos sete leitões*, sow with the seven piglets, a nightly apparition (one may now perform the most entertaining associations between this concept and some creative Thelema in honor of Kenneth Grant, Salve!). In Portugal this is usually regarded as a form of the Devil, tormentor of night travelers, but it is also a common form for an *Encantado* or his treasure. Northern Portuguese folklore does also mention the similar "chicken with golden chicks" as a possible form for an *Encantado* treasure.

One other interesting element in some of these treasures is the apparent indications of specific hours and moments of the day when they can be accessed (16, 18, 29, 31, 70, 97), which, when thought of in the context of this book and its preoccupation with the open hours, does make a lot of sense.

2. Also noteworthy is the fact that many of these treasures are attributed to specific names and apparent historical characters, locking them quite firmly in time. Of the numerous names and references dropped I have managed to find the following (I apologize for the history lesson):

Treasure 24 – Any reference to a D. Ramiro will always be quite vague, as Ramiros is something of which Iberia has no shortage. However, I am tempted to think that this might be Ramiro II of León (900 – 965). This particular Ramiro is quite relevant in Portugal as he was the first man to call himself king of the land of Portucale, making him the first king of the first Portugal, in 931 (if my counting is correct, the current Portugal, officially founded in 1139, is the third Portugal). Of this Ramiro there are also numerous Portuguese legends regarding his illegitimate love for a *Moura* girl named Zahara, sister of the *Mouro* King Alboazar, lord of the castle of Gaia on the shore of the Douro.

Treasure 29 – As with D. Ramiro, there is one particular Sertorius who stands out in Iberia, Quintus Sertorius (122 B.C. – 72 B.C.). This is probably regarded as the second Portuguese (and Iberian) hero, only falling short of the Lusitanian leader, war chief and apparent god-made-man Viriathus (*regnator Hiberae magnanimus terrae*), today probably credited with all the values and virtues of what might be considered the perfect hero. Sertorius was actually a renegade Roman general who would come to lead the Lusitanian some fifty years after the treacherous death of Viriathus and as such would come to enter the hearts of the Iberian peoples as one of their mythical heroes and ancestors. Of him there are abundant legends, such as the one where he was frequently seen consulting with a white fawn previous to battle.

Treasure 50 – This black bishop is probably a reference to the homonymous Portuguese legend of the Black Bishop.

Shortly after King Afonso Henriques (1109? – 1185), the first and founding king of the current Portugal, had imprisoned his mother after having waged war against her for the right to claim autonomy for his lands (there is more here than psychoanalysts will ever care to unravel), the Pope ordered him to release her, under the penalty of excommunication.

As the bishop of Coimbra (at the time the capital of Portugal) was loyal to the Pope, the king decided to have him removed and have a new bishop nominated from among the clergy sympathizing with his position, and ended up selecting a black man, named Çoleima, just to spite the Vatican. This bishop became known as the Black Bishop.

The legend goes on among excommunications, kidnapping and attempts of murder, all performed by the King, as he adds insult to injury and ends up being readmitted into the Church by sheer power of son-of-a-bitchness.

This legend has been largely disproven by historians, but in it there is something which is always curious, namely the nomination of a black man as a bishop when in the Vatican the Cardinals were still deciding on whether black men had souls or not.

Of the black priestess (treasure 52) on the other hand, I know nothing...

Treasure 54 – Pelágio probably refers to Pelagius of Asturias (685 – 737) the founder of the kingdom of the Asturias, the last Christian bastion left in Iberia after the *Mouro* occupation. This makes this king the starter of the *Reconquista* movement which birthed all the Iberian Nations, and as such, stands as ancestor to them all.

Under the perspective of the *Mouros* as the inhabitants of the remotest of times, Pelagius can be thought of as the First Man, the man at the edge of time, cutting straight at the border between "Us" and the "Others".

(Treasure 127 might also refer to Pelagius.)

Treasure 67 – This may be a reference to a knight of the Order of Calatrava, founded in the year of 1150 by Alfonso VII of León and Castile (1105 – 1157). This was a powerful and truly fearful military order, designated to fight the *Mouros* and protect borderlands, eventually becoming one of the most relevant fighting bodies in Iberia.

CROSS OF THE ORDER OF CALTRAVA

Treasure 126 – Analyzing the time frame of these most notable figures presented so far, there are a number of princesses named Urraca to which this treasure may refer. Unfortunately, unlike the previous figures, none of them rises to a mythical level which would make her relevant to the point of being safely attributed to this treasure.

The first of these is Urraca of León and Castile (1079 - 1126). As the *Reconquista* waged in the Iberian Peninsula, two Burgundy knights presented themselves in the court of Alfonso VI of León and Castile (1040 - 1109) to offer their services in the battle against the *Mouros*; these were Raymond (1070 - 1107) and Henry (1066 - 1112), cousins.

In return for their services King Alfonso would give his daughter, Lady Urraca, in marriage to Raymond, while Henry was given Lady Theresa (1080- 1130), illegitimate daughter of the king. From these marriages would be born Alfonso VII (1105 - 1157), son of Raymond and future king of León and Castile, and Afonso Henriques, son of Henry (*Ibn-Arrik*), the founding king of the current Portugal.

The second Urraca is Urraca of Portugal (1151 - 1222), daughter of King Afonso Henriques and spouse of Ferdinand II (1137 - 1188), King of Léon and Galicia, son of Alfonso VII.

The third is Urraca of Castile (1187 - 1220), daughter of Alfonso VIII of Castile (1155 - 1214) and consort queen of Portugal by marriage to King Afonso II of Portugal (1212 - 1223), grandson of Afonso Henriques.

Of course, all of the previous cases may be problematic due to the fact that these were all in fact queens, and, as such, maybe not the ideal candidates, as *The Book* clearly reads "princess".

Of princesses we then still have Urraca Henriques (? - ?), daughter of Henry of Burgundy and sister to King Afonso Henriques; Urraca Afonso (1130), illegitimate daughter of King Afonso Henriques; Urraca of Zamora (1033 - 1101), Daughter of Ferdinand I of León and Castile (1015 - 1065) and sister of García II of Galicia (1042 - 1090), one other early nobleman to claim the title of king of Portucale as an attempt to silence the growing independent movement in those lands; and Urraca Afonso of Léon (1190), bastard daughter of Alfonso IX of Léon (1171 - 1230), granddaughter of Urraca of Portugal and, as such, great-granddaughter of Afonso Henriques.

Take your pick dear reader...

Treasure 160 – Again there are a vast number of historical Gonçalo Viegas who can fit into this treasure. Gonçalo Viegas de Riba Douro (1175 – ?), great nobleman and knight of the land of Portucale, member of the ancient Riba Douro lineage; Gonçalo Viegas de Portocarreiro (?– ?, he got married around 1253) nobleman and knight of the kingdom of Portugal (the king at the time was Sancho II, son of Afonso II); Gonçalo Viegas de Marnel (? – ? alive in 1050), nobleman and lord of Aveiro (Center North of Portugal); Gonçalo

Viegas Barroso (1160 – ?), great nobleman, lord of vast territories in Braga and Barcelos (Northern Portugal); Gonçalo Viegas de Lanhoso (1197 – 1219) third grandmaster of the Order of Avis (at the time called the Order of Évora), sometimes considered the Portuguese offshoot of the Order of Calatrava, who perished in the Battle of Alarcos.

CROSS OF THE
ORDER OF AVIS

Again, grab a history book and take your pick...

3. Taking into consideration the deep significance of this disenchantment ritual (as extensively explained in the commentaries to Chapter VII of the "*Book of St. Cyprian,*" Book I), this list of treasures actually suggests a slightly different outcome when compared with the first one, which is strongly bonded to *castros*, fountains and standing stones, connecting it to the most remote antiquity.

What we are presented with here are mythical ancestors, founders of nations, royal houses and noble lineages, still existent today and very much alive, put together with strange and unrecognizable *Mouro* kings and their nameless enchanted warriors. These are all dwellers of the two sides of the border of time and consciousness, between Us and the Others.

In the mundane sphere, Iberia, this crossing from remote unconsciousness to current and waking consciousness is represented by the *Reconquista* movement, of which all these characters are specific and fundamental players. Through their integration into the occult treasure hunter, through the unraveling of their treasures, the adept can reconcile the eternal mythical duality of the Christian and the *Mouro* (which he should have attained with the first list of treasures) and rise beyond them both. He then takes the crowns, jewels, and weapons of these two eternal rivals and establishes himself as one such godly man, a ruler and founder of nations, universes in themselves.

4. Similar to this great specification in characters and *Encantados*, we find that the great majority of the locations mentioned in this list are actually extremely easy to find on a map of Galicia. In all of these treasures a village, a town or even a city where the treasure may be sought is always mentioned, even though their exact location might still be a serious problem. This is a great contrast to the first list of treasures, as most of those are located in wild, ruined and uncivilized places, vestiges of old cultures and peoples, again, in accordance with the conclusion of the previous point.

5. In this list of treasures there are thirty-two references to *haveres/averes*, meaning, a treasure specifically belonging to a *Mouro* (35, 37, 45, 63, 70, 71, 93, 98, 99, 101, 111, 113, 120, 126, 131, 132, 138, 141, 144, 146, 148, 154, 155, 156, 157, 158, 160, 163, 165, 166, 171 and 173).

6. Having had problems correctly identifying all these locations, Enediel Shaiah adds the following comment:

There are a few other places in this list whose location is still uncertain, and for this reason we have omitted them. We also confess that many names presented here did cause us many doubts, for some of these are occasionally repeated in the various Galician provinces or simply do not seem to exist at all. Either way the result is the same, these places can only be considered as mere curiosities of magical literature, which are also fed by the faith which, in the villages of Galicia, *The Book of St. Cyprian* inspires, this ever since the conditions to have it printed have presented themselves at an early date. Otherwise it would not inspire so much confidence.

SOURCES

J. Leite de Vasconcelos: *Tradições Populares de Portugal – Bibliotheca Ethnographica Portugueza*, Livraria Portuense de Clavel & C.ª, Porto, 1882.

DIABOLICAL SPIRITS WHICH INFEST HOUSES WITH LOUD NOISES AND THE REMEDY TO AVOID THEM

1. THIS IS INDEED QUITE A CURIOUS TEXT; should it actually be original to *The Book*, it reveals an extraordinary erudition and bibliographical knowledge by its mysterious author. Should it not be original we at least can be sure that it is of a Portuguese origin, or at least it was adapted for a Portuguese audience, given its mention of certain obscure Portuguese authors and very specific elements of Portuguese folklore. Still, sidelining all of this, it strikes me as, to say the least, irrelevant and on some occasions even contradictory to the whole first part of *The Book*.

2. As no man is without error, and some of these references are quite obscure, we should do our best to clarify them.

Firstly, one should mention that the reference to Saint Augustine's *City of God* is actually incorrect. The mentioned section is actually in chapter VIII, not VII. The original:

> Hesperius, of a tribunitian family, and a neighbor of our own, has a farm called Zubedi in the Fussalian district; and, finding that his family, his cattle, and his servants were suffering from the malice of evil spirits, he asked our presbyters, during my absence, that one of them would go with him and banish the spirits by his prayers. One went, offered there the sacrifice of the body of Christ, praying with all his might that that vexation might cease. It did cease

immediately, through God's mercy. Now he had received from a friend of his own some holy earth brought from Jerusalem, where Christ, having been buried, rose again the third day. This earth he had hung up in his bedroom to preserve himself from harm. But when his house was purged of that demoniacal invasion, he began to consider what should be done with the earth; for his reverence for it made him unwilling to have it any longer in his bedroom. It so happened that I and Maximinus bishop of Synita, and then my colleague, were in the neighborhood. Hesperius asked us to visit him, and we did so. When he had related all the circumstances, he begged that the earth might be buried somewhere, and that the spot should be made a place of prayer where Christians might assemble for the worship of God. We made no objection: it was done as he desired. There was in that neighborhood a young countryman who was paralytic, who, when he heard of this, begged his parents to take him without delay to that holy place. When he had been brought there, he prayed, and immediately went away on his own feet perfectly cured.

The mentioned John the Deacon refers to Johannes Hymonides, a IXth century monk. Unfortunately a copy of his *Life of St. Gregory the Great* is quite hard to find (even digitally) and so far I was not able to confirm this reference.

Father Possevino is likely to be Antonio Possevino (1533 - 1611), a Jesuit controversialist and bibliographer, but again, the book and characters elude me, as Tolosa can both refer to locations in Portugal, Spain or to Toulouse in France. However, Antonio Barreto may be the Portuguese version of the name Antonie/Anthony Batt/Bratt, a theological author sometimes found associated with Possevino, but this is highly unlikely as Possevino is quite older than this Anthony/Antonie.

Cardano is very clearly identifiable as Gerolamo Cardano (1501 - 1576) an Italian mathematician and physician. The mentioned Book XVI is entitled *De rebus praeter naturam admirandis*, and it's stock full of occult information, sigils and such curious stories.

EXTRACT FROM CARDANO'S *DE VAERITATE RERUM*, BOOK XVI

The mentioned chapter XCIII is entitled "Daemones et Mortvi", and the original quote reads as follows (I think...):

> *At obiiciet quispiam, quód in familia Torellorum, nostra adhuc aetate manet. Seb libet historiam narrare. Est familia nobilis, ac inter primas Parmae, Torellorum nuncupata possident, ut audio, arcem in qua aula est. In e a sub camino solet uideri anus iam centum annis, quoties è familia aliquis obiturus est. Referebat mihi aliquando illustris matrona Paula Barbiana, quae ex e a familia erat, dum ac cenaremus Belzoiosij, quandam puellam aegrotasse, uisam anum, existimasse omnes illam perituram at contrá accidit seruata enim est, fed alius incolumis repené è familia mortuus est. Referunt, hanc anum cuius nunc umbra uidetur, olim fuisse praediuit em, & ob pecunias interfectam a nepotibus suis, & in frusta diuisam proiectam que in latrinam.*

Johannes Trithemius (1462 – 1516) shouldn't be a real mystery, as this is a quite reputed author in certain occult circles. The mentioned book is the *Chronicon insigne Monasterii Hirsaugiensis*, and it does contain the famous, and lengthy, story of the Hudekin:

His temporibus, spiritus quidam malignus, in dicecesi Hildeshemensi, multo tempore multis uisibiliter apparuit in habitu rustico, pileo caput opertus, unde & uulgo pileatum appellan bant eum rurales, hoe est, ein Hedeckin, lingua Saxonica. Iste spiritus Hukin multa mirabilia fecit, & delectabatur esse cum hominibus, loques, interrogas, & respondens familiariter omniibus, aliquando uisibiliter, aliquando inuisibiliter apparens.

The references to Alessandro Alessandri's *Genialium Dierum* all check out, the only omission being that what is meant is chapter IX of Book II, as the work in question is made up of six books. In truth, the three stories mentioned actually make up the whole chapter IX of Book II. And indeed the reference to André Tiraqueau seems to be correct, as this author penned a commentary to Alessandri's above mentioned book.

The mentioned Cassianus is actually John Cassian (360 – 435), a Christian Theologian born in Romania but established in Marseille. The mentioned quote is from the *Collationes patrum in scetica eremo*, referred to in English as *Conferences*, taken from part VII, chapter 32:

Nonnullos (immundos Spiritus), quos faunos vulgus appellat, ita seductores et joculatores esse manifestum est, ut certa quaeque loca seu vias jugiter obsidentes nequaquam tormentis eorum, quos praetereuntes potuerint decipere, delectentur, sed derisu tantummodo et illusione contenti fatigare eos potius studeant, quam nocere; quosdam solummodo innocuis incubationibus hominum pernoctare.

The reference to presbyter Manuel Bernardes (1644 – 1710) seems to bind this text unequivocally to a Portuguese source.

This is quite a significant mystical author of his age, still considered one of the greatest Portuguese classical prose writers of all time. The reference is also correct, being part of the chapter in question, entitled "Greed", devoted to the discussion of several cases of demonic and spiritual possession with some references back to Alessandro Alessandri and many classical authors.

The actual reference to Apollonius of Tyana may be hard to locate, as the author gives absolutely no hint or clue of it, nonetheless, the following extract from the *Life of Apollonius of Tyana* does fit the bill:

Now while he [Apollonios of Tyana] was discussing the question of libations [in Athens], there chanced to be present in his audience a young dandy who bore so evil a reputation for licentiousness, that his conduct had once been the subject of coarse street-corner songs... Apollonios then was talking about libations... when the youth burst out into loud laughter, and quite drowned his voice. Then Apollonios looked up at him and said: "It is not yourself that perpetrates this insult, but the Daimon, who drives you on without your knowing it."

And in fact the youth was, without knowing it, possessed by a Daimon; for he would laugh at things that no one else laughed at, and then he would fall to weeping for no reason at all, and he would talk and sing to himself. Now most people thought that it was the boisterous humour of the youth which led him into such excesses; but he was really the mouthpiece of a Daimon, though it only seemed a drunken frolic in which on that occasion he was indulging. Now when Apollonios gazed on him, the Eidolon (Ghost) in him began to utter cries of fear and rage, such as one hears from people who are being branded or racked; and the Eidolon (Ghost) swore that he would leave the young man alone and never take possession of any man again. But Apollonios addressed him with anger, as a master might a shifty, rascally, and shameless slave and so on, and he ordered him to quit the young man and show by a visible sign that he had done so. "I will throw down yonder statue," said the Daimon and pointed to one of the images which was in the King's portico, for there it was that the scene took place. But when the statue began moving gently, and then fell down, it would defy anyone to describe the hubbub which arose thereat and the way they clapped their hands with wonder. But the young man rubbed his eyes as if he had just woken up, and he looked towards the rays of the sun, and won the consideration of all who now had turned their attention to him; for he no longer showed himself licentious, nor did he stare madly about, but he had returned to his own self, as thoroughly as if he had been treated with drugs; and he gave up his dainty dress and summery garments and the rest of his sybaritic way of life, and he fell in love with the austerity of philosophers and donned their cloak, and stripping off his old self, modeled his life in future upon that of Apollonios.

Athenodoros Cananites and Pliny the Younger are actually very easy references to confirm, one should nonetheless add that it is in point 27 of book 7.

Of the *The Life of Saint Ambrose*, written by Paulinus of Milan, around the Vth century, all the information seems to also be correct.

The St. Germanus mentioned is Germanus of Auxerre, as Antissiodorum is merely the original Latin for Auxerre. The reference also is in accordance with the *Life of Germanus* written by Constantius of Lyon in the Vth century.

3. It is probably relevant to underline that some of the descriptions of ghosts given in these accounts do fit quite well into general Portuguese lore (not exclusively of course) and one should ponder if this was the reason why these references in particular were chosen. Beyond the more spiritually oriented soul of Purgatory, or other forms of *Almas Penadas*, which may take on a great variety of forms and occupations, one may find many other kinds of curious apparitions in Iberian folklore. Of these, the *Aventesmas* fit quite well into some accounts in this chapter.

This word by itself may be problematic, as it also describes, as in Chapter II of the story of Victor Siderol, a startling figure, but it is in the second meaning we are now interested. Of this one may still find some variation, such as *Abentesma*, *Aventisma*, *Abejão*, *Abujão* and a number of others. These are usually described as tall and pale figures, dressed like priests, which have the peculiarity of the more you look at them the taller they become. The point of this description is that you never get to see their head, and, as your eyes go up its body and your head leans back to enable you to see farther up, they constantly grow out of your sight. The lore and information on how to deal with these dangerous apparitions is somewhat lacking, as it is never explained or understood what is the purpose of such visitations, only that, should one encounter one, you should flee in search of the town Calvary and climb it, having to stay there the whole night as the *Aventesma* will not be able to touch you there. One other interesting idea says that one should actually keep looking up to the farthest extreme possible, so as eventually the *Aventesma* will make an arch over you; when this happens one should remove one shoe and throw it through the arch – if the shoe passes through it one is safe, if not then one should flee.

One other point which should be clarified is the mention of *fradinhos de mão furada*. These are a type of Portuguese *Duende* and, as their name indicates, can be recognized by their friar-like hoods and by having a hole in the palm of their hands (like the *pesadelo* described in the orison of St. Bartholomew, see the comentaries to "The Cross of St. Bartholomew and St. Cyprian" in the "True Treasure of Black and White Magic" section, Book II, page 323). This, in my opinion, is the strongest element in attributing this text to a Portuguese source.

These *Duendes* in particular, even though they are usually paired with the wilder *Trasgos*, do constitute what would be called household spirits, having the ability to actually be helpful (which a *Trasgo* generally is not). The symbolism of the hole is complicated to ascertain with clarity, as a XVIIIth century text, attributed to António José da Silva, a satirist, states that this is due to their unselfish distribution of wealth among those they favor; their hands have holes for they cannot hold anything for themselves:

Some call me the Little Devil with a Hole in The Hand and others the Little Friar, for some of us have their hands so leaky with liberties that in many of the houses we live in we boil the honey, make the olive oil grow, increase the wealth, multiply happiness and, most of all, when our company deserves it, we discover hidden treasures for the owner of the homes in which we live.

This however becomes problematic given the extreme fluidity of *Duende* lore in Iberia, as no one type of *Duende* is explicit or exclusive to any one region, and their characteristics overlap with one another. In the present case, taking the Portuguese *Fradinhos* and *Trasgos* as distinct in this context, if we go to, for example, the Asturias, one finds their *Tragus* described with a hole in the palm of their left hand, being that one way of ridding a house of one is to ask it to collect grains in his palm, which he will not be able to do due to this physical issue.

This hole may also be related to Christ's wounds and suffering on the Cross, as *Duendes* are in truth souls who have experienced some form of bad death, and as such are in suffering.

SOURCES

Alexandri ab Alexandro: *Genialium Dierum*, (digital version).

Hieronymi Cardani: *De Rerum Varietate – Libri XVII*, (digital version).

Ioannem Tritehemivm: *Chronicon insigne Monasterij Hirsaugiensis*, Ordinis S. Benedicti, (digital version).

John Cassian: *The Conferences of John Cassian*, (digital version);

José Diogo Ribeiro: *Turquel Folklórico, Revista Lusitana*, Vol. XX (1917) p.54.

Manuel Bernardes: *Nova Floresta ou Sylva de varios apophtegmas e ditos sentenciosos espirituais, e moraes : com Reflexoens, em que o util da doutrina se acompanha com o vario da erudiçaõ, assim divina, como humana*, (digital version).

Owen Davies: *Grimoires – A History of Magic Books*, Oxford University Press, New York, 2010.

Philostratus: *Life of Apollonius of Tyana* (digital version);

Saint Augustine: *The City of God*, (digital version).

Teófilo Braga: *O Povo Português nos seus Costumes, Crenças e Tradições*, Vol. II, Publicações Dom Quixote, Lisboa, 1994.

Xoán R. Cuba, Antonio Reigosa, Xosé Miranda: *Dicionario dos seres Míticos Galegos*, Edicións Xerais de Galicia, Huertas, 2008.

OCCULT POWERS OF HATE AND LOVE

DISCOVERED BY MAGICIAN JANNES AND PRACTICED BY ST. CYPRIAN

1. THIS FINAL LIST OF SORCERIES BEARS A CURIOUS mark upon it. Even though it does not fall off the track from the previous lists (which can at times be terribly repetitive), this one, besides what you would call "normal" folk sorcery recipes, does seem to include a few others which are explicitly said to have been acquired in other regions of the world by traveling Portuguese, another mark of the Empire.

Of course the adoption of foreign magic into any traditional system is more than frequent and these are merely another example. Anyone with the knowledge for it may easily spot various other instances of foreign influence in *The Book*, but what is remarkable here is the immediate assumption of this fact (which may just be a way of attributing the glamour of foreignness to it). Further still, the presence of this list in the third part of *The Book*, specifically entitled "The treasures of Galicia", makes it seem somewhat out of place. Most likely this title of the third part of *The Book* is meant to underline the story of Victor Siderol and the subsequent list of treasures, whose relevance cannot be understated.

2. Also the Magician Jannes is most likely a reference to one of the Pharaoh's magicians who contended with Moses, although in some Brazilian editions this name has been substituted by that of the *Bruxa* of Évora.

Interestingly, a direct connection can be made between Jannes (and Jambres) and Cyprian through Armenian sources, where legends of Cyprian (referred to as Bishop Kiprianos of Antioch) are actually remarkably common. One of these has Cyprian acknowledging his own wickedness by mentioning that Jannes and Jambres at least respected the finger of God, a thing that he did not.

This legend is the base of the *Kiprianos*, an Armenian talismanic book of prayers.

SOURCES

James Russell: "An Armenian Spirit of Time and Place": Švot, *Proceedings of the 2013 Harvard/AIEA/SAS Workshop on Armenian Folklore and Mythology*, Belmont & Watertown (2013).

POINT IV

1. Monserrate is likely a reference to the Monserrate palace, gardens and the surrounding forests in Sintra (the mountain of the Moon). As this palace was built in 1858 it might actually fit with the production of the current version of *The Book of St. Cyprian*, and what might actually be meant is that these said scrolls were discovered during the building of the palace. But these are all unsubstantiated conjectures.

2. Keeping in line with the rest of *The Book*, we may note that, when it is mentioned that this sorcery may be used for "good", it is immediately implicit that what is meant is inflaming love in someone. This book is groundbreaking in assuming and proclaiming that love and sex, for their own sake, are inherently good.

POINT VII

1. The name of Piaga Ambongo, it should be mentioned, also features in the Brazilian play *Um Não Sei Quê Que Nasce Não Sei Onde* by Maria Jacinta, written in 1969, where he is referred to as a black sorcerer who died between 1800 and 1900. This reference is not without interest, as the sorcery in question, using navelworts and *erva-de-saião*, is actually mentioned in this curious play, together with a few other elements present in *The Book of St. Cyprian* (such as donkey testicles, sorcery VIII of this same section), even if the book seems to not be directly mentioned.

The insistence on the African origin of this sorcerer may be problematic in the current case if we analyze the orison following the recipe, which has no mention of Africa, but rather to the Brazilian Tupi natives and the *Pajés*. This issue has been solved in some Brazilian editions (such as the remarkable N. A. Molina book) where Piaga Ambongo is simply mentioned as being a native Indian.

2. Regarding the sorcery itself, one should pay particular attention to the instruction which mentions that this recipe may be applied to any person of any gender.

Also, do know that what seems to be intended by the "etc." at the end of the orison is for one to continue the line with the rest of a "Salve Regina", which begins precisely with "Mother of mercy".

POINT VIII

Donkey rape!

POINT IX

1. This sorcery stands out quite remarkably by its unusual functioning. This appears to be the only one in *The Book* which resorts to the usage of playing cards without being a form of divination. The two orisons are also quite interesting as these are meant for two completely different saints, St. Lucia and the Virgin Mary.

2. The "chaplet" which is mentioned as the final instruction for this sorcery is a kind of short *terço*, consisting of seven Mysteries with seven Hail Marys each. There are a number of these one can offer to any saint or spirit, but the most commonly prayed for the Virgin Mary is the "Chaplet of Sorrows", which relates to the Seven Sorrows of Mary, in which each Mystery is pain experienced by Mary.

Opening prayer:

Most Painful Virgin, we would be ungrateful if we did not make efforts in promoting the memory and cult of Thy Pains. Thy Divine Son hast bonded to the devotion of Thy Pains, particular graces for a sincere penitence, timely aids and succors for all necessity and dangers. Reach to us, Lady, from Thy Divine Son, by the merits of Thy Pain and Tears, the grace of (make your request).

Creed, Our Father and three Hail Marys in honor of the Holiest Trinity.

1st sorrow: The Prophesy of Simeon

For the sorrow Thou felt upon hearing Simeon's prophesy, that a sword of pain would pierce Thy Heart, Mother of God, hear our prayer!

Our Father, seven Hail Marys, Gloria Pater

2nd sorrow: The persecution of Herod and the escape of the Sacred Family

For the sorrow Thou felt when escaping to Egypt, carrying in the virginal bosom the Baby Jesus, so as to save him from the fury of the impious Herod, Immaculate Virgin, hear our prayer!

Our Father, seven Hail Marys, Gloria Pater

3rd sorrow: The loss of the Baby Jesus in the Temple of Jerusalem

For the sorrow Thou felt when the Baby Jesus was lost for three days, Holiest Lady, hear our prayer!

Our Father, seven Hail Marys, Gloria Pater

4th sorrow: The meeting of the admirable mother with her son, carrying the Cross, on the path of the Calvary

For the sorrow Thou felt when seeing the beloved Jesus with the Cross on his shoulder, on the way to the Calvary, Virgin Mother of Pain, hear our prayer!

Our Father, seven Hail Marys, Gloria Pater

5th sorrow: The crucifixion of our Lord

For the pain Thou felt when witnessing the death of Jesus, crucified between two thieves, Mother of Divine Grace, hear our prayer!

Our Father, seven Hail Marys, Gloria Pater

6th sorrow: When Mary received the body of Jesus in her arms, having been taken down from the Cross

For the pain Thou suffered when receiving in Thy arms the inanimate body of Jesus, taken down from the Cross, Mother of Sinners, hear our prayers!

Our Father, seven Hail Marys, Gloria Pater

7th sorrow: When the body of Jesus was deposited in the tomb, leaving Mary in sad solitude

For the sorrow Thou felt when the body of Jesus was left in the tomb, leaving Thou in the saddest of solitudes, Lady of All Peoples, hear our prayers.

Our Father, seven Hail Marys, Gloria Pater

Final prayer:

Give us, Lady, the grace of comprehending the ocean of anguish which made Thou the "Mother of Sorrows", so as we may participate in Thy suffering and console Thee with our love and our joy. We cry with Thee, oh Queen of Martyrs, in the hope that one day we will have the joy of being with Thee in Heaven. Amen.

Although not as common as the "Chaplet of Sorrows," one may also offer the "Chaplet of Joys" (also called the "Seraphic Chaplet" or the "Franciscan Rosary"). This chaplet has the particularity of having 72 Hail Marys in it, which, besides the C/Q/Kabbalistic connections, corresponds to the number of years the Virgin Mary is said to have lived in this world.

CHAPLET OF JOYS

1st joy: Incarnation of the Divine Verb

We accompany Thee, Holiest Virgin in the joy Thou had when from Thy purest loins the Divine Verb incarnated.

For this mystery we beg Thee to keep forgiveness at our reach and the grace to imitate Thy holiest virtues.

Our Father, ten Hail Marys, Gloria Pater and the Antiphon: My merciful Jesus; Virgin Mary Mother of God and ours; Reach to us from Thy beloved Son, grace and mercy.

2nd joy: The Visitation of the Mother of God to her cousin Saint Isabel

We accompany Thee, Holiest Virgin in the joy Thou had when Thou visited Thy cousin Isabel and when the glorious Baptist was sanctified.

For this mystery we beg Thee to keep forgiveness at our reach and the grace to imitate Thy holiest virtues.

Our Father, ten Hail Marys, Gloria Pater and the Antiphon: My merciful Jesus; Virgin Mary Mother of God and ours; Reach to us from Thy beloved Son, grace and mercy.

3rd joy: The birth of Jesus

We accompany Thee, Holiest Virgin in the joy Thou had when Thy Divine Son was born in the manger.

For this mystery we beg Thee to keep forgiveness at our reach and the grace to imitate Thy holiest virtues.

Our Father, ten Hail Marys, Gloria Pater and the Antiphon: My merciful Jesus; Virgin Mary Mother of God and ours; Reach to us from Thy beloved Son, grace and mercy.

4th joy: The devotion given to the Divine Child by the three wise men

We accompany Thee, Holiest Virgin in the joy Thou had when Thou saw Thy Son worshipped by the wise men of the orient.

For this mystery we beg Thee to keep forgiveness at our reach and the grace to imitate Thy holiest virtues.

Our Father, ten Hail Marys, Gloria Pater and the Antiphon: My merciful Jesus; Virgin Mary Mother of God and ours; Reach to us from Thy beloved Son, grace and mercy.

5th joy: Finding Jesus in the Temple

We accompany Thee, Holiest Virgin in the joy Thou had when thou found Thy Divine Son amongst the doctors.

For this mystery we beg Thee to keep forgiveness at our reach and the grace to imitate Thy holiest virtues.

Our Father, ten Hail Marys, Gloria Pater and the Antiphon: My merciful Jesus; Virgin Mary Mother of God and ours; Reach to us from Thy beloved Son, grace and mercy.

6th joy: The joyful resurrection of the Savior

We accompany Thee, Holiest Virgin in the joy Thou had when Thou saw Thy Divine Son glorious and resurrected.

For this mystery we beg Thee to keep forgiveness at our reach and the grace to imitate Thy holiest virtues.

Our Father, ten Hail Marys, Gloria Pater and the Antiphon: My merciful Jesus; Virgin Mary Mother of God and ours; Reach to us from Thy beloved Son, grace and mercy.

7th joy: Coronation of the Immaculate Virgin in Heaven

We accompany Thee, Holiest Virgin in the joy Thou had when Thou wert crowned Queen of the Heavens and Earth, of the Holy Church of Christ and defender of sinners.

For this mystery we beg Thee to keep forgiveness at our reach and the grace to imitate Thy holiest virtues.

Our Father, ten Hail Marys, Gloria Pater and the Antiphon: My merciful Jesus; Virgin Mary Mother of God and ours; Reach to us from Thy beloved Son, grace and mercy.

Final prayers:
Two Hail Marys, one Our Father and one Salve Regina

CHAPLET TO THE HOLY SPIRIT
(for good measure)

Send Thy Spirit and all shall be created and Thou shall renew the face of the Earth.

V. God, come in our aid.
R. Lord, aid us and save us.
Gloria Pater

1st Mystery – Come Holy Spirit of Wisdom, free us from earthly things and bring us the love and dedication for the things of Heaven.

Come Holy Spirit, fill the hearts of Thy faithful and ignite in them the fire of Thy love, come and renew the face of the earth.

(repeat this last evocation seven times and in the end one more for Mary)

Oh Mary, who by the work of the Holy Spirit Thou conceived the Savior, pray for us.

2nd Mystery: Come, Spirit of Understanding, illuminate our minds with the eternal light of truth and enrich it with saintly thoughts.

(Come Holy Spirit, etc., seven times and the evocation of Mary)

3rd Mystery: Come Spirit of Counsel, make us accepting to Thy inspiration and guide us in the path of salvation

(Come Holy Spirit, etc., seven times and the evocation of Mary)

4th Mystery: Come Spirit of Fortitude, give us strength, constancy and victory in the battles against our spiritual enemies.

(Come Holy Spirit, etc., seven times and the evocation of Mary)

5th Mystery: Come Spirit of Science, be the master of our souls and aid us in putting Thy saintly teachings into practice.

(Come Holy Spirit, etc., seven times and the evocation of Mary)

6th Mystery: Come Spirit of Piety, come inhabit our hearts, take charge and sanctify all its affections.

(Come Holy Spirit, etc., seven times and the evocation of Mary)

7th Mystery: Come Spirit of the Saintly Fear of God, reign in our will and make us willing to suffer all before offending Thee

(Come Holy Spirit, etc., seven times and the evocation of Mary)

Point XI

One should be careful while performing this operation, especially when passing the *trovisco* through fire. This is because, traditionally, burning *trovisco* may be the cause of extreme bad luck, being that this is a divinely consecrated plant on account of the legend which states that Our Lady dried her child's diapers over it.

This plant is also magically used in the North of Portugal by market vendors (usually women), with the purpose of helping them sell out their wares and free them from evil influences. To do this, while on the way to the market, one should cut some *trovisco* and place it in one's basket of merchandise, saying the following prayer while cutting it:

Praised be
Our Lord Jesus Christ!
Come now with me
And help me sell all this.

But one should always be careful when cutting any *trovisco*, as it is said that wandering souls like to take refuge in patches of this plant (one should pray for the souls whenever one of these patches is found), which may shed some light on one of the orisons to St. Barbara mentioned above (point VII in the "Mysteries of Sorcery" section, book II, *Generous Saint Barbara*, etc...).

SOURCES

José Diogo Ribeiro: *Turquel Folklórico, Revista Lusitana*, Vol. XX (1917) p.54.
Teófilo Braga: *O Povo Português nos seus Costumes, Crenças e Tradições*, Vol. II, Publicações Dom Quixote, 1994, Lisboa.

Point XII

1. This is the only direct mention of Jeronimo Cortez Valenciano in *The Book of St. Cyprian*, even though other recipes and sorceries in this book do relate directly to the works of this author (like point XXVI of the "Mysteries of Sorcery" section). The entry in question reads as follows:

Secret to pull a tooth, or all of them, without the patient feeling it, which is proven

Take a live lizard and place it in a very well covered new pan, so as he does not escape, place it to dry in an oven and as soon as it is well roasted make it into a powder and rub this powder on the gums, the jaw or tooth which is in pain, be it rotten or not and the flesh will be soothed in such a way that with your hand, using very little force, you will be able to take out every tooth without any pain.

Unfortunately, both in this entry and in the one from *The Book* it is not possible to determine the exact species of the lizard.

2. Again we have in this sorcery a non-specification of gender.

Point XVI

1. We are presented here once again with a rare sorcery of great earth-shattering magical power, quite in league with the also remarkable points I, IV and V of the "Mysteries of Sorcery".

Indeed who would have thought that to capture the heart and attention of a woman all that is truly required is an orgasm.

One could go on and explain the basis of sexual magick, and the qualities and energetic significances of the female orgasm but it would all mean nothing. Plainly, we as men should all just shut up and give our women an orgasm. There is no ritual, no magical secret, no word of power, no nothing that will ever be more than a mere shadow in comparison with the power of properly generous lovemaking. Dear reader, should you be a man, you would do better to read a pamphlet on female genital anatomy than to read a whole library of the occult.

Make your woman quiver in pleasure, hold her in a lover's embrace (I believe that these days this is referred to as "cuddling") and pray to God and the Saints that those beautiful eyes upon which you gaze at that moment never leave you. Treat her right and lovingly, you will be loved in the measure of which you are a lover.

Dear reader, never think this a joke, for this is a most serious matter.

Point XVIII

1. One should underline the remarkable lesson of religious tolerance and acceptance given by Cyprian, which might come into contradiction with some other statements in *The Book*:

"I aid thee because my religion, which is the Christian one, says that all are children of the same Omnipotent God, and we should not enquire about the beliefs of our suffering brothers."

2. Interestingly, in a couple of books by the Brazilian publisher Pallas this sorceress is actually referred to as the *Bruxa* of Évora (page 414), and the moral of the story is actually inverted, with Cyprian aiding the sorceress with a demonic

love sorcery, for which she was missing the ingredient of rue, which her mother, *Bruxa* Bambina (suggesting an Italian origin), had in the past used.

3. The use of burning snake skin may contain some connections to other accredited virtues of this substance, which may also have to do with the snake head powders used in point VII of the "Occult Powers" section and point IV of the "Mysteries of Sorcery".

According to Valenciano:

Secrets and virtues of the skin snakes usually cast off

The skin of a snake once burned and placed on any wound will heal it, and should there be any iron spike pierced into the flesh it usually attracts it until it comes out.

Do know that whoever brings with him snake skin powder will be protected from leprosy and any venom. And know that these powders have great virtues and many properties, you must however, burn this snake skin when the Sun is on the sign of Aries, which is from the 21st of March until the 20th of April.

Also in the *Perpetual Lunarium*, Valenciano mentions the following:

It is also said that the skin a snake sheds, dried and made into a powder and given as food with some bread is extremely efficient in preventing abortion.

POINTS XIX & XX

These two most remarkable procedures should be put together with the most advanced and mighty magical arts mentioned in points I, IV and V of the Mysteries of Sorcery and point XVI of this very section.

This appears to be the most secret method of breaking and undoing the previous sorceries, this from the woman's perspective, logically.

I assure you, dear reader, these are most effective methods and will cause such horror and affliction to their victims that they border on the cruelty of the most gruesome of animal sacrifices described in this book.

But still, there is a serious warning I would like to offer the fair lady sorceresses reading this book: Do know that there exists a certain quality of men who do greatly enjoy the scent of an unwashed woman. This sorcery could possibly backfire and you might find yourself in an even greater predicament than when you started... and yet, I cannot find it in me to feel the slightest pity, for if you choose to perform this sorcery you are a most cruel and heartless woman!

POINT XXI

1. This is one of the most interesting points in *The Book*. Putting it together with all that has been discussed so far regarding sexual liberty a very clear image of some of the deeper significance of this book should begin to form in the mind of the reader. Not only does *The Book* advocate the goodness of love and sex, for the sole sake of love and sex, independent of gender or reputation, it now offers advice for the consummation of pleasure for pleasure's sake.

Regarding this contraception method in particular, it seems to me that what is implied is that each woman intending to use this method should search for a sponge of the same size as her own palm, being that, apparently, there is some sort of correlation between the size of a woman's palm and her vagina. I for one will have to take the Saint's word on this...

But... dear reader, modern age has given us an abundance of ungodly birth control devices and techniques, and, should the option be available, do go for the condom. You can get these just as freely as sea sponges and they are better in every respect (even if all the Devil's sorcery and magical art cannot help you with lasting more than five minutes, a condom will).

2. If we now pay close attention to the initial introduction to the narrative, and place it together with Cyprian's narrative of the *Flos Sanctorum*, one issue does seem to contradict itself. The fact that the woman in question is mentioned as having been burned as a Witch by Diocletian doesn't really make much sense, as Diocletian was a persecutor of Christians and not of what these would later call Witches.

POINT XXIII

This particular point should be noted with attention. So far I have only found this procedure in one single version of *The Book*, the old *Livraria Ecónomica* version in the Portuguese National Library. Such is quite understandable; it is a delicate topic and a procedure which is still criminalized in many countries.

This book has managed to survive many regimes and dictatorships, and the disappearance of such delicate matters from its pages seems to me to have been a matter of survival.

POINT XXV

1. Regarding the ingredients of this sorcery a few things should be said. By reading the mention to the chest hairs in the short activation prayer, these are probably meant to be used as a direct physical connection to the heart, as "threads of the chest". One could probably as easily say threads of the bosom, or even directly, threads of the heart.

Also, and this is a serious piece of advice, cork oak is a fiercely protected tree, at least in Portugal. Even if one owns such a tree, it still requires a specific legal permit to just trim it. If you attempt to acquire some roots of this tree, even if it belongs to you, you risk serious problems with the law.

Of course, should you get into trouble, you can always try the orison of the Just Judge, but I would simply leave this tree alone if I were you. They are too sacred, magnificent and useful to have their health jeopardized by the whims of men.

2. The last remark in this point should also be underlined, as most of these sorceries are clearly meant for unmarried lovers. Analyzing the logic of the short prayer, a married woman is one who already is united with her partner "through love and flesh", but we are assured this sorcery is still valid.

3. Together with point II of this same section, these are the only two love sorceries which call upon St. Cyprian directly. Such is actually quite strange as this is one of the great saints who may be traditionally called upon for such matters, particularly by men. One other orison of this kind, originating from Brazil, goes as follows:

"St. Cyprian, bishop, archbishop, my Lord Jesus Christ's confessor; St. Cyprian I beg thee to slow down the heart of (NN) for me."

SOURCES

Riollando Azzi; O Casamento na sociedade colonial luso-brasileira – uma análise histórico-teológica, Perspectiva Teológica, 24 (1992) 49.

Point XXVI

1. This is once again a particular development of a much wider tradition.

Viper heads feature with great relevance in Portuguese sorcery, with particular incidence in the Gerês region to the North, be it as an ingredient for some magical recipe or as a talisman.

Vipers as a whole, or just their heads, are thought to bring luck, bless a household and attract wealth; you may use them as a necklace or a bracelet; if you dry a viper head on the ashes of a fireplace and place it inside your jacket it will make you fortunate in your daily life; by preserving a viper in aguardente[201] you thus produce a potent medicine for rheumatism and so on. Their tongues, worn around the neck, are also good to keep the "bad airs" away.

One other folk tradition mentions that a viper head acquired on the first Friday of March gives its owner complete immunity from sorcery, while also providing great advantages in games of chance.

Now, as is logical, this particular object has fallen somewhat out of use

---

201. Fire water, a strong Ibero-American distilled drink. If you can't find any I believe vodka will work just as well.

due to the increasing difficulty in its acquisition, as since the Bern Convention in 1979 (Convention on the Conservation of European Wildlife and Natural Habitats) its commerce has been banned... still... I remember seeing preserved viper heads openly on sale in a small *ervanario* during my careless youth in the early nineties (an herbs store, and a proper one too, not those modern "medical" ones). I believe that back then they went for 70.000 *Escudos*, what today would be 350 Euros. I can only imagine what they go for these days...

2. Teixeira de Aragão offers the following recipe for a viper head *bolsa*:

> Place inside a green bag a viper head, seven pieces of twine with three knots on each end, a pinch of virgin salt, fumigate this with holy olive oil and place inside it a piece of paper with the following, written in rat's blood:
>
> *O azeite de Deus é bento que alumeia o Santissimo Sacramento,*
> *Vá o mal d'esta casa para fóra e vanha o bem para dentro.*[202]

2. From what I've been able to gather, rattlesnake heads are used for similar ends in Brazil.

SOURCES

A. Thomaz Pires: *Miscellanea III, Revista Lusitana vol.3* (1895) p.366.
José Diogo Ribeiro: *Turquel Folklórico, Revista Lusitana,* Vol. XX (1917) p.54.
Teixeira de Aragão: *Diabruras Santidades e Profecias,* Vega, Lisboa, 1994.

POINT XXVII

This sorcery to me is the very definition of gruesomeness. I will not judge anyone who chooses to perform it, but honestly, if you choose to do so, you are in serious need of evaluating your life and the choices which have led you here, for I am pretty sure you took a wrong turn somewhere.

That said, it does seem like a remarkable piece of magical artillery, quite literally a magical grenade: volatile, unstable, powerful, and dangerous.

---

202. As this is meant to be written, we have no real need to concern ourselves with pronunciation, and as such I have opted to present the original (old fashioned) Portuguese. Nonetheless, one should know what is being written, as there is always a need for intention and understanding:

The olive oil of God is blessed which lights the Holiest Sacrament,
Be gone evil from this house and let then good enter.

Point XXIX

Beyond the doubt of unfaithfulness, methods of knowing the whereabouts and state of being of absent people are common and a constant preoccupation both in the system in this book and the very environment it spawns from, relating once again to the ever present drama of emigration presented in the comment to point XVII of the "Mysteries of Sorcery".

Apart from the typical and traditional Cartomancy methods, a very versatile technique does also bear significant weight in Portuguese divination, and is particularly useful for these same kinds of concerns. This is called *andar ás vozes*, seeking voices, the interpretation of the words of random passersby. This is a remarkably ingenious, simple, and symbolically charged technique, which may be used by anyone without the slightest inconvenience. It can be performed in any number of situations, but it is frequently associated with certain religious activities (processions, pilgrimages, feast days, or simple mass).

One would attend these, either alone or with a few companions, while remaining absolutely silent through the whole event, and pay close attention to what is being spoken around you, as well as all that is heard on the way from and to your own home. Upon arriving home the silence may be broken and one may begin to interpret, either alone or with one's companions, what was heard in light of the problem at hand.

More frequently this can be done just by standing at your own window and saying the following:

"Court of heaven hear me! Court of heaven speak to me! Court of Heaven answer me!"

The first words heard after reciting the above will contain the sought answer.

Also common in this type of divination is the appeal to St. Zachariah, the father of John the Baptist. Being that this saint was spoken to by the archangel Gabriel, and as a consequence of his disbelief was made mute, he is clearly in the realm of words and communication. To do this one needs only to stand by the window and say the following prayer:

My St. Zachariah
my blessed saint!
thou wert blind, deaf and mute,
thou had a son
and thou called him John
Declare to me in the voices of the people...

One finishes this prayer by adding the name of the person or the issue at hand and then listens and interprets the random words, either rising from the street or the ones heard by actually going out in search of them. Vasconcelos mentions that this orison should be said three times and done on three consecutive nights.

ST. ZACHARIAH – SEPTEMBER 23ᴿᴰ

ST. HELENA – AUGUST 18ᵀᴴ

Still related to this method, but already somewhat removed from it, is the following prayer to St. Helena, also meant for divination on the state of health of an absent loved one.

Saint Helena, queen of the Scene
Thou wert a Moura, to Christendom thou returned,
In the sea thou dined, the cross of Christ thou found.
Where thou found it, there thou left it.
Three nails thou took from it.
One thou left in the sea to consecrate it,
Another thou gave to thy son Constantine
To be a victor in wars and battles.
The other thou placed on thy saintly breast.
Give me in one of the signs I ask thee
The certainty that (NN) is living or dead:
Roosters singing
Children crying
Dogs barking
Doors opening or closing.

This orison should be prayed in the silence of night, and the praying person should wait for any of the requested signs after it is finished. If in fact any rooster sings, a child cries, a dog barks, or a door is heard opening or closing, the person in question is still alive; if on the other hand none of these signs manifest, then that person is dead.

It should be noted that these kinds of signals (dogs barking, roosters singing and such) are somewhat common in many kinds of workings either as signals to be interpreted or as proof that a prayer was actually heard by the spirit it was meant for. Of this there is a remarkable example from the Inquisition process of one D. Paula Thereza (1731) in which these signs are requested "*by the love of Barabbas, Satan and Caiaphas*".

Also, St. Helena, being the patron of archeologists, is also a proper saint to call upon for the finding of lost things (be it objects, people, or information), an aspect further cemented by certain orisons where one actually calls upon both Helena and Anthony to help you find a good suitor.

Other simpler methods for these same kinds of concerns revolve around the typical forms of botanical divination traditions, such as cutting an *Erva de Nossa Senhora* (Our Lady's herb, a common name which may refer to a few plants, but in this case I assume it is most likely to be the *Hylotelephium telephium*) and placing it on the roof of your house. As the herb grows greener, withers, or dries, so does the absent person become healthy, sick, or dead.

SOURCES

J. Leite de Vasconcelos: *Annuario para o Estudo das Tradições Populares Portuguezas*, Livraria Portuense de Clavel & C.ᵃ, Porto, 1882.

J. Leite de Vasconcelos: *Tradições Populares de Portugal – Bibliotheca Ethnographica Portugueza*, Livraria Portuense de Clavel & C.ᵃ, Porto, 1882.

Jaime Lopes Dias, *Crenças e Superstições da Beira*, Alma Azul, Coimbra, 2002.

Teixeira de Aragão: *Diabruras Santidades e Profecias*, Vega, Lisboa, 1994.

Teófilo Braga: *O Povo Português nos seus Costumes, Crenças e Tradições*, Vol. II, Publicações Dom Quixote, 1994, Lisboa.

ART OF DIVINING THE FUTURE BY THE PALM OF THE HAND

1. WE ARE HERE PRESENTED WITH THE GENUINE QUIROMANCY section of *The Book*, the veritable *Buena Dicha*. I cannot help but think that the introductory text to the Astrology section in the first part of *The Book* should actually be transported to this one.

That being said, this section might have its value for the astrological attributions it offers regarding the various features of the hand, but it nonetheless is a gross simplification of what is actually an ancient, complex and versatile art.

2. Interestingly, I've come across this exact section of *The Book* in an antique book dealer as a standalone pamphlet by *Livraria Económica*, the same

publisher of this version of *The Book of Saint Cyprian*. As none of these possess a publishing date I have been unable to determine which is the original, but given the lack of an obvious connection between this technique and the rest of *The Book*, I have a tendency to believe that the original is the pamphlet. Given this instance, one must also question how much of *The Book's* content was just collected from previously published chapbooks.

SOURCES

J. Leite de Vasconcelos: *Opúsculos – Volume VII – Etnologia*, Imprensa Nacional de Lisboa, Lisboa, 1938.

ALCHEMY

WHAT APPEARS TO BE SUGGESTED IS THAT THIS SECTION is simply an excerpt of the mentioned *Crimini Falsi* by Cecilio Rodigenio.

I for one have never been able to find or locate anything about this book or its author, though it must be noted that most of the information given in the text does seem to check out.

Firstly, the title is probably misspelled; it should most likely be *Crimine Falsi*, which, being the case, should be a reference to the 1317 decree by Pope John XXII, *De Crimine Falsi Titulus VI. I Joannis XXII* against forgery and alchemy.

Not being able to provide a reference for this text, all I can do is to try to clarify the somewhat obscure references in it, with the exception of Arnaldus of Villa Nova and Ramon Llull, for they are far from obscure.

João André is most likely the Portuguese adaptation of the name Giovanni d'Andrea 1270/1275 – 1348), a great medieval Italian canonist. The information given regarding the fact that this was the author's master does make sense, as Giovanni d'Andrea was made a teacher in Padua, Pisa, and Bologna. Thus, all one needs to do now is search for a certain Rodigenio among all the students he lectured.

Bernard Trevisan is a semi-legendary Italian alchemist of the XVth century. This may cause some issues, given the dates of birth/death of Giovanni d'Andrea, but it is still possible that the life of this mysterious Cecilio did overlap with the lives of these two.

Of Guillermo Aragosio, the mysterious botanist from Trevigi (Trevisto, I believe) who it turns out is named Antonio, and Ausonius I found a reference in the book *Teatro Crítico Universal* by Benito Jerónimo Feijoo, a great Galician philosopher and Benedictine monk, which basically just refers back to an unnamed book by Cardano. The information given by Feijoo doesn't actually add much, as it is apparently just an analysis of this same story, and it is more precisely located in Volume III, Discourse VIII, entitled *Piedra filosofal*, of the mentioned book.

I also did manage to find a small fleeting footnote reference of a certain Ettore/Hectore Ausonius as an apparent author of a book on astrology, the astrolabe and also something on Kabbalah, but in all honesty I cannot confirm this is the same as Hector Ausonius mentioned in *The* Book.

The final reference is logically to Bodin's *Demonomanie des Sorcieres*, more precisely to book three of this work. This last reference is actually the one which may provide more food for thought. Analyzing it as a narrative, it ends up falling in line with other aspects of the content of *The Book of St. Cyprian*, mainly the story of Victor Siderol. Once again, it appears that *The Book* argues that it is quite fine to deal with the Devil, but only if you manage to cheat him in the end.

THE SORCERESS OF ÉVORA

1. THE MENTIONED MANUSCRIPT BY AMADOR PATRÍCIO is actually the book *Historia das Antiguidades de Évora*, "History of the Ancient Things of Évora". More precisely, the excerpts presented in *The Book* were taken from the first part entitled: *"Where one reports the events which happened in Évora until the time it was conquered from the Mouros by Giraldo, in the time of King Dom Afonso Henriques; and all which happened from that time to the present shall be related in the second part, which we make lighter by presenting in the end of this one the list of Kings of Portugal, with their generations and descendents"*. The first printed edition of this book was made by the University of Évora in the year of 1739 which jeopardized the date of 1614 given in *The Book of St. Cyprian*.

As far as I have been able to determine, Amador Patrício was a pseudonym of Francisco José Freire (1719 − 1773) from the Congregation of the Oratory (the same as Manuel Bernardes mentioned in the "Diabolical Spirits" section), one of the founders of the literary *Arcádia Lusitana*, a movement set on battling the baroque spirit and installing a neoclassical aesthetic in Portuguese literature.

The book itself is a precious lead for all those who wish to explore the mysteries of *Yeborath*, the city at the crossroads, as it very appropriately ties the history of this city in with both biblical and classical mythical narratives, drawing a most entertaining apocryphal mythical and magical geography and history among an insane mash of names and concepts. In this book the classical knowledge and ideology of Francisco José Freire is more than obvious, as the Gods and Giants walk though Portugal and the Alentejo, shaping its ground and topology. A creative Typhonian eye will be able to see their power still there, just waiting to be tapped.

A most entertaining entry in this book reads as follows: *We have shown how Évora was founded 200 years after the Deluge, and what happened in it during these 200 years we know not, for it was still uninhabited, even if before the Deluge it is certain that it was inhabited by the Giants, which lived in that area up to what is now the Collegio da Companhia; for in the mount of Count Bastos, by digging in that tower which is mostly a ruin, a large rock was found, which had the following letters:*

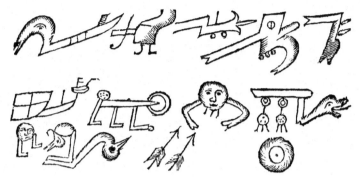

These letters, which must have been the ones used by the Giants of those times, in our Portuguese mean the following:

Briarêo, and Tiphéo (Typhon)
Entered into council,
To wage war on heaven.

(...)

This rock with letters was made into a foundation for a gate which gives entrance to a courtyard at the back of the Church of the Collegio, which, by uncovering it further one may very easily see that that rock has other letters, as follows:

Which in our Portuguese reads:

Our brother Adamastor
Did not join us
For he had another love

Which would now lead us straight to Camões, Fernando Pessoa and so on until the end of all written words...

Some might see this book as pretentious, but I for one just see it as brilliant. There is something about it which reminds me greatly of Kenneth Grant.

2. Salvaterra most likely refers to Salvaterra de Magos, a municipality in the Ribatejo region of Portugal, already quite removed from Évora. A *Salvaterra* is a short sword or scimitar, and as such this town is actually called "Magicians' Blade" or "Magicians' Sword". Apart from this I see no other relevance in this reference.

3. Regarding the narrative presented, when we consult the original book we see that what we have here is actually a collage of two different stories, both of them from the same book 9 of the first part of the *Antiguidades de Évora*, which specifically deals with the *Mouro* kings of Évora.

The first of these is logically the story of King Praxadopel, from the year 760, or 4722 of the creation of the world.

The construction which is mentioned in the narrative as the Castelo Giraldo is actually an ancient *castro*, predating the *Mouro* occupation by many long centuries. It is named as such after Giraldo the Fearless who is said to have occupied the site during his "campaigns" in the Alentejo.

Giraldo is one of those characters who crosses both history and myth and can be rightfully placed among the halls of the sacred ancestors along with the kings of the *Reconquista*.

Frequently described as hard to deal with, this early Portuguese nobleman went into business by himself and formed his own army, walking along the thin and sharp blade between the king of Portugal, the king of Leon, and the Almohads. His unconventional battling methods made him an expert in conquering Muslim cities, and it is important to mention that this was the man responsible for the final conquest of Évora for the Portuguese King Afonso Henriques. To this end he disguised himself as a minstrel and insistently courted the daughter of one of the city guards, eventually winning her heart and managing to have her allow him into the city. Once there he proceeded to murder her, murder her father, and open the city gates to the rest of his army. This story is still today marked in the Évora Coat of Arms.

Giraldo is one of those ambiguous beasts that emerge occasionally in the world. A mix of madness, intelligence, brutality, cunning, and bloodlust, to which the particular conditions of their world provide them with the opportunity to rise to the heavens. Without a doubt he was a monster, but without a doubt he was great. He was all but perfect for the Iberia of his time.

Coat of Arms of the city of Évora, displaying Giraldo the Fearless and two decapitated *Mouro* heads

Curiously, in the original book, the strange chamber found by the workers preparing the foundations for the castle is in no way related to Lagarrona, merely to Montemuro, and this point appears to be an original addition and alteration by the author of *The Book of St. Cyprian*.

This mentioned Montemuro, of which no additional information is given in *The Book*, is, on the other hand, actually a very well described and developed character in the second part of the *Antiguidades de Évora*. He is initially mentioned on page 55 of the original as a wise Necromancer who Helen of Troy consulted in search of a way to restore her beauty as she approached her old age (for, according to Amador Patrício, she and Menelaus lived in the Alentejo). Later the story of Montemuro, also Monteromúr or Montero-múr, is related in detail. This, it turns out, is actually the story of Oedipus transported to Northern Portugal and Galicia, with the characters of Laius, Jocasta, and Oedipus being substituted by Dolpo and his unnamed wife and son. Montemuro is then the child of the incestuous relation between mother and son, whose unnatural origin gifted him with great wisdom and magical powers.

After he revealed to his parents their blood relation, triggering their tragic ends, he and his son, also named Montemuro, decided to leave their lands and search for a new home. Montemuro ended up stopping in a town today known as Montemor-o-Velho (Montemor the old), in the district of Coimbra, while his son continued his journey to the town today known as Montemor-o-Novo (Montemor the young), in the district of Évora.

Shortly after this Montemuro the son died, and Montemuro the father then decided to travel to his son's town in order to reclaim his wealthy possessions, to which the town's folk did not agree. Finding himself in such a situation, while walking to Évora, he found the mounts near the city to be very welcoming and ended up taking residence there. It was in this mount that he was buried, together with all his magical books, in the same grave and house found much later by the men of Praxadopel when building the Castelo Giraldo.

The description of the house/temple seems to me remarkable beyond measure. There appears to be something very specific being hinted at here, although I am not able to say what for certain. The whole conjunction of symbols seems somehow logical and appropriate for "*Mouro* Magic": the serpent-human monsters, the women, the severed heads, the toads and lizards. All are commonplace in *Mouro* legends and iconography.

4. The second part of the narrative, the story of Lagardona, (which starts at "Not far away from this place") can be found in the original on page 290 and it is actually just a side tale of the whole story of King Alvado. The story itself is not particularly remarkable, or at least not more than the whole original book, but if we are to take a wider look at the global tradition of *The Book of St. Cyprian* and its remarkable offshoots, this gains something of a completely different relevance.

On all accounts this seems to be the literary *début* of the *Bruxa de Évora*, the Witch of the crossroads, a character which by now has her own story and merits, having arrived at the point of sometimes being considered as one of Cyprian's masters, with the mention that his magical knowledge arises from the manuscripts he inherited from her. Naturally this creates a problem regarding geography, seeing as Cyprian's (orthodox) story never mentions him traveling to the Iberian Peninsula, and even stranger is the fact that she, mostly in Brazilian editions, is actually most often mentioned as having lived in Babylon. But anyway, historical and geographical exactness was never something that greatly preoccupied many grimoire writers, as a few books under her name do now exist in the Brazilian market, many of which share a lot of content with *The Book of St. Cyprian*.

Apart from all this, the *Bruxa* herself has joined the legions of the Pomba Giras, and can now be worked with directly under the name Pomba Gira Bruxa de Évora, although it may be argued that this name may just refer to a particular designation of an already established Pomba Gira.

Alternatively, regarding this Pomba Gira, if we analyze the Portuguese Inquisition records from the XVIth century, we can see that the large majority of Witchcraft processes originate precisely from Évora (at the time the second largest Portuguese city after Lisbon), with Francisco Bethencourt presenting the number of 24 cases from Lisbon, 9 from Coimbra and 61 from this city (which amounts to almost 65% of the total). This number by itself may be enough to suggest a most remarkable and living magical atmosphere existing in Évora in the late Middle Ages and early Renaissance, but if we now examine the penalties ascribed to these practitioners we also see that the majority of them are that of *degredo* (24 out of the 61 from Évora; with Lisbon only banishing 3 and Coimbra 0). It then becomes clear that the overwhelming majority of Witches being transferred from Portugal to Brazil and Africa are precisely the Witches of Évora.

Pomba Giras and Exus are known to be spirits of outcasts and outsiders, spirits of marginality, and the existence of the Pomba Gira Bruxa de Évora suggests that this is the Quimbanda crystallization of this particular Portuguese magical current, the current of the outcast Witches of Évora.

These are the unspoken Portuguese mothers of Umbanda and Quimbanda, old and tired like their Pomba Gira suggests (considering the remarkably sexualized character of most Pomba Giras the appearance of the Pomba Gira Bruxa de Évora image as an old decrepit woman is indeed strange) and running full of *Moura* blood, masters of St. Cyprian, the King of Magic.

5. One should also meditate on the bizarre description of the disenchantment ritual performed by Lagarrona. Once again there is something about it which to me seems to suggest more than the fancies of the imagination of a neoclassicist.

And finally, there is a mystery that still remains, and that is the reason behind the selection of these two particular sections to incorporate in *The Book*.

Surely if the author wished to present the *Bruxa* Lagarrona then this second part would be the appropriate point to do so, but why the first part? There are plenty of other stories of sorcery and mystery in *Historia das Antiguidades de Évora*, so why Montemuro?

The only reason I can find is that such a selection would tie Lagarrona to the *castro* of Castelo Giraldo, and that the author of *The Book of St. Cyprian* might have been hinting at something very specific with this *castro*, much like he does with those to the North of Portugal in the first list of buried treasures. What this might be I cannot say, for I have no contact with Lagarrona, be her the *Bruxa* or Sorceress of Évora or the Pomba Gira by that same name. But if there is anything that this strange maneuver definitely accomplished it was the bringing into the light this same *Bruxa*, endowing her with sufficient autonomy to generate her own cult, legend, and magic.

The mystery remains for those to whom this *Bruxa* might call.

6. Following is the map of some of the locations mentioned in this narrative. Unfortunately I could not find what today is called Matacabelo, and strangely I found two locations for Lagardona, both quite near to Évora.

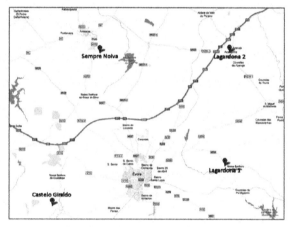

MAP DATA ©2014 GOOGLE

Again, it should be underlined that Amador Patrício is not shy about redefining the origins of the names of such places, as the Sempre Noiva, for example, is a location which owes its name to a completely different set of events.

SOURCES

Alexandre Parafita: *A Mitologia dos Mouros – Lendas, Mitos, Serpentes, Tesouros*, Edições Gailivro, Canelas, 2006.

Amadeo de Santander: *O Livro da Bruxa ou A Feiticeira de Évora*, Editora Eco, Rio de Janeiro.

Amador Patricio: *Historia das Antiguidades de Évora – Primeira Parte*, Officina da Universidade, 1739, Évora (digital edition).

Francisco Bethencourt: *O Imaginário da Magia – Feiticeiras, Advinhos e Curandeiros em Portugal no século XVI*, Companhia das Letras, 2004, São Paulo.

Jerusa Pires Ferreira: *O Livro de São Cipriano: Uma Legenda de Massas*, Editora Perpectiva, 1992, São Paulo.

Maria Helena Farelli: *A Bruxa de Évora*, Pallas Editora, Rio de Janeiro, 2006.

Nicholaj de Mattos Frisvold: *Pomba Gira & the Quimbanda of Mbúmba Nzila*, Scarlet Imprint, 2011.

FINAL CONSIDERATIONS

AFTER ALL WE HAVE SEEN, why is *The Book of Saint Cyprian* cursed? Why is reading it, owning it or even touching it a sin? Why is it said that it attracts misfortune, or even worse, the Devil himself? Why do they say reading it makes you mad? Why was it banned by church and state during Salazar's regime? What is this horror, this shadow hiding in the hearts of both the miserable and the mighty alike? What makes this book more than paper and ink?

As a grimoire or a magic book it is certainly not more sinister than other pearls of the genre, crueler, maybe, but definitely not more sinister. There are no sigils or infernal demons, only the mundane preoccupations of lowly men.

My dear reader, I am so sorry to have to tell you this, but you and I are both damned. If you have read this book and resisted its whispering madness, its cold grip of fear, its loud and heartfelt warning to drop it, to turn away and erase it from your mind, you have, my dear beloved friend, fallen through the cracks and you did not even notice it.

Look around.

Do you smell brimstone?

Don't look now, but the Devil is grinning over your shoulder.

The Devil is pinching your cheek...

The Devil is sniffing your hair...

The Devil is licking your ear...

The Devil...

The Devil...

The Devil...

For you see, it is not about *The Book*, it is not its sorcery, its magic or its Witchcraft. All of that ends up just being noise; it's as ridiculous or as serious as YOU want it to be. It is the same great nothing as the whole world!

Why, in all these years of dread, didn't anyone try to debunk this book, why did they not try to disprove or rationalize it? Why was the response to it always fear - one hundred years of fear?

This book holds such a key, such an idea that it has made this "paradise planted on the seashore" and its "people of gentle ways" cower in the darkness at the mention of its name. You may not see it now, but this book is blight, a plague on the world, an infection of the mind which has made political regimes and religious institutions tremble in the realization of their impotence in destroying it, leaving fear as the only way of containing it, such fear, such horror, so as none would dare even touch it.

For the publication of a new edition of *The Book of Saint Cyprian* is, independent of the country and the language, always a visceral scream of rage.

It is the power of the miserable and hungry against the world, the might of dirty calloused hands carrying life-giving agricultural tools on a march to lynch their lord. For its magic is wholly different, its magic is LIBERTY!

You can look back at it and here and there, unsuspectingly, with little or no emphasis, gently insinuating between the lines, you can see it revealing itself. It proclaims the right of thought, the right of love, the right of sex, the goodness of lust, sexual equality, never judging orientation or preference and going as far as offering methods of contraception and abortion. Its sorcery is free and loving, fit for men and women seeking men and women.

It hijacks religion from the clergy and throws it openly into the hands of the hungry people, it breaks open the gates of Purgatory where the Church had hidden our beloved dead and our departed ancestors from us and invites them to share the world and join our prayers and love-filled hearts. Among convoluted arguments, animal sacrifice, death and sex, it generates a whole new fringe order, laying waste to all preconceived notions.

It sits Jesus and the Devil side by side and laughs at their ridiculous duality, forcing them to hold hands as if stubborn children and come together in our prayers and our worries and walk in the world of mundane affairs as a whole truly Catholic Divine.

It shows us the keys and tells us to choose, for there is nothing to choose, there is no right and no wrong, there is no sin, there is only virtue.

It brings us new commandments: to take our fill of men and women, for all love is good; be a decent person, a good and charitable person; don't be a fucking jackass; take a shower and get a dog!

This is what *The Book* proclaims, the great and mighty Liberal Black Magic, the magic of freedom.

Oh! You have fallen through the cracks, dear beloved reader, my dearest friend, you have fallen up, out of the rules of society, out of the law and into the threshold of the gate of choice. You are now a *Bruxo* or *Bruxa*, a Sorcerer, or whatever you want; you have been branded and are now on the fringe. All the power the clergy holds is now yours; the dead, the saints, the Devil, and everything in between – they are all within your reach, all you need is to Will it.

Look now over your shoulder, kiss the Devil standing there. Now look over your other shoulder and kiss Jesus standing there. Grab their hands as if you are all innocent children and, free from fear, walk with joy and love across that gate.

Like Siderol, you now hold *The Book*, and your destiny awaits.
He had his story, what will you make of yours?

With love, tired but not yet dead,
José Leitão

ANNEX I
WITCHING WITH KING MANUEL

THE TWO FOLLOWING TEXTS, although of a completely different nature, have much to give and teach if they are examined together.

The first of these is the XXXIIIrd title of the fifth book of the Manueline Ordinances: "*Of sorcerers and vigils performed in Churches*".

Issued by King Manuel and printed between 1512 and 1521, the Manueline Ordinances in their essence were meant to cover quite literally every aspect of law and government in the country, being one of the first complete and unified legal codes of the Portuguese kingdom. These in fact consisted of a great update to and expansion of the Afonsine Ordinances (after King Afonso V, the alchemist king), which were found to be wanting given the particular circumstances of the growing Portuguese empire. Later, these would be further expanded by the Philippine Ordinances, issued by Philip the II of Spain and I of Portugal, the ruler of the unified Iberia after the disappearance of the Christ-like King Sebastian.

Analyzing this continuum of the Portuguese Ordinances, the rule is firstly set by the Afonsine, compiled at an uncertain date somewhere in the XVth century. This, as all other Ordinances to follow, is divided into five books. The first deals with administrative and legal offices; the second with the relation between church and state, donations and the royal and noble taxes upon these, and also all the special legislation regarding the Muslim and Jewish populations (who at this time enjoyed wide tolerance in the country); the third deals with the exercise of law and due process; the fourth with civilian rights; and the fifth with crime and punishment. Naturally sorcery, deemed an illegal practice, is approached in this fifth book, in which are explained the penalties to be applied to the various practices and practitioners according to their social class, and what among these may be tolerated and regulated. In the Afonsine Ordinances this is in title XXXXII, simply entitled "On sorcerers".

Boiling down its content, this first text does not fall far from the later Manueline Ordinance (presented below), although it is much more vague and general, keeping away from most of the details given in the later Ordinances.

One major difference in tone and orientation is that the Afonsine Ordinances frequently resort to Divine Law and Sin, as understood by the Christianity of its time, in order to justify the evilness and implicit crime of sorcery. While this still echoes strongly in all subsequent Ordinances, from the Manueline onwards there is a much clearer concern in making the language of the document appear more secular and legally oriented, keeping away from the direct mention of crimes against "Our Lord and His Commandments".

Also notable in these early Ordinances is the frequent reference to and quoting from "the law of King John my grandfather". This refers to King John

I (1357 - 1433), the first king of the second Portuguese dynasty, victor of the Battle of Aljubarrota alongside Nun'Álvares Pereira, the Constable Saint[203]. King John I was the first known king to have brought sorcery into legislation in 1385, as mentioned before, and although his laws were never organized into a single document, like the Ordinances, they stand as predecessor and foundation to them all.

Going forth into the Philippine Ordinances, we find that the text regarding Sorcery is pretty much the same as in the Manueline. Some sentences have been changed into a clearer and less archaic structure and the single title of "Of sorcerers and vigils performed in Churches" has been divided into three parts: Title III – On Sorcerers; Title IV – On those who bless dogs or other animals without the authorization of the king or the prelates; Title V – On those who perform vigils in churches or vows outside of them.

Besides of all these changes, which were aimed at greater clarity, the only remarkable novelty in this document is an apparent leniency towards women, which, in certain circumstances, are ascribed lighter penalties. But regarding that which is considered a crime, the text is in its essence the same as the Manueline Ordinance.

Also worth mentioning is the addition in the Philippine Ordinances of title LXX "So as slaves do not live on their own and blacks do not make dances in Lisbon", which, among other things, is meant to target the suspicious festive gatherings of black slaves in and around Lisbon. Finally, also interestingly in the text of these two later Ordinances, although not explicit, is that the last points in the chapter (title V of the Philippine) are clearly intended to target hidden Jews, which by this time had been banned or forced to conversion.

As it has become somewhat of a tradition, this is the kind of document one can look upon to try to find the traces of the banned practices of ages past, precisely in the words of those who banned them.

The second text presented below is the "Auto[204] of the Fadas" by Gil Vicente (1465 - 1536), and this demands attention and respect. One should not go any further without at least trying to understanding who Gil Vicente is, this man of that rare quality who can be called a gift from the Gods upon the world.

Although there is still some controversy regarding his exact identity (apart from his body of work all the rest seems to be mere speculation) he is nonetheless, rightly, the father of Portuguese and, partly, of Spanish theater. His work represents the transition from the Middle Ages into the Renascence, from the explosion of ideas and knowledge arising from the seafaring contact with

---

203. Canonized as Nuno of Saint Mary by Pope Benedict the XVIth in 2009. His feast day in on the 6th of November.

204. An *auto* is a type of play made popular in the XVth and XVIth centuries in Iberia; it usually consists of a single act and has a moralistic intent.

new worlds and nations, laying waste to all millennial preconceived notions. His work is at the maelstrom of the new social and world order arising from the Empire and the first wave of Globalization, at the collapse of the old world into the new[205].

Working in the vein of the *auto*, his plays frequently revolve around character-types: nameless figures who merely represent a social class, a profession or a quality and who are properly addressed as such. Being the puppeteer of such straw men he uses these characters as mirrors to debate and challenge the society of his time (and tragically for us all, not only of his time). Hence, frequently his characters are pinned together with *Bruxas*, angels, demons, and fey folk, as symbols of the virtues and vice of his XVIth century society. It is his close attention to this point in particular that has made his work into an extremely detailed reservoir of late medieval popular traditions, legends, and beliefs, being nowadays cited and quoted by folklorists, anthropologists and ethnographers as a sure and secure academic source.

The play in question, the *Auto of the Fadas*, follows a very simple line: a sorceress named Genebra Pereira enters the royal court to appeal to the king over the persecutions placed upon her trade; she explains to the king the necessity and goodness of her work, citing examples of members of the court who have resorted to her services; to demonstrate her power she summons the Devil, who is revealed as an untreatable rascal speaking in strange tongues. She demands that he bring her some *Fadas* from the *"lost islands"*, which the Devil misunderstands and instead fetches some infernal friars; one of the friars gives out a sermon about love inspired by Virgil and the Devil then agrees to fetch the *Fadas*. These, upon arriving, proceed to give out fortunes and readings, predicting the fates and characters of all the audience members, by relating all the men to land animals and the ladies to birds.

This play, however remarkable, has fallen somewhat out of fashion among modern academics, mainly due to the use of the character-type of the sorceress (*Feiticeira*), which is thought to no longer have relevance or meaning in modern society (little do they know...). Although Witchcraft and general devilry is extremely common in Gil Vicente, the model of the sorceress is not the most usual, with the other great example of this being found in the *Comedy of Rubena* (1521), where a sorceress equally summons devils (Legião/Legion, Plutão/Pluto, Draguinho/Dragon and Caroto) and *Fadas* (Ledera and Minea) to do her good work. But even given this fact, which establishes the sorceress as her own character-type, in the current case of the *Auto of the Fadas*, given her role as magical match-maker, she is usually equated with the procuress (which the sorceress in question does call herself on one occasion), another very popular Gil Vicente character-type which reduces the *auto*'s relevance in the academic eye.

---

205. In this sense Gil Vicente is a poet of the crossroads.

Finally, it should also be important to understand what a *Fada* is.

Logically this would be the Portuguese correspondent to the English *fairy*, but language here offers us a much deeper significance.

Fada is the one who fates, who determines the *fado*, the tragic existence of all. To be *fadado* equally means to be fated for some tragedy or to be under the influence of a *Fada*. This concept then leaps over into the confusing multileveled cultural mess of the fairy godmother, your personally appointed *Fada*, the one who determines your *fado* at the hour of your birth.

This personal *Fada* in many ways resembles the ancient concept of personal daemon, or the Christian equivalent of the guardian angel, to whom one may appeal for a change in one's *Fado*. But these concepts, however, must not be confused, as a *Fada* is always something extremely exterior to the individual and not easily appealed to (even with all the anti-Semitism, this is not a Walt Disney production). The breaking of one's *fado* is usually not done through the interception of a *Fada* (although they can write you a new one), rather, it is accomplished by a powerful action, through a magical act of Will in which you claim your fate as your own, away from the predeterminations of mighty beings. Alternatively, as in the case of *Mouras*, *fado* may be broken by the same magical act, but performed by a third party as an act of (damnable) love.

Logically, the comparison between *Mouras* and *Fada* is unavoidable, but *Fadas* have over the years lost much of their folk appeal and have become largely a literary device. The (rare) *Fadas* of Portuguese folklore then have a much more ethereal character to them, more fateful than comfortin;, they are almost at the level of Gods, extremely removed from mundane contact with humans (for that you have *Mouras*). Given these attributes, it then makes sense that they are the ones most qualified to read the lots/lucks/fates of humans, for they are their masters and keepers, and it is precisely in this function that they appear in the *Auto of the Fadas*.

But no matter how remarkable, what truly makes this play particularly relevant for us at this point is the fact that Gil Vicente was actually the court playwright of King Manuel.

Given that this play is thought to have been performed for the first time between 1511 and 1527, there is a high probability that it was written and acted out for the viewing of King Manuel himself (it should also be noted that all of the various names mentioned in the play were those of court members who would actually be attending the play). We should then meditate on the exact motive behind this *auto*, as in it, whenever the sorceress Genebra Pereira addresses the king, she is actually addressing King Manuel himself, not a character, but the royal person in the flesh, the issuer of the Manueline Ordinances against sorcery.

It is then likely that this play is a direct response to the laws being issued and newly enforced in the kingdom by the king's *meirinhos* (lawmen), a criticism by one of the nation's greatest social critics of all times, given straight to the king's face.

It is remarkable to see how both these texts, the Ordinances and the *Auto*, can actually establish a vivid dialogue between themselves, as they address the same problem from apparently opposing positions, enabling a truly rare direct insight into a historical drama.

The Fifth Book of the Ordinances Title XXXIII

Of sorcerers and vigils performed in Churches

We establish that any person of any given quality and condition, who, from a holy or non holy place, a *pedra d'ara* or an altar cloth, or a part of these, may take, or any other holy thing, shall die a natural death.

1. And the same for any person who inside a circle, or outside of it, or at a crossroad calls up evil spirits, or to any person offers as food or drink anything, either for good or for bad of another, or of another unto him, may he die a natural death. But in these two above cases an execution will not be performed until we disclose firstly, so as to know the quality of this person, the way in which such things were performed, so as we may mandate exactly what is to be done.

2. Likewise to any person who in order to divine may cast lots, or rods to find water, or see in water, or in crystals, or in mirrors, or in swords, or in any other bright thing, or on the shoulder blade of a lamb, or divine with figures or images made of any metal, or of any other thing, or perform divination with the head of a dead man, or that of any animal, or carry with them a tooth or a hangman's noose, or any other limb of a dead man, or perform with the above mentioned things, or with each one of them, or any other (which may not be mentioned here), any kind of sorcery, either to divine, or to harm any person or property, or do any other thing so as a person will wish good or bad to any other, or to bind a man or a woman so as to prevent carnal contact. Who performs the mentioned things or any one of them, we order that they be publicly lashed with a knotted rope and paraded around the town or place where such crime took place, and they shall be branded on both cheeks with iron that will be made for that occasion with an **.ff.** so as it will be known by this iron that they were judged and condemned for this evil, and may they further

be permanently *degredados* to the island of São Tomé, or to one of the other islands of that county, and beyond this corporal punishment, they will pay three thousand *reaes* to he who accused them.

3. And given that we are told that in our kingdom and lordship, among the rustics such superstitions are common, such as passing a sick person through a thorn bush, or a young oak, or a *lameira virgem*[206], and afterwards bless them with a sword that has killed a man, or pass the Douro and Minho three times. Others cut their loneliness[207] in a wild fig tree. Others cut the shingles on the edge of a door. Other have the heads of *saludadores*[208] casted unto gold or silver or in any other thing. Others preach to the possessed. Other take images of some saints to the edge of some water, and then pretend to throw them inside, so as if given a certain period of time the saint does not given them water or any other thing they ask of him, they will throw him in. Others roll boulders and throw them into the water so as to make it rain. Others cast on a sieve. Others offer cake to eat so as to learn of any theft. Others have herbs in their homes, believing that by having them they will have the good graces of lords, or shall be fortunate in all things they may undertake. Others pass water over the heads of dogs to gain some profit. For of such superstitions and other similar things we should not admit, we order and defend that no person perform the said things nor any one of them; and any person who does otherwise, should he be a peasant or lower, may he be publicly lashed with a knotted rope and paraded around town, and further pay two thousand *reaes* to he who accused him. Should he be a vassal or squire or higher, or the wife of any of these, may he be *degredado* to each one of our places in Africa for two years, and further

---

206. Translator's note: a plant I believe, although I cannot say for sure.
207. Translator's note: uncertain translation.
208. The Philippine Ordinances add the following:

Head of *Saludadores*, i.e. of *Benzedores*.

One calls *Saludadores* to those who in Spain and Portugal say they are descendents of St. Catharine and St. Quiteria, and carry upon their arms paintings of their heads, and in their pocket engraved knives, which they embedded with blue or black ink, and maybe as a hoax, use these to perform blessings, perhaps similarly to what Moreas says, of medals of St. Blaise and St. Athanasius, etc. This superstition was punishable by law so as to prevent the delusions of the people.

pay four thousand *reaes* to he who accused him. And these same penalties for all those who proclaim anything that is still to happen, saying and demonstrating that it was revealed by God, or any saint in a vision, or in a dream, or in any other way, and this according to the different qualities of persons: lashings and two thousand *reaes* for the peasant and those of similar fate, and the vassal and those above two years of *degredo* and four thousand *reaes*. But in all of this there is no sentencing to astrologers who by the science and art of astrology may foresee the births of people and say things according to the judgment and laws of their science.

4. We further defend that no person should bless dogs, or creatures or any animal, without firstly consulting with our authority or that of the prelate, so as they may do so, and anyone performing otherwise may they be publicly lashed if he is a peasant or lower, and pay two thousand *reaes* to he who accused him, and if he is a vassal or squire or higher, may he be *degredado* for one year to each one of our places in Africa, and pay two thousand *reaes* to he who accused him.

5. We further mandate that no person make vows or vigils of sleeping, eating and drinking in churches, nor gather to eat and drink for reason of a mass they had prayed, which is the mass of Saturday, nor save devotion on Saturday or Wednesday, not being this an ordered observance of these mentioned days by the church and by constitution of the prelate, and any person who any of these things mentioned on this chapter performs, may they be arrested, and from jail pay five hundred *reaes* to he who accused him.

6. And similarly we defend that no vows of eating and drinking be made, outside of churches, and proclaim that they are so done out of devotion for any saint, under the penalty that all which may be earned from that vow be paid in double from jail by those who so requested and received it, this not counting the vows of the holy spirit which are made at the time of Pentecost, for only these are conceded to be performed, and no other.

7. However in those places where it is custom to eat when carrying the dead, on those one may do so without any penalty, never eating inside the church.

Auto of the Fadas[209]

Characters:
    A Sorceress
    The Devil
    Two Friars
    Three Fadas

In the following farce we have that a sorceress, fearing arrest over the use of her trade, complains to the king, showing him for what reasons are her sorceries so necessary. And entering the royal halls she finds herself very embarrassed, saying the following:

> .Jesus he who brought here
> this airhead
> with cackling laugh
> I don't know how I'll go about
> such shame I feel.
> For I am so embarrassed
> cowering and fearful
> what am I to do in this hall
> for I am so embarrassed
> with all this beauty
>
> Oh what shall I do of this fearfulness
> oh shameful of me
> how I am flushed
> blushed and colored
> but urgency brings me here
> to where I see no place
> on which a man may piss
> nor do I even dare to sneeze
> for no one is free
> among these people

---

209. Translator's note: It should be noted that Gil Vicente was a poet of rare skill, and that this play was set out in a beautiful rhythm and rhyme. I was unable to replicate this point in the current translation.

<table>
<tr><td>She approaches the king
and queen and says</td><td>My lords although thou art
with health and pleasure
many years may thou prosper
the boughs which are born
may God make them grow
as thou wishes</td></tr>
<tr><td>To the prince and
infants</td><td>Oh what varnished jewels
oh what flowers of heaven
oh what perfumed roses</td></tr>
<tr><td>To the ladies of court</td><td>My good Jesus what golden saints
great joys may I see from thee
and good fates</td></tr>
</table>

I am Genebra Pereira
who lives there in Pedreira
neighbor to Joam de Tara
single for I only knew love in my old age
without husband or nobility
I was raised in gentleness
inside the bowels of the court
and over the sorceries I make
they say I am a *feiticeira*

Genebra Pereira however
never harmed a soul
but rather for wanting to do good
I roam the crossroads
at those hours when those of good *fado*
sleep a restful slumber.
And I am in the company of a hanged man
speaking in his hear
such this old woman will show
much better then she can say

For now Estevam Diz
says that thou such defends
oh I give thee to Jesus Christ
for it is to be taken from me
all which I have done
in my forty years.
Stopping many harms

by such proven banishments
calling up ten dead men
so as to learn a truth

And by mercy
of ill married women
to see them well matched
I roam naked the church yards
without any company
save that of a *sino-saimão*
stuck inside the heart
of a black cat and nothing else
this my lord is not for evil
for it is to do good

Other times coming to me
young men with broken hearts
wishing rather to be dead
than to have such passions
I ride my goat
and I go to Val de Cavalinhos[210]
and in this I break my face
on all those olive trees
calling on friars and nuns
who are dying of love.
oh if thou but saw the terrors
I experience in this labor
Pereira would not fear
so much the lawmen

I am always in this toil
a single man comes to me
wanting to marry Constança
with no shred of hope
sad and dying of passion
and I with lion's blood
stirred with the tail of a fish
and there with the bile of an owl
is the boy served.

---

210. Translator's note: This place is actually mentioned several times and in several texts of various periods as a famous gathering place of the Witches' Sabbath. It is currently named Vale de Santo António in Lisbon.

Further comes an excommunicated friar
who will bless him from the *quebranto*
I further do the same
and in such my lord do I see pleasure

He comes so as to say
Gonçalo Silva to me
and tell me he is besides himself
for Francisca da Guerra
doest thou wish me to be such a bitch
so as not to ask the Devil
to free him from the cliff
Where his spirit lays?
And what if Gaspar de Brito comes to me
over Caterina Limão
should I not go on my goat
to bewitch to Limeira?

And if in this way
Marichal comes to me
over Guiomar de Ataúde
seeking my health
I must put myself at risk
and if Dom Francisco pleads to me
to bewitch Beneni for him
unless I am heartless
I cannot deny him such.
And to Martim de Sousa
dying for Perimintel
I cannot be unfaithful

Sorceries such as these
are my lord works of great piety
and nothing else is the truth
know Thy Majesty
who is Genebra Pereira
who always wished to remain single
to have greater graces.
now I know not what to do
with this black *meirinho*
Face of St. Sardoninho[211]

211. Translator's note: this saint is sometimes called upon on some *benzedeira*

Oh do I love and wish
if such is Thy Highness' wishes
to see the sorceries I perform
right here in this hall
thou shall see them fresh.
And thou my lady queen
infants and courtesans
raise thy hands to the heavens
stay strong and don't be frightened
of all the evil things thou shall see

Wait just a little
stay still as such
I will arrange the clay bowl
the lamp and the bag
And thou shall see the flames.
If thy skin trembles
of fright and terror
and thy suitors are there
then get close to them
cover thyselves with love

The sorceress brings in a clay bowl[212] and a black bag containing her sorceries, which she starts to perform by saying:

Bowl bowl
who wert made under the moon light
under the seven stars
with the spittle of a damsel
I had thee kneaded.
oh precious spittle
from such precious lips
give now the pleasure
to those who wish thee so good
and provide now good *fadas*
at the crossroads

This path goes that way

---

workings to speed up births. To the best of my knowledge he is not an official Catholic saint and I know nothing else of him.

212. Translator's note: the original Portuguese is *alguidar*; those familiar with Afro-Brazilian cults will recognize this tool.

this one goes this way
thou art in the middle bowl
that here a cross will never be

Although thou art crossed
entering from here and leaving from there
be welcomed honorable lady
the road goes through the road
blessed is the cat that birthed
black cat black is the cat
black goat roams the wilderness
black is the crow and black is pitch
black is the king of chess
black is the sole of the shoe
black is the bag I untie

these are the entrails of a frog
here in this napkin
here is the tit of a sow
the beard of a stolen goat
the bile of an excommunicated dead man
pebbles from the foot of the gallows.
Cake made from fallowed wheat
and with two mice from my house
sowed by my hand
harvested grinded kneaded
on the back of the bowl

Come close to me
what doest thou wish to eat my cherub?
Froth from a possessed man
who gave them to thee?
I gave them to thee
bile of dead man my comfort
horned cake thou knows all
tip of a nail wing of a bat
dragon's breath all I carry
I don't swear nor banish
but a black cock
sang on my dung pile
and the holy words being said
behold Devil goes behold Devil comes
with his trousers hanging.

A Devil arrives at the sorceress' call, speaking to her in the Picard language[213] in the following way:

Devil	.Ó dame jordene
	vu seae la bien trovee
	tu es fause té huméyne
	sou ye vous esposee.
Sorceress	.What language is that?
	my word he speaks gibberish
	look here Turkish fool
	speak to me the tongue of Portugal.
Devil	.Tu as fet biauco de mal
	aveu in frayre jacopim.
Sorceress	.Thou so greatly hurts me
	may thy speech be clear
	what say thee that I do not understand
	does thou mock me
	well I swear to God who is grace
	to the Devil I ask thee
	being so big and being there.
Devil	.Macarele de limosim
	tripiere de sancto Ouim
Sorceress	.Give the Devil that Latin
	for I do not understand what he says.
Devil	.Tu nas oy tene vergonhe.
Sorceress	.What have I done?
Devil	.De tois le sães en aute vois.
Sorceress	.Thou should tell me later
	what all that means.
Devil	.Tu aspete de bem la mer.
Sorceress	.What may *pété* mean
	what language is this?
Devil	.Tan sant y xi noble en trapisu
Sorceress	.Thou Devil sees what thy came for.

---

213. Translator's note: The Picard language that is to follow is not in any way accurate, what is indeed meant here is simply to have the Devil speak in an unfamiliar language, as most of the audience of this play would probably only know Portuguese and Castilian (which is used further down without any hint of confusion) and for this reason I have chosen not to translate these lines. If you are familiar with Picard, or even just French, you might be able to make out a few words... but don't strain yourself, that is not the point.

Devil	.E la ribald orrem
	y puis gessa venu.
Sorceress	.Then why did thou come
	if not for my services?
Devil	.Dime tos xem que tu veus
	fame dum vilhem cocu.
Sorceress	.Who has seen a German Devil
	I plead to thee scoundrel
	evil *quebranto* break thee
	if thou does not speak in any other way
	by the life of Genebra Pereira
	old thief and procuress
	who calls upon the name of Jesus.
Devil	.Eu eu que dile tu.
Sorceress	.I banish thee cursed one
	member of the wrath of God
	by the earth and by the heavens
	and by thy cursed sign
	thou shall answer me.
Devil	.Oh what cursed woman
	what does thou wish infernal one?
Sorceress	.I wish to understand thee
	my rose come closer
	my *quebranto* give me the faith
	do not talk to me as such
	and I shall worship the ox's bottom
Devil	.Te toy te toy
Sorceress	.Speak Portuguese
	so far I have been jesting
	thou shall go as I order.
Devil	.I shall when thou so says.
Sorceress	.Go then to the lost islands
	in the sea of feathers or vines
	bring three sea *fadas*
	and pick them right
	go now with haste
Devil	.Tu as destaque la pendus.

The Devil departs and the sorceress returns to her sorceries saying:

Sorceress	.What does thou do relics of mine
	In this clear water immersed?
	thou require to be stirred
	With the filth of a swallow.

The messenger returns and instead of the *fadas* that the sorceress had ordered him to bring, he brings two infernal friars; one of them is playing a bagpipe and the other used to be a preacher while living but also a philanderer, and he immediately says:

Friar	.What great torment thou gives me[214]
	by bringing me here to this place
	ita vere
Devil	.What say thee?
Friar	.This place makes us sadder
	than the whole of hell.
Devil	.Per quam regula diremos.
Friar	.For we know this to be very certain
	quia dedit Deus potestatem
	the ladies who so much kill us
	we also worship
	Greater are the pains
	that I have for these gentlemen
	for I know that it is love
	and not the infernal fires
	the greatest of torments.
	How the suffering is sufficient
	of the infatuated torment
	if love is sharp
	that caution does not kill it
	and it drowns one's thoughts
	this is what I know
	and I used it when I lived
	may this give thee faith
	this is what I studied
	this is my library

---

214. Translator's note: It should be noted that the friar speaks largely in Castilian with some occurrences of Latin, as does the Devil when addressing him. I have translated the Castilian as this would be an easily understandable language for the audience, the Latin I have left as it is.

such contemplations
were always my lectures
in this I spent my years
giving my sermons
the greatness of my sins
with painful tears
inside my oratorio
contemplating the beautiful
after certain verses
I would say this invitatory

the saintly temple of love
where we lose our souls
come all and let us worship
come beautiful
to the sad devotion
where passion kills
and life always falls
into yet greater prisons
and such damnation
over greed we gain it
come all and let us worship

we worship and exalt
those who killed us
opera manum suraum
are the sighs we whisper
in hoc vita lachrimarum
to those who treated us so badly
for we hold them as goddesses
come all and let us worship

the first third sixth and ninth
praying this fate
for I always
of this crowning fact
was given unto love and death
contava de deum laudamus
with my eye on Cupid
saying that to thee we worship
those of us who ran out of fortune
with so much time having served.

They approach the sorceress, and as she sees them she says:

Sorceress	.Bad service and bad torment
	come here by the hair of thy beard
	I sent thee for *fadas*
	and thou brings me a bagpiper
	and what's the purpose of these friars?
Devil	.Vus ma ves dexem.
Sorceress	.May thou live as thus amen.
Devil	.E pene foy xiaa
Sorceress	.Thou comes in a bad time
	for thy foolishness
	did I not tell thee *fadas?*
Devil	.Fradas
Sorceress	.Fadas
Devil	.Friars
Sorceress	.I may yet have some use for thee
Friar	.Give us something to do
	or send us back to hell
Sorceress	.And what should that be? Let the Devil solve
	that
	I had no propose for thee
	what trade does thou have
	thou and thy musician?
Friar	.Over here I used to be a great preacher
	over there I was made a weaver.
Sorceress	.Well then say a sermon
	very brief to these ladies
	at this time be quick
	choose the theme don thief
Friar	.Amor vincit omnia
	loco et capitulo
	jam per elegatis

Discrete illustrious and beautiful ladies
unto whose service it is more than fair to perish
the topic of the theme means
that love conquers all
oh what marvelous words
oh what words of such knowledge
written by the great poet Virgil
learn them ladies for they are a great relief

for those who feel defeated by love

For these are words of such mystery
that they blind or illuminate the human reason
shedding the life off of any heart
for thou have rule over love.
Many times Valerius writes such
that thy power is not human
but a great supernatural force
that forces the forces of our hemisphere

He blows his nose.

Somebody silence those children

Amor vincit omnia prodent siters
and this love may come by three different accidents
of which thou are not to be blamed.
One is of the fault of thy gaze
and the beauty which gazes with thee
the other oh wretched of us is the grace
which all things beats and kills

The other accident which greater is the torment
roses of the world of so dreadful feeling
are the deceptions of the sweet feeling
of certain detour now and again.
Oh bringers of such storm
bright clouds raining down sighs
over those tormented who to serve thee
do not doubt death nor fear insult

We see the discreet and noble person
of Gonçalo da Silva biting the ground
for thus is his blindness from this continuous war
as if he was a race horse
for this is so precious thy Lisbon
because thou ladies mortally sin
convert to Dominum for thou art killing people
with sweet wags made in Pamplona

This poor man is walking on the edge
Calataud over Anriquez so much
that it is said about him oh Easter candle
that thou used to be wax and now thou art but
a wick
oh gracious creeks of the Nile
pietate vestra super omnes gentes
free him from such cruel bothers
that even if he was thick now he is but a wick

I do not want to forget don Luís de Meneses
who Lady Leonor de Castro has been killing
that by now he seems like a barge of Port
three or four months with no sustenance.
Abandon such tricks of thy setbacks
ladies ne oerdas animam vivam
for thy good do they captivate themselves
ut non dessoletur for they are Portuguese

Oh Cristovam Freire most loyal knight
who lady Ginebra he took as his God
he is now as a greyhound of Porto de Mós
but skin and bone roaming these lands.
And many other lords whose name I do not
wish to say
quia non debemus de plaza decir
who suffer the wounds of the sad concealing
of which they suffer the most horrible of
torments

Why then my ladies doest thou not confess
that thou make the living die in thy service
thou make the dead over there sigh
only because they art not where thou art.
Amor vencit omnia and thou art the cause
orbis terrarium et semitas maris
oh beautiful goddesses judged per Paris
where one writes the lives thou squander

Promise to lord Juan de Salaña
that he has the keys to thy paradise
may God give him graces out of such theft
the keys or thee or him or his cane.

Now it is no longer time for predictions
he who wished to hear my sermon
may he go to hell with great devotion
and in this way save himself

All things that I am usually ordered
I deliver thou should know
all the evil thou may do
do it my ladies for thou have the blessing of
the good *hadas*

Sorceress   .Well now evil creature
fetch me now the *fadas*
from the sea good and ghostly
and reverse this bitterness

Where does thou come from? From Almoinha
what brings thee? Flour
take it back for it is not mine

look at all the honorable people
what did that thief bring me
one who was living in sin
a proven pimp
and a thug of a friar.
Thou very well knows how I am disturbed
By such people of improper ways
Even more than flies bother me
I cannot bear to hear or see them

The sorceress takes a few beads out of her bag

For the carnal union
of friar Graviel with Marta
his spiritual daughter
let these new clothes come
that I am tired of waiting.
And let it bring the *fadas*
oh my lady litany
may thou aid me now
black goat go through the vine
go through the vine my sister
we plead to thee audi nos

When thou goes to church
do not forget the pride
having taken my advice
oh lashes of my advice
which my grandparents broke in
we plead to thee audi nos

The litany of Pereira
written on the skin of a rat
ink from the drop of a duck
roasted by the hand of the walnut tree
oh picottah of Ribeira
which my grandparents broke in
we plead to thee audi nos

The *fadas* arrive singing the following song:

Which of us is more tired
of this tiresome journey
which of us is more tired.

Sorceress	.Chicks chicks chicks ducks ducks ducks be more than welcome my damsels fresh and fried flounders
Devil	.Oo fauxe buxiere malvada vaxites a buxions.
Sorceress	.Thou returns to such terms excommunicated harrier.
Devil	.Mi gene memie mi.
Sorceress	.Be quiet and let me do the talking
She asks the fadas:	.How is thy sea so deep and open?
The fadas respond singing:	.Our sea is prosperous our life tearful after this journey which of us is more tired of this tiresome journey
Sorceress	.Can thou not speak unless by singing?

The fadas sing:	.We left walking
	with tear sobbing
	without knowing how nor when
	would be the end of our journey
	which of us is more tired
	of this tiresome journey
Devil	.Melior cantale quien
	y le hoyssos de villee
Sorceress	.Be quiet crow of Noah
	that thou hast no idea
	of what is singing badly or good

My river flowers
peace of this my soul
queens of all sea life
honor now this pilgrim.
Fate in a beautiful way
these ground with good *fado*
that God shall repay them doubled
for this he will see.

The *fadas* fate the king and queen each in their turn. The first one says:

.The *fados* that gave being unto the stars
when the earth was still empty
may they make thy path joyful
wherever their light shines on thee
and those *fados*
that for fortune are determined
may they bring thee thine among the many
and the instruments of long life
be them doubled

The *fados* that gave dew to the roses
may they visit the flowers of thy path
and all concern with sad concerns
may it have no place in thy highnesses.
And those *fadas*
who keep the creeks painted green
paint thy lives of joyful colors
and the fortunes of good venture
may thy be kept.

Second fada	.The things that make the earth birth white lilies and divine veins may they surround thy widows and let always victory lull thee to sleep. And the first *fada* who made fortune thy great dispenser and made our seas and heaven with good measure may her give thee the joys of life in a new way
Third fada	.The news we bring from the waves of the sea art that on earth there is little truth as truth thou have bad news as new thou shall accept them. Now it shall be proven take thy highness any thou so wishes that these lots are all true take from those seven planets the one which suits thee best

Here they predict the lots, firstly to the king.

to the king	Jupiter. This chosen planet chosen for it is deep the highest good in the world.
to the queen	Sun. Great wealth gave God to the earth but if this one doesn't come never would there be a dawn.
to the prince	Cupid. This God is greatly beloved for he has dominion over every heart.
to the infanta Lady Isabel	Moon. This lady Diana has in heaven her abode and from the Sun her beauty.

to the infanta Lady
        Beatiz

Venus.
To this planet alone
do all the stars gaze
for he is brighter than them.

From here on there are the lots of the gentlemen, given as animals.

Camel.
This one joyful news brings
and carries his own sad ones
every time he departs from here.

Marten.
This animal is free
on the outside he seems soft
but on the inside not so much.

Sagittarius.
This one has two hearts
aching over one sadness
that will never end.

Stoat.
This animal is praised
in general all over the world
and here he is treated so badly.

Goat.
This animal feeds
on the harshest of plants
for daring to venture.

Ferret.
This is skilled in silence
for he is so proud
that he becomes desirable.

Podengo.
This animal raises
the hunt for it is he who finds it
yet it is always someone else who makes the kill.

Mouse.
This pretty animal
I know not what he does
for there are always animosities.

Turtle.
Whoever has this animal
should not leave him
for he is neither meat nor fish.

Chameleon.
This strange animal has
such strange food
that he never gets tired of wind.

Wolf.
This one dies with reason
for he has such opposition
that he takes death well.

Hedgehog.
This fooled animal
takes care to love hidden
and he is the most known
of candies.

Mountain hog.
This animal takes refuge
in the most hidden wildernesses
and there they still find him.

Deer.
This greatly brave animal
in keeping himself had his intention
but love took his wind.

Roe.
The leaping of this gallant
could not save him
from an evil he must endure.

Lamb.
This one should a love come over him
soon he shears himself
and a new one he immediately finds.

Porcupine.
Of these there are few in the earth
he should be preserved
from fortune and love
without war.

Bear.
This animal is venturous
and fortunate for he has suffered
to suffer is a good part
and it is tolerable.

Ground hog.
This is never satisfied
nor content will he ever find himself
for he desires that which is and isn't.

Cat.
This is a home animal
and he does not wish well to Cupid
he loves to be a husband
with money.

Lion.
This is a very strong animal
he never knows terror
but he fears love
and never does he give it.

Unicorn.
This kind is very elusive
and is hunted with a damsel
and for no other reason
is he captivated.

Dromedary.
This one carries great baggage
And he demands his share
But he does not ask properly.

Horse.
This furious animal
can fall hopelessly in love
for he does not love in a single place.

Greyhound.
This delicate animal
I know not why he tires of life
he brings those he guards.

Hare.
This one has life in little care
and it is good that he thinks it cheap
for he wishes to wound who kills him.

Howler Monkey.
This animal understands
all which he may care
however his non speak
hides and hurts those who understand.

Bull.
This one not being guilty
is wounded
and the greater the wounds the greater his
flame.

Rabbit.
This caged animal
is such a lively lover
that he shall die by the cane.

Fox.
Of this thou should take care
for he pretends to be limp or hurt
and even sometimes dead
while he is hunting.

Elephant.
Only this animal
has veins in his heart
where his tears are.

Panther.
This light animal
if in three pounces does not kill
he abandons the prey.

Old horse.
The life of this animal
is at night the work
in the morning the hay.

Galician horse.
This is a good server
he serves well with a saddle
but is better for work.

Mongrel.
This one is false and gentle
sneaky
when thou sees this dog
always have a stick in thy hand.

Weasel.
This is not quite a ferret
nor genet nor squirrel
he is a vagrant animal.

The lots of the ladies are given by birds.

Hawk.
This bird has cruelty
and no mercy
he who wishes to take it
has a lot to sigh.

Heron.
This bird is fearful
and beautiful
she is not gained with tricks

but only through feats.

Blackbird.
This bird is a lover
most declared
and she makes her nest in the square
and all with most grace.

Nightingale.
This bird has her loves
with flowers
solely two months out of the year
however she loves with no mistake.

Eagle.
This one vanquishes the sun with her sight
and she blinds all others
that with her have great faith.

Sparrow-hawk.
This bird is most light
and flattering
she loses her love for no reason
she is beautiful and altered
in a great way.

Starling.
this bird is of the kind
that goes to greatest height
and she trusts venture
with reason.

Dove.
This bird seems like a saint
for she is sly
but in the certain she is false.

Turtledove.
This one desires to marry
but she wants to choose so well
that I fear she will be left
without a husband.

Peacock.
This bird is such a lover
of the beauty she has
that I know for certain that for no one
she has feelings.

Phoenix.
This one does not have a partner
she leads her life in the wild bushes
and she does not kill anyone
she only kills herself.

Swan.
This bird follows the extreme
for she sings against reason
when she kills her heart.

Magpie.
This bird never rests
she is gallant and very joyful
but in the hour of no mistake
she is not talkative.

Ádem[215].
This one is taken to be royal
she is so wild and elusive
that she doesn't want to see any living thing.

Goshawk.
This pretty bird
she plays like she awaits
but by God she keeps herself very well.

Kestrel.
This bird is always sieving
and she never gives any flour
thou art the same my lady.

Swallow.
This bird is joyful
and trusted

215. Translator's note: uncertain translation but maybe the Indian runner duck.

her loves come and go
she has no certainty.

Lark.
This one is never sad
she rises in the air at every hour
and sings for another cries.

Owl.
This bird follows such dread
and has all others frightened
for at each time she changes.

Seagull.
Only this bird fills herself
with luck
she does not fear sea nor torment
she is born free and lives absent.

Partridge.
This bird is greatly appreciated
and warned
and if someone fools her
I swear to God that she will have a good hunt.

Crane.
This bird is always vigilant
she never has a restful sleep
for she dreams night and day
of being married.

Buzzard.
this bird it is said she saw
but she can see no greater good
than the lady who now has it.

Thus finished the lots, all leave with their music and this farce is ended.

FINIS.

SOURCES

José Camões: *Fadas – Vicente*, Quimera Editores, 2005, Lisboa (digital edition);

Maria João Amaral: *Rubena – Vicente*, Quimera Editores, 2005, Lisboa, (digital edition).

Maria José Pallas: *Figuras literárias de magas e imagens de Sabat na obra de Gil Vicente*, Revista da FCSH (1994/1995) 297.

Ordenações Afonsinas, (digital edition).

Ordenações Manuelinas, (digital edition).

Ordenações Filipinas, (digital edition).

Teixeira de Aragão: *Diabruras Santidades e Profecias*, Vega, Lisboa, 1994.

ANNEX II
THE NORTHERN CONNECTION

AT LAST, WAVING OUR GOODBYES, one should also mention the Cyprian traditions of Scandinavia, even if these are somewhat tangential to our current preoccupations.

The Scandinavian Wittenberg Books, Black Books, or *Svarte Boken*, also commonly called the *Cyprianus*, are in themselves another riddle. These are an entirely different branch of the grimoire tradition, which by itself just makes their existence, in this so distant region of Europe, all the more remarkable.

Although in terms of content these are very different from the Iberian Cyprian books, in all other aspects they present themselves as surprisingly similar, particularly with the Portuguese *Sorcerer's Treasure*. Both are compilations of sorceries, remedies, and spells with oral and traditional roots, being, like their Iberian counterparts, interestingly fluidic. This is of course due in part to the fact that traditionally a *Cyprianus* is generated by the writing down (usually by hand) of lists of magical formulas, spells, and folk remedies, being that commonly every new copy is made from a previous older one.

Regarding their origins, most legends place these books in the University of Wittenberg. This is an interesting aspect of the whole puzzle, as it was at this university that Martin Luther taught theology and actually posted his ninety-five theses on the reformation of the Catholic Church.

According to local folklore, in this university priests were said to learn the hidden secrets of the Bible and gain knowledge of other such hidden things, symbolized by the Black Book, becoming thus *svartebokprest*, Black Book Priests.

While a common man could only gain possession of a Black Book at the cost of his soul, a Black Book Priest could do so with impunity, for, as an ordained priest, he had the power to keep the Devil at bay and even control him. This once again reverberates with the Iberian St. Cyprian book, where the whole first part is meant as set of instructions to the priesthood, suggesting that indeed *The Book*, as with many other grimoires, was meant to be used by priests.

This legendary Wittenberg is once again a similar theme to the *Cueva de Salamanca* in Iberia, as there is even mention that, as the black arts were studied at Wittenberg, one of the students would be randomly selected to become the Devil's property.

The association of Wittenberg with the Devil's school does deserve some careful consideration, even more so as the Black Books exist in, mainly, Protestant countries. By analyzing the content of the Black Books one cannot help but denote the Catholic tone of some of their prayers, and, as far as the rest of their content goes, they are in all aspects offensive to Protestant theology, even moreso than to Catholic. However, we find them associated with the very birthplace of Protestantism and Wittenberg as the university where both the Devil and Martin Luther (should they be different people) gave their lectures.

One could make the dangerous leap that this is an actual folk denial of Protestantism in favor of Catholicism, making Martin Luther the Devil himself and the Black Book Priests the keepers of the secrets of the Bible. This might be highlighted by the fact that the Black Books are sometimes thought of as the 6th and 7th Books of Moses, which Martin Luther had kept out the Bible when he translated it so as they could not be used by the simple folk, reserving their power for the priesthood alone.

Think what you will about Catholicism, it surely has its terrible faults, as does all of Christianity and maybe even more; I will certainly not be the one to defend it, but one must admit that, with all its rituals, fetishistic remnants, mysterious inconsistencies, and incompetent pagan cover ups, it does hold strong in the hearts of the simple rural folk. These are not concerned with theology, philosophy or grace by faith alone, rather, they are concerned with disease, hunger and pain, and they are concerned with the proper prayer, the proper saint and the proper divine name to call upon for help, something Catholicism provides with abundance.

While analysing the Scandinavian legends regarding the Black Books one might also notice that this Cyprian, author of these books, is immensely removed from the canonical Sorcerer Saint of Antioch. Surely they are meant to be the same character or at least have the same origin, even if the Black Book users may not realize it.

As far as Denmark goes, there appear to be two distinct reports of Cyprian. One says that he was an exceedingly evil Dane, evil enough to get kicked out of Hell by the Devil. Apparently upset by this event he dedicated himself to writing nine books on black magic, whose content is the base for the Scandinavian Black Books. The other, also present in Norway, describes him as a gentle and orderly person, who, while passing by the Black School of Norway, made a pact with the Devil and became a Sorcerer – once again, a common theme with Giles of Santarém. His book is said to have been written during his later years as he repented such evil actions and that its purpose is to show how evil is performed so as one may counteract it. The legend goes on to say that his book is in fact divided into three parts, the *Cyprianus*, *Dr. Faustus*, and *Jacob Ramel*.

In Germany, tradition seems to agree with that first Danish report; the following account is given by Benjamin Thorpe:

> In ancient times there lived in one of the Danish isles a
> man named Cyprianus, who was worse than the Devil;
> consequently, after he was dead and gone to hell, he was
> again cast forth by the Devil and replaced on his isle.
> There he wrote nine books, in the old Danish tongue,
> on Witchcraft and magical spells. Whosoever has read all

these nine books through becomes the property of the Devil. From the original work three (or nine) copies are said to have been made by a monk, and mutilated copies of these have been dispersed all over the world. A count, who resided in the castle of Ploen, is said to have possessed a perfect copy, which he caused to be fastened with chains and buried under the castle; because in reading through eight books he was so troubled and terrified that he resolved on concealing it from the sight of the world. One of these books still exists in Flensborg. Some spells from the nine books are still known among aged people. Whoever wishes to be initiated therein must first renounce his Christianity.

One other remarkably different account describes Cyprianus as a beautiful Mexican nun who lived in 1351 (just a reminder, America was officially discovered in 1492). After refusing the advances of a depraved clergy member she was locked in a dungeon where she wrote her book of magic with shreds from her clothing and her own blood.

Similarly to Iberia, the idea of a hidden and lost, true and final *Cyprianus*, to be found out there in the world, clearly transpires from some of these accounts.

One other similarity with these books is related to their intrinsic magical properties, which are given by themselves and not necessarily by the virtue of their written content. In order to obtain one, should you not be a Black Book Priest, popular lore states no other way than by making a pact with the Devil. The method of performing such pact is even described in some books and it usually consists of denying God and performing certain religious rites backwards. After the ritual is performed the Devil appears and hands you the book (similar to the account of Jonas Sulfurino), this after you sign one other book he carries with your own blood.

Once you acquire one of these books it becomes impossible to get rid of it, as even destruction will prove useless seeing as the book will always return to its owner. Apart from trying to make a "holy" fire (by burning sacred texts) to try to destroy a Black Book, the proper method to permanently unbind yourself from one is by writing in it your name in your own blood and leaving it in a concealed place at church together with four shillings.

These books then, wherever in the world, suggest themselves as the response of Tradition faced with modernity, the oral faced with the written, always at the border and at the limit. Confusing and muddled, they are by definition incomplete, as one must never confuse the shadow with the body. And yet, there can also be no doubt that there is a spirit about them, something very concrete and living emanating from what otherwise would be a pile of paper and ink.

It is my opinion that these books point to something hidden, that they are the tip of the iceberg of something grand and mysterious. They are the gate and the path back, calling those who can hear its voice under the fear and ridicule society casts on all truly magical books.

They will not conform, for what they represent is invincible, unbreakable, and unbendable to the limited reason of Man.

SOURCES

Benjamin Thorpe: *Northern Mythology – Comprising the principal popular traditions and superstitions of Scandinavia, North Germany and The Netherlands – Compiled from original and other sources*, Vol. II, Edward Lumley, London, 1851.

Kathleen Stokker: *Remedies and Rituals – Folk Medicine in Norway and the New Land*, Minnesota Historical Society Press, St. Paul, 2007.

Mary S. Rustad: *The Black Books of Elverum*, Galde Press, Lakeville, 2010.

Owen Davies: *Grimoires – A History of Magic Books*, Oxford University Press, 2010, Oxford.

Oh crawling serpent
Day and night in that lament
Raise yourself from the ground,
Let us break your enchantment!

Excerpt from a Moura folktale, from Bolideira, Chaves

BIBLIOGRAPHY

GENERAL

Aleister Crowley: *Magick: Liber Aba: Book 4*, Weiser Books, York Beach Maine, 2000.

Alexandre Parafita: *A Mitologia dos Mouros – Lendas, Mitos, Serpentes, Tesouros*, Edições Gailivro, Canelas, 2006.

Alexandre Parafita: *O Maravilhoso Popular – Lendas, Contos, Mitos*, Plátano Editora, Lisboa, 2000.

Alexandri ab Alexandro: *Genialium Dierum*, (digital version).

Amadeo de Santander: *O Livro da Bruxa ou A Feiticeira de Évora*, Editora Eco, Rio de Janeiro.

Amador Patricio: *Historia das Antiguidades de Évora – Primeira Parte*, Officina da Universidade, 1739, Évora, (digital edition).

Andrew D. Chumbley: *The Leaper Between – An Historical Study of the Toad-bone Amulet; Its Form, Functions and Praxis in Popular Magic*, Three Hands Press, Lammastide, 2012.

António Pinelo Tiza: *Inverno Mágico – Ritos e Mistérios Transmontanos*, Ésquilo Edições e Multimédia, Lisboa, 2004.

António Quadros: *Poesia e Filosofia do Mito Sebastianista*, Guimarães Editores, Lisboa, 2001.

Benjamin Thorpe: *Northern Mythology – Comprising the principal popular traditions and superstitions of Scandinavia, North Germany and The Netherlands – Compiled from original and other sources*, Vol. II, Edward Lumley, London, 1851.

Bernardo Barreiro: *Brujos y astrólogos de la Inquisicion de Galicia y el libro de San Cipriano*, Extramuros Edición, S.L., Sevilla, 2010.

Camilo Castelo Branco: *Noites de Lamego*, (digital edition).

Cipriano di Antiochia, Stefano Fumagalli: *Confessione – La Prima Versione del Mito di Faust Nella Letteratura Antica*, Meledoro, Milano, 1994.

Cruz de Caravanca, *Editora Pensamento-Cultrix*, São Paulo, 2011.

Dalila L. Pereira da Costa: *Corografia Sagrada*, Lello & Irmão Editores, Porto, 1993.

Dalila L. Pereira da Costa: *Da Serpente à Imaculada*, Lello & Irmão Editores, Porto, 1984.

Dalila L. Pereira da Costa: *Dos Mundos Contíguos*, Lello Editores, Porto, 1999.

David Beth: *Voudon Gnosis*, Fulgur Limited, London, 2010.

David Rankine: *The Book of Treasure Spirits – A grimoire of magical conjurations to reveal treasure and catch thieves by invoking spirits, fallen angles, demons and fairies*, Avalonia, London, 2009.

Devoção às Almas do Pugatorio, Editorial Missões, Cucujães, 2010.

Devocionario – Manual arreglado por algunos padres de la Compañía de Jesús, Imp. Del Corazon de Jesus, Bilbao, 1889, (digital edition).

Éliphas Lévi: Transcendental Magic – Its Doctrine and Ritual, Martino Publishing, Mansfield Center, 2011.

Francisco Bethencourt: O Imaginário da Magia – Feiticeiras, Advinhos e Curandeiros em Portugal no século XVI, Companhia das Letras, 2004, São Paulo.

Gabriela Morais, Fernanda Frazão: Portugal, mundo dos mortos e das mouras encantadas, Vol. I, Apenas Livros, Lisboa, 2010.

Gabriela Morais, Fernanda Frazão: Portugal, mundo dos mortos e das mouras encantadas, Vol. II, Apenas Livros, Lisboa, 2010.

Gabriela Morais, Fernanda Frazão: Portugal, mundo dos mortos e das mouras encantadas, Vol. III, Apenas Livros, Lisboa, 2010.

H. P. Blavatsky: The Secret Doctrine – Part 5: Synthesis of Science, Religion and Philosophy, Kessinger Publishing, 2003.

Hieronymi Cardani: De Rerum Varietate – Libri XVII, (digital version).

Ioannem Tritehemivm: Chronicon insigne Monasterij Hirsaugiensis, Ordinis S. Benedicti, (digital version).

J. Leite de Vasconcelos: Annuario para o Estudo das Tradições Populares Portuguezas, Livraria Portuense de Clavel & C.ª, Porto, 1882.

J. Leite de Vasconcelos: Opúsculos – Volume V – Etnologia, Imprensa Nacional de Lisboa, Lisboa, 1938.

J. Leite de Vasconcelos: Opúsculos – Volume VII – Etnologia, Imprensa Nacional de Lisboa, Lisboa, 1938.

J. Leite de Vasconcelos: Tradições Populares de Portugal – Bibliotheca Ethnographica Portugueza, Livraria Portuense de Clavel & C.ª, Porto, 1882.

Jake Stratton-Kent: Geosophia – The Argo of Magic, Scarlet Imprint, 2010;

Jake Stratton-Kent: The True Grimoire, Scarlet Imprint, 2009.

Jennifer Larson: Greek Nymphs – Myth, Cult, Lore, Oxford University Press, New York, 2001.

Jeronymo Cortés: Fysiognomia, e Varios Segredos da Naturesa, Lisboa, 1699, (digital edition).

Jeronimo Cortez Valenciano: O Non Plus Ultra Do Lunario, e Pronostico Perpetuo, Geral e Particular para Todos os Reinos e Provincias, Lisboa, 1857 (digital edition).

Jerusa Pires Ferreira: O Livro de São Cipriano: Uma Legenda de Massas, Editora Perspectiva, São Paulo, 1992.

Jaime Lopes Dias, Crenças e Superstições da Beira, Alma Azul, Coimbra, 2002.

John Cassian: The Conferences of John Cassian, (digital version).

José Camões: Fadas – Vicente, Quimera Editores, 2005, Lisboa (digital edition).

José Leite de Vasconcelos: Signum Salomonis; A Figa; A Barba em Portugal – Estudo de Etnografia Comparativa, Publicações Dom Quixote, Lisboa, 1996.

Kathleen Stokker: Remedies and Rituals – Folk Medicine in Norway and the New Land, Minnesota Historical Society Press, St. Paul, 2007.

Kenneth Grant: *Aleister Crowley & the Hidden God*, Samuel Weiser, New York, 1974.

Kenneth Grant: *The Magical Revival*, Starfire Publishing Limited, London, 2010.

Manuel Bernardes: *Nova Floresta ou Sylva de varios apophtegmas e ditos sentenciosos espirituais, e moraes : com Reflexoens, em que o util da doutrina se acompanha com o vario da erudição, assim divina, como humana*, (digital version).

Manuel J. Gandra: *Portugal Sobrenatural – Deuses, Demónios, Seres Míticos, Heterodoxos, Marginados, Operações, Lugares Mágicos e Iconografia da Tradição Lusíada* – Vol. I, Ésquilo Edições e Multimédia, Lisboa, 2007.

Maria Helena Farelli: *A Bruxa de Évora*, Pallas Editora, Rio de Janeiro, 2006.

Maria Helena Farelli: *Antigo Livro de São Marcos e São Manso – Os Tesouros da Feitiçaria*, Pallas Editora, Rio de Janeiro, 2010.

Maria João Amaral: *Rubena – Vicente*, Quimera Editores, 2005, Lisboa (digital edition).

Mary S. Rustad: *The Black Books of Elverum*, Galde Press, Lakeville, 2010.

Michel Giacometi: *Filmografia Completa* – 01,RTP Edições, 2010.

Moisés Espírito Santo: *A Religião Popular Portuguesa*, Assírio & Alvim, Lisboa, 1990.

Nicholaj de Mattos Frisvold: *Exu & the Quimbanda of Night and Fire*, Scarlet Imprint, 2012.

Nicholaj de Mattos Frisvold: *Pomba Gira & the Quimbanda of Mbúmba Nzila*, Scarlet Imprint, 2011.

Ordenações Afonsinas (digital edition).

Ordenações Manuelinas (digital edition).

Ordenações Filipinas (digital edition).

Owen Davies: *Grimoires – A History of Magic Books*, Oxford University Press, New York, 2010.

Pinharanda Gomes: *História da Filosofia Portuguesa – A Filosofia Arábigo-Portuguesa*, Guimarães Editores, Lisboa, 1991.

Reginaldo Prandi (org.): *Encantaria Brasileira – O Livro dos Mestres, Caboclos e Encantados*, Pallas Editora, Rio de Janeiro, 2004.

Rezai Pelas Almas do Purgatório, PAULUS Editora, Porto, 2011.

S. Liddell MacGregor Mathers: *The Key of Solomon the King (Clavicula Salomonis)*, Weiser Books, San Francisco, 2006.

Saint Augustine: *The City of God* (digital version).

Samuel Liddell MacGregor Mathers (trad.), *Aleister Crowley: The Goetia – The lesser Key of Solomon the King*, Weiser Book, San Francisco, 1997.

Teixeira de Aragão: *Diabruras Santidades e Profecias*, Vega, Lisboa, 1994.

Teófilo Braga: *O Povo Português nos seus Costumes, Crenças e Tradições*, Vol. II, Publicações Dom Quixote, Lisboa, 1994.

Vanicléia Silva Santos: *As Bolsas de Mandinga no Espaço Atlântico: Seculo XVIII*, Universidade de São Paulo, São Paulo, 2008 (PhD. thesis).

Various authors: *Actas da 1ª Xornada de Literatura oral – Afigura do demo na literatura de tradición oral*, Asociación de Escritores en Lingua Galega, 2005.

Various authors: *Conjure Codex - A compendium of invocation, evocation and conjuration*, Volume I, Issue I, Hadean Press, 2011.

Various authors: *Memento Mori - A collection of Magickal and Mythological Perspectives on Death, Dying, Mortality and Beyond*, Avalonia, London, 2012.

Various authors: *Diabolical*, Scarlet Imprint, 2009.

Victorino d' Almada: *Elementos para um dicionário de Geographia e Historia Portugueza - Concelho d'Elvas e extinctos de Barbacena*, Villa-Boím e Villa Fernando - *Tomo Primeiro*, 1888, Elvas (digital edition).

Xoán R. Cuba, Antonio Reigosa, Xosé Miranda: *Dicionario dos seres Míticos Galegos*, Edicións Xerais de Galicia, Huertas, 2008.

BOOKS OF SAINT CYPRIAN

Adérito Perdigão Vizeu: *O Antigo e Verdadeiro Livro Gigante de São Cipriano (Capa Preta)*, Editora Eco, Rio de Janeiro. (Br)

Anon: *El Gran Libro de San Cipriano*, Berbera Editores, Mexico, 2012. (Mx)

Anon: *El Libro de San Cipriano*, Indigo, Barcelona, 2002. (Es)

Anon: *El Libro Magno de San Cipriano - Tesoso del Hechicero*, Editorial Humanitas, Barcelona, 2010. (Es)

Anon: *El libro de San Cipriano - y otros Rituales de Potencia*, Editoral EDAF, Madris, 2010. (Es)

Anon: *El Libro Infernal - Tratado Completo de las Ciencias Ocultas*, Biblioteca Esotérica Herrou Aragón.

Anon: *Il Libro Infernale - Tesoro delle Scienze Occulte*, Edizioni Mediterranee, Roma, 2010. (It)

Anon: *Il Libro Infernale - Tutti i segreti, gli incantesimi e le stregonerie*, Keybook, Lavis, 2008. (It)

Anon: *O Livro de São Cipriano - O Tesouro do Feiticiero*, Moderna Editorial Lavores, 2001. (Pt)

Anon: *O tradicional Livro Negro de São Cipriano*, Pallas Editora, Rio de Janeiro, 2006. (Br)

Anon: *O Verdadeiro Livro de São Cipriano - Os tesouros do feiticieiro - com as suas magias, esconjuros, artes de adivinhação, presságios, orações e preces para todas as circunstâncias*, Livros de Vida Editores, Mira-Sintra, 2007. (Pt)

Anon: *São Cipriano: antigo e verdadeiro livro de sonhos, cartomancia e receitas*, Pallas Editora, Rio de Janeiro, 2006. (Br)

Anon: *São Cipriano, o Bruxo - Capa de Aço*, Pallas Editora, Rio de Janeiro, 2011. (Br)

Antônio Maria Ramalhete: *O Breviário de São Cipriano*, editora Eco, Rio de Janeiro. (Br)

Dr. Israel Ben Yesha: *De las Tinieblas a la luz: San Cipriano*, Editorial de Juan, L'Hospitalet de Llobregat. (Es)

Eugenia Moyano: *San Cipriano - Su Historia, Conjuros y Rituales*, Ediciones del Lagarto, Buenos Aires, 2006. (Ar)

Joaquim V. Guimarães: *O Livro Negro de São Cipriano*, Editora Eco, Rio de Janeiro. (Br)

Jonás Surfurino: *El libro de San Cipriano – Tesoro del Hechicero*, Biblioteca Esotérica Herrou Aragón.

Jonás Surfurino: *El libro de San Cipriano: libro completo de verdadera magia, o sea, tesoro del hechicero*, Nabu Press, 2011. (Mx)

Jonás Sufurino – *La magia Suprema – Negra, Roja e Infernal de los Caldeos y de los Egipcios*, Biblioteca Esotérica Herrou Aragón.

Júlio Alcoforado Carqueja: *O Livros de São Cipriano das Almas*, Editora Eco, Rio de Janeiro. (Br)

Maria Helena Farelli: *O Livro Encarnado de São Cipriano*, Pallas Editora, Rio de Janeiro, 2011. (Br)

Max Scholten: *El Libro de San Cipriano*, Distribuciones Mateos, Barcelona. (Es)

N. A. Molina: *Antigo Livro de São Cipriano – Gigante e Verdadeiro Capa de Aço*, Editora Espiritualista, Rio de Janeiro, 1993. (Br)

Pierre Dumont: *São Cipriano – O legítimo – Capa de Aço*, Madras Editora, São Paulo, 2010. (Br)

Profesor Norel: *Los Misterios de San Cipriano*, Editorial Siete Llaves, Buenos Aires, 2000. (Ar)

S. Cipriano: *Grande Livro de S. Cipriano ou tesouros do Feiticeiro*, Edições Afrodite, Lisboa, 1974. (Pt)

S. Cipriano: *Gran Libro de San Cipriano o los tesoros del Hechicero*, Akal Ediciones, Madrid, 1993. (Es)

PSEUDO-BOOKS OF SAINT CYPRIAN

Amadeo de Santander: *O Livro da Bruxa ou A Feiticeira de Évora*, Editora Eco, Rio de Janeiro.

Athanásio: *O Livro do Feiticeiro Athanásio*, Editora Eco, Rio de Janeiro, 2004.

ConjureMan Ali: *Saint Cyprian – Saint of Necromancers*, Hadean Press, 2011.

Cunha Simões: *Os Estranhos e Poderosíssimos poderes de São Cipriano*, Cunha Simões, Alcanena.

Cunha Simões: *São Cipriano – Egoísmo Saudável – Orações Diarias*, Cunha Simões, Alcanena.

Stephen Skinner & David Rankine: *The Grimoire of St. Cyprian – Clavis Inferni*, Golden Hoard Press, Singapore, 2009.

PAPERS

A Thomaz Pires: *Miscellanea III*, Revista Lusitana vol.3 (1895) p.366.

Arlindo José Nicau Castanho: *A construção da imagem do Fausto, de Cipriano de Antioquia a Fernando Pessoa*, Artifara – Revista de línguas literaturas ibéricas e ibero-americanas, nº1 (Julho-Dezembro 2002) secção Monographica.

Daniela Buono Calainho: *Jambocousses e Gangazambes: Feiticeiros Negros em Portugal*, Afro-Ásia, 25-26 (2001) p.141.

Didier Lahon: *Inquisição, pacto com o dêmonio e "magia" africana em Lisboa no século XVIII*, Topoi, v.5,n.8, jan-jun. 2004, pp.9-77.

Donald Warren, Jr.: *Portuguese Roots of Brazilian Spiritism*, Luso-Brazilian review, Vol. 5 (1968) p.3.

F. Adolpho Coelho: *Notas e Parallelos Folkloricos – I Tradições relativas a S. Cypriano*, Revista Lusitana, Vol, I (1888-1889) p.166.

F. Adolpho Coelho: *Notas e Parallelos Folkloricos – II As doze palavras retornadas*, Revista Lusitana, Vol, I (1889) p.246.

Francisco Martins Sarmento: *A Mourama*, Revista Guimarães, 100 (1990) p.343.

Francisco Martins Sarmento: *A propósito dos "Roteiros de Tesouros"*, Revista Guimarães, vol V (1888), p.5.

Helena Ulhôa Pimentel: *Cultura Mágico-Supersticiosa, Cristianismo e Imaginário Moderno*, Revista Brasileira de História das Religiões 12 (2012) p.173.

J.S. Wingate: "The Scroll of Cyprian: An Armenian Family Amulet", *Folklore*, 41 (1930) p. 169.

James Russell: "An Armenian Spirit of Time and Place": Švot, *Proceedings of the 2013 Harvard/AIEA/SAS Workshop on Armenian Folklore and Mythology*, Belmont & Watertown (2013)

José Augusto M. Mourão: *A oração a Santa Bárbara (semiótica da acção, semiótica da manipulação)*, Revista Lusitana – Nova Série, n.º 3, Lisboa, Instituto Nacional de Investigação Científica, 1982-1983, p. 22.

José Diogo Ribeiro: *Turquel Folklórico*, Revista Lusitana, Vol. XX (1917) p.54.

Juliana Torres Rodrigues Pereira: *Feitiçaria no Arcebispado de Braga: denúncias a Ana do Frada à Visitação Inquisitorial de 1565*, Cadernos de Pesquisa do CDHIS 24 (2011) p.587.

Maria José Pallas: *Figuras literárias de magas e imagens de Sabat na obra de Gil Vicente*, Revista da FCSH (1994/1995) 297.

Mariana Gomes, Isabel Dâmaso Santos: *Tradição devocional de Santo António*, Centro de Tradições Populares Portuguesas "Professor Manuel Viegas Guerreiro", Universidade de Lisboa.

Mundicarmo Ferreti: *Encantados e Encantarias no Foclore Brasileiro*, VI Seminário de Ações Integradas em Foclore, São Paulo, 2008.

P. A. D'Azevedo: *Superstições Portuguesas no sec. XV*, Revista Lusitana vol.4 (1896) p.187.

P. D'Azevedo: *Benzedores e Feiticeiros do Tempo D'El-Rei D. Manuel*, Revista Lusitana, vol.3 (1895) p.329.

Pedro A. de Azevedo: *Cartas de tocar ou de pactos com o demonio*, Revista Lusitana vol.13 (1910) p.66.

Pedro D'Azevedo: *Costumes do Tempo D'El-Rei D. Manuel*, Revista Lusitana vol.4 (1896) p.5.

Peter Missler: *Tradicion y parodia em el Millionario de San Cipriano, primer recetario impreso para buscar tesoros en Galicia (Las hondas raíces del Ciprianillo: 1ª Parte)*, Culturas Populares – Revista Electrónica, 2 (2006) p.8.

Peter Missler: *Las hondas raíces del Ciprianillo – 2ª parte: los grimorios*, Culturas Populares – Revista Electrónica, 3 (2006) p.15.

Peter Missler: *Las Hondas Raíces del Ciprianillo. Tercera parte: las 'Gacetas'*, Culturas Populares – Revista Electrónica, 4 (2006) p.17.

Riollando Azzi: *O Casamento na sociedade colonial luso-brasileira – uma análise histórico-teológica*, Perspectiva Teológica, 24 (1992) 49.

INDEX

A

Act of Contrition 18, 235–236
Adelaide. *See* Cyprian of Antioch, Saint: and Adelaide
Adonis 71, 320–321
Afonso Henriques, King 388–389, 414, 416
Afonso V, King 423
Afro-Brazilian syncretism xxiv, 244, 340
Afro-Portuguese syncretism 362
AGLA 260–261
Alchemy 212–213, 413
Aldao, Alfredo Rodríguez. *See* Shaiah, Enediel
Alessandri, Alessandro 184, 185, 394
Alfonso VI, King of León and Castile 389
Alhambra Decree xvii, 377
Almas Penadas 239–241, 244, 396
Altamira, Guttierre de 170, 386
altar stone. *See* pedra d'ara
Alvado, King 215, 218, 417
Ambongo, Piaga 193, 399
andar ás vozes 410–411
André, João 212, 413
aniline 209
Ánima Soa 241, 242, 377
Anima Sola 241–242
Antioquía xxxi
anti-Semitism xviii–xx, 377, 426
Apollonius of Tyana 186, 394–395
Apple of Cain 39
Aragão, Teixeira de xxxiv, 298, 348, 409
Aragosio, Guillermo 212, 413
Arbutus unedo. See Apple of Cain
Aristolochia gigantean. See root of mil-homens
Arnaldus of Villa Nova 212, 413
astrology 53–57, 278–296, 412
ATR (African Traditional Religion) xxi–xxiii
Ausonius, Hector 212, 413–414
Auto das Fadas xx, 424–426
auto de fé xix
Aventesmas 153, 396

B

bad death. *See* má morte
Barabaia, Dom João de 270
Barabbas 84, 85, 112, 123, 412

cat 183, 327
    black, as omen 129
    black, in spells 82–85, 197, 330
Catholic Catechism 239–240, 241
Catholic Monarchs xvii–xviii
chaplet 194, 399–403
chiromancy. *See* quiromancy
Chumbley, Andrew D. 261
Cistus ladanifer. *See* laudanum
clematis 83
Clematis campaniflora. *See* clematis
Clotilde. *See* Cyprian of Antioch, Saint: and Clotilde
Coelho, F. Adolpho xxviii, xxx
Commelina diffusa. *See* Grass of Saint Lucia
Commelina erecta. *See* Grass of Saint Lucia
Commelina nudiflora. *See* Grass of Saint Lucia
Constable Saint 424
contraception 203–204, 407, 422
cordão-de-são-francisco 73
cork oak 205–206, 407–408
Coronopus didymus. *See* mestrunços
Cortés, Gerónimo. *See* Valenciano, Jeronimo Cortez
coruja. *See* owl
coscinomancy 59, 299–300, 327
Crataegus laevigata. *See* hawthorn seeds
Crataegus monogyna. *See* hawthorn seeds
Crimini Falsi 212, 413
crossroads 26, 226, 243, 248, 266, 338, 414, 418
    city at the. *See* Yeborath
Cueva de Salamanca xxxi, 457
Cueva de San Cíprian xxxi
Cupressus sempervirens. *See* cypress
Curdled Sea 22
Custodian Angel 65–67, 311–312, 318
cypress 323
cypress apple 81
Cypriani Magjej septe horar Magicae xxviii. *See also* Book of St. Cyprian, The
Cyprian of Antioch, Saint xxv, xxx–xxxi, 62–63, 66–67, 199–202. *See also* Book of St. Cyprian, The
    and Adelaide 104–105, 327, 344
    and Barnaby 119–121, 344, 364, 376
    and Clotilde 93–97, 327, 328, 337, 344
    and Elvira 105–110, 190, 327, 344
    and Justina 3–7, 15–16, 234–235
    and St. Gregory 16, 65–66, 125–127, 235
    and the Devil 69–72, 109–110, 263, 346
    cross of 81–82, 323

E

Eboracum 338
Echium plantagineum. **See** Paterson's Curse
Edoun Ara 362
egg 340, 365
    in spells 85, 86, 122, 199, 207
elderberry 361
El Libro Magno de San Cipriano xxxiv, 224, 235, 254, 262. **See also** *Book of St. Cyprian, The*
Elvira. **See** Cyprian of Antioch, Saint: and Elvira
emigration xxxii, 360, 410
Encantados/Encantadas 226, 244, 267–271, 273, 386, 387, 390
    Brazilian 267, 269
enchanted vial 117–118
Equisetum. **See** snake grass
Ericaceae Calluna. **See** heather
Ericaceae Erica. **See** heather
Eruca sativa. **See** roquette
erva de Nossa Senhora. **See** Our Lady's herb
erva-de-saião 193, 399
erva-do-diabo 190
escalheiro. **See** hawthorn seeds
Eshu/Elegua xxiii, 241, 365
esparto 84
evil eye 350, 351, 352, 378
Évora 338, 414, 416, 418. **See also** Bruxa of Évora
    coat of arms 416
exorcism 21–25, 32, 73, 186, 225, 226, 235, 238, 244, 312, 324
Exortação da Guerra xxix
Exu 274, 348, 418

F

fada 265, 266, 274, 426
fado 266, 426
fairy lore 70, 265, 270–271, 272, 329, 338, 426
fate. **See** *fado*
Fatuellus 329
Fatuus 329
Faust xxv, 216
fava beans 327
    in spells 82
    in stories 93, 105, 109, 127
fennel 101, 117, 361
Ferdinand I, King of León and Castile 386, 389
fern seeds 87–89, 328, 329
Ferrabraz. **See** Barabaia, Dom João de

invisibility 83, 327, 332-333, 361

J

Jannes 189, 398
jet 113, 300, 350-351
John III, King xviii
John II, King 377
John I, King 424
John the Deacon 183, 392
Justina. *See* Cyprian of Antioch, Saint: and Justina

K

key 25, 353, 356, 357, 366
Key of Solomon the King, The xxvii
Klip Dagga. *See* cordão-de-são-francisco

L

Lady of the Goat Foot 274-275
Lagardona 218, 417-419
Lagarrona 214, 216-218, 417-419
lamb 73, 198-199, 427
Lantana microphylla martius. See northern rosemary
laudanum 43, 64, 100
leek 366, 379
Légua Boji 269
lemon 227, 366
Leonotis nepetifolia. See cordão-de-são-francisco
Lethe xxxi
Levi, Eliphas 230, 360, 383
Libro Infernal xxvii. *See also* Book of St. Cyprian, The
lightning 103, 226, 340, 345, 361
lightning stone 355, 362-363
Linum crepitans. See Galician linen
Lion's Ear. *See* cordão-de-são-francisco
Llull, Ramon 212, 413
Lobisomen 65, 226, 376
Luther, Martin 457, 458
lycanthropy 272

M

Macrochloa tenacissima. See esparto
magical herb 119-121
magnetism 116, 195, 253, 308
mallow 117, 128
má morte 239, 244
Manuel I, king of Portugal xviii, xix, 377, 423

snake skin 199, 200, 406
sow with the seven piglets. *See porca dos sete leitões*
Spanish fly. *See* cantharidin
spirit of hartshorn 83, 117, 127
squill 202
stag-beetle. *See vaca-loura*
stingray 195
Stipa tenacissima. See esparto
St. John's Eve 329, 361, 365
St. Peter's mother 366
strawberry tree. *See* Apple of Cain
Sulfurino, Jonas xxvi, 262, 378, 459
sunken city. *See* Antioquía
sweet gale. *See* northern rosemary

T

talismans 113, 196, 207-208, 321, 351-357
terço 225-226, 244-246, 399
Theophilus of Adana xxvi
Thursday 376
Thymelaea villosa. See trovisco
timing, magical 121
tiny devil 85-86, 328, 337
Tiraqueau, André 394
toad 99, 110-112, 114, 347-348, 349
toque das almas 225
Trasgos/Trasgus 244, 397
treasure 387-391
    disenchantment of 33, 36-37, 172, 271-273, 312
    Guides 258
    hunting 258-259, 273, 385
    lists of 38-47, 173-182
    riddles 386
Trevisan, Bernard 413
triangle 33, 172, 260, 262, 320
Trithemius, Johannes 184, 393
trovisco 195, 404
Tuesday 376
Twelve Words Said and Returned 311, 318

U

Umayyad occupation 98, 338
Umbanda xix, 194, 244, 418
Umbilicus rupestris. See navelwort
University of Wittenberg 457-458
Urginea maritima. See squill

Lightning Source UK Ltd.
Milton Keynes UK
UKOW06f0710311217
315211UK00014B/1283/P